THE
ADVENTURES
OF
$\mathcal{S}$ayf
$\mathcal{B}$en$\mathcal{D}$hi
AN ARAB
FOLK
EPIC
$\mathcal{Y}$azan

THE ADVENTURES OF Sayf Ben Dhi Yazan

AN ARAB FOLK EPIC

TRANSLATION & NARRATION BY
LENA JAYYUSI

INTRODUCTION BY
HARRY NORRIS

A **PROTA** Book

INDIANA UNIVERSITY PRESS
Bloomington & Indianapolis

This book is a publication of

Indiana University Press
601 North Morton Street
Bloomington, Indiana 47404-3797 USA

http://www.indiana.edu/~iupress

Telephone orders 800-842-6796
Fax orders 812-855-7931
E-mail orders iuporder@indiana.edu

Authorized 4-volume Arabic edition published
in Cairo by Maktabat Al-Jumhuriyya [n.d.]

Christopher Tingley, Style Editor
Poetry translated by Salma Khadra Jayyusi and
John Heath-Stubbs

First reprinted in paperback in 1999
Copyright 1996 by PROTA (Project of Translation from Arabic)
All rights reserved

The paper used in this publication meets the minimum requirements
of American National Standard for Information Sciences—Permanence
of Paper for Printed Library Materials, ANSI Z39.48-1984.

Library of Congress Cataloging-in-Publication Data

Sīrat Sayf ibn Dhī Yazan. English. Selections
    The adventures of Sayf ben Dhi Yazan : an Arab folk epic /
translation and narration by Lena Jayyusi ; introduction by
Harry Norris.
        p. cm.
    The selections in this volume cover the first 500 pages of
the authorized 4-volume Arabic ed. published in Cairo by
Maktabat al-Jumhūrīyah with no publication date.
    "A PROTA book."
    Includes index.
    ISBN 978-0-253-33034-5 (alk. paper)
    I. Jayyusi, Lena. II. Title.
PJ7760.S5A24 1996
398.22'089'927—dc20   95-41559

ISBN: 978-0-253-21342-6

3 4 5 6 7   12 11 10 09 08 07

Contents

THE ADVENTURES OF

Sayf Ben Dhi Yazan

Acknowledgments

I am pleased to present this English version of *The Adventures of Sayf Ben Dhi Yazan*, one of the most beautiful and fascinating Arab folk romances. The idea of rendering into English this romance, or part of it, was suggested to me by Lena Jayyusi even before I founded PROTA, the project for the dissemination of Arabic literature and culture through translation and scholarly studies, in 1980. When I taught the tale to an intelligent and creative class at the University of Utah in 1977, I became convinced of the tale's absolute suitability for English-speaking readers.

Because it is a very special kind of literature, rendered in a language somewhere between written Arabic and the Egyptian vernacular, the tale proved exceedingly difficult to translate. However, thanks to the expert hands that worked on it, we were able to produce a smooth and exciting text. I should like to thank Lena Jayyusi for her meticulous and artistic handling of the work. Her decision to divide the text into translation and narration enabled us to include a larger portion of the romance than would otherwise have been possible. My thanks go next to Christopher Tingley, PROTA's principal style editor, for his great enthusiasm and his painstaking work on the manuscript and the indexes. My collaboration with the poet John Heath-Stubbs, a folklore enthusiast himself, on the translations of the poetry passages that appear throughout the romance was highly enjoyable and illuminating. I thank him most sincerely for his help. Heartfelt thanks go to Professor Harry Norris for his introduction to this folk romance and for much expert advice on other matters. My gratitude also goes to Hasan El-Shamy, Professor of Folklore at Indiana University, for many helpful suggestions so generously given.

The donors to our project merit equal appreciation. I acknowledge first of all Dr. 'Abd al-'Aziz al-Maqalih, president of the University of Sanaa, who enthusiastically welcomed the project and secured funds from the Yemeni authorities to enable us to begin the translation. In need of further support, we were aided by Shaikh Sultan al-'Uweis of the United Arab Emirates, a great benefactor of literature, who rallied to my call for help with a grace equal to his well-known generosity. Finally, warm thanks to Dr. Daniel Varisco, who secured funds for us from the American Institute of Yemeni Studies. This timely grant allowed us to put the final touches on a labor which, though arduous, we all loved.

SALMA K. JAYYUSI
GENERAL EDITOR, PROTA

Introduction

HARRY NORRIS

The *siras* (Ar. plural *siyar*), Arabic for "folk-epic," "geste," or "romance," were composed in Middle Arabic during the Mamluk period, that is some time between the thirteenth and sixteenth centuries. As such, they span the age which saw the rise of the Ottoman Empire in the Middle East. Their originality and their marked individuality cast doubt upon a common notion that Arabic literature began to fall into rapid and steep decline during this age. In a few respects, the *siras* represent a continuation of the high artistry of classical Arabic narrative as illustrated in the *maqamat* rather than in the colloquial, or vulgar; but they do reflect a genuine vernacular taste for the exotic. They have been written down and survive in manuscripts which are now to be found in many of the world's libraries where Oriental manuscripts are preserved. They have also been printed in recent times in various parts of the Arab world, notably in Egypt, Syria, Algeria, and Tunisia.[1] These *siras* are still cherished by storytellers in cafés, villages, and nomad camps. One famous modern writer who has referred to the *sira* bards is Taha Husain. He described their art in the childhood memories set out in his *al-Ayyam* (Stream of days).[2]

The best-known *siras* consist of highly colored, somewhat rambling though skillfully structured panoramas, which are like giant semimusical frescoes (in Western music, Honegger's *Le Roi David* comes to mind). They tell of heroic feats, escapades, bizarre landscapes, brief or long-lasting love affairs, sincere friendships and demonic hatred, supernatural forces and dark spells, and have a barely disguised Islamic mission. Several are terminated by the heroic death of the principal character. Two of the supreme heroes, 'Antar and al-Zir Salim (Muhalhil), were famous historical poets of the pre-Islamic age, the former of partially black origin, the latter an important participant in the battles of the War of al-Basus in the fifth century. On the other hand, Abu Zayd al-Hilali (who was also dark skinned), his kinsman Dhiyab, and the heroine Jaziya would appear to be largely mythical and stylized personalities, though their foe, al-Zanati Khalifa, has in fact been identified with a historical Berber ruler in the Maghrib. All these are in the repertoire of bards in Egypt, Tunisia, Jordan, and other parts of the Arab World. The *sira* of Dhat al-Himma is about an Amazon warrior whose exploits are semihistorical. They are intimately linked to actual wars between Arab tribes and the Byzantines, and they show similarities with the Byzantine folk epic of *Digenis Akritas* and the adventures of the Arab commander, Batal Ghazi, near Constantinople. He has his own cycle in Ottoman literature. The *sira* of the Mamluk ruler Baybars al-Bunduqdari (al-Malik al-Zahir, 1260–1277) is in part a historical romance, composed some time before the reign of Qansawh al-Ghawri (1500), who refers to it specifically in his own writings. This *sira* mentions battles against the Crusaders and against the Mongols.

Such *siras*, along with others, share much of the language and literary art to be found in the Mamluki *One Thousand and One Nights (Alf Layla wa-Layla)*. Indeed, some late versions of the *Nights* contain the adventures of *'Ajib wa-Gharib, Sayf al-Muluk,* and *'Umar ben al-Nu'man,* which are *siras* to all intents and purposes, even if they are not conventionally deemed to be a part of the *sira* cycles. At least one Egyptian scholar has seen the *Nights* as a kind of "anti-sira."[3] Another literary genre that shares common features with the *siras* are the "shadow plays" of Ibn Daniyal.[4] The subject matter is often remarkably similar, as the following poem by Ibn al-Farid (alluding to these plays) makes clear.[5]

> Thou seest how the birds among the boughs
> Delight thee with their cooing, when they chant
> Their mournful notes to win thy sympathy,
> And marvelest at their voices and their words
> Expressing uninterpretable speech.
> Then on the land the tawny camels race
> Benighted through the wilderness; at sea
> The tossed ships run amid the billowy deep.
> Thou gazest on *twin* armies—now on land,
> Anon at sea—in huge battalions
> Clad all in mail of steel for valor's sake
> And fenced about with points of swords and spears.
> The troops of the land army—some are knights
> Upon their chargers, some stout infantry;
> The heroes of the sea force—some bestride
> The decks of ships, some swarm the lancelike masts.
> Some violently smite with gleaming swords,
> Some 'neath the arrows' volley drown in fire,
> Some burn in water of the flaming flares.
> This troop thou seest offering their lives
> In reckless onslaught, that with broken ranks
> Fleeing humiliated in the rout.
> And thou beholdest the great catapult
> Set up and fired, to smash the fortresses
> And stubborn strongholds. Likewise thou mayest gaze
> On phantom shapes with disembodied souls
> Cowering darkly in their dim domain,
> Appareled in strange forms that disaccord
> Most wildly with the homely guise of men;
> For none would call the jinnis homely folk.

One of the most colorful and typical Islamic representations of manly endeavor (*muruwwa*) within the *sira* corpus is that of *Sayf Ben Dhi Yazan,* "the knight of the Yemen," available here in English for the first time.[6] Those who love *Morte d'Arthur* or who are familiar with the genius, in verse, of Ariosto and

Tasso (both of whom left their mark on Tudor England and on later ages) will be struck by the similarity of the imagery, the chivalrous criteria, the all-pervading magical atmosphere, and the bright colors characteristic of the late medieval imagination; the imagery of Chaucer in "The Squire's Tale" draws upon similar Oriental and Mamluk inspiration.

What, then, distinguishes the *Sirat Sayf Ben Dhi Yazan* from other works of this genre? It is shorter than *Sirat 'Antar* and is saturated with the magical to a degree unmatched elsewhere. Whereas 'Antar's adventures initially focus on tribal Arabia before his later adventures and missions take him to Spain, Africa, Oman, Byzantium, Syria, and Iraq, most of *Sirat Sayf Ben Dhi Yazan* takes place within the Yemen or in the Nile Valley southward to the Nile's mountainous source. Geography is subordinated to vast expanses of sky, monster-infested rivers, celestial bodies, Pharaonic monuments, and cities and horizons that recall the Alexander romance. Much of the plot is built around "the search for a bride," for example, Sayf's quest for "The Book of the History of the Nile" in order to gain the hand of Shama. This theme seems to be borrowed from Persian literature, where the Iranian epic contained, from early times, the mythical motif of a hero traveling to a distant land to win such a bride. Such a story was told in the Achaemenian period, according to Alexander's chamberlain, Chares of Mytilene, with reference to Zariadres and Hystaspes, while Firdawsi calls the brothers Zarer and Gushtasp. The search for a bride comes to involve further, subsidiary feats characterized by fantastic religious ritual.[7] In the *sira* of Sayf, for example, "The Book of the Nile" is no ordinary book. It possesses talismanic properties, controlling the flow of the water in the Nile, and it is guarded by pagan magicians after Jabalqa, a magician of ancient times, hid it from mankind. The latter's name recalls that of a city, one of two situated at the end of the earth, which had been founded by Alexander and which is mentioned in *Pseudo-Callisthenes* and in the Arabic and Persian romances based upon the exploits of Alexander. Aided by the Almighty, by the priestess 'Aqila, and by his half sister 'Aqisa, Sayf obtains "The Book of the Nile," then exerts himself to control waters, remove obstacles, and subdue nations. In order to attain his objective, Sayf must first have in his hands seven instruments of power, some of which will be described in this shortened version, while others can be found in the full version of the *sira*: "The Book of the Nile"; the sword of Asaf, who was vizier to King Solomon; the magic horse called Barq al-Buruq; the pick of Japeth, which can rend mountains asunder; the magic stone of Kush; the tablets of two subjugated *jinn*, Khaylajan and his brother; and the powers of the *'ifrit* called Rahaq al-Aswad after he has been totally subdued. Sayf achieves his dream of a glimpse of a vision of Paradise in the Mountains of the Moon, wearing "The Book of the Nile" as a protective breastplate; his steed is a magic horse that resembles the hippogriff, the flying steed depicted by Ariosto in his *Orlando Furioso* (first printed in 1516). The steed also recalls the ebony horse in *One Thousand and One Nights*, as well as Chaucer's flying steed of brass in "The Squire's Tale," the Arabian intrusion at the heart of the *Canterbury Tales*. Sayf's military objective is to break the power of Ethiopia's ruler so that he will be incapable of cutting off the Nile's waters from Egyptian towns and villages. Here, too, there are similarities between the *sira* and *Orlando Furioso*, where Ariosto tells us that

> The soldan, king of Egyptian land,
> Pays tribute to this sovereign, as his head,
> They say, since having Nile at his command
> He may divert the stream for other bed,
> Hence with its district upon either hand,
> Forthwith might Cairo lack its daily bread.
> Senapus him his Nubian tribes proclaim;
> We Priest and Prester John the sovereign name.[8]

Rahaq clears the bed of the Nile. Blessed by God, and by now fulfilling the role of the "Sword of Islam" against the pagans, Sayf turns his efforts toward subduing them in order to acknowledge the prophethood of Muhammad. Having achieved this, Sayf abdicates and is succeeded by his son, Masr, as the reader of the fuller version will see. In the *sira* of 'Antar, the eponymous hero dies heroically, his corpse being propped up on his horse in the manner of the Cid in his final moments, while his tribe, the Banu 'Abs, finds safety in its rocky homelands. In fact, that *sira* is extended further, as the exploits of 'Antar's daughter continue the martial feats of her father. Sayf, on the other hand, survives, retiring to meditate and contemplate the majesty and power of the Almighty who has spared him and guided him throughout his life of adventure. This provides a unique conclusion to this particular *sira*.

According to the narrator, "When King Sayf had ended this ode, he bade farewell to his son and to those who were present, going to dwell in this mountain behind the castle; and there he sat, worshipping Almighty God, he and those who were with him, close comrades of his, kings and sages, who had remained with him. King Masr ruled Egypt then, the governors obeying his command on land and at sea; and the same loyalty was shown to Dummar. The people were happy and contented. As for King Sayf and those who were with him, they remained there worshipping Almighty God, until at length they were visited by the 'vanquisher of the self' [*hazim al-dhat*], the one who also sunders men from their fellows. When King Sayf died, his son Masr was present and buried him in the ground, writing upon his tomb, 'This is the tomb of the *Juyushi* king [the commander of armies of men and *jinn*?]. The mercy of Almighty God be upon him and upon those Muslims who have departed. He ruled justly all his days until he tasted the cup of death. Glory be to Him who never dies and who will remain for all eternity.'"

The majesty of the Almighty and the wonders He has created are constant themes throughout the story of Sayf, bringing to mind the play entitled *Aladdin*, composed by the Danish poet Adam Oehlenschlager and published in 1805. This play, as its title indicates, draws upon *One Thousand and One Nights* for its inspiration; but it also draws upon sentiments expressed in the Arabic *sira*, especially the Islamic belief in a tremendous supernatural power which underpins the entire universe. To cite the Danish poet:

> Lift up your hearts to the eternal power,
> feel near to Allah, observe His work!
> Though joy and sorrow alternate in the earthly light,
> here the pillars of the world stand unmoving
> thousands and thousands upon thousands of years,
> unmoving in their strength,
> with radiant splendour and constancy.
> They represent the indestructible.[9]

So much of the landscape in this *sira* is of an Egyptian character, or is derived from literary and especially geographical works or books which tell of marvels to be seen in Africa, that one is prone to forget that the historical Sayf Ben Dhi Yazan (Abu Murra or Maʿdikarib) was actually a Persian-backed ruler of the Yemen. He attained fame in Arab history through his defeat and expulsion of the Ethiopians who invaded his country following the persecution of the Christians of Najran by a predecessor, Dhu Nuwas, who is thought to have been a convert to the Jewish faith. In Muslim tradition, the Ethiopian disaster began with the rout of Abraha the Ethiopian outside Mecca in 570, the "Year of the Elephant" in which the Prophet was born. Sayf ruled later as a Persian underling, but increasingly managed the affairs of his country as an independent ruler. It was left to later writers such as the romancer Wahb ben Munabbih (d. 732) and Ibn Ishaq (d. 768), the biographer of the Prophet, to integrate Sayf into the annals of Islam. Although it is now lost, we know that Hisham ben al-Kalbi composed a work entitled "The Book of the Yemen and the Affair of Sayf" (*Kitab al-Yaman wa-amr Sayf*). In the twelfth century, Nashwan ben Saʿid al-Himyari, in *Shams alʿUlum* and the ode *al-Qasida al-Himyariyya*, was one of those who transformed the record of the rule and achievements of Sayf into a national folk epic and Arab saga, albeit markedly Yemeni in its national loyalties. By that date, Sayf's exploits were no longer limited to the Arabian Peninsula; he had sailed to Ethiopia to wage war. The conflict had become ethnic between the sons of Shem and Ham, the "red" Arabs, and the "black" peoples of Ethiopia and the Sudan.

Verses 93 and 94 in Nashwan's ode encapsulate Sayf's victory over the Ethiopians:

> Sayf Ben Dhi Yazan brought down Persia's sons. He had emigrated [to Byzantium, unsuccessfully seeking help], then turned [to Persia for help] and was successful. The Ethiopians became slaves of the Arabs, who bought and sold them for loss or for gain.

Sayf was to fulfill other roles besides that of fighter for Islam in *jihad*. He was to become identified in particular as the national hero of the Yemenis, whose exploits were to counterbalance those of other heroes born among the "northern" Arabs. As such, he became the ideal of the sons of Qahtan, as opposed to those of 'Adnan. Hence, the Berbers of North Africa, who claimed to have originated from the Yemen in pre-Islamic times, took Sayf as the model for their heroic fight against the blacks (pagan and nonpagan) to the south of the Sahara, while the Somalis, who saw themselves as "Yemenis," regarded both Dhu Nuwas and Sayf as heroic fighters against their traditional enemy, the Ethiopians. Hence, Sayf came to be endowed with the feats of the first prince (Tubba'), who personified the ancient heroes of the Himyaris. In this *sira*, such a dichotomy and ethnic distinction can be seen in the fact that the great enemy of Sayf Ben Dhi Yazan is also called Sayf Ar'ad. The latter has been identified with two different Ethiopian sovereigns who are important for the dating of the composition: 'Amda Syon (1314–1344) and Sayfa Ar'ad (1344–1372). Both these rulers posed a threat to the Muslim kingdoms neighboring Ethiopia at that time. Their fate was of concern to Mamluk Egypt, whose rulers were worried about a potential alliance between Christian Ethiopia and crusading and post-crusading Europe; this may be traced in the famous legend of the "Kingdom of Prester John." It was believed that the latter, Gabra Masqal, "Servant of the Cross" ('Abd al-Salib), was able to divert the Nile waters from Egypt. 'Amda Syon, moreover, is none other than the Senapo in Ariosto's *Orlando Furioso*. Aspects of the *sira* which seem to relate Mamluk romance to that of Renaissance Italy have already been mentioned.

The *Sirat Sayf Ben Dhi Yazan*, like all the other Arab *siras*, consists of pure prose, rhymed verse (*saj'*), and strategically spaced poems. The latter appear occasionally, particularly as we approach the denouement, some extending over a page or more. The prose, however, is paramount, and particularly so in this *sira*, where dialogue continues over extended stretches of the narrative; direct speech, introduced by "he said" or "the narrator said" (*qala 'l-rawi*), is also characteristic. There is always an implicit dialogue between the storyteller and his audience, who are presumed to be present even if the *sira* is recited among a very small circle or read, as a book, by a solitary individual.

Indeed, the narrator is the crucial arbiter and all but dictates the flow of the narrative. To cite an unpublished paper presented by Mahmud Sulayman at a conference on popular *sira* in Cairo in 1984:

> The story-teller greatly interferes in the form of the narrative, as such, and in its language. Secondly, he is the determining arbiter in the method of the recital in regard to its sundry linguistic aspects. Thirdly, the narration of the story joins together, linguistically, dialogue, that is the language of the theater, and the language of the narrator himself. Fourthly, the narration has not been fixed, from the aspect of form, in accordance with what we find in poetry and in the theater. Fifthly, both lucidity and obscurity, or vagueness, are intimately joined together in the story-teller himself. Sixthly, and lastly, the presence of the story-teller is epitomized in the elevation and the lowering, the voice raising and the whispering or the unvoicing, the absence and the presence. All such appear when he follows the dialogue.

(From "Grammatical Idioms in *Sirat Sayf Ben Dhi Yazan* and Their Connection with the Level of Guidance and Direction.") Parallelism also marks the style, as it does so often in Arabic literature.[10]

In several of the "bedouin" *siras*, there are to be found genealogical histories and a boasting of prowess which is typical of the pre-Islamic age. The entire milieu of camels, horses, and tents conveys a desert environment, be it in Arabia itself or North Africa. *Sayf*, however, is enclosed within the parameters of a quite different world. It is more truly a "romance" within the accepted norms of "romantic literature." Much of it seems to be unconnected with everyday life, and the lines separating the world of magicians and *jinn* from that of humankind are all but nonexistent. Symbolism has precedence over realism. Gory battles give way to magical spells and marvelous machinery. In this respect, *Sirat Sayf Ben Dhi Yazan* is a partial model for the *sira* of Sayf al-Tijan,[11] and it also seems to be linked, in some manner, with the story of "Hasan of Basra" in *One Thousand and One Nights*, a fact observed by E. W. Lane in the last century.[12]

Occasionally in such *sira* literature, it is possible to spot direct borrowings from other works of literature in Arabic. There is little doubt, for instance, that the Pharaonic and pseudo-Coptic elements echo, if they do not actually quote, the compositions of al-Mas'udi (d. 956). Closest of all is a passage in *Sayf Ben Dhi Yazan* referring to the source of the Nile and the monsters that have to be faced in order to reach it; it echoes *Akhbar al-Zaman*, a work also attributed to al-Mas'udi. It is very doubtful whether al-Mas'udi was in fact the author; it was probably written by a certain Ibrahim ben Wasif Shah, who lived in Egypt during the tenth and eleventh centuries.[13] Other literary models may be traced to the earliest storytellers in Arabic: 'Ubayd ben Sharya (a seventh-century contemporary of Caliph Mu'awiya), and Wahb ben Munabbih, to whom reference was made above. These writers furnished portraits of pre-Islamic Yemeni kings who reached "the land of darkness," "the flowing river of sand," "monsters who followed the sun's course in the sky," "the fount of life," and "the rivers of Paradise"; and they described sundry adventures amidst the stars and the world of the *jinn*. Sayf Ben Dhi Yazan's exploits occasionally remind one of certain Russian heroes or of Tatar folk tales. This is not surprising when one knows that there were many links between Mamluk Egypt and the Golden Horde, via the Volga region, and that the kindred story of *Sayf al-Muluk* has been a popular romance among the Tatars.

It is not difficult, even in the general context of comparative literature, to discover correspondences between the *sira* of Sayf and other world romances of a similar type; and where the origin is Oriental, it is hard to imagine that any one Islamic or non-Islamic culture inspired the themes or the plot. So much give and take was there over the centuries that one is frequently liable, on the basis of diffusion alone, to pursue a fruitless search, affording no conclusive evidence to prove or disprove a particular theory.[14]

It is harder still to assess how this *sira* has contributed to Arabic literature. Interest in it has been revived in the media in recent years, helped by the abridged and edited version of it published in Egypt by Faruq Khurshid.[15] Certainly, the exploits of Sayf Ben Dhi Yāzan, at least in oral form, left their mark on the dynastic claims of the medieval kings of Kanem and Borno in West Africa; and this underlies apparent allusions to some kind of composed *sira* in Arabic geographic and diplomatic works and documents of the later medieval period.[16] The work has been especially popular in certain towns in the Maghrib (e.g., Chechaouene in Morocco and Tlemcen in Algeria), while elements in the plot have possibly influenced the literature of Malaysia and Indonesia and parts of East Africa. This is not unexpected, as all these areas were in close commercial contact with Cairo, with the Yemen, and with southern Arabia generally.

The concept of the Amazon warrior is known in other *siras*, and it is also found among Arab writers referring to the legend of a remote "Island of Women," whose inhabitants lived independently, waging war and only infrequently sharing the bed of their spouses. They were also possessors of an unmatched beauty and of magical powers which gave them an equality to, and at times a superiority over men. All their feats and arts ran counter to the traditional social mores of Islamic society. In western Europe, via Italy and possibly Spain, the age of the post-Renaissance reveled in such Amazons. This can be seen in Ariosto's *Orlando Furioso* and in the personality of the warrior enchantress, Armida, who appears, for example, in the libretto of Handel's opera, *Rinaldo*, of 1711:

> That supernat'ral pow'r which helps my art
> Long e'er your coming told me why you came.
> Rinaldo and the beauteous Almirena,
> High on the summit of yon dreadful hill,
> Slaves to the fierce Armida's pleasure lie.
> Thither no mortal courage can arrive;
> Unless high heav'n shall please to lend a force,
> Equal to that of hell, which guards her palace.

The passage is from act 3, scene 2, which shows how the abode of Armida—surrounded by magic and forces both magnetic and destructive—protects the Amazon sorceress. She loves the hero, Rinaldo, whose religious quest to liberate the Holy Land is at risk and subject to the conflicting emotions that determine or inhibit his actions.

Sayf Ben Dhi Yazan, aided by forces of the supernatural and inspired by divine guidance, was indeed such a force. Nowhere in *sira* literature is the magical and the demonic given such a high profile in the plot. And nowhere else is eroticism, bordering on the explicit, allowed such a prominent place in the narrative. A passage where Sayf is all but seduced by his mother, Qamariyya, when she challenges him to wrestle with her naked, alone in single combat, is almost startling in its explicitness. Its juxtaposition with other passages telling of ascetics, of spiritual discipline, of Prophetic example, and of feats of gallantry and skill in weaponry by male and female combatants apparently reflects the taste and accepted morality of the Mamluk age. Yet, Rudi Paret detects a weakness here and remarks in his article on the *sira*: "If we were to cut out of the *sira* all the passages that deal with or are connected with spirits or magic, we should have barely half of it left."[17]

The popular folk epics have been viewed as medieval prototypes for some features of the modern Arabic novel and modern Arabic drama. Such is the view of the Russian Arabist, I. M. Filshtinsky, whose comments reflect the approach of East European scholarship, which regarded *sira*, the *Nights*, and the "shadow play" as essential components of Arabic literature. Filshtinsky rejects the "class" snobbery of Arab littérateurs who eschewed them and whose views were so often slavishly followed by "Orientalists" in the West:

> Folklore elements constituted an essential part of popular romances about legendary or half-legendary heroes of ancient times. For example, the hero of *Sayf ibn dhi-Yazan*, one of the pre-Islamic South-Arabian Himyarite princes, had incredible adventures, shared by magicians and witches; and so had the aforementioned Abu Zayd, who participated in fantastic campaigns.
>
> The narrative in popular romances abounds in lively scenes with dialogue, in which scholars see the embryo of the drama.[18]

NOTES

1. For a comprehensive treatment of such narratives, see the recently published, 3-volume work by M. C. Lyons, *The Arabian Epic: Heroic and Oral Story-Telling* (Cambridge: Cambridge University Press, 1995). The study includes an introduction (vol. 1); a comparative index (vol. 2); and texts (vol. 3). A summary of the *sira* of Sayf Ben Dhi Yazan appears in volume 3, pages 586–641, under the title: "Sirat Faris al-Yaman al-Malik Saif b. Dhi Yazan."

2. Taha Husain gives a detailed description of the performance of the *Sirat Bani Hilal* by a reciter (*sa'ir*) in the village where he grew up. Much later in the same work, *al-Ayyam* (chap. 16), he describes at length the "magical literature" which intrigued him and his friends. These works included "Hasan of Basra," from *One Thousand and One Nights*, and *Sayf Ben Dhi Yazan*. For a nineteenth-century description of the public recitation of romances in Egypt, see Edward William Lane, *An Account of the Manners and Customs of the Modern Egyptians Written in Egypt during the Years 1833–1835* (London: East-West Publications, 1978), chaps. 22 and 23, especially the latter. This seems to be the only account of this period that makes mention of *Sayf Ben Dhi Yazan*.

3. See Ferial Jabouri Ghazoul, *The Arabian Nights: A Structural Analysis* (Cairo: Cairo Associated Institution for the Study and Presentation of Arab Cultural Values, 1980), pp. 75–89.

4. Paul Kahle, ed., *Three Shadow Plays by Muhammad Ibn Daniyal*, translated by A. J. Arberry, compiled by Derrick Hopwood and Mustafa Badawi (Cambridge: Cambridge University Press, 1992, E. J. W. Gibb Memorial), pp. 7–8.

5. Ibn al-Farid's descriptions of the battle scenes are especially characteristic of the *Sirat 'Antar* in the *Marhala Malhamiyya* ("epic" inflation of the content in its latter sections) of that *sira*, especially where Africa and Byzantium are the focus of geographical

interest. On Ibn al-Farid, see Julia Ashtiany, ed., "'Abbasid Belles-Lettres," in *The Cambridge History of Arabic Literature* (Cambridge: Cambridge University Press, 1990), pp. 253–60. See also M. M. Badawi, "Medieval Arabic Drama: Ibn Daniyal," *Journal of Arabic Literature* 13 (1982).

6. See also the extensive resume in M. Lyons, *The Arabic Epic*, Cambridge: Cambridge University Press, 1995. *Sayf Ben Dhi Yazan* has been translated into Russian, though only in a partial translation (*Zhizneopisanie Sayfa syna tsaria zu Yazana*, translated by I. M. Filshtinsky and B. Ya. Shidfar [Moscow: Nauka, 1975, 1987]). The classic study by Rudi Paret, *Sirat Saif b Di Yazan, ein arabischer Volksroman* (Hanover, 1924), offers a detailed analysis of plot and background as well as useful indexes of names, cities, countries, and motifs. For a more concise survey of the story, see J. Chelhod, "La geste du roi Sayf," *Revue de l'Histoire des Religions* (1967), pp. 181–205. For Arabic readers, the most complete published study to date is Thurayya Manqush and Dar al-Hurriyya, *Sayf Ben Dhi Yazan bayn al-haqiqa wa'l-ustura* (Baghdad, 1980).

7. Ernst E. Herzfeld, "Archaeological History of Iran," *Schweich Lectures of the British Academy* (1934), pp. 65–66.

8. See Francis M. Rogers, *The Quest for Eastern Christians* (Minneapolis: University of Minnesota Press, 1962), pp. 106–107. Ariosto and *Sayf* depict expeditions to the source of the Nile. The salvation in Ariosto's work of the King of Ethiopia from the ravages of creatures that descend and devour his victuals could have been influenced by the story of the destruction of Abraha's army at Mecca.

9. The full title of the work, as given in Theodore Martin's 1857 translation (London: J. W. Parker), is *Aladdin, or, The Wonderful Lamp: A Dramatic Poem in Two Parts, by Adam Oehlenschlager*. This particular passage is used in part of the fifth and concluding movement of Ferruccio Busoni's immense piano concerto, *Opus 39*.

10. Although mentioned only in passing, the style and form of *Sayf Ben Dhi Yazan* is admirably analyzed in Danuta Madeyska's study, in Polish, of *siras: Poetyka Siratu, Studium O Arabskim Romansie Rycerskim* (Warsaw: Warsaw University, 1993; there is a summary in English on pp. 197–200). On parallelism, see A. F. L. Beeston, "The Role of Parallelism in Arabic Prose," *Cambridge History of Arabic Literature*, vol. 1 (Cambridge: Cambridge University Press, 1983), pp. 180–85.

11. For *Sayf al-Tijan*, see the French translation by A. Perron, *Glaive des couronnes* (Paris, 1862).

12. Edward William Lane, *The Thousand and One Nights, Commonly Called, in England, The Arabian Nights' Entertainments* (1839–1841; London: East-West Publications, 1981), vol. 3, chap. 20, nn. 64 and 83, and chap. 25, nn. 11, 15, and 16.

13. See M. Cook, "Pharaonic History in Medieval Egypt," *Studia Islamica* 57 (1983), pp. 79–99.

14. On this whole subject, see Dorothee Metlitzki, *The Matter of Araby in Medieval England* (New Haven: Yale University Press, 1977), pp. 140–60.

15. Faruq Khurshid, *Sayf Ben Dhi Yazan (al-Malhama al-Sha'biyya)* (Cairo: Dar al-Shuruq, 1402 [1982]).

16. All these relations have been discussed in my article, "Sayf Ben Dhi Yazan and the Book of the History of the Nile," *Quaderni di Studi Arabi* 7 (1989), pp. 134–37. For an introductory survey of Ethiopia's relations with the Muslim world—especially during the period most relevant to the story of Sayf's exploits—and a discussion of the reasons for the composition of the *sira*, see I. Hrbek, ed., *UNESCO General History of Africa*, vol. 3, abridged edition (New York: UNESCO, 1992), pp. 279–84.

17. See the *Encyclopaedia of Islam*. In most respects this is the best short introduction to the *sira* by a leading authority.

18. Quoted from I. Filshtinsky, *Arabic Literature* (Moscow: Nauka, 1966), p. 223.

Translator's Introduction
LENA JAYYUSI

One of the remarkable things about this folk tale, seen from the vantage point of the late twentieth century, is that it attests to the shifts, plays, and transformations of language and concepts that are characteristic of human experience and perception. The hero at the heart of this narrative is based on a real historical figure who, according to folk tradition, was an Arab king of the Jewish faith (recast as a Muslim in the folktale), who lived in the sixth century A.D., prior to the rise of Islam, and who is viewed as one of the first genuine Arab heroes. Although the narrative reveals the central role of identity in human practice, it reveals, at the same time, its complexity, its multiplicity, and its open-ended character.

The figure of Sayf Ben Dhi Yazan is presented in the tale (together with other characters) as a Muslim (a believer in Islam), prior to the actual advent of Islam. In the narrative, the *Shehadeh*, one of the five fundamental tenets of Islam, is transmuted: it bears witness to Abraham as God's Friend and to the Prophet Muhammad as the seal of all prophets who will come "at the end of time" bearing the message of Islam, the true religion. Thus the tale may be seen as a reworking of the historical "story" of Sayf Ben Dhi Yazan of Yemen in such a way as to leave a narrative space for some of its real-world particulars; at the same time it affirms the primacy of Islam as the true and final word of God, and Islam's continuity with the earlier monotheistic traditions.

The actual historical details surrounding the life of the real Sayf Ben Dhi Yazan cannot be definitively determined or confirmed since no written sources dating from that period survive. However, according to both oral tradition and accounts of Arab historians writing in the tenth century, the historical Sayf had fought (and briefly won) battles against Ethiopian Christian forces. In those accounts of that conflict, both religious and ethnic divisions had simultaneously been involved: on one side Jewish Arab, on the other Christian Ethiopian. But in the fourteenth century, at the time that the oral tale seems to have made its appearance in the form we know today, a predominantly Muslim Arab Egypt under Mamluk rule (foreign, yet Muslim), was anxious about the threat posed by Christian Ethiopia. Sayf's enemies in the tale are, however, pagans who worship the stars. Thus, in the transformations worked on the "historical" story, which produced this narrative of an Arab hero—a Muslim *prior* to the advent of Islam, battling foreign pagans—one can perhaps locate a "space" for the two other monotheistic religious constituencies of Egypt (and the Arab world) at the time the tale was popular. Furthermore, it provides a space for emphasizing equally the primacy and virtue of both the Muslim *and* the Arab identity of the central characters. In this version, Sayf, as the pre-Islamic Muslim, can fully embody Arab virtues and character, which are sung repeatedly in the abundant verse that is woven into the tale. Thus both the religious and the ethnic dimensions are attended to in a way that may refract the tensions and accommodations within the society and culture of the time.

The selections in this volume are drawn from the first 500 pages of the 4-volume edition of the epic published by Maktabat Al-Jumhuriyya in Cairo (n.d.), which totals nearly 2000 pages. These 500 pages represent one cycle of the tale's events, what can be called the "founding cycle." This cycle can be read as an allegory of the establishment of Muslim Arab dominion and empire. It recounts Sayf's adventures and tribulations as he establishes his sovereign rule in the service of God and in accordance with the tenets of Abraham and Muhammad. His battles, loves, journeys, and pursuits, his mistakes, misfortunes, and victories are chronicled here. They culminate in his victory, the demise of his scheming mother, the union with women who represent various territorial constituencies (and different meanings in his life), the forging of alliances with monarchs from Persia to China, and the destruction of paganism in these territories. The rest of the tale chronicles the adventures and pursuits, not only of Sayf the king, but also of his sons: as Sayf fulfills the prophecy and overcomes all enemies of Islam, the focus of the narrative becomes the sustenance and maintenance of righteousness and Muslim dominion.

Another set of identities which the tale reveals to contemporary eyes in a distinctive way involves gender. One of the most striking features of the gender landscape delineated here is the absence of the hard dividing line between "woman" as private, emotional, and reactive, if not passive, and "man" as a public, rational, and active agent that one finds in western notions of the culture of the Arab world. This construction of "woman" (as opposed to the depiction of an individual woman who may step outside of its boundaries) is also, of course, one that predominates in contemporary western epics from Tolstoy's *War and Peace*, to Lew Wallace's *Ben-Hur*. Here, by contrast, we have women who can ride into battle, become strategists for survival, and exact retribution, on the one hand, and men who weep for love, recite emotional verses, or give in to curiosity that defies wisdom, on the other. Neither women nor men in this tale are distilled out of pure elements of emotion or reason, weakness or strength, the now dichotomous renderings of "male" and "female" that mark popular culture and institutions. Rather, the gender identities of both male and female are melded of the same combinations.

Nevertheless, the narrative exhibits a very interesting progression: while women who "rule" and are politically "powerful" or autonomous may still be cast as virtuous, desirable, and "successful," they shift position within the founding cycle so that "power" and leadership come to reside primarily in the hands of the men they marry. This is in marked contrast to western fairy tales and narratives as we know them today, in which women who are powerful are also figures of evil or darkness (the brothers Grimm, for example, as well as the

Disney renderings of them). In the Sayf epic, the women simply do not retain power, and Sayf's mother, who insists on it, is doomed. This suggests that gender distinctions are embedded more in a vision of social organization and the division of labor than in a conception of wholly distinct "natures."

The treatment of women in the Sayf tale demonstrates that the oral narrative is a "living" field of negotiated identities, positions, and practices. The puzzles and paradoxes that one finds as one reads the epic offer indications of the process by which the tale itself came to be formed. This is not surprising when one remembers that the oral tale, disseminated and transmitted in popular venues, was thus situated within the living fabric of everyday culture. One feature of the tale that is especially salient here is the characterization of Sayf's mother, which does not fit into the patterns of characterization of the "mother" figure in Arabic tales, either traditional or contemporary. She is the major individual villain (as opposed to the "collective" villain, i.e., paganism) of the story, constantly attempting to kill her own son in order to usurp his power and position. In Arabic Islamic literature, this kind of motif is quite rare, though it is not uncommon in western tales (e.g., Hansel and Gretel). Within this founding cycle of the tale, the advantage alternates between Sayf and his treacherous mother until she finally meets her fate at the hands of his jinni half-sister, 'Aqisa.

But what could such an anomalous characterization suggest? If we place it within the context of the other developments of the story, in which women's worldly position (not their gender characteristics) shifts, might it be an index of an ongoing negotiation, even conflict, over gender roles that was taking place in Egypt at the time? Might it not reflect some popular cultural responses to the real-life story of Queen Shajar al-Durr, which had unfolded in Egypt in the mid-thirteenth century, within recent historical memory? Like the figure of Qamariyya, Sayf's mother in the epic, the real-life Shajar al-Durr had been a foreign-born slave girl who married a sultan after conceiving his child and who acceded to power on his death. Shajar al-Durr then ruled on her own for some three months, until she married the military commander Aybak, who took the title to the throne. Subsequently, lest she be removed from power, she had this second husband, the sultan, killed in the bath when she learned that he was planning to take a second wife. The parallel with significant elements of Qamariyya's role and character in the tale is striking. Shajar al-Durr's story provides a potentially rich source for the themes of betrayal and power/gender conflicts that surface in the Sayf epic. One can thus discern the interplay of various literary, folkloric, and historical sources, and the hybridities they engender, within the oral tale.

A final point needs to be made here about the constructions of identity within this tale. One of the salient identity distinctions that emerges is that of race and ethnicity: black and white, Ethiopian and Arab. As with gender, these categories within the tale are more fluid and multiple than one might expect. The narrative tells, early on, the biblical story of Noah's sons and Noah's cursing of Ham. In the Sayf tale, this narrative (which is also a Quranic narrative) is used to explain the origin of the black peoples of Africa and thus to mark the "difference" between the peoples of the region. Yet it does not appear within the tale as a *systematic* marker of moral or even aesthetic differences. In this treatment, it is the Muslim dimension of identity and its discourse of universality that is implicitly privileged—the union of Sayf and Shama, the glowingly beautiful daughter of the black King Afrah, Sayf's first love and his first wife, is a politically and culturally charged union that had been foretold. It portends the fall of Ethiopian power, but is nevertheless a union which is in part accomplished and sustained through the allegiance and assistance of great black warriors and kings who are sung for their prowess, defeated only by Muslim fortitude and God's aid. It is a union which, more than anything else, signifies the fall of paganism and the ascendance of Islam, proclaiming, at the same time, that Islam is the message that unites and includes all who would believe.

The version made available here is composed of part translation and part retelling of the "founding cycle" (the latter is indicated in the text by a ragged right margin). The choice of sections for direct translation was based on their textual quality as well as their thematic importance. The translated sections are either central to the development of the tale's fundamental themes and concerns or particularly rich in detail, language, and imagery. The Great Battle, for example, establishes a very important principle: the primacy in battle of the Muslim warrior over the pagan and his superior righteousness manifested in his valor, prowess, and mercy. In this battle, the conversion of the great Ethiopian warriors to the side of Sayf and Islam is accomplished, and the moral superiority of one side over the other is demonstrated. Linguistically and from a comparative literary perspective, it is an important section, since the literature of battle was always important in Arab history. Tales of battle, moreover, can lend themselves superbly to two elements that are particularly pronounced in oral literature: the alliterative and the visual. A battle scene is a site of exaggerated sound as well as of striking images.

The Garden of Delights and the City of Maidens, also very rich in narrative texture, treat a key theme in classical Arabic literature: love. They represent the pursuit, winning, temporary loss, and reclaiming of Munyat Al-Nufus, the central love in Sayf's life. These two sections also address a significant point of tension that arises within the tale itself (and that may perhaps be taken as an indication of its relevance in everyday life): that of polygamy. The narrative in these sections attempts to resolve the issue and to work out the relationship between men and women and their respective roles.

Some of the sections chosen for translation (Quest for the "Book of the Nile," The Sword, Kings and Magicians) are particularly complex and developed narratives of the fantastic that elaborate a mythic world of humans and *jinn*, physical and metaphysical, rational and magical, closely intertwined together, as they might have been within the popular imagination of the day. These figures, events, and developments within the tale are not set up in opposition to "religious" conceptions (indeed they could not be, given their Quranic grounding) but are, rather, very much embedded in them. Here again, popular cultural narratives are different from the more ascetic and sociolegal preoccupations of Muslim religious authorities, as well as from western dichotomies between the "magical" and the "sacred" that were the outcome of the cultural conflicts and contestations through which modern western Christianity was able to establish itself in Europe.

I have attempted to maintain a continuity of tone and style between the translated and narrated sections. As many significant narrative and descriptive details as possible have been included in order to preserve scenic settings, atmosphere, and character, as well as the sense of unfolding action. This approach allows the "story world" to remain consistent and vibrant across both translated and narrated sections. The translated sections include the verse.

As one reads the Sayf epic, scenes unfold before one's eyes, as though one were watching a film. The tale is, in this respect, very cinematic. The language used and the details rendered construct a vivid and colorful scene for the reader or listener. Oral tales depend on the description of actions and their contexts, as much as on dialogue. The importance of scenic description is embedded in the roles of narrator and listener: for the narrator, memory of the narrative trajectory may be enhanced by its repeatedly visual rendition. At the same time, the details of the visual descriptions provide each narrator with a space for "creative" rendition that nevertheless maintains the integrity of the story line. And it is, in part, the visual details that transport the listener to the scene and evoke the pleasure of imagined lives and experiences that keep him or her interested in the minute-by-minute flow of the tale. In the Garden of Delights, for example, there is the rich tapestry of the description of the physical environment and setting; in the Great Battle there are the manifold actions and sounds of battle. The language used is minutely descriptive and active, and it is precisely through alliteration and repetition (necessary for the memorizing of an oral tale) that the visual character of the action is amplified. The battle scene becomes not only vivid through the detail provided but *familiar* through the repetition that accompanies each round of the battle. One has to remember that, as told, this tale would have been accompanied by phonetic expression—voice and gesture would have added a further dimension to the scenes described for the listeners. That interactive dimension is important, particularly where alliteration, rhyme, and repetition are concerned, but also with respect to visual imagery. For here, gestures would have contributed to the virtual materialization, not so much of the described scene in front of the listener, as of the listener within the imagined scene.

The Adventures of Sayf Ben Dhi Yazan thus embodies two significant properties of an orally rendered folktale. First, an oral tale can be subtly reworked to incorporate contemporary events and concerns that may not have been as important at the time earlier versions of the tale began to circulate. An oral tale has no author, nor is it treated as authored. Over time, it is a transmutable cultural object, so that it becomes difficult to locate a base or essential version, as is the case with an authored written narrative, although one can perhaps speak of essential elements and figures. As a cultural object, it is distinct from the written tale.

Second, every "reading" of a tale is located *within its own context* and reflexively reveals it. The oral tale, in this way, is uniquely suited both to exploring the unfolding cultural and social contexts, contradictions, and preoccupations of the period and to critically rendering one's own cultural categories of other times and places. It remains then, for the present-day reader of these pages to undertake a journey of exploration that will, assuredly, yield puzzles and pleasures not encountered elsewhere.

THE ADVENTURES OF

Sayf Ben Dhi Yazan

AN ARAB FOLK EPIC

1

King Dhi Yazan

Once, in times long past, there was a king of great power and renown, feared by one and all. This king was of the tribe of Banu Himyar, whose fame and reputation spread wide among the people of those days. His name was King Dhi Yazan, and he ruled over the land of Yemen and had a wise minister called Yathrib.

Now this Yathrib was not only wise but an eloquent man of good lineage, and he was very dear to King Dhi Yazan, who gave him command over all his army. He had read the ancient books and old heroic tales, and had found—in the Torah, and the Bible, and the writings of Abraham the Friend of God, and the scrolls of David— the name of our master Muhammad, God bless him and grant him salvation, who was from the clan of Quraysh of the tribe of Banu Hashim; and he had read, too, of how this Prophet would spread the true faith of Islam, rooting out the religions of unbelievers and tyrants through the length and breadth of the land. When he had read these books, he saw the truth and followed it, abandoning all error, and believed in the Prophet Muhammad and became one of the Faithful.

The days and years passed, and then, one feast day, King Dhi Yazan went out of the city to celebrate the feast together with all his troops and all those who dwelt in the city, not one being left behind. When he saw the mighty array of his troops, he commanded them to parade there before him and be counted; and when this had been done, his men came to the king, saying: "O valiant and mighty king, you have four hundred thousand knights, and four hundred thousand warriors bearing heavy arms, and four hundred thousand men with shields and armor, and four hundred thousand with bows and battle-axes, all of them like raging lions."

When the king heard this, he rejoiced, saying: "In the name of the idols and al-Lat and al-ʿUzza, no great king, from the East to the West, has such a mighty army." Then, turning to Yathrib, he said: "Tell me Yathrib, from the depth of your knowledge, is there any king on earth who has such a kingdom as I, or such numbers of warriors, or greater glory?"

"O great and glorious King," replied Yathrib, "there is in the East a king called Baʿlabek, who is valiant and powerful, feared by free man and slave alike. He has men and warriors, knights and champions, fearless as lions and more numerous than the grains of sand. This king has built a dome outside the city, and in it he has placed a hoard of all manner of jewels and precious metals. It is built of gold and silver, and within are a hundred thousand vessels and ornaments, and a hundred and twenty lanterns of glass to light it, and the crescent on its summit is a gem of twenty carats. All around this dome is an orchard filled with various fruits that grow by Almighty God's power, and on the branches perch birds praising God in all tongues. Alongside is a stately palace, lovely enough to remove all care and sorrow from the heart of the beholder, and there it is that his women dwell."

When King Dhi Yazan heard this, the light before his eyes turned to darkness, and he swore in the names of al-Lat and al-ʿUzza that he would march against King Baʿlabek and slay him, blotting out his name and memory from all the lands.

In the coming days King Dhi Yazan busied himself in dispensing the affairs of his kingdom; then, remembering Yathrib's words, he summoned up his resolve and ordered his minister to make his troops ready for a journey to battle and conquest. And when Yathrib had done as he was commanded and all was ready at last, the king mounted his horse and gave the order for the great march eastward to begin.

For three full days the troops marched on, with King Dhi Yazan and Yathrib riding at their head; and on the fourth day they drew near God's Holy House. Then lo, Yathrib, the king's minister, dismounted and approached that House, falling to his knees and saying: "To the Sovereign God who created this world from nothing, and to Him alone, is it fitting to kneel." When King Dhi Yazan saw Yathrib act in this fashion, he was greatly perturbed; and when Yathrib had finished his prayer, he said: "My Minister, why have you done this, when I never saw you, in all your life, do such a thing before? Why have you acted in this way?"

"You must know, O King," answered the minister Yathrib, "that we have come to God's Holy House, the dwelling place of His noble angels, and of His mighty prophets and messengers, peace be upon them. This is the House of God who formed the seven heavens and filled them with angels, who unfolded the seven tiers of earth, making them fast with the lofty, immovable mountains. This is the House of Him who created the sun and the moon and the rock, and the circling planets, the dark night and the golden morning, and the foaming sea—the whole world, through all its length and breadth—and who provided a cause for all things."

"This is the One who created us," the king said then. "And do we worship idols?"

"O King," said the minister, "He it is also who created those idols."

Then the king asked his minister who could have built such a place in the desert, with no servant or any to help him. "Know," replied the minister, "that when Almighty God commanded Adam to come to the Ka'ba and build the Holy House, Adam took the stones from the mountain close by, with the strength Gabriel gave him by God's leave; and when he had laid the foundations, Gabriel erected the pillars and showed Adam how to build, and so Adam, through Gabriel's instruction, erected the house. Then Gabriel told Adam to make pilgrimage each year to that House, along with the angels, till at last Almighty God created Noah. And Noah exhorted his people to embrace the true faith; then, when they would not follow him, he called down God's wrath upon them, and God answered his call, commanding Noah to build a ship and take one pair of each living creature on board, one male and one female. And Noah did as he was commanded.

"Then God sent a great flood, raising this House up into the heavens, and moving the black stone to Mount Abu Qubays, till at last the waters had covered the peaks of the mountain ranges and the ship floated over the spot where this House had been built. And Noah and all who were with him were saved, but God drowned the others of his tribe. Then God commanded the rain to cease, and the land to become dry, and mountain and city appeared once more; and Almighty God ordered Noah to obey his commandments."

When the king heard this, he asked Yathrib what he should do concerning the Holy House, and Yathrib told him he should dismount and circle it with reverence. At that the king commanded his army to dismount and pitch camp; then, as they busied themselves raising the tents and banners, and preparing the food, he circled the Holy House, gazing on it and contemplating it till he was lost in awe and admiration. Then the wish took hold of his heart to take it down piece by piece and bear it off to his own land; for by this means he desired to exalt himself above all other kings, from the East to the West, and to become the mightiest king indeed.

When the king spoke of this to Yathrib, his minister said: "O great King and wise Sovereign, this House has a God to protect it against all harm, and none can take it down. Do not therefore attempt this, lest you have cause to rue it."

"In the name of al-Lat and al-'Uzza," said the king then, "I must indeed take it down."

"King of all time," replied the minister, "the prophets and angels it was that built this house, at God's commandment and by His will."

Then the king, falling into a fury, summoned the masons and architects and builders of his kingdom, and they were ten thousand strong. And when they appeared before him, he told them that when the sun rose the next day they should begin to take down the House stone by stone, using the greatest care not to break a single stone; for if any did so, his head would be struck off. But when King Dhi Yazan woke the next morning, he found his body bloated and diseased, and uttered such a cry as shook the corners of the place and brought the elders of his council running to his side, filled with amazement at his condition. Then the king instructed that Yathrib be summoned forthwith.

"King of all time," said the minister, "this is the work of the Lord of this House. If you do not hold back from taking it down, and do not believe in the God of Zamzam and al-Maqam, then you will perish utterly."

"I swear before you," the king said then, "and before all those gathered here, that I repent of my resolve to take down this House, and that I believe in its Lord and Sovereign."

And when King Dhi Yazan woke next morning, he was sound of body once more; and, gazing at the House, he saw it to be still more beautiful than before. Then he once more summoned his masons and architects, and once more he commanded them to begin their work at dawn; and again, when he woke from his sleep, he found his body bloated, but much more bloated than the first time, so that it appeared a mere lump of flesh, without hands or feet or eyes, like a flayed mouse. And once more, with screams and cries, he summoned Yathrib and asked his counsel.

"King of all time," said Yathrib, "without peer in this age, you first professed faith in the Lord of this House, then went back on your word. Repent of your resolve to take it down, and believe in God, and in the prophet Abraham, His Friend."

Then the king once more made his profession of faith, declaring he would never again seek to take down the House. But again, when he woke and found himself sound of body, he resolved to take it down; and yet again next morning, for the third time, he woke to find himself bloated, to a degree still greater than the first times. And when Yathrib came to him, the king said: "My Minister, I shall never again attempt to act in this fashion, or seek to do the impossible."

"Twice you have made profession of your faith," said the minister, "and twice you have gone back on your word. If you do not truly, this third time, repent of your wicked resolve, and do not truly believe in Almighty God, the Lord of this Holy House, and in the Prophet Abraham, His Friend, you shall be destroyed and sent into perdition with all other unbelievers; but if you believe, having faith in the message of Abraham, the Friend of God, and in all the prophets and messengers, then you shall be saved and receive your reward at last, dwelling in Paradise as one of the blessed."

When King Dhi Yazan heard all this, he professed his faith truly and firmly before his minister, declaring: "I witness that there is no God but God, and I witness that Abraham is the Friend of God." And he believed in all the principles of Islam because of what he had seen of Almighty God's power. Then he commanded his whole army to profess the Faith, and they all became Muslims by heartfelt conviction.

That night, when King Dhi Yazan was asleep, a voice called out to him in his dreams, saying: "Dhi Yazan, adorn the walls of the Holy House with hangings, for you dwell beneath its blessings, and the blessings of those who shall make pilgrimage there from the four corners of the earth." And when he woke, he summoned Yathrib, who was now dearer than a brother to him, and Yathrib told him to do as the voice had commanded.

Then King Dhi Yazan commanded that the walls of the House should be covered with goat hair. But as he slept that night, the voice called out again, saying: "Hang the walls of the House with something other than this."

"O King," said Yathrib, when the king told him of this dream, "you are sovereign over all the earth. These hangings are not worthy of the House, nor of you."

And so the king commanded that the walls of the House be hung with silk; but the voice called out to him yet a third time in his sleep, saying: "Hang the walls of the House with something other than this." And again the minister counseled the king to heed the voice's bidding. Then the king commanded that the silk hangings be embroidered with pearls and silver and gold thread, and so it was done.

Then, when a few days had passed, King Dhi Yazan, sound of body and free of all disease, gave orders for the eastward march to resume; and when they had gone a distance of seven parasangs, they came upon a green and fertile valley, filled with fine fruits and sparkling waters, and with graceful gazelles and all manner of birds singing and praising God. And there King Dhi Yazan ordered his men to dismount and pass the night.

Next morning Yathrib approached the king and, kissing the ground before him, addressed him thus: "O fortunate King, may your morning be blessed, and may God bring you ever greater prosperity and success. This land, so goodly and fragrant, pleases me and I am minded to build a city here. Know too, O valiant King, that I have read in the ancient books and chronicles and heroic tales how Almighty God will send a Hashimi Qurayshi prophet named Muhammad—God bless him and grant him salvation. The highest prophet he is, and the seal of the messengers, and he will remove from Mecca to this good and fragrant land and here make his abode and his grave. I ask the King's leave to build a city here, and call it by my name."

When the king had given his permission, his minister thanked him, wishing him blessings and health and prosperity a thousandfold. Then he departed and began forthwith to lay the foundations of the city and to establish its dwellings and palaces, and raise its walls; and when this was done, he settled men and women and children of his clan to live in it. Then it was that he wrote a book for them, enjoining them to preserve it from generation to generation, and to give it to any who should remove from Mecca and the Holy House; and to that man to whom these letters spoke, the city and all its great places would belong. Then the minister gave the city his own name, calling it Yathrib.

His people took the book accordingly, placing it in a secure coffer enclosed

within a dome, and guarding it from generation to generation, till God sent
forth the glorious prophet Muhammad; and when the Prophet Muhammad
was given the Message, and his own people turned against him, he left Mecca
and removed to Medina, after the most dazzling prodigies had been per-
formed at his hands, and he came to this city. Then, when he entered the
place and settled there, the citizens brought out the book and gave it to him;
and when the Prophet, God bless him and grant him salvation, took it and
opened it, the letters spoke to him. With that the people of the city placed
their lives and their families and their wealth at his service, and these were the
Helpers of the Prophet. All this was to happen later, after Yathrib had built
the city.

As for King Dhi Yazan, when the city had been built and named and all
were settled there, he gave the order for his mighty army to march on once
more, and rode at their head like a raging lion toward the land of King
Ba'labek.

Many days they marched over plains and hills, till at last they came to the
place where King Ba'labek dwelt; and there Dhi Yazan ordered his men to
surround the city and pitch their camp. When news came to King Ba'labek
that King Dhi Yazan had come down upon the city with all his army, he was
greatly perturbed and sent an emissary to Dhi Yazan with a letter asking
where he had come from and what his purpose was. Accompanied by fifty
knights, the emissary presented himself before Dhi Yazan with courtesy and
ceremony and was well received in his turn; and when King Dhi Yazan's reply
reached Ba'labek, he was pleased, commanding that Dhi Yazan's army should
be fed and entertained for three whole days. Then, on the fourth day,
Ba'labek rode out with a group of his own dignitaries and knights to meet
Dhi Yazan; but Dhi Yazan met him halfway, taking his turn now to entertain
his guest and honor him, setting a great banquet before him. Then Ba'labek
again asked Dhi Yazan why he had come to that land, and Dhi Yazan told
him he had come to see whether Yathrib's account of his might and magnifi-
cence were true or not. At this King Ba'labek was amused and delighted, and
he invited King Dhi Yazan to review his troops and visit his palace.

Next day King Ba'labek paraded his men before King Dhi Yazan, who was
astounded at their number; for they were more numerous than the grains of
the desert sand. Then, on the third day, he sent emissaries to conduct King
Dhi Yazan and his kin, his dignitaries and knights, to his palace, there to
witness for themselves its splendor and the glory of his realm. When they
entered the city, King Dhi Yazan and his men found themselves in a great
orchard, and within that orchard stood a lofty palace, amazing in its work-
manship and ornament. It was a full ninety cubits long, and, likewise ninety
cubits wide, built of marble blocks studded with pearls and emeralds, with ten
gates of Andalusian brass that dazzled the eye with their brilliance, and the
turrets of the palace glittered with gold and silver.

Then King Ba'labek greeted Dhi Yazan with great ceremony, bidding him be seated alongside him on a chair of ivory inlaid with shining gold, and set before him a banquet served in dishes of precious stone and red gold, without peer in their time. And when they had eaten and made merry, King Ba'labek showed King Dhi Yazan all the wealth of his treasury.

By this time Dhi Yazan was lost in admiration and wonder, and he turned to King Ba'labek, saying: "O fortunate King, I have seen your warriors, and your wealth and treasures; all that now remains for me to see is your valor. Either you shall overcome me, or I you, and whoever wins the victory shall possess this kingdom." And King Ba'labek, who was a fearless fighter and a mighty and indomitable rider in battle, gave his consent to this.

Next day the place for the contest was determined, and the knights gathered on their horses to view the combat. The first in the field was Ba'labek, brandishing in his hand a sword that shone like a flame; and then King Dhi Yazan came to meet him, bearing a lance as heavy as an engine of siege or the mast of a ship, and the two fell one upon the other, jarring together like two mighty mountains.

All day long they fought and jousted, lunged and retreated, till the hour of sunset approached and they parted for the night, each of them safe and sound. Then, on the morrow, they met in combat once more, and all that day they fought fiercely and proudly, with neither gaining advantage over the other or giving way; and at nightfall they parted to go to their rest, the knights and troops wondering at their skill and valor in battle. But on the third day, when they had met still another time in fearful combat, King Ba'labek felt his strength wane and his will fail, and he turned and fled into the desert, anxious to escape the jaws of death.

By noontide on the second day, as he walked on in the heat of the sun, all at once he saw a cloud of dust in the distance; and within the hour the dust lifted to reveal a ferocious lion, with eyes flashing, fangs bared and claws sharper than misfortune, glaring and glowering at him. When the lion saw Ba'labek approach, it leapt at him with a fearsome roar and tore into him, dealing him a mighty blow with its paws. Such was the end of Ba'labek.

As for King Dhi Yazan, after Ba'labek had fled, he took possession of all his wealth and treasures, laying claim to his kingdom and slaying his warriors. Then, appointing a governor to rule over the kingdom on his behalf, he took twenty full loads of Ba'labek's wealth, struck camp, and set off toward the lands of Ethiopia and the Sudan.

So they marched on through the desert, for many days and nights, till they came upon a green and beautiful valley, with lush trees and bushes, abundant water and rushing sparkling streams, birds of every kind singing and praising the Eternal One, flowers laughing in every corner, and a musky fragrance blowing from all sides, truly a garden of delights.

So taken was King Dhi Yazan with that place that he straightway resolved to build a city there, making it his royal seat and a home for his people ever after; and, having made his wishes known to his minister and received his approbation, he set his masons and architects to the task of building a grand and well-fortified city. When they had completed their work and a mighty and splendid city stood there before his eyes, he was filled with joy and sent forthwith for all his kinsfolk, and all his knights and people, to move there with their families. Then they, at his bidding, came to dwell with him, and he called the new city al-Madina al-Hamra' (meaning, the Red City); and they all lived there in happiness and contentment, with an abundance of good food and drink.

So the time passed; then one day, King Dhi Yazan summoned his minister and, having bade him be seated, said: "See all this beauty God has given us. I mean to plunder all other realms, so that no adversary shall be left to stand against me across the face of the earth; Ethiopia shall be mine, and its kings shall be subject to me and render me tribute. My desire is to be sole sovereign and live out my days in glory and splendor."

"Do as you wish, King of all time," said Yathrib, "but let me first cast the sands and make my divination; for I have read in the ancient books and great heroic tales that there shall be a king from among the noble Tubba'i kings at whose hands the curse of Noah will come to pass. It may be that you are he, O valiant and fearless King."

But when the minister cast the sands and examined them closely, he saw this was not the king at whose hands the curse of Noah should come to pass, but that it would be one of his flesh and blood, bearing his name, who would uphold the Islamic creed and bid people worship the All-Knowing Sovereign; and he saw how the whole of Ethiopia and the Sudan would come to serve the descendants of Shem, son of Noah.

And so the minister informed his king of what he had seen, reciting it in a long poem that chronicled their journey and adventures, and counseling him to lay aside all dishonorable intent and fight only those who stood against him. He assured him too that the prophesied king, begotten by him, would in due season settle the land of Egypt, so that Arabs and foreigners would dwell there together in concord. This king, he said, would make the Nile flow through Egypt, and God's rule and decree would be paramount.

When the king heard these strange verses, he was filled with a wondering awe and had it written down in gold characters, keeping it as one of the precious things in his treasury, so that it became famous to all. And so it was the king was dissuaded from his intent.

The days went by, and word of King Dhi Yazan reached the king of Ethiopia and the Sudan, who was sovereign over this whole region and was called Sayf Ar'ad (meaning, Sword of Thunder), because his voice was like the very thunder. A mighty and fearless king he was, at whose words hearts trembled, and whose bidding was done by one and all. He was sovereign over all the kings of Ethiopia and the Sudan, exacting tribute and respect from each of them, feared by everyone, and his city was called al-Dour. Vast and splendid it was, half on land and half in the sea, and this king had six hundred thousand armored knights.

He had also two accursed demonic wizards to counsel him, one named Saqardyoun, the Ill-Fated, and the other Saqardis; and he had a minister called Bahr Qafqan al-Rif, who had read in the ancient books the same things as the minister Yathrib and likewise had secretly professed Islam. For in those days the people in the lands of Ethiopia and the Sudan worshipped the stars, and Saturn above all, rather than the Almighty.

One day King Sayf Ar'ad summoned his two wizards and the minister Bahr Qafqan al-Rif, saying: "See how these coarse and ignorant Arabs have settled in our lands without seeking our leave. I have resolved to conquer them and destroy their dwellings, to slay them to the last man, both young and old, and seize their wealth and their women."

"If you will take my counsel," said the wizard Saqardis, "do not ride out against them. Do not confront them, for I fear lest the curse of Noah should come to pass at their hands."

"And what is this curse, wizard of all time?" asked King Sayf Ar'ad.

With that Saqardis recounted the story. "Know, King of all time," he said, "matchless among your peers and in this age, ruler over all Ethiopia and the Sudan, that there was in ancient times a prophet called Noah. He exhorted his people to follow him and heed his commands; and when they would not do so, he called down God's wrath upon them, so that rain fell from the sky, and the waters sprang up from beneath the earth, and all who stood against him were drowned. Only Noah survived, together with those of his kin who followed him. Then, one day, he fell asleep in the afternoon hours with his sons Shem and Ham seated beside him, and a breeze blew over him so that his private parts were exposed; for in those days they did not wear drawers. At that Shem came forward and covered his father, but Ham looked at his father's private parts and laughed, and Noah awoke from his slumber and dreams to find the two young men quarreling, with Ham seated at his feet and Shem seated by his head. When he saw Ham grinning and Shem angry, he asked them what the matter was, and his son Shem told him what had happened. Then Noah looked angrily at Ham and called down God's wrath upon him (and his prayer was always accepted by God), saying: 'May God blacken your face and the faces of your descendants, and make your progeny serve the progeny of your brother Shem, the child of your own mother and father.' And now we fear lest this curse should come to pass upon us, at the hands of this king who has come to our domain."

When King Sayf Ar'ad heard this, he was struck dumb for a full hour; but while he was in this condition, a company of men came in and kissed the ground before him, saying: "King of all time, as we were making our way to your city, we came upon another city, fortified and Meccan, in the Red Land, which we had never seen before. A lovely and splendid city it is, with trees blossoming and fountains gushing, its gardens filled with graceful gazelles and warbling birds, its towers soaring high and its walls raised firm, its watchfires gleaming from afar; and we were obliged to pay tribute to its king."

When King Sayf Ar'ad heard this, he fell into a fury and, turning to his cowering counselor Saqardis, rebuked him for holding him back from conquest. At that Saqardis counseled the king to defeat his foe by trickery and deceit rather than war and combat. "O valiant King and mighty Sovereign," he said, "so it is you should do: send him a splendid gift, including one of your loveliest and best-trusted concubines; but first give her a small phial of deadly poison, instructing her that she should, once alone with him, slip it into his food or drink, so that he may die forthwith. Then, when he is dead, his people will depart without battle or combat, and our purpose will be achieved without fighting. Such is my considered opinion, in the name of exalted Saturn."

The king was delighted at this plan and had a gift of great value prepared forthwith, including silks and brocade, precious wares and ornaments, beads and ostrich feathers, horses and camels, and slaves and servants, too. Then, going in to his chambers, he had all his concubines set before him; and there was one among them of great beauty and grace. When he saw her, the king said to himself, "Our goal is accomplished," and he had her brought to him, then told her his plan and gave her the phial of poison. The concubine was willing and eager to do his bidding and, taking the phial of poison, deftly concealed it among the locks of her hair; and the king, pleased at her resourcefulness, placed his hand among her locks, but could not find it. And at that he rejoiced in his heart.

Now this concubine had come to him from foreign lands, from a city called Qamar, and the king had therefore called her Qamariyya. Sayf Ar'ad now had Qamariyya dressed in resplendent robes and adorned like a bride, then he sent her off with other maidens as part of the gift destined for King Dhi Yazan.

As for King Sayf Ar'ad's minister, he was originally from the land of Hijaz; and when a great drought came there, his father migrated with his son, Bahr Qafqan al-Rif, crossing plains and hills till they reached the land of Ethiopia and the Sudan. There they settled, and Bahr Qafqan al-Rif learned the language of the place and adopted the local customs, winning for himself high standing and respect, and marrying a king's daughter from among them. King Sayf Ar'ad had come to favor him greatly and had made him his minister and the first in the land after himself, consulting him on every matter great and small, for he was a man of skill and learning.

This Bahr Qafqan al-Rif, having read the ancient books, as the minister Yathrib had done, had learned of the true faith, and how a prophet from the tribe of 'Adnan would be sent forth at the end of time to destroy the worship of Saturn, and of fire, and of all the idols, and that his name would be Muhammad, God bless him and grant him salvation; and so he had put aside the worship of Saturn and secretly professed Islam. When he saw what King Sayf Ar'ad had done that day on the counsel of Saqardis, his indignation was roused and he resolved to foil their plan. Repairing to his house, he wrote a long letter to King Dhi Yazan, informing him of everything and warning him

against Qamariyya and her poison; and he told him how he, too, was one of
the Faithful.

Then he summoned one of his most trusted slaves and bade him take the
letter to King Dhi Yazan swiftly and in secret, warning him not to let
himself be known to any of Sayf Ar'ad's men, black or white, and to be sure
to arrive before King Ar'ad's emissaries came with the gift and the concu-
bine. The slave set off forthwith, crossing, with great speed, hills and valleys,
wilds and thickets, till he reached Hamra' al-Habash. But it so happened
that King Sayf Ar'ad's emissaries nevertheless came there first, for they had
set off before him.

When these emissaries had explained their mission at the gates of the palace
and had told of the mighty king who sent them, they were brought into the
presence of King Dhi Yazan, where they kissed the ground before him and
gave him their sovereign's greetings. Then they went on to present him with
the precious gifts they had brought with them. King Dhi Yazan was delighted
with the gifts; but when he saw the concubine Qamariyya, radiant in her
beauty and resplendent in her fine robes, love for her struck his heart and
distracted his mind.

Instructing his men to honor King Sayf Ar'ad's emissaries and lavish royal
hospitality upon them, he resolved to go straightway to the quarters where
Qamariyya had been taken, eager to quench his passion and delight his heart,
for he was consumed by love for her. But his minister Yathrib, understanding
what had happened and fearing lest the king should come to harm, counseled
him to hold back a while. "It may be," he said, "that this concubine is sent by
way of a stratagem, a gift in appearance but in reality a trick; for have we not
entered the lands of Ethiopia and the Sudan, and built this city here where we
dwell without leave? These are people who worship the sun and the stars,
Saturn above all. They do not fear the Almighty, and we cannot know what is
in their hearts and minds. Let us be patient in this matter, lest we perish
utterly in the same manner that the throne was lost to Balqis, Queen of
Sheba. It may be that this concubine comes bearing a deadly poison, which
she will slip into your food or wine to slay you." And Yathrib continued to
counsel King Dhi Yazan in this fashion.

As they were thus conversing, they were told of the arrival of Bahr Qafqan
al-Rif's emissary. When he was brought into the king's presence, he kissed
the ground before him, wishing him lasting wealth and prosperity, then gave
him the letter he bore. Then the king passed the letter to Yathrib, who read it
and understood it, and turned to the king, saying: "It is as we said, great
King—what you have received is only in appearance a gift; in fact it is a
cunning trick. The concubine Qamariyya, who has the face of a houri, has
come only to do you harm. She has with her a small phial of deadly poison
and was sent by that basest of wretches, King Sayf Ar'ad, to slay you, for fear
that the curse of Noah should come to pass at your hands. Beware, noble
King, of this concubine, and do not trust her."

Then the light before King Dhi Yazan's eyes turned to darkness; and, commending his minister Yathrib for his wisdom and prudence, he asked him what was to be done. "Summon the concubine here before you in your palace," Yathrib counseled him then, "threatening to slay her forthwith unless she delivers the phial of poison into your hands."

King Dhi Yazan thereupon unsheathed his sword and, entering his palace, went in to Qamariyya, who shone like the very sun. When she saw him, she rose to her feet and greeted him with sweet words, kissing the ground before him. But he paid her no heed; rather, with his sword raised as if to slay her, he demanded she give him the phial of poison provided by King Arʿad so she might slay him. At that she smiled and spoke honeyed words, saying: "I swear by God, valiant King, that whoever is like you will be a great king indeed." Then she put her fingers in her hair, brought out the phial of poison and handed it to him, saying within herself: "What cannot be accomplished today will be accomplished tomorrow. Now he will trust me and love me the more, and I shall be able to slay him."

And indeed, when the king took the phial from her hand, his love for her grew still stronger and, powerless to stay his passion, he joined with her that very hour, finding her to be a virgin untouched by any other man; and she straightway conceived by him.

When Dhi Yazan found that Qamariyya was carrying his child, his love for her took stronger hold yet upon his heart, so that he could not bear to be parted from her and gave her charge over all his affairs—over his women and his kinsfolk, and over all his wealth.

Now it was that King Sayf Arʿad began to send secret messages to Qamariyya, saying: "Did I send you to become his consort or to slay him?" And Qamariyya sent word back to him to be patient, promising she would slay Dhi Yazan when the chance offered and assuring him this would not be long delayed.

So the days passed, and, when Qamariyya was six months pregnant, King Dhi Yazan fell gravely ill and took to his bed—and none but God knows whether this was by some wicked deed wrought by Qamariyya, or by His own will and decree. Then the king, summoning all his dignitaries and counselors and kin to his side, said: "I have gathered you all here to make known my will and testament. To wit, first that you should hold firm in your faith in the One True God and the message of Abraham, the Friend of God, and believe in Muhammad, God bless him and grant him salvation, who will appear at the end of time. And second, know, all of you, that this concubine is carrying my child. She shall rule over you after I am gone, till she has given birth and reared the child up to a proper age. If the child be a male, then he shall rule over you; and if the child be a female, her husband shall rule over you. Remember, too, it is the custom for kings to give their daughters in marriage only to men of the realm, and never to strangers."

When the men heard this, they said to the king: "We hear and obey. We shall do your bidding to the letter." Then it came to pass, a few days later, that King Dhi Yazan departed from this world to the next, and he was buried with all due rites and ceremony.

2
Wahsh
al-Fala

After the death of King Dhi Yazan, Qamariyya sat upon the throne; and when her time came upon her, she went into labor and bore a son who was lovely as the full moon rising on the fourteenth night of the month, with a green mole on his cheek as there had been on his father's, a sign by which the Tubba'i kings have been known from time immemorial. When Qamariyya saw his beauty, a fierce jealousy seized hold of her, and she said to herself: "If this boy should live, he will wrest the kingdom from me and rule over all in my stead; but be patient, Qamariyya, it may be that Saturn will come to your aid." Then she began ceaselessly to pray to Saturn for the boy's death. Nor did she suckle the child in proper fashion, intending that his bowels should run dry and he should perish. But by God's will the boy grew, becoming each day more comely in his beauty, while the wicked woman, knowing nothing of God's almighty power, grew ever more jealous and furious and morose.

So things continued for forty days. Then the ministers of state and all the dignitaries met, saying: "Queen of all time, show us our king, so that we may see him and serve him and protect him." She went off accordingly and, returning straightway with the boy, set him down on the royal throne in the presence of the ministers and nobles, who one and all rose to honor him.

Meanwhile Qamariyya watched from behind a screen, filled with envy and rancor. "I must slay this bastard," she thought to herself, "consigning him to his ruin and perdition. Then I may remain on the throne, with none to contest my sovereignty." When she heard the men say: "You have acceded, O fortunate King, to your father's kingdom, and we are all your slaves," her heart came close to breaking in two; ready to burst almost with rage and grief, she took the child into the palace, then, setting him on the floor, she took hold of a weapon, a scimitar, feeling neither terror nor remorse. In her right hand she raised the scimitar, while with her left she seized his head; but as she was about to strike his head from his body, her arm froze by God's decree. And at that very instant the midwife entered and, standing there before her as she struggled to move her arm and slay her son, cried out: "What are you about?"

"I mean to kill this fruit of sin," said Qamariyya. "For when he grows older, he will wrest the kingdom from me."

"If you slay him, you will rue the day," replied the midwife, "for you will be found out and will pay with your own life. And what crime has this boy committed that you should slay him?" Then she proffered Qamariyya a better plan, that she should take the boy out into the desert, there abandoning him to live or die as his fortune would have it.

That night the midwife came to Qamariyya, saying: "Queen of all time, bring a necklace of precious stones and two thousand dinars." And when Qamariyya had brought her these things, she set the necklace round the boy's neck, and dressed him in a costly robe of embroidered silk unlike any other, then asked for a camel and two of the best horses, set some provisions on the camel and mounted one of the horses, while Qamariyya with her son mounted the other. And so they left the city for the open country.

Four days and four nights they rode; then, on the fifth day, they came to a valley that had once been the site of a prosperous city but was now a barren waste. There Qamariyya placed her child under a thorn bush, with the bag with the two thousand dinars set beneath his head, then, feeling no pity, abandoned him there and made her way joyfully back to her city.

Now just at the place where Qamariyya had left the baby boy, there chanced to be the couching place of a gazelle which had just given birth and was now gone to graze in the wilderness. A hunter had marked her, and had followed her back to this bush, but when she fled from him, he had instead seized her young he found there; and at this moment it was that Qamariyya had come and placed the boy beneath the bush. When the gazelle returned and found her young gone and the baby boy left by Qamariyya in their place, she suckled him, for he was hungry; and when the hunter returned, intent on capturing the gazelle, he found there, to his amazement, the baby boy. "What manner of gazelle is this," he said to himself, "that gives birth to a human baby!"

With that he took the bag of money, and the child, and returned full of joy to his wife, who heard her husband's story with astonishment. "This child," the hunter said, "must be the son of some great king, for I found a bag with a thousand dinars* beneath his head, and he has the appearance of one of royal

---

*The discrepancy in the number of dinars mentioned here no doubt reflects the oral nature of the narrative.

lineage." So comely was the boy! Then he told his wife to keep the necklace safe but to use the money for their needs, and he resolved to take the baby next day to the king of that land.

Now this hunter lived in a walled city called al-Dour,** ruled over by a mighty and valiant king called King Afrah, who was feared by all his neighbors. He worshipped Saturn and owed allegiance to the king of Ethiopia and the Sudan, King Sayf Ar'ad, but was second to none but him alone, commanding a fearless army of ten thousand knights.

Next morning the hunter said to his wife: "This child, I say, is the son of some mighty king. I shall take him to King Afrah, so that he may bring him up in his kingdom; for he has a better right to him than we. For us this money will be sufficient." With that he took the child, and, going full of joy to the palace of King Afrah and standing there beneath the walls, he called out to the king, who had him brought before him and asked him what it was he wanted.

"Know, goodly King," replied the hunter, "that I am a hunter of gazelles and other beasts. Yesterday I went out as is my wont and set a trap, and a gazelle came walking proudly and fell into it; but then, tearing her way free, she fled into the desert, and, furious at her escape, I followed her trail to a bush. There under the bush I found this baby with a bag with a thousand dinars beneath his head and a necklace of precious stones round his neck. Then I said to my wife: 'This child must surely be the son of some mighty king. The proper course is to present him as a gift to King Afrah.' Now I have told you my story as you asked me."

Hearing this, King Afrah took the baby and set him on his lap. When he looked into its face, it smiled at him; and when King Afrah saw the baby smiling, God put love into his heart. He noticed, too, the mole on the child's right cheek and was filled with amazement at his beauty.

At that moment a great commotion was heard in the court, and the king was told that the wizard Saqardyoun, brother to the wizard Saqardis, had arrived with his retinue. The king thereupon rode out to meet him, with much pomp and ceremony, and brought him back to his court. (Now this Saqardyoun, as we have seen, was counselor to Sayf Ar'ad along with his brother, and was a wily and wicked sorcerer, known as the Ill-Fated.) After bidding Saqardyoun be seated alongside him, he showed him the child, saying: "See this boy, brought to us by a hunter who found him in the wilderness, sucking at the teats of a gazelle."

When Saqardyoun heard this, he was struck dumb. Then he looked into the face of the baby, seeing the mole glowing on his right cheek and the face radiant as the full moon; and at that moment God put hatred into his heart, driving all mercy from it. "King of all time," he said, "who ever heard of a

---

**Al-Dour appears to be used in error here for the city of al-Hadid, al-Dour being the city of King Sayf Ar'ad.

gazelle giving birth to a human child? This boy is, I am sure, the mere fruit of adultery; his mother has committed adultery with some great king, and now, fearing shame and dishonor, has abandoned him in the desert, in the couching place of a gazelle. Do not bring him up in our country, for he is not of our race; he, you see, is white, while we are black. The proper course is to kill him, for I fear lest the curse of Noah should come to pass at his hands, bringing destruction to us all." Then the wizard Saqardyoun told King Afrah the story of Noah's curse upon his son Ham. "I have read," he said, "in the ancient books and great heroic tales, that black people will spring from Ham's line, and that from the line of Shem will spring a boy child at whose hands Ethiopia and the Sudan will suffer many tribulations, and so will many priests and sorcerers. He will become a mighty potentate, ruling over both men and jinn with the help of the sword of Asaf, son of Birkhiya, the minister of God's prophet, Solomon, son of David. This Asaf built himself a great and splendid palace in a desolate spot, placing within it a bed of ivory inlaid with shining gold; and when his end drew near, he lay down on this bed with his sword hung above his head, telling the servants of the palace that this sword should be kept for one man alone, King Sayf Ben Dhi Yazan, who would recite his lineage and take possession of the sword by the might of his arm. Such are my fears, O King."

At this King Afrah smiled. "Wizard of all time," he said, "pray tell us the origin of the black people of Ethiopia and the Sudan." And Saqardyoun accordingly told King Afrah of their strange and wonderful beginnings.

When God's prophet Noah died (said Saqardyoun), his sons disputed among themselves as to who should be their father's successor; and when the succession went to Shem, Ham quit the land in a rage, wandering through field and forest till he came to this country, which was ruled by a mighty king called Karkar. This king had an only daughter of great and radiant beauty, and he had decreed that she should choose her own husband, building her a splendid palace outside the city, from which she could look out across the land. One day, as she sat there looking out, it happened that Ham approached on foot, and at first sight of him her heart was filled with passionate love, so handsome was he; for no one had ever seen a black man before. There and then she called out for her servants to bring Ham before her and sent in haste for her father. Ham was accordingly brought before her, and when her father arrived, she said: "It is my wish that you should give me in marriage to this black man." When he saw Ham, King Karkar was struck with admiration, and that very night the marriage ceremony was performed and Ham came in to his bride, who was called Qamar Shahiq; and he enjoyed her beauty and took her virginity, so that she conceived.

After seven months had passed, her father's end grew near; and, gathering his knights and dignitaries around him, he appointed his daughter sole heir and successor to his kingdom, with her husband next in line to her, to be obeyed in everything. Then, a few days after, King Karkar died and was buried with all due rites and ceremony. Thereafter, Queen Qamar Shahiq handed over her throne to her husband, who became sovereign over the length and breadth of the land, and then she gave birth to a boy who was black as coal, and she was filled with delight. Later she bore a daughter and another son, both likewise black, and when they had grown up, they married among the white people of the city and their children were born black; and so it continued through the years that followed, till all the inhabitants of the city became black, and they in their turn married with their white neighbors round about, till the whole population of the land was black. Such was the tale Saqardyoun recounted to King Afrah. "Slay this boy now," he said in conclusion, "before the worst comes to pass."

Now all this took place in the presence of the hunter. And when the king turned to him, asking if he had found anything on the boy, the hunter told him of the bag of money and the precious necklace. Then the king gave him the money and told him to return to his home, he himself keeping the necklace for the boy.

At that moment ululation and joyful song was heard in the palace, and a messenger brought the king the glad news that his wife Queen Dahshana had given birth. At this King Afrah was overjoyed and went straightway to his wife, to find she had given birth to a baby girl lovely as the full moon, with a mole on her cheek just like the mole on the cheek of the boy. Rejoicing, King Afrah carried his daughter to where the boy lay and set her down there beside him, marveling at the two moles.

At this Saqardyoun fell into a frenzy of rage, frothing and foaming at the mouth and crying that the union of the two moles would herald the destruction of the lands of Ethiopia. "If you will not slay the boy," he said then to King Afrah, "then you must slay your newborn daughter." The king, enraged at his counselor, refused to do so; but he resolved, nevertheless, to rear the children apart from one another in separate apartments, assigning different nurses and maids to serve them day and night; and he called the boy Wahsh al-Fala (meaning Beast of the Wild) because he had been found in the wilderness. So it was that things came to pass.

Then one day, as Wahsh al-Fala's nurse was drawing drinking water from the spring, she heard a voice saying: "Maiden, bring Wahsh al-Fala here to me, so that I may rear him till he is three years of age." The woman paid no heed; but the voice called out again, and yet a third time, saying: "If you do not bring him to me of your own free will, I shall take him by force."

Hearing this, the girl was afraid, and she brought the boy to the spring and left him there; and when she returned an hour after, she found no trace of him. Then she went to tell King Afrah of this, and the king was filled with gloom and forebodings, while Saqardyoun was overjoyed.

Three years passed, and it happened one day that King Afrah, on his way to his court, heard a voice saying: "King Afrah, I bring you glad news. I it was who took the boy Wahsh al-Fala and reared him among my people for three years, but now I return him to you. Guard him with all care, for I shall destroy any who harms him. And know, King Afrah, that this boy is a king and the son of a mighty king. He is now my foster son, and I am at his command."

And so King Afrah took the boy to his wife and told her what had happened, saying: "Take this boy, Wahsh al-Fala, for he has been restored to us." And the queen took the boy into her arms, and kissed him, rejoicing in her heart.

Now the reason for what had happened was this. When Qamariyya left the boy beneath the bush in the wilderness, it chanced that one of the queens of the jinn was passing and had her daughter with her. Her husband was one of the great kings of the jinn, known as the White King, who dwelt on the Bitter Mountain by the source of the Nile. They had been blessed with this one girl child, who was radiant as the sun and called by her father 'Aqisa. Her mother, bent on an errand, had come down into the plain in the noonday heat to take some rest, and as she lay beneath a thorn bush to sleep, she heard a baby's cry. When she discovered him there, her tender feelings were aroused and she suckled him with some of her milk; then, when he had taken his fill, she left him there where he was and, taking up her daughter, returned to her husband.

When the White King heard of the baby she had suckled then left on the barren plain, he reproached her for leaving the child in such a desolate and arid spot—all the more as he had become her nurseling child. So angry was he that he drew his sword; and when the queen saw that, she hurried back to the place where the baby had been. But that very day the hunter had borne the child away. When she did not find him, she searched for him far and wide, till at last she heard he was with King Afrah; and, going there and taking possession of the boy, she returned to the Mountains of the Moon, near the source of the Nile. When she reached her home, her husband's heart was gladdened, and she began to suckle the child every day, bringing him up alongside her daughter 'Aqisa.

When three years had passed, she took the boy and returned him to King Afrah, who, as we have seen, received him gladly. He set aside quarters for the boy and assigned servants to look to his every need, attending himself to his instruction; and so he brought him up till he had reached the age of seven. Then the boy began to show a passion for horsemanship and the chivalrous arts of war, spending all his time in these pursuits, so that by the time he was fourteen years of age, none could surpass him in prowess or valor or beauty.

One day, as King Afrah was seated on his throne, the wizard Saqardyoun entered and was greeted with ceremony by the king, who honored him and bade him be seated beside him. Then the king told Saqardyoun of Wahsh al-Fala's return and of the jinn queen who had fostered him and was now his protector. At that the counselor became distraught, saying to the king: "You must keep this boy from your daughter. Never let them meet, or Saturn's wrath will fall upon you and the lands of Ethiopia and the Sudan will be destroyed." The king pretended to assent to this; but as the days passed, he began to take Wahsh al-Fala by the hand and seat him next to him among his kinsfolk in the assembly.

Now it was Wahsh al-Fala's custom to go riding every day outside the city, where he would tilt at all his comrades and unseat them, striking and slaying any who approached him with hostile intent, till the whole city began to go in fear of this youth, and a group of them went to the king to complain. But the king, feeling pride in him, let him do as he wished, till the complaints grew loud and numerous. Then Saqardyoun was filled with gloom and foreboding at the boy's deeds and prowess, and rage hardened his heart ever more. Going to the king, he threatened that unless the boy were sent into exile he would tell King Sayf Ar'ad, the High King, that King Afrah was harboring an enemy in his domain; and then King Sayf Ar'ad would send a mighty army to depose Afrah and cast him out, blotting out all memory of him. And King Afrah, knowing Saqardyoun had power to do this, gave his assent.

Now King Afrah had in his service a mighty and renowned knight who lived in a castle in the wilderness, three days' ride from the city. This knight was known as 'Atumtum Kharaq al-Shajjar (meaning, Piercer of Trees), the reason for this being that he had in his park ten enormous trees, and when he went riding he would take his spear in his hand and cast it at one of the trees, so that the spear pierced it. He was known far and wide on this account, and knights and champions from all lands came to seek him out. King Afrah had come to hold 'Atumtum dearer than a son, and to him it was that he turned when confronted by Saqardyoun, summoning him to come straightway into his presence. 'Atumtum hastened to his king, riding with a company of his own men, and when he arrived, King Afrah greeted him and honored him, treating him with lavish hospitality for three days. Then, on the fourth day, 'Atumtum turned to King Afrah, saying: "King of all time, why have you summoned me? If you have some enemy who has offended you, let me go to him and destroy him, though it should be King Sayf Ar'ad himself."

"Know, my son," replied King Afrah, "that this boy Wahsh al-Fala is dearer to me than my own children. Take him to your castle and there protect him and honor him, teaching him your skills in horsemanship and combat and imparting some of your valor and fortitude to him." Now all this happened while Saqardyoun was absent from the court.

'Atumtum accordingly took Wahsh al-Fala back to his castle and began to teach him all he knew. Each day they would ride out, and 'Atumtum would train Wahsh al-Fala in the knightly arts of cutting and thrusting, striking and unseating, attack and retreat, and the ways of chivalry and horsemanship, valor and endurance. And so, when Wahsh al-Fala reached fifteen years, he had learned all there was to be known of the arts of war, on horseback or on foot.

Then one day 'Atumtum said: "My son, there is one thing left for you to learn. Come with me and see." With that they went to a tree so vast, soaring up through the very clouds, that they walked beneath its shade for a full hour; and nine others there were like it, each with a hole bored through its midst. And when Wahsh al-Fala, astonished at the sight of these holes, was told how they had come about, his amazement grew still further, and he asked to see for himself. He watched 'Atumtum perform the feat, then said: "Give me your spear, father, and let us see what I can do." With that he took the spear and bore down against the tree, thrusting his spear through it; and lo, its point came out a full hand-span on the other side. And as his horse galloped past, he leaned over and plucked it out with ease, then wheeled round and pierced the tree from the other side, plucking out the spear once more from the opposite side, as his horse galloped by a second time; and so he continued, without halt or weariness, till he had pierced forty holes in the tree. At that 'Atumtum showed him a still vaster tree, indicating that he should try his hand there; and after a brief rest Wahsh al-Fala mounted his horse, brandishing his spear aloft, and cried out: "See, O Saturn, here is Wahsh al-Fala!" Then he thrust at the tree with all his might, and this time the spear went right through the tree with the force of a catapult, striking the castle walls and bringing many stones toppling down. When 'Atumtum saw these deeds, he was overcome with awe and wonder, and he flew into a fit of rage and fear, frothing and foaming at the mouth, no longer knowing what he was doing.

"Who knows," he stormed at Wahsh al-Fala, "it may be you are the one at whose hands Noah's curse will come to pass. Know, boy, that this land is not yours, nor your father's, but ours from time immemorial, since the days of our father Ham. Quit our country this instant, basest of scoundrels, and prepare to die if ever we find you here again!" And so Wahsh al-Fala, bewildered and angry, quit the place and fled for his life, walking out into the wilderness with his heart full of sorrow.

So he walked for two days, across wilds and plains, eating from the plants and drinking from the streams; then, on the third day, he came to a cave where, to his surprise, he heard a human voice. Approaching the cave, he saw within an outlandish man, ugly of countenance, with sparks flying from his eyes, who asked Wahsh al-Fala who he was and where he was going. And when Wahsh al-Fala told him his name and sadly recounted his misfortunes, the outlandish man began to smile. "My son," he said, "I have long awaited you."

"And how is that, friend?" asked Wahsh al-Fala, astonished.

"Know," said the outlandish man, "that my name is 'Abd Lahab (meaning, Servant of the Flame). From my great reading in the ancient books, I learned there was a treasure in this cave, concealed since ancient times and guarded by jinn, and among this treasure an enchanted whip to be taken only by a youth called Wahsh al-Fala, who shall come as a stranger out of the wilderness."

"And what is the quality of this whip?" asked Wahsh al-Fala.

"Know," replied the outlandish man, "that I am skilled in the secret sciences, and have learned this whip was fashioned by mighty wizards. Sharper it is than the edge of a sword, and any who is struck by it dies forthwith. But none can take possession of it, save a youth named Wahsh al-Fala. Go down now my son—indeed, you are dearer to me than my kin—and bring me the whip, and I will guard you against all the dangers to be found there."

So Wahsh al-Fala went down into the place where, as 'Abd Lahab had told him, the whip hung above a bed of ivory inlaid with shining gold, while 'Abd Lahab himself sat murmuring spells and incantations. When Wahsh al-Fala had taken hold of the whip, the outlandish man asked him to hand it up to him, meaning to trick him; but Wahsh al-Fala said: "First help me come up out of this place, and then take it." For in his heart he feared treachery from 'Abd Lahab. Then, when he was back in the upper part of the cave, he found the means to strike him with the whip, and lo, the outlandish man's head was struck from his shoulders.

Joyful and glad of heart now at this treasure, Wahsh al-Fala went on his way through the wilderness. Two days he walked; then, on the morning of the third day, he came upon a splendid and lofty city and saw that all the inhabitants, men, women, and children, were standing on the walls, weeping and wailing, dressed in the black of mourning. Before the city he saw two mounds on which two great tents had been pitched, one of them a bridal tent; and when, curious and astonished at the sight, he made his way to this, he found within a bride of the most wondrous beauty, decked out in the finest robes, but weeping copious tears and lamenting the fate that had forced her, a king's daughter, to leave kin and loved ones and marry a demon of the jinn. She looked at him, beardless youth that he was, while he, returning her gaze with a thousand sighs, saw that she had a green mole on her cheek exactly like his own. He could not endure her sorrow and affliction, for she had stolen his heart and mind and aroused his passions; and she too was filled with love and passion for him, and with wonder at his beauty. "O, handsome youth," she said, "whose face is like the moon, who are you and from where have you come?"

"I am Wahsh al-Fala," he said, "and I have come through the wilderness from the city of King Afrah. And who, lady, are you?"

"Know, friend," she said, "that I am Shama, daughter of King Afrah, who is ruler of this city, and that the people on the walls are my kinsfolk." And at this Wahsh al-Fala's ardor grew still stronger, and amazement seized his heart, for this was the daughter of the man who had reared him from infancy.

Now these things had come about for a strange reason, all on account of the wizard Saqardyoun. When King Afrah would not slay Wahsh al-Fala, or send him into exile, but had rather sent him away to 'Atumtum, Saqardyoun was bitterly vexed and began to plot in secret. Wishing to acquaint his brother with how matters stood, he left the city and began to walk through the wilderness, when, all of a sudden, he came upon an old friend, a treacherous and wicked sorcerer called 'Abd Nar; and when 'Abd Nar asked him the reason for his gloom and anger, Saqardyoun recounted the whole story from beginning to end, saying that he wished to keep the boy and King Afrah's daughter apart to prevent the union of the two moles. Then the sorcerer told him to leave matters in his hands and returned to his home, leaving Saqardyoun relieved and comforted.

Then this sorcerer seated himself in his place of sorcery and began to mutter spells; and lo, the ground heaved and rumbled, and an enormous, ugly giant, with sparks flying from his eyes, rose up. "Go straightway to King Afrah's city," said the sorcerer then, "and there call out in a thunderous voice; and when they all come running, young and old, to know what it is you want, tell them: 'You must bring out the king's daughter, dressed in all her finery, and set her in a tent outside the city, and tomorrow I shall come to take her. Unless you do this, I shall destroy you utterly, every last one among you.'"

And so the giant, who was called the Snatcher, flew off to King Afrah's city to do the sorcerer's bidding; and having flown round it, he called out in a thunderous voice that shook the very mountains and made every heart tremble. Then, when the people of the city came out to know what it was he wanted, he told them just what 'Abd Nar had told him to say. Terrified, they went in to King Afrah, who was weeping bitterly for his daughter, and told him that if he did not do as the giant commanded, they would seize Shama themselves and deliver her to him, so that he should then leave them in peace.

That night Shama's mother and her women, wailing and weeping and lamenting, dressed and adorned her, then, along with the king and all her kin, passed the night in taking their leave of her, while everyone in the city grieved with them. Then, on the morrow, two tents were set up outside the walls, and Shama was led into one while her mother and her women sat in the other, awaiting the arrival of the Snatcher.

At this point it was that Wahsh al-Fala had come upon Shama in her tent, as she wept there over her misfortunes, and so the two met for the first time; for though they had long known of one another, neither had set eyes on the other. And when Shama told him what had passed, and told him of the giant, he said: "Apple of my eye, have no fear. You shall see how I deal with this giant."

As the two of them sat there together and the people of King Afrah's city watched from the walls, believing Wahsh al-Fala himself to be the giant, lo, a cloud of dust swirled up in the distance and the sky darkened; then, soon after, the giant was towering over them and, picking up Shama's tent, he thrust it to one side. When he saw Wahsh al-Fala seated there alongside Shama, he was filled with rage. "What business have you here," he roared, "seated beside my bride and wife? May you never see the light of day again!" With that he shrieked out at him so that Wahsh al-Fala trembled and felt the ground ready to give way beneath him; but he summoned up his resolve and looked at the giant, seeing that he was hideously ugly, with legs like the masts of ships and hands like lumps of mud, with a mouth as wide as a road, and nostrils like trumpets, feet like mounds of earth, and each ear like a door.

Then Wahsh al-Fala stiffened his resolve and, striding up to the giant, struck him with the magic whip (since the weapons of men cannot wound the jinn unless they are enchanted); and the blow fell on the giant's left hand, which dropped to the ground as though it had been sawn off. At that the giant cried out: "Ah! You have slain me, son of perdition!" Then, picking up his severed hand, he set it back on his arm, pressing it against his wrist for fear the smoke would escape—for the jinn have no blood, being formed from fire by Almighty God's will. And with that the Snatcher spread his wings and flew off forthwith.

When the people of the city saw this, they were struck with wonder and joyfully flooded out, with the king at their head, to Shama's tent. There they strewed petals over Wahsh al-Fala's head, while the king embraced his daughter with great joy, thanking Wahsh al-Fala and praising him for his deed, then leading them back together to the palace. Then the entire city was decked out and there was great rejoicing, with the king instructing that a great banquet, to last for three days, be given for all the citizens. As for Wahsh al-Fala, King Afrah set aside special quarters for him, and showered gifts and fine robes upon him. The only one not content was Saqardyoun, who had returned from his meeting with the sorcerer to find the city decorated, and everyone rejoicing at Wahsh al-Fala's victory over the giant; and he retired to his room crazed with rage and sorrow.

That night Shama could not sleep, for she had given her heart to Wahsh al-Fala, who was like the full moon in his beauty, and she loved him still more after he had saved her from the giant. She rose accordingly and made her way to Wahsh al-Fala's chamber. He, for his part, was now enchanted with her, his heart and soul in a tumult and, unable to contain his passion, he began to sing of her beauty and of his love for her. Then Shama heard him and went in to him, and so they sat conversing for a full hour, totally lost one in the other. Then Shama said: "In the name of Saturn, if you truly love me, ask my father for my hand in marriage, in the presence of all his men of state."

"Dearest heart," he replied, "I hear and obey." But when he went into the king's court the next day, although his heart was filled with his love, he was too abashed to speak of it; and that night Shama again came to him, asking why he had not spoken to her father of marriage.

"Dearest heart," he said, "I was too abashed. But tomorrow I shall speak." Yet next day the same thing happened.

Then, on the third day, Wahsh al-Fala went into the court to find it full of dignitaries and ministers, and Saqardyoun was there also; and so he stiffened his resolve and began to address the king, wishing him health and prosperity and happiness.

"Young man," said King Afrah, "tell me your wish, so that I may straightway grant it."

"I seek the hand of your noble daughter, the Lady Shama," said Wahsh al-Fala, "and ask you not to refuse me."

At this the wizard Saqardyoun flew into a rage, warning King Afrah against consenting to the union of the maiden and the young man, lest the lands of Ethiopia and the Sudan be conquered and destroyed.

"But," said the king, "he it is who yesterday saved my daughter from the demon giant, turning our grief to rejoicing."

"Tell the young man," replied Saqardyoun, "that she has left the matter in the hands of her counselor."

And so King Afrah did as Saqardyoun had instructed him. But when Wahsh al-Fala asked for Shama's hand from Saqardyoun, Saqardyoun said: "Indeed, knight of all time, Shama shall marry none but you. But have you forgotten brides have a price, and the price for a king's daughter is a very high one?"

"Ask what you will," said Wahsh al-Fala, "and I shall provide it."

"We demand neither money nor gifts," said Saqardyoun, "neither horses nor camels. The price we ask is that you bring us the head of a wretch named Sa'doun al-Zinji, who lives three days' ride from here in a castle called al-Thurayya. Unless you bring us his head, the marriage will never take place."

"Let it be so," said Wahsh al-Fala, "though I should drink from the cup of death." And with that he returned to his chamber deep in thought.

Now this Sa'doun al-Zinji was a mighty knight and a fearless champion, whose fame had spread throughout the land, and he was feared by all the neighboring kings. He had beneath his command eighty strong men with no fear of death, and as for Sa'doun, he was the mightiest of them all, able to face an army single-handed. His custom was to raid caravans and plunder them, slaying the men and women, so that all had come to fear him. When word of his deeds had reached King Sayf Ar'ad, the king had twice sent against him an army of five thousand men, who were defeated and put to flight. Then, accordingly, he had sent an army of thirty thousand heavily armed men; and when Sa'doun had seen how numerous they were, he had withdrawn with his men to his castle, which was built on a high mountain ledge with a narrow path that led up to it. And there he remained safe from attack, while terror of him reigned throughout the land. Indeed, the wizard Saqardyoun, in demanding Sa'doun's head, intended only that Wahsh al-Fala should meet his end.

That night Shama came to Wahsh al-Fala's chamber, saying: "This cursed wretch designs only that you should meet your death. Let us leave this place together, you and I, and live in contentment under some other king till the end of our days."

"God forbid," he replied, "that I should flee with you in such a fashion." And so Shama returned to her room racked with distress. As for Wahsh al-Fala, he could neither eat nor drink, so tormented was he with love, nor could he sleep; and rising that very night and donning his armor, he mounted his horse and rode out toward Sa'doun's castle.

As he rode on next morning, a knight in glittering armor, mounted on an Arab steed and bearing a long lance, came galloping toward him like an angry lion, crying: "Where are you bound, son of perdition? Prepare to meet your end!" With that he bore down on him with his lance, while Wahsh al-Fala, wheeling round on his steed like the wind, galloped to meet him in his turn, and they were locked in mortal combat the whole morning, like two raging seas.

Then Wahsh al-Fala began to chafe at being held back from his goal by this knight and bore furiously down on him with a loud cry, striking him on the breast with his lance and thrusting him down from the saddle. But as he strode toward him, minded to slay him there and then, the knight cried: "Stay your hand, mighty knight, lest you regret your deed."

"And why should that be, basest of knights?" asked Wahsh al-Fala.

"Because it is I," replied the bold knight, "the Princess Shama, daughter of King Afrah."

At this Wahsh al-Fala was astonished, saying: "Why have you done this?"

"To make proof of your prowess and valor, king of knights," she replied. "Take me with you now, and together we shall strive to attain your goal."

"Never shall it be said," replied Wahsh al-Fala, "that Wahsh al-Fala was powerless to defeat Sa'doun al-Zinji without the aid of the Princess Shama."

And so Shama left him once more and rode off into the wilderness, her love and passion stronger yet. As for Wahsh al-Fala, he rode on for two full days, and on the evening of the third day, he drew near the castle, finding its gates locked. But as he pondered what he should do, all of a sudden twenty fierce knights came thundering out of the night on black steeds, bearing with them the booty from a caravan they had raided, with their captives set trussed on their horses; and so Wahsh al-Fala slipped in among them by the castle door and entered with them. Then the men set their booty and their captives down in the castle courtyard and went into the building.

When they did not return, Wahsh al-Fala resolved to follow them and, stepping forward to the place from which they had gone, he saw a stairway. But as he set his foot on the first step, it slid from beneath him and he fell into a pit filled with daggers, two of these piercing his side, one on the left and the other on the right. Then, as he struggled to free himself, a figure appeared, calling: "Have no fear, hero of all time." And this person drew near and plucked the daggers from his sides.

"Who are you, pray, valiant knight," Wahsh al-Fala asked then.

"I am the Princess Shama, daughter of King Afrah," came the reply.

"And how is it, queen of all women?" asked Wahsh al-Fala, "that you are here?"

"I feared for you," she replied, "since you do not know the ways of this castle. And so I slipped in with the men as you did, and stood watching to see what you would do; and now here I am by your side. Test each step with your sword before you set your foot on it."

So he did, till he reached the top, then he leapt over the wall into a wide marble passageway, with Shama following in her turn. Then they saw before them the inner gates to the castle, shut on one side and open on the other, and Wahsh al-Fala stood behind the gate that was shut and looked inside.

There sat the eighty men, forty on each side facing one another, with their leader Sa'doun al-Zinji, tall and strong, his eyes sparkling with fire, seated at their head. He turned to his men, saying in a voice like thunder: "Let someone among you go down to check the captives. I fear one of them may free himself and cut loose the others, for my ears are ringing and my eyelids twitching." At that one of the men straightway leapt to his feet and went out grasping his sword; and Wahsh al-Fala waited till he drew near, then, swift as lightning, struck him on the right shoulder with his sword, so that the blade came out beneath his left arm. Then Shama dragged the dead man away and laid him down by the wall.

When the man did not return, Sa'doun sent another after him, and when still the same thing happened, he sent a third. But when he was minded to send a fourth, his men refused, telling him he should go to see for himself; and at that Sa'doun became like a raging lion, and they all rose with him, unsheathing their swords.

When Wahsh al-Fala saw this, he took his position in the middle of the passageway, his sword gleaming in his hand. And as the first of Sa'doun's men was about to step out from the hall, he saw Wahsh al-Fala and stopped in his tracks, saying: "There is the hunter that slew our brothers."

At that Sa'doun plunged forward, roaring: "You there, are you man or jinn? And what is it you seek?"

"I am a man," replied Wahsh al-Fala, "and I come seeking your head as the price for my bride Shama, daughter of King Afrah."

When Sa'doun heard this, the light before his eyes turned to darkness. "Who is Shama," he cried, "and who is King Afrah? Since you have come for me, I shall slay you here in this very castle." Turning to his men, he forbade them to intervene between him and his adversary, then went to his quarters and returned in his armor, like a lion of steel, fuming and snorting in his rage and resolution. And with that they set to, locked in mortal combat, like two raging seas.

With sword and lance they fought, till their weapons were blunted and they themselves exhausted; and in this exchange of blows, it chanced that Sa'doun was first to strike home. When Shama, standing outside, saw this well-aimed blow, she was filled with terror for Wahsh al-Fala's life, knowing that Sa'doun had struck the land of Ethiopia like a searing thunderbolt. Grasping the hilt of the dagger she had with her, she aimed its point toward Sa'doun's head and flung it, as the two fighters were locked together there, and the dagger pierced Sa'doun's hand, sapping his strength and resolve at the very moment Wahsh al-Fala was closing in for the mortal blow. But when Wahsh al-Fala saw the sword fly from Sa'doun's grasp, and saw how his strength and resolve failed, he stayed his hand, and turned to Shama, saying: "May your hand never fail you, nor your enemies mark you." And to Sa'doun he said: "Take up your sword and fight, Sa'doun. Never shall it be said that Wahsh al-Fala overcame you through treachery."

"Champion of all time," said Sa'doun, "to whom were you talking then?"

"To the Princess Shama," replied Wahsh al-Fala, "daughter of King Afrah." At that Sa'doun asked him to have her come in, and Shama entered the castle. And when Wahsh al-Fala again bade Sa'doun pick up his sword, Sa'doun refused, saying: "God forbid, king of champions, that I should fight against you when you have spared my life." Then, putting his hand behind his back and inclining his head, he said: "Strike my neck, gallant knight, and go safe to your bride and your people."

"Rather come," said Wahsh al-Fala, "and fight me on the plains beyond the castle."

To this Sa'doun consented, forbidding any of his men to follow; and so the three went out into the fields. Then Sa'doun proposed the two of them should wrestle three bouts there in the wilderness, and whoever won all three should decide the other's fate: to be slain, or to be taken captive, or to be released and pardoned. And when Wahsh al-Fala agreed to this, the two doffed their armor and their clothes, remaining in their drawers, then discarded their weapons and leapt into a clinch, wrestling together like two mighty trees.

When he saw Wahsh al-Fala's slender build and grace of movement, Sa'doun rushed at him and, lifting him by the waist with one hand, dashed him down on the ground, meaning to make an end of him. But Wahsh al-Fala, vexed and enraged that Sa'doun should so raise him up with one hand before his beloved Shama, and knowing this mighty man was likely to slay him, fell on his feet like a lion, then leapt forward at him, stretching out his hand to grasp Sa'doun's ear and twisted it with all his might. At that Sa'doun crashed to the ground like a heavy rock, and Wahsh al-Fala, seeing his chance, leapt on to his shoulder and drew his dagger, meaning to end the contest and so attain his goal.

"Do not be so hasty," said Sa'doun. "This is the first bout only of three." At that Wahsh al-Fala drew back abashed to continue their fight, and again Wahsh al-Fala was victorious; but in the third bout he felt his strength begin to wane, and, invoking God's help against this valiant champion, he stretched out his hand to Sa'doun's belly, grasped one side of it and squeezed with a grip like a vice. Now this was the place where Sa'doun's kidneys were, and so he fell powerless to the ground, while Wahsh al-Fala set his knees once more on the other man's shoulders and drew his dagger to slay him.

"Gallant knight," said Sa'doun, "matchless in your age and time, are you minded to slaughter me as you would slaughter a cow in this wilderness?" At that Wahsh al-Fala stayed his hand and rose to his feet; whereupon Sa'doun also rose, then fell on to his knees with his hands behind his back, saying to Wahsh al-Fala: "Now strike off my head, for so it should be done, king of champions."

Then Wahsh al-Fala, abashed, turned and straightway flung Sa'doun's sword back to him and released him, swearing he would never slay such a champion as Sa'doun, even to save his own life. And at that Wahsh al-Fala and Sa'doun embraced like brothers, their hearts open one to the other, and together with Shama they returned to the castle, where the three of them feasted and made merry for three days.

When it was time for Wahsh al-Fala and Shama to depart, Sa'doun insisted on going, too, to King Afrah's castle, so that Wahsh al-Fala could wed his beloved; and to this Wahsh al-Fala gladly agreed. At that Sa'doun instructed his men to make ready for the journey; and so, having donned their armor and their weapons and packed up everything of value in the castle, the eighty men followed behind Sa'doun and Wahsh al-Fala and Shama as they rode off joyfully to King Afrah's castle.

Now all this time it had been the custom of King Afrah and the wizard Saqardyoun to go out each day, on the plain beyond the city, and one day King Afrah wondered aloud what had happened to Wahsh al-Fala; to which Saqardyoun was swift to declare that he must now be dead, slain by Sa'doun, beyond all hope of return. But as he spoke these words, a cloud of dust swirled up in the distance, then cleared some time after to reveal eighty fierce men, bearing keen swords and long spears, mounted on horses graceful as gazelles. At their head rode a tall and mighty knight in full armor, and at his side rode another knight in full armor, his face smooth as a blade and lovely as the full moon.

When King Afrah recognized Sa'doun, he was alarmed and turned to Saqardyoun, saying: "This is your doing. Here is Sa'doun, come to wreak vengeance on us for sending Wahsh al-Fala to seek his head." And with that he turned his horse and fled into the city, with Saqardyoun and the troops who were with them hard on his heels. Then they barred the city gates and took up their positions on the ramparts, preparing for the siege.

But when the riders drew near the city, and King Afrah saw Wahsh al-Fala at Sa'doun's side, conversing together with him (Shama, for her part, had slipped quietly back to her quarters), he was reassured and ordered the gates to be opened. As Sa'doun entered the city with his men, the crowds flocked to see him, lining the roads to King Afrah's palace, for his fame had spread far and wide. But once inside the palace, when the king invited all present to be seated, Sa'doun and his men remained standing; and at last Saqardyoun had no choice but to rise to his feet, declaring that he had demanded Sa'doun's head only so that Wahsh al-Fala should bring Sa'doun himself to court, and that his presence there was bride price enough.

After much feasting and merrymaking, Sa'doun requested that tents be prepared for himself and his men outside the city, rather than quarters assigned them in the palace. A magnificent pavilion was accordingly set up for him, fit for a king, and there Wahsh al-Fala chose to spend his nights in the company of his friend, setting out from it each day to attend the king's court.

Now after a number of days had passed in this fashion, Wahsh al-Fala presented himself one morning at court, then remained standing after all others there had taken their seats; and when King Afrah asked him what it was he desired, Wahsh al-Fala reminded him of the matter of the Lady Shama. With that Saqardyoun intervened once more, saying: "You have brought the price we demanded of you, and Shama is surely yours. But there remains the wedding gift, noble knight."

"And what shall that be," asked Wahsh al-Fala.

"Honored knight," said Saqardyoun, "you must bring us the Book of the History of the Nile. That shall be the wedding gift for the Princess Shama."

"And where is this book to be found?" asked Wahsh al-Fala.

"I do not know, by Saturn," replied Saqardyoun. "But unless you bring it, you shall never be married."

"And what is the use of this book?" asked Wahsh al-Fala.

"Whoever possesses it," said Saqardyoun, "shall have dominion over the lands of Ethiopia and the Sudan, and all the kings of the time will bow down before him."

So Wahsh al-Fala promised to bring the book or else renounce all claim to Shama; and with that he departed, with his friend Sa'doun at his side.

That night, as Wahsh al-Fala sat in his chamber in the palace, Shama entered weeping and sad of heart; then, having greeted him, she reproached him for the impossible undertaking he had accepted, begging him to bear her off there and then, so they could be together till the end of their days.

"Never will I do such a thing," answered Wahsh al-Fala, "though I were to drink the cup of death. We are of the Arab race: what we promise we fulfill, and, if we are able, we give pardon. If we have said yea we do not then say nay, and if we have said nay we do not then say yea."

When Shama heard this she was convinced; and so they bade one another farewell with tears, and she went away, her heart filled with grief at the thought of the separation to come. Then Wahsh al-Fala, unable to sleep or to drink or taste food, rose that very instant and, girding himself with his weapons of war, mounted his horse and rode off into the night.

3
The Quest for the Book of the Nile

Wahsh al-Fala went on across the plains and hills for sixty days, cutting a path through the barren wilderness and meeting no living creature on his way. Then he drew near to a high mountain surrounded by a garden pleasant to the eye, full of tall trees and running rivers, green branches and gushing waters, and birds that sang praises to God the Creator.

High on the side of this mountain was a hermitage, and Wahsh al-Fala walked on till he reached this, saying to himself: "It may be that Almighty God will bring me some good from this place." And as he stood at the door, he heard a voice within invoking the All-Merciful and Compassionate One, saying: "You who are All-Compassionate and All-Bountiful, have mercy on your servant, a mortal man. You are eternal and all things on earth pass away."

When Wahsh al-Fala heard this voice, he was reassured in his heart but, still not knowing if this were man or jinn, stepped toward the door of the hermitage and called out: "Peace be upon you, you who dwell in this place, whether humankind or jinn; for I have seen no other in these valleys."

Then lo, the one within said to him: "Peace be upon you likewise, and God's mercy and blessings. Welcome, King of the land of Yemen and other regions, who shall be father of the ruler of these domains, and of him who shall turn the course of the Nile from the land of Ethiopia to the land of Egypt, vanquisher of tyranny and sedition, ruler of Sanaa and Aden, and of the deserts of Ethiopia and all they contain of towns and villages, King Sayf Ben Dhi Yazan. Alight from your horse, King of all time, and tether it to that rock below the hermitage; then come up to me in this place, so I may converse with you, and you rest yourself from the cares and hardships of travel; for you must be weary after riding two full months."

"Uncle," said Wahsh al-Fala, "who is it you are addressing, since I am known among men as Wahsh al-Fala?"

"You speak truly, King of all time," said the other. "But know that name was given you by King Afrah. As for your true first name, it is Sayf, given you by the All-Conquering Sovereign."

At that Wahsh al-Fala felt reassured and, dismounting from his horse, unbridled it and left it to graze in that spacious land. Then he went up to the hermitage and, entering it, found it to be a place exquisitely adorned; and the hermit rose to meet him, saying: "Greetings and welcome."

When Wahsh al-Fala approached the hermit to kiss his hand, he saw him to be dark of complexion and tall of stature, with a mole in the place between his eyes.

"Sir," said Wahsh al-Fala, "this is a name I have heard from no other."

"My son," said the hermit, "your true name is indeed Sayf Ben Dhi Yazan, vanquisher of infidels and ill-omened persons. You will bring in the rule of justice and champion Islam, and at your hands the curse of God's prophet Noah, peace be upon him, will come to pass. But you, my son, who is it you worship?"

"Sir," he answered, "according to my understanding, the one to be worshipped is God. And yet I have, up till now, found no divinity I can acknowledge. I have seen the Sudanese worship Saturn."

"My son," said the old hermit, "none is rightly to be worshipped save God the All-Glorious and Exalted, who created earth and heaven and by His power made the seas move and the rivers flow. He is the One True God, the All-Victorious One. Resolve, King Sayf, to worship God, and to place your trust in no other."

"Sir," said Wahsh al-Fala, "what should I say that I may be one of the Faithful?"

"Sayf, my son," said the other, "you must repeat these words: I witness that there is no God but God, and that Abraham is the Friend of God, and that Muhammad is the Messenger of God; and he will be the last of the prophets and their seal, who shall be sent at the end of time— from the lineage of Mu'ad Ben 'Adnan he is—God's blessing on him and his clan, and his noble companions, the first in charity and good deeds."

When the king heard these words, he was overcome with joy. "I ask you to instruct me," he said, "and to teach me what God has taught you."

"Place your hand in my hand," replied the other. So Sayf Ben Dhi Yazan placed his hand in that of the old man, saying: "I witness that there is no God but God, and I witness that Abraham is the Friend of God and the father of the prophets, and I witness that Muhammad is the Messenger of God, the seal of prophets and messengers, and he is the prophet of the end of time, whom God shall send from the lineage of 'Adnan."

Then the pious shaykh, whose name was Shaykh Jiyad, said: "You have done well, son of a generous race. But where are you journeying, that you come upon me to receive such good fortune at my hands?"

"I asked," he said, "for the hand of Shama, daughter of King Afrah, in marriage; and the price required of me was Sa'doun's head. Then they asked for her wedding gift, which was to be the Book of the Nile. And here I am journeying, as you see, with none to guide or direct me to it."

"If you were to traverse the earth from furthest East to furthest West," said Shaykh Jiyad, "you would not find your way to that book, except by the Providence of the All-Bountiful Sovereign. But since you have entered the religion of Islam, son of noble kings, it is our duty to help you. Stay with me tonight, so that you may attain an exalted station and receive some means of help."

"Uncle," said Sayf, "do with me as you wish, for I shall not depart from your counsel."

Then the shaykh rose and conducted him to a spring, saying: "Perform your ablutions with me." He instructed him as he performed his ablutions, and after that bade him be seated so as to spend time in pious supplication and praise and worship of God, whose wish and will is all things. Then the shaykh stood up, spread out his palms, and said: "O God, grant us our sustenance, for you are the best Provider." And Sayf looked and lo, two loaves of bread appeared before them.

"Take one of these, Sayf," said Shaykh Jiyad, "but do not eat until you have said: 'In the name of God the Merciful, the Compassionate.'"

"By God, shaykh," said Sayf, "this is a usage unlike any other." With that he invoked the name of God and ate, as the shaykh did likewise, and they spent the night invoking God's name and asking forgiveness for their sins.

In the morning, Shaykh Jiyad said: "King Sayf, my son, place your trust in God, and go and see to your task, in which God will aid and champion you. As for your horse, leave it in this place, for you have no need of it. Rather, climb this mountain and descend on the other side, where you will find a mighty running river: keep it on your left, and walk on the right bank. If you grow thirsty, drink of its water, and if you grow hungry, eat from the plants there; and walk on in this way for three days, till you come to a vast flat land where there is a mighty sea whose limits cannot be discerned. When you reach it, stand on the shore till the setting of the sun. Then you will see a sea monster vast of body and full of fury. Know, my son, that this creature was created by Almighty God, who made it to be hungry for the sun. When this beast sees the sun rising in the east, he turns his face toward it, wishing to snatch it, but he cannot overtake it; and when the sun sets in the west, he turns there too, wishing to seize it with his mouth and devour it, but again he cannot overtake it. Then, in his rage, he beats his head on the ground till he stuns himself; and then sleep overcomes him and he slumbers till the time of the sun's rising, waking from his sleep to find the sun has risen from the east. And so once more he turns toward it, wishing to snatch it, but the sun will already have risen high in the sky. Then he follows its course till it sets, and so it goes on. This is a beast that can be ridden, mettlesome and huge. As soon as you come to him, climb up onto his head, or his back, or any other part of him; for if you sat within his very eye, it would be nothing to him because of his enormous bulk. He will bear you to the other side, for there is none to bear you across that sea but he, and cross it you must in order to attain your goal. Once you have reached the further shore, you will find ahead of you her who sits awaiting you, O King, by the decree of the Almighty Sovereign, the Beloved and All-Forgiving One, who is the One True God, the All-Victorious One."

"Sir," said King Sayf, "who is this who sits waiting?"

"Have no fear," said Shaykh Jiyad, "no harm will come from her. Had I not known that God makes changes and transformations among His creatures according to His will, I would have told you what the sorceress 'Aqila will do, and what will come about from her daughter Tama, who shall be your second wife, and also from Shama, your first wife. But my son, you are to fight against infidels, so if you go into battle, invoke the name of God the All-Highest Sovereign, in order that He may grant you victory, through the power of His blessed name, over those that err."

"And what should I say, Uncle," asked Sayf, "when I am hard pressed in the field?"

"Say 'God is great! God is great!'" he replied. "Never cease from saying 'God is great!' and strike among the infidels with the edge of your sword, praying for victory from the Almighty, the Beloved One. He will grant you triumph, and no harm or destruction in war shall touch you."

At that King Sayf was convinced and stayed a second night with him. And Shaykh Jiyad spent this night instructing him in the principles of Islam and the worship of the All-Knowing Sovereign, till God lifted the darkness and the smiling day drew near.

"My son," said the shaykh, "go your way now, with the blessings of Almighty God."

"Sir," he said, "I desire you to pray for me."

"Place your trust in God," said the other, "and do not cease from invoking His name, for He to whom prayer is due is ever present, and He sees you."

Then King Sayf bade Shaykh Jiyad farewell and, placing his trust in the All-Bountiful Sovereign, made his way on foot across the plains and lowlands; his horse he had let loose before the hermitage, unharnessing it and leaving it to roam freely, for the shaykh had said to him: "Leave it and do not concern yourself about it. It is in my keeping, and the All-Merciful and Compassionate will provide sustenance for the horse and myself alike."

Sayf Ben Dhi Yazan was full of wonder at the shaykh's faith and, bidding him farewell, went on by the side of the river, as we have said, for three days; and on the fourth day he reached the vast plain of which Shaykh Jiyad had told him. It was evening when he arrived, and gazing at the sea, he could not see the further shore, for it was distant and out of sight, nor did he see any promontory by which he might come there. "I wonder," he said to himself, "where the furious beast may be of which the pious shaykh told me." Then he sat down, performed his ablutions as the teacher had instructed him, and invoked the name of the Lord of Creation and begged forgiveness for his sins till nightfall. Then, all of a sudden, he perceived the approach of that furious creature, which was like a mountain in its bulk.

When it reached the shore, it dragged itself forward till half its body lay on the land; and even so, had there been a walled city there, it would have been torn down by the monster. Sayf, perceiving how the beast was, invoked the All-Bountiful and Almighty God, then waited patiently till it dashed its head upon the ground, again and again, for it was mighty and powerful; and when sleep overcame it, it lay there in that place.

All this happened while Sayf stood and looked on. Then, seeing how things were going, he rose onto the monster as though he were ascending a high mountain, and sitting down among its scales, he invoked the name of God the All-Glorious and All-Powerful till morning broke. Then the creature turned its head toward the further shore, wishing to snatch the sun as was its wont; and at that instant Sayf leapt from its back onto the ground and saw it dashing its head against the shore. With that he left the place, saying: "Praise be to the One who made it and all other creatures, the One who made heaven and earth, the world and all things, He who is Ever-Living and Eternal."

With that Sayf walked on through the plains and deserts, from the morning till the afternoon. Then, all of a sudden, he perceived a cloud of dust swirling up before him, which cleared to reveal a knight clad in steel, mounted on a horse as yellow as gold, with a long tail. This knight, girded with a sword that was like the messenger of death, bore a dark spear, well-made, well-balanced; his face was covered by a visor and the eyes sent darts flying from beneath the brows. Proudly he sat in the saddle, like a lion among lions. This knight approached Sayf Ben Dhi Yazan and called out to him: "Stop there! Do not move! Know this day is your last." Sayf made no reply, responding only by parrying the blows and thrusts he received, paying no heed to charge or attack; and each time the horse bore down on him, he would fend it off with his hand alone, without blow or thrust. For a full hour this went on; and if the knight struck Sayf with the sword, or lunged at him with the spear, this would do him no harm, for Sayf would parry the blows and thrusts, well aimed though they were.

Then the knight, amazed by all this, said: "Youth, will you not strike me as I have struck you, and fight me as I have fought you?"

"Youth," said Sayf in his turn, "I perceive you are no warrior; you have no power to fight and do combat, nor do you have the valor for strife and conflict. A mere novice you are, who should never mount such a steed. Seeing me on foot, you said in your ignorance: 'I shall assail that knight and match myself against him.' I look upon you with contempt, as a mere witless boy with no endurance or courage to fight with me. Had you been accomplished in combat and chivalry, you would not have opposed yourself to me, commanding me to halt and then assailing me, while you were on horseback and I on foot. Such is not the custom of noble knights. Had the one who did this been accomplished in combat and chivalry, I would surely have laid him out on the sands; for so it is, I would have you know, that I deal with champions." And with that he grasped the horse's neck with his right hand and lifted up the knight with his left, saying: "So do men do who have knowledge of combat." Then he set the other down again in the saddle, so that the knight was amazed and ever more troubled.

"You speak truly," he said, "King of the kings of Yemen, lord of the regions of Sanaa and Aden, destroyer of infidels and ill-omened persons, purifier of the earth from sorcery and strife. Are you not, my lord, King Sayf Ben Dhi Yazan?"

"Such I am," he replied. "And what ignorant youngster, pray, are you? Who is your father, and what might his name be among knights and champions, that you should know me and seek me out in battle?"

"I am no man," came the reply, "nor am I a champion, but rather a maiden among maidens, whose accomplishment is chastity and modesty. I have journeyed to these deserts, lord among champions, and fought with you, out of fear and love for you. I am the Lady Tama and my mother is the sorceress called 'Aqila. The reason I came out to meet you is this. When my mother had raised me, I said to her: 'Find out for me what man I shall marry.' So she cast the sands and figures appeared. 'Your husband,' she said then, 'will be from the land of Yemen—he is King Sayf Ben Dhi Yazan.' 'And how shall we come together,' I asked, 'since he lives in a distant land?' 'He will ask,' she said, 'for the daughter of King Afrah in marriage, and the Book of the Nile will be required of him as her wedding gift; and so he will come to find it in this land, and I shall help him in this. He will suffer the sorest hardships, but I shall rise up and aid him. Through this it is that you shall marry him.' My mother continued in this manner, striving each night to instruct me in the things I should know, till the day came when she said: 'King Sayf has requested marriage, and the counselor Saqardyoun has opposed him. And so Sayf has made his way from the castle of al-Thurayya, accompanied by his beloved.' Then I asked my mother to discover who this maiden might be, so that the signs might become manifest. 'As for the maiden,' she said, 'she is his bride Shama, and in her concern for him, for fear he should drink from the cup of death, she went with him to Sa'doun's castle and delivered him from death when he fell into a snare, and after that they were reconciled with Sa'doun.' Then she added: 'Sayf has asked for Shama a second time, and they have demanded the Book of the Nile from him. He is journeying to these lands but has halted at the hermitage of Shaykh Jiyad, who has taught him to invoke God's name and to proclaim the Oneness of the Lord of Creation. This very night he is riding the sea monster which will bring him across the sea, and tomorrow morning he will come to this land; and I fear lest he should meet death and destruction.' 'What fate do you fear for him, mother?' I asked. 'This city has Watchers,' she said, 'and if a stranger enters, they raise the alarm, crying: 'Citizens of Qaymar, a stranger has entered your city. Pursue him!' Then, when the people of the land come out, a being called the Hidden One comes from the walls, to lead them where their enemy is, so they can pursue him, and bring him back and slay him.' Then she said: 'Tama, my daughter, all these Watchers and this Hidden One are the work of skilled sorcerers, set to protect the Book of the History of the Nile. For all the citizens of Qaymar, together with their king, Qamroun, worship this book, which was handed down to them from their fathers and forefathers, and they have made it their god. If King Sayf Ben Dhi Yazan should come, and the Watchers and the Hidden One shriek out against him, he will be confused and will fall into their hands. And when King Qamroun comes, Sayf will be torn into a thousand pieces by the people of the city, and by the ministers and counselors.' 'Mother,' I said then, 'what is to be done, since you have promised you will give me to him in marriage and that you will help him take possession of the Book of the Nile? Tell me what the plan shall be, and what is to be done, so I may carry it out. For if I saw him in danger, I would lay down my own life for him.' 'Mount your horse,' my mother said, 'and don your battle attire, then go out as though to hunt or fowl, riding east toward that plain. Should you find a person coming alone from there, with none at his side, then charge at him, as though you were minded to slay him. Strike at him too with the sword, for it will do him no harm, harassing him ceaselessly till he snatches you from the saddle with his left hand and grasps the horse with his right. If he does this, then know that he is the one we seek. Tell him to beware and not to make his way through the gates of the city, but to come below the tenth tower, where I shall raise him up on a catapult. It may be that God will bring us solace after tribulation.' When I heard these words of my mother I was convinced, and straightway mounted my horse, making for the desolate plains, till I saw you as she had said, and did battle with you as I did, and all that happened happened. Now I have told you, King Sayf, of all the things my mother said concerning you, and I have found her words to be true in every detail. As for you, O King, tell me what you are minded to do and what plans you have laid."

"Your words do not convince me," said King Sayf. "They seem indeed mere idle talk. I think you are rather some knightly champion come seeking combat with me. You struck blows at me, thrusting as an enemy would; and now, when you see defeat and shame draw near, you pretend to be a maiden, spinning me a long tale of which I can make nothing at all. The things you speak of are no concern of mine. I know nothing of the Book of the Nile, nor have I come seeking it, nor am I he of whom you speak. You have veiled your face, and this is something I have never seen."

"You speak truly," she said, "and indeed my mother forewarned me of this. 'He will not believe anything of what you say,' she told me, 'until you lift the veil from your face.' Thus shall I prove the truth to you, valiant youth." With that she raised the veil from her face to reveal a countenance like the full moon, round as a shield of bright crystal, with cheeks on which roses were strewn, fashioned by the All-Forgiving Sovereign, and eyes like the eyes of the gazelle, with glances darting arrows and lances that had power to strike the boldest of men, and a neck like a pillar of precious stone set on a bosom smooth as marble, on which were set breasts before which a lion might bow its head.

When King Sayf Ben Dhi Yazan saw all the comeliness and beauty with which the Lady Tama had been endowed, he was dazzled and filled with amazement. "Turn away your face, lovely and exquisite beauty," he said, "for you have ensnared me and confused me with love, adding to my tribulations."

"Have no fear," she said, "you see only that with which God will make your heart glad. I shall return from here to my mother the sorceress 'Aqila and tell her of your coming. As for you, do not approach the gate of the city, but rather, leaving the gate on your left hand, walk toward the towers. Pass nine of the towers, then stand before the tenth; there you will find a long plank of wood jutting out from the tower, with a rope attached to it, and hanging from the rope there will be a chest. Climb into this and lie down inside, then pull the lid down over you and close it from within with your feet."

"I hear and obey," he said. Then Tama mounted her horse and, returning to the city of Qaymar, went in to her mother to tell her King Sayf was come and bid her make shift to prepare the marriage.

"I hear and obey," her mother replied.

Now the reason for these things was that the lord of this city of Qaymar, King Qamroun, worshipped the Book of the Nile, which was worshipped, too, by all his people. He had lodged it in a place of which we will speak in due season, and he had three hundred and sixty wizards well versed in the arts of sorcery, magic, and conjuring of spirits, presided over by the sorceress 'Aqila, the mother of Tama, whose age exceeded a hundred and fifty years. For a long time she had been blessed by neither girl child nor boy child; but when she was well steeped in age, a certain wizard cunning and adept in magic possessed her, a mighty and skilled sorcerer named Tabhoun. When she had become the companion of his bed, he wished her to show him the tablets that were in her keeping, but she said: "These are secrets to be revealed neither to free men nor slaves."

Still he pressed her and the matter ended in strife, after which battle and conflict ensued. The sorceress 'Aqila was more powerful than he in the secret sciences, but seeing him mighty and unassailable, and fearing he would slay her, she prepared a poisoned lance to use against him and, catching him unawares, overcame him with it, piercing him through the eye and slaying him. He had presided over a hundred and eighty wizards, who now came to the sorceress 'Aqila and fought against her; but them too she defeated, and they offered her their allegiance and became subject to her. She likewise had had a hundred and eighty followers, so now it came to pass that there were three hundred and sixty wizards, all under her command.

Each day one of these wizards would come to be at the king's service, then be guardian of the book for a further day. Then, when he had served these two days, he would remain without duties of guardianship or sorcery for the rest of the year. 'Aqila ruled over all of these wizards, because King Qamroun placed trust in none but her and did nothing without asking her counsel; for she was most knowledgeable and wise in the affairs of the kingdom of the Maghrib and all its districts and towns and villages.

Now when the due time came, she knew King Dhi Yazan had died according to God's decree, leaving behind him his son, the noble knight Sayf, and that this son it was who would take possession of the Book of the Nile so that the river would flow at his hands thereafter by the leave of the Glorious Sovereign. He would marry 'Aqila's daughter, and should she try to stand against him she would be defeated, since God's destiny was greater than her power or the power of any other. She wished accordingly to conciliate him so that she might be in good standing with him, and her affection for him grow stronger through giving him her daughter in marriage; for she had learned he was destined to marry her daughter in any case. And all these things came to pass by the will of the All-Creating Sovereign.

When Tama returned to her mother and told her King Sayf was coming, she said: "Welcome and greetings to him." Then she rose and, placing two wooden poles one in front of the other, like the masts of a ship, she took one of these and hung a pulley with a rope around it, a rope of great length, with wooden guards so that the chest should not touch the walls and none should seize hold of it. She herself would haul at the rope, and the two wooden masts would tilt together outside the walls, causing the chest to rise upwards like a catapult, and come down inside the city without touching the walls, either ascending or descending. And Sayf came and saw the chest, as Tama had told him, and placed himself within it. The sorceress 'Aqila and her daughter Tama were inside the tower, and a horse also; and when 'Aqila hauled at the rope, the chest rose and came down inside the city.

Now the sorceress 'Aqila had a place over which she had cast a spell, using all the power she had in such things; and when King Sayf came down into this she rose to meet him and bade him be seated, greeting him like one of her own kin, honoring him with courtesy and making him welcome. She ordered her servants to bring food, then seated herself beside him, conversing and jesting with him. And Tama was pleased at this, hoping this heralded her own well-being and good.

Now while this was happening, lo, the Hidden One cried out: "Qamroun, this night, under cover of darkness, a stranger has entered your city; and he it is who will steal the Book of the History of the Nile. Pursue him! Cut him to pieces with your swords! If you see him, do not let him live! Quickly, quickly, before all hopes are dashed!"

All the inhabitants of the city, the people and soldiers and guards, heard this, and King Qamroun straightway mounted his horse, with the great officers of state mounting theirs behind him, and likewise the people of his kingdom and his chamberlains and lieutenants. All the citizens raised a hubbub with their shouting and weeping and wailing, the tumult rising from every nook and corner, the men and women alike crying out.

Then the search began throughout the city and its precincts and markets, through stalls and houses and mansions and all manner of places, in search of the enemy. But they found no sign or trace of him, so that King Qamroun grew crazed with anxiety and his heart was fit to burst; and he returned to his quarters close to madness and death.

All this took place as the sorceress 'Aqila sat entertaining King Sayf, unaware of what passed. But he turned to her, saying: "How is it, sorceress 'Aqila, that I hear such a tumult and hubbub in the city, and the sounds of people crying in confusion? What is the reason for all this?"

"Sir," she said, "the Hidden One has betrayed your entrance into the city. He is telling King Qamroun to look for you, and now they are searching; but I shall let none discover you. You must do now as I tell you and follow my counsel to the letter, for though I rule over the three hundred and sixty wizards here in this city, at the court of this great king, each of them seeks his own glory and wishes to raise his standing with the king so that he may be exalted over me. If they learn where you are, and find you here with me, I shall be considered a traitor by the king. But I cannot abandon you, since my daughter Tama is so enamored of you. For her sake I must help you and put you in possession of this Book of the Nile, letting none find a path to you." And King Sayf accordingly told her to do as she saw fit.

Meanwhile the search went on in the city. Then the sorceress 'Aqila turned to her daughter, saying: "Light of my eyes, I wish you to help me."

"Tell me your wish," said Tama, "and I shall help you."

"Rise," she said, "and go to our neighbor Khalid al-'Ibadi, saying: 'Do you have a fish we could cook for our meal, for we have honored guests who eat neither mutton nor beef.'" And Tama rose and returned with her neighbor, a fisherman who bore a large fish.

"By Saturn, sorceress," he said, "this is the only fish I have."

"Very well," she replied. Then she gave the fisherman a dirham and he went on his way. As for the sorceress, she cut open the belly of the fish and skinned it, and wrapped King Sayf in its skin up to his armpits, leaving his neck and head free; then she tied him up under the armpits. Now she had a bird called the roc. She slit open its breast, and set its legs over King Sayf's shoulders, then placed his hands inside the bird's breast and tied the whole with a long rope, letting it all down into the well in her house. "Remain where you are," she said, "till I return." Then she tied the end of the rope to a peg which she hammered into the ground and made ready to ride to the court, saying to her daughter Tama: "Look after him till I return." And with that she locked the gate on King Sayf and Tama, mounted her mule, and went her way to court.

When King Qamroun saw her, he rose to meet her, saying: "Sorceress of all time, come to my aid, for the world is closing in on me and I see my reign drawing to an end."

"Do not be troubled, King of all time," she replied. "Your reign is secure and Saturn's blessing will fall upon you. But tell me, O King, what is the reason for all this anxiety?"

"The reason, sorceress," he said, "is that the Hidden One has come and cried out to us, telling us of an enemy here within the city, a noble king who seeks to rob us of the Book of the Nile. We are troubled on this account, and so I have summoned the wizards, saying: 'Find out where the enemy is. If he has entered the city, then why did the Watchers not cry out? And if he has entered by some way other than the gates, then where can he lie concealed?' Then the wizards said: 'This, O King, is a weighty question, which cannot be solved except at the hands of the sorceress.' 'Can you not learn of this without her help?' I asked. 'We can learn of it, O King,' they replied, 'but still, she it is that you should ask.'"

Then the sorceress realized that these wizards were in truth her enemies and if they learned what she had done, they would bring it to light. "If I do not destroy all these wizards," she thought, "they will set a snare for me and expose me."

"King of all time," she said then, "you have three hundred and sixty wizards dwelling in this city, each ruling his own district with his own court. Why do they not perform their duty, telling you of your enemy and helping you attain your desires?"

"Sorceress," he replied, "here you are yourself now."

"And I am minded," she replied, "to view the Hidden One."

With that she rose, and the king with her, and they went to the Hidden One, and lo, they found it cracked and its neck twisted backwards as though it had been broken. "O King," said the sorceress, "the crack in this Hidden One means its power is ended, and it will serve no longer."

"That I see for myself," he replied. Then he demanded of his men of state: "What have you to say about this crack in the Hidden One?"

"O King," they replied, "we know nothing of such things. This is a matter for the wizards. Summon them to the court tomorrow morning, and they will show proofs and reveal who the enemy is."

"Let us return to the court, O King," said the sorceress, "and I shall make all plain."

So the king returned to his palace and seated himself, with the sorceress 'Aqila seated beside him, and said: "Did you not hear the voice of the Hidden One last night?"

"I heard it, O King," she said, "but I paid no heed to it. What, O King, have the wizards to say of this?"

"They were present here," he replied.

"Choose sixty of the wizards," she said, "to cast the sands in your presence so you may watch how they go about their business. Then confine the others in some place till we see the proofs from them also."

So the king did as the sorceress bade him, confining three hundred of the wizards and summoning the other sixty. Then he said: "Cast the sands, all of you." And they cast the sands a first time, and a second, and then a third, saying nothing all the while.

"What have you seen in the sands?" asked the king. "What has been revealed to you?"

"Give us your pledge of safety," they said.

"You have it," he replied.

Then they said: "The enemy who has entered our land was within a wooden chest, which flew up with him and cast him down into the city; and now a fish has swallowed him, and a roc has swooped down on him, so that two-thirds of his body remains in the belly of the fish, with the remaining third seized by the bird.

The bird is in a dark place, and the fish is submerged in water with the bird hanging over him. The fish will not release him, nor will the bird leave him. And so he remains."

Then the king turned to the sorceress 'Aqila, saying: "Do you hear what these wizards have to say? The enemy entered a flying chest, and now a fish has swallowed him and a bird has seized him, yet he is still alive. I understand nothing of all this."

"I told you wizards," the sorceress 'Aqila said, "to abstain from heavy foods, and yet you paid no heed. Such food weighs on the brain, making the actions clumsy and the mind slow-witted."

At that the king roared at the wizards: "Out of my sight, you dogs!" And so they left, banished from his presence and in great terror.

Then the sorceress bade the king disband the court, saying: "Have no fear, King of all time, I shall help you attain your desires." With that she mounted her mule and returned from the court to her house, then went down into the well where King Sayf was and drew him out.

When he saw her, he felt reassured in his heart and asked her what she had done that day.

"I summoned the wizards," she said, "and confused them so they had no power to see you. And tomorrow I shall play a trick still greater than the prodigies I worked today."

King Sayf was cheered by her words, and he thanked her for her care for him. Then she called for food, and they ate and drank their fill, conversing together till the day drew to an end and night approached with its gloom. Then the sorceress 'Aqila said: "King Sayf, I wish to ask you something under your pledge of safety."

"Ask all you wish, mother," he replied. "I am your son and there are no hidden secrets between us."

"You came to this land," she said, "pursuing a goal of your own. And when you have gained your ends, you will return in peace to your own land, without having done what we wish of you."

"What is it you wish of me," he asked, "when I have gained my ends, and you have helped me accomplish them?"

"I wish to give you in marriage to my daughter Tama," she replied, "for I have long promised you to her, turning away all suitors who came for her with a show of their wealth. You it is who are my choice; and I have told Tama of her marriage to you, that you will be her husband, and she your kin. 'You shall marry none,' I told her, 'but King Sayf.'"

"Mother," replied King Sayf, "if my destiny is to be joined to her, and she is to have sustenance at my hands, then so it shall be; but I have taken a bounden oath that I will marry none before Shama, King Afrah's daughter. As for Tama, your daughter, she is the very life of my soul, but she will respect my reasons."

"My son," said the sorceress, "there is no need to tell me this, for I have known of it from ancient times. You speak nothing but the truth."

And so they spent the rest of the night in safety and contentment, till the dawn broke. Then the sorceress said: "Bring what you have, Tama." But when Tama brought her a gazelle she had, her mother said: "Have you nothing else?" And when she was told there was nothing else, she said: "Bring the eagle's wings you have, so I may attain my goal."

"I hear and obey," said Tama. Then she went to fetch the eagle's wings and gave them to her mother. The sorceress took them and tied them to a stick, then spread them wide as a bird would spread them in flight and set them on the back of the gazelle, so that it became like an eagle, spreading its wings to the right and to the left; then she tied the stick with a rope round the beast's girth and tied the end of the rope to a pulley. And when she then pulled on the rope, the gazelle rose up toward the roof with the wings on its back, as though about to take flight. After this she set one pulley in front of the gazelle, before its head, and one at its back, behind its legs; and, bringing a plank of wood, instructed King Sayf to lay himself down on it while she tied the ends of the plank to two ropes and passed them through the pulleys. Finally she seized hold of the first rope, her daughter seizing hold of the other, and together they lifted King Sayf from the two ends, so that he and the plank together came to rest beneath the gazelle's belly, with his head beneath its breast and his legs beneath its tail, both he and the gazelle suspended in the air. Then she made the ropes fast to iron pegs on the right and left side of the house, and said: "Remain so, O King, till I have been to the court and done what I have to do; for today there will be a new reading of the sands." So saying, she donned her gear and mounted her mule to ride to the court, where she dismounted, gathered up her skirts and went into the presence of King Qamroun. There she found a full gathering of ministers and governors, all consulting over the present threat to them, exchanging talk and suppositions, one saying one thing and one another.

When they saw the sorceress 'Aqila approaching, they rose to their feet; and when she gave them her greeting, they all returned it in a state of confusion. She thereupon told them to be seated, both officers of state and others, then took her own place, so that they all grew calmer. Then she greeted King Qamroun, and said: "King of all time, how is it I see all the wizards sitting idle here?"

"We awaited your coming," he replied, "to come and give us sound counsel so we may take captive this enemy who has entered our city without our knowledge and is minded to rob us of the Book of the History of the Nile. Now you are come, tell us the wise course to take."

"I am indeed come," said the sorceress 'Aqila. "Stir yourselves then, wizards, and cast the sands in the sight of all present; and let us see, wizards of all time, what proofs you are able to produce. Here I stand, and I give you my leave. But do not talk nonsense as you did yesterday."

"We hear and obey," they said. And with that they cast the sands, viewing the signs from every point of view; but though the truth was revealed to them, they were struck dumb, so remarkable was the sight that met their eyes. A full hour they read the signs, astounded by them, wishing to be sure of the account they gave. But all this brought them no joy; rather they were filled with terror and panic, knowing the tyrannical nature of their king. Gazing at one another, they mixed the sands together yet again, all at their wit's end; and when those gathered saw these things, they were yet more astonished.

As for King Qamroun, he became like a madman, and was minded to deal cruelly with them. "What think you, sorceress of all time," he said, "of these wizards who cast the sands, saying nothing of what they have seen, then mix them together yet again?"

"Be patient a while longer, King of all time," said the sorceress 'Aqila, "till they have gathered everything together and give a clear testimony of what they have seen." Then she addressed the wizards. "If no meaning has revealed itself to you in the sands," she said, "then cast them once more. Examine them at your leisure, then tell us what you have seen, hiding nothing from us." Finally she said: "King of all time, do not be hasty, for each casting will produce its own signs and patterns."

At this the king was grudgingly silent, his mood growing ever more sullen and angry. As for the wizards, they cast the sands with great care, and remained awhile lost in thought, the shapes multiplying and changing beneath their hands; and when still the same reading came as before, they mixed the sands yet again and continued to cast them and mix them, with the king growing ever more furious, till they had done it seven times. Then the king shouted at the top of his voice: "What have you seen, dogs of wizards and witless fools, concerning my reign?"

"Know, O King," they said, "that the enemy we seek is within the city. He entered through flight in a wooden chest, but now a beast of the wild has seized him and is flying with him over the earth, soaring toward the lofty heavens. This beast has four legs, like the buffalo and other cattle, and two great wings spread wide. Its form is small, like that of a gazelle or goat or some other beast of the kind, and its wings are spread out to the right and the left. These wings have joints of rope and iron to the right and the left, and he himself is laid on a piece of wood, with the breath of life still in him. So we have seen in the patterns of sand, and it is the truth we speak."

When the king heard these words, he went almost out of his wits, turning to his officers of state in amazement, and crying: "Did you ever hear, any of you, of a beast of the wild snatching up a man and soaring up into the heavens with him—a beast with four long legs like a buffalo or a gazelle or a goat, with long wings spread out, joined to iron and ropes?"

"O King," the whole company said then, "this is something we never heard of, neither we nor our fathers and forefathers. These words are mere ravings. None has ever seen such a thing, or indeed conceived of it."

"Time and again," the sorceress 'Aqila told the wizards, "I have forbidden you heavy foods that cloud the mind, like onions and greens, garlic and radishes and leeks. How often have I not told you to eat foods that lead to health, like clear honey? And yet you paid no heed, eating only the things you desired. Your better qualities are lost, and there is no virtue left in you. What you have told us passes all understanding. It is beyond the mind of any to grasp."

When King Qamroun heard this, he rose to his feet and drew his sword, brandishing it till death crept along its exquisite blade. "You dogs," he cried then to the wizards, "what is this you have told us? Where is the profit in the sands you cast, and the arts you show here, if the enemy does as he wishes in my city, and can seize the Book of the Nile from beneath my hand?" With that he struck one of them across the neck, sending his head spinning from his shoulders, then struck a second and cleft him in two, so that the two pieces fell to the ground, then he struck yet a third, laying him out flat on the earth; and at that the wizards scattered before him, fleeing the court in an agony of fear and shame. And when the king saw the wizards seeking flight in this fashion, he pursued them and overtook three of them, giving them too the cup of death to drink, while the rest fled, scarcely able to believe they had escaped to safety.

The king turned back from his pursuit in a furious rage, feeling all paths were blocked before his eyes; and he returned to the court at his wit's end, giving no answer to any who spoke to him there. Then he turned to the whole company, saying: "Return to your homes. I am better served without you and your counsel!" With that they all departed, and he remained seated there alone, so beside himself with rage he hardly knew where he was.

Meanwhile the sorceress 'Aqila, her snare so well set, sat watching all that had passed with patience and fortitude, yet exulting and rejoicing in her heart at what she had done. Then she left the court, mounted her mule and went to her house, where she found her daughter Tama awaiting her as though on fire with impatience. Then she went up to the roof of the house, with her daughter accompanying her, untied the ropes and the pulleys and released King Sayf, reassuring him as she brought him down, and laughing over what Qamroun had done to the wizards, some of them so violently and unjustly slain.

"What is it you contrived, mother of wizards?" asked King Sayf and Tama.

"I have done a deed," she said, "at whose greatness even champions would stand abashed, which would turn the hair of children white. The wizards of this city know all that passes; when they cast the sands, they find you out and know the paths you take, though layers of earth cover you. And so, my son, the only way to combat them is to trick them and bring them to utter confusion so we may achieve our ends without war or combat. Today I have brought their work to nought, confounding their arts and turning the tables on them. Six have been slain this very day with the keen sword, and the rest I shall destroy also by such means." Then she commanded the servants to bring them food, and she and King Sayf and Tama ate. Then, when they had eaten, they sought rest in sleep till the smiling day broke and the night departed with its gloom.

Then the sorceress 'Aqila rose and said to Tama: "Bring the gazelle we had yesterday." And when she had brought it, 'Aqila took hold of it and slew it over a brass dish into which she drained the blood, adding to it a measure of water, so that the blood filled the vessel before her. Then she brought a gold mortar and placed it, upside down, in the middle of the dish, so that the blood surrounded it. Finally, she set all these things in the middle of a larger vessel and poured in milk, so that the milk surrounded the smaller vessel with the gold mortar. Then she instructed King Sayf to stand within the gold mortar, saying: "Remain as you are till I return from the court."

With that she mounted her mule and left her home for the court; and she was like a venomous serpent. When she arrived at the court, she was the first to give greeting, and all there rose to their feet, King Qamroun making her welcome together with all the men that were with him. Then, when she had sat a full hour in her place, she turned to King Qamroun, saying: "King of all time, what news do you have? Have you learned anything of our enemy, from what country he comes and how he entered this city? Have the wizards been dumb, or have they striven to make him known to all?"

"Sorceress 'Aqila," said King Qamroun, "for these things we look to you and to the wizards that lie under your sway. It is for you to command or forbid. Now you are here among us, do as you will."

"I am indeed among you now," she replied, "and here too are the wizards. I shall command them to cast the sands and make our enemy known." And with that she turned to the wizards, saying: "Cast the sands, and make shift in your business."

"We hear and obey," said the wizards. Then they cast the sands and examined them, scrutinizing every detail with diligent care for a full hour; after which they swept them up and once again cast them and gazed at them, then swept them up yet once more; this they did three times in all. Then they said to the sorceress: "Mother of wizards, we are all your subjects. You it is who rule over us, and for you it is to command or to forbid, since none of us holds sway over you. Gaze yourself at the signs and separate truth from falsehood. None of us has power as you have power, or knowledge as you have knowledge. Do not give us over to the destruction of the king, for none but you is sovereign over us."

"Indeed I have power to divine," said the sorceress. "And yet I should like to see what you have observed and learned, and how it comes you have won lands and your own court with the king; for when there was need of you, you failed, accomplishing nothing for the king. And from this the king may know that you give him no good counsel and have no power to attain his goal."

"Sorceress 'Aqila," said King Qamroun, "if these wizards have no knowledge of the matter, is that good cause to yield, giving the enemy leave to usurp our sovereignty and rob us of the book we venerate? I shall not let these wizards be. Rather I shall slay them all."

"Calm yourself, O King," said the sorceress, "till I attain your goals for you, and fulfill your wishes. This is a plot we shall soon unravel." Then she asked the wizards: "What did you see in your sands?"

"Sorceress," they replied, "this enemy has amazed our minds and bereft us of reason; for what we see is beyond any sound mind to understand, astounding whoever hears it. We have seen that our enemy dwells here in the heart of the city, standing atop a mountain of gold, which itself stands in a sea of blood. Around the sea is a wall of brass, and around the wall a flowing river of milk, and around the milk another wall of brass. Our enemy stands on that mountain with shoes on his feet, and his two hands are set on the top of his head. You are a sorceress, and a person of wit and understanding. Tell us how we may be delivered from our plight and make our escape."

"Mother of wizards," said King Qamroun then, "do you hear the words of these false wizards? They trifle with my authority, pretending to true arts, yet showing no proper proofs. Where in our city can we find a mountain of gold, a sea of blood, a wall of brass, a river of milk? These are mere fancies to cloud the mind."

With that he rose and drew his sword, striking one of them and slaying him, and then a second, and then a third. But the sorceress approached him and spoke sharply to him, angrily staying his hand.

"Why do you slay them," she asked, "when they have committed no offense worthy of death? You seek your enemy and I shall bring him before you. As for the wizards, they are my children at last." Then she bade the wizards depart, saying: "Your enemy, O King, cannot escape our hands. We shall surely take him captive. Yet I fear for the future, for I am old now and my mind begins to fail; soon I shall die and dwell beneath the earth, and then the king will find none to carry out his business. None of those I have instructed is of any worth. Such is the fear that seizes me in your presence, O King Qamroun."

"If matters stand so," replied King Qamroun, "all the more likely it is that the enemy will enter my city and rob us of the Book of the History of the Nile. Is that not a shame and a scandal for you?"

"King of all time," said the sorceress, "have no fear things will so come to pass. I shall take your enemy captive and deliver him into your hands, so you may make an example of him before the kings of the earth."

"And when will that be?" he asked.

"When the present month ends," she replied, "and the new moon rises. Let us go to the book now and consult it in these matters. It will surely make known the proper course to follow."

"Do as you see fit," the king said then, "for I shall not reject your counsel."

Now this book was the deity of the people of Qamroun's city, and they knew no other god, believing it brought them fire and made the waters flow, so that they would plant their crops in the soil and the water would come to irrigate it. Whenever the new moon rose, they would come in to it and kneel down before it, rather than before the Lord of Lords, the All-Forgiving Sovereign, who brought down the rain from the clouds and mist and created Adam from clay. This book was placed in a chest of black ebony, inlaid with patens of red gold, and the chest was set within a coffer of teak inlaid with patens of silver. Above this was a high wooden altar draped with a curtain of colored silk, and over all was a strongly built dome of white marble, entered by a gate of Chinese iron with locks of steel. The keys to those locks were in King Qamroun's keeping, for he would trust no man with them, and none but he could open the dome. When the new moon rose, the dignitaries of the city would all assemble, the ministers and princes and governors and chamberlains, so that any man of standing in the kingdom would be there that day with the king. The king would first come and unlock the gate of the dome, then raise the lid of the coffer, then draw out the chest and open it, then look on the book and fall on his knees before it, rather than to the Lord of Lords. When the officers of state, the princes and the ministers, saw him kneel in this fashion, they would know he was doing obeisance to the book; then they too would fall to their knees, and their vassals, seeing them do so, would do likewise. Such was their belief; for these people were like cattle and had no Imams to guide them in the principles and laws of religion. Rather their wizards dealt in magic and sorcery, and their kings venerated that book, praise be to the Great Mover of all things.

When it was day, the sorceress 'Aqila said to King Qamroun: "Now I shall uncover the truth and rid you of suffering and harm." And with that she went to her house, and her daughter Tama welcomed her, asking her what she had done.

"Nothing but good has come to pass," she said. "Go to King Sayf and give him the glad news, then bring him down from the top of the mortar." And so Tama went to Sayf, and brought him down and took him to her mother, who rose smiling to meet him.

"King Sayf, my son," she said, "I have done a great work today, and but for me the king would have struck off the heads of the wizards. Nine of them already he has slain, and all on account of the trick I played."

"But what possessed the king," asked King Sayf, "to slay the wizards who were his friends? And what use has he for this book?" Then she told him all the things we have recounted. These people had, she concluded, no other object of worship, and when the time came to go before the book, the people gathered all together and went to the dome to kneel before it. Any who was tardy would be considered impious, possessed of neither faith nor conviction; and if King Qamroun were to learn that any in his kingdom had been tardy taking his place, on the day the dome was unlocked and the book revealed, he would vent his wrath on him, bringing torment down upon him and making him rue what he had done.

"And when," asked King Sayf, "will they gather to go in to the book and kneel before it?"

"O mighty adversary," she said, "tomorrow will pass, and then the day after will be the day of the assembly."

Then Tama brought them food and, when she had entered, seated herself beside King Sayf and gazed into his face to see his beauty, and his radiance, and the fineness of form with which Almighty God had endowed him, so that her heart inclined to him in love and her wonderment increased. Then they set to the food and ate their fill and drank together and made merry, with Tama still amazed all the while at how handsome King Sayf Ben Dhi Yazan was, her passion and feeling rising ever higher. "Mother," she said. "Tomorrow morning let us go to the dome and kneel before the book with the ministers and chamberlains."

"And why should we perform these rites, you and I?" she replied. "What obliges us to do such a thing, when worship is a matter for men? Who has heard of women going to kneel before the book?"

At that King Sayf turned to Tama, saying: "Sister, I wish to go with your mother, to see the people gathered there in that place, and what they do in their worship of this book."

"Light of my eyes," replied Tama, "what good will come to you from this? I have heard you worship the Great and All-Bountiful God, claiming the worship of the book is false and contrary to reason, a wrong and wayward thing. Have no part of the matter therefore, for you are not one of the people of this land. You are white-skinned, while everyone else here is black; if you take your place among them they will surely know you, and then they will slay you and make you dwell beneath the earth, while I remain, long weeping and mourning over you. You are more precious to me than the book, and all I own in this city, and all of my friends and kin."

"Know, King Sayf," said the sorceress then, "that the wizards are now confounded, standing in terror of the king's power, so that none is left to oppose you or stand between you and the king. Tomorrow morning I shall know what stratagems to use against him, and I shall snare him with the fine trappings of falsehood, so turning his eyes from you. Then, when he lets you be, holding back from his pursuit of you, I shall devise a means for you to take the book and so attain your goal, and I shall send you hence in safety. Such is the dearest service I can do you at this time, and I know such service will not be wasted on a man of your stamp. My wish is to give my daughter Tama in marriage to you, and give you possession, O valiant King, of all her exquisite beauty."

When King Sayf heard the words of the sorceress 'Aqila, his heart was filled with joy. "Sorceress of all time," he said, "may I never lose you, nor lose sight of your radiant face. Everything in you is pleasing to me, and if time grants me my desire and I win to high standing, I shall requite all your good and kindly deeds with the like."

"My son," replied the sorceress 'Aqila, "you wish to reward me, and yet nothing is beyond my reach; for if I desired wealth I could straightway have it, and if I wished sovereignty over a land, I could attain every wish through my craft, and if I have need of servants, the hordes of the jinn stand utterly at my command. But if you are indeed minded, King of all time, to requite me with a good deed and a token of your esteem, leaving nothing with which I may reproach or blame you, then my wish is that you take my daughter Tama in marriage, so she may become a wife to you as Shama will be."

"Sorceress," said King Sayf, "you know this is in the hands of destiny. If my lot lies with her, then none can gainsay it, and such is indeed my very desire; but you know I am engaged on a matter here. If I accomplish it, then all I have desired and hoped for will be attained."

With that he left the sorceress engrossed in her divination and magic, and turned to Tama, saying: "What do you say, Tama my beloved? Will you not persuade your mother to take me with her to bear away the book, so I may observe how the people of these lands conduct their worship? My wish is to spy out the realm of King Qamroun and number his troops, learning how many knights he has, and noting his champions and valiant men. My heart is set on the matter, for to be told of such things is not like seeing them with one's own eyes."

"And why should you concern yourself with such perilous matters?" asked Tama. "Do you not fear you will be discovered, when our object is to keep you concealed?"

"Tama," said King Sayf, "I can know no rest till I have done this, though I should drink from the cup of death."

"And I cannot consent," said Tama, "that you, the man I have chosen, should place yourself in such peril. Rather I shall hide you in the depths of my heart. Stay with me and rest in my house."

"Indeed, Tama," said Sayf, "whatever happens I am yours, and know that, if fate so wills, you shall be my wife. And therefore your duty is to help me attain my ends, for I have no support but you in this perilous enterprise. I ask you to intercede with your mother, so I may go with her, and see where the book is kept, and so fulfill my hopes and aims; and if your mother does not consent to this, I shall attend to the matter myself."

Hearing this dispute, the sorceress 'Aqila said to her daughter: "What is it he asks? Let me know, so I may satisfy his desires and set all my heart to serving him."

"Mother," said Tama, "he wishes to go with you to the court, to be safe and secure in your company, so he may observe with his own eyes King Qamroun's court and his troops, and the officers of his kingdom, and his knights, that he may discern which are courageous and which are cowards among them. I have warned him against such a course, but he pays no heed and will do only as he himself wishes."

"My son," said the sorceress, when she heard these words, "why should you concern yourself with such grave matters? This is a mighty king, ruler of many lands and provinces, and if he should learn of you he will not stay his hand from you; if he takes you captive, he will not permit you to live. I cannot abandon you. Rather I shall fight all who draw near you, laying down my own life if any seeks to harm you; for you, my son, are a stranger here, solitary and alone. But if you so wish it, I shall not hold you back; rather I am at your service. Only, if you come with me, do not speak to any, or answer any who speak to you."

"And why," asked King Sayf, "should I be minded to speak with people, or they speak with me, when I do not know them, nor they me?"

With that the sorceress rose, saying: "Take off your clothes." And when he had done so, she brought a bottle filled with a red ointment, and said: "Rub this over your body." He did as she instructed him, and he became as red as an Ethiopian in color. Then she dressed him in the clothes of one of her slave boys and gave him a leather bag filled with magical writings, and instruments of her craft, and astrological charts, and all the equipment for casting the sands: all the means she needed for divination and magic. And when she was finished with her work, she said: "My son, carry this bag on your shoulders, as though you were one of my slave boys. Walk with me, but take care not to reveal yourself."

"Mother," he replied, "the matter is in God's hand."

And so the sorceress mounted her mule and, taking Sayf with her, proceeded to the court. Then she dismounted and, still accompanied by King Sayf as though he were one of her servant boys, went in to King Qamroun and greeted him; and when he had risen to meet her, returning her greeting with a great show of esteem, she seated herself in her place and the slave boys stood in attendance on her.

Then King Qamroun turned to her, saying: "Sorceress of all time, I have not tasted food this night, nor have my eyes enjoyed sleep for the cares that have entered my heart. I suffer torments thinking of this enemy."

"King of all time," said the sorceress, "drive these cares and sorrows from your heart. Leave the matter with me; I will cast the sands and give you news of the enemy." And with that she turned to King Sayf, saying: "Bring the bag, boy, so I may see what new things have come to pass." So King Sayf stepped forward and handed her the bag, and she opened it and took the sand tray, then returned the bag to him, saying: "Stand here before me." And he stood among the slave boys, as she bade him, like a raging lion.

The sorceress cast the sands and examined the signs, gazing at the sands for a full hour and working out the figures falsely. Then she smiled, saying: "Know, O wise and fortunate King, that your enemy has entered our land and was minded to rob us of our book, but could not do so because of the manifest miracles the book can work—among them the power to preserve itself from an enemy, though he were a great and mighty king. When the enemy entered the city and heard what had passed between you and your wizards, and learned you were a great king, he feared for his life. The awesome powers of the book struck him with terror, lest he fall into your hands and have his head struck off. His only course was to flee into the plains and deserts. Now I have told you, King of all time, so drive these sorrows from your heart. This book is safe, I warrant you, and your enemy has been powerless to seize it; nor could he do so were he to ride on the back of a cloud."

"Sorceress of all time," said King Qamroun, "what talk is this? It is known to me, and to you and the other wizards, and to all in this land, that if this enemy once enters our city, he will leave only when he has gained possession of the book. The matter is manifest to all; for our enemy is a mighty king and a noble knight, pledged to take the Book of the History of the Nile and so win fame. He will turn the Nile from these lands to the lands of Egypt."

"Be patient, O fortunate King," said the sorceress, "for the Hidden One has said this enemy is a man solitary and alone, nor have I read in these sands that he is anything other than that; and when he fled, he took nothing with him from these lands and deserts."

"I do not believe a word of all this," King Qamroun said then. "This is the day of the new crescent moon. Rise and come with me, so we may open the dome and the altar, and you may approach the chest with the book to see if it is there or if it is gone."

"The matter is in your hands," said the sorceress 'Aqila. "Rise, King of all time and let us proceed."

With that King Qamroun and the sorceress 'Aqila rose, accompanied by the ministers and governors, the rulers and dignitaries, who rode with them to the dome and the altar where the book was kept; and the king, riding with the sorceress 'Aqila, was in haste to be first to arrive there.

"If the book is indeed there, O King," said the sorceress, "then we have attained our object, and no enemy or envious man will have come near us. But if it is gone, then I shall pledge myself to retrieve it with all speed."

"Sorceress," said the king, "this cannot be, for the book will have been taken by a mighty king who, by its power, will make the great Nile flow, will use it to irrigate lands and regions, and so become a king of great renown. Do not say that if it is gone, it will return, for such a thing is unheard of. All our care will have been of no use."

"If so you think," said the sorceress, "then even if the book is there, it will surely vanish in due season."

All the while King Sayf heard these words but paid heed to no one, for his heart was full of thoughts of Shama, daughter of King Afrah. He found no release from the snares of his love for her, saying to himself: "I must seize the book this very day, taking no account of blame or rebuke."

The sorceress, seeing his state, drew near, saying: "My son, let me tell you a thing of which you must beware."

"And what is that?" he asked.

"On this day," she said, "the king will open the dome so as to inspect the chest. It awaits you, who are destined to seize it, and none can keep it from you. If you enter the dome with us, the people of the city will not know you, nor will King Qamroun; and though the Watchers of the Book will all know you, they have no power to deny you. Because the chest with the book is yours by fate, the moment you cross the threshold to enter the dome and stand within, the chest will spin three times round on its base, there in the middle of the dome, and will be raised from its place, coming to rest between your feet. But when that happens, and the king and the ministers of state see you, the crowds will rush at you, shredding your flesh with the edges of their swords, like flocks of cotton; hundreds and thousands they number, and you, my son, are solitary and alone. Since you are my helper, I cannot keep them from you, for if I make a show of resistance, they will accuse me of treachery. Therefore take due warning, my son, and do not enter the dome."

"Have no fear on this account," said King Sayf. "Do not speak of it."

"Now I have given you my counsel," she replied. "Peace be upon you."

With that she left him and went on her way, but her heart was troubled on his account, for she knew he would not heed her words whatever she might say. She went on till she caught up with King Qamroun, then remained by his side, riding on her mule, while the high officers of state rode behind; and so they continued till they reached the dome. When the doors were opened, the men and the youth stepped forward, and the people entered behind the king and his ministers and his retinue, the soldiers and peasants and all the people of the kingdom. And when they opened up the altar and looked into the chest, they found the book unharmed, and knelt down before it, rather than before the Lord of Creation.

All this while King Sayf stood at the door of the dome, minded to enter, but wavering between two courses. "My son," the sorceress 'Aqila had said, "do not enter this place"; and he had promised to take heed of her warning, pledging his solemn oath. Yet he could no longer hold back now he knew where the book was, and he was resolved to take it whatever might happen. Besides, he yearned for his country and longed to take Shama for his wife, and so accomplish his desire; and stronger yet was his wish to prevail over the accursed sorcerer, Saqardyoun, who was the cause of all this trouble. All this while he remembered the sorceress and her warning to him not to enter. Then, steeling his heart and mind to the deed, he crossed the threshold of the dome, where he found the people all kneeling together; and he gazed at them, wishing to do as they did, but kneel rather before God, the Lord of Creation. For he said within himself: "Every man who kneels does so to his own God, and I kneel before Almighty God."

But as he was about to fall to his knees, all at once the base trembled and rose higher, and the chest holding the book fell, spinning round three times and sliding from its place with a screeching sound, till it came to rest at last between his feet. When King Qamroun saw this, he was deeply troubled, as were all those present, the champions and soldiers and ministers and dignitaries and chamberlains and lieutenants, for they all knew this was the enemy come to seize the book, who had revealed himself now before all their eyes. Neither fear nor caution would serve him any longer.

King Qamroun, seeing him, cried out at the top of his voice: "Here is the enemy! Seize him and cut him to pieces with your swords! Here is the enemy who has come to our city, minded to seize our book, on whose account I slew the wizards."

At that the men surged forward, champions at the ready, and the elephants were made to kneel. Each drew his keen blade, and they straightway bore down on King Sayf to give him the cup of death to drink; and when King Sayf saw what they were doing, he knew he had risked his life by his impatience in entering that dome. Holding back would no longer serve; for were he to remain silent, he would drink the cup of destruction, and nothing could save him in his fearful plight but the power of God, the Exalted Sovereign, and his own courage in facing the champions and striking with the edge of the sword. Accordingly, he flung the bag to the sorceress 'Aqila, who was watching him and moving toward him; then, seeing one of the chamberlains approaching him sword in hand, he cried out in the man's face and flung a punch at him, striking him on the chest and flinging him on his back. Then he seized his sword and roared at his base enemies like a lion of the forest, growling and snarling and roaring just as the lion does. He raged or grew grimly surly, passing from one mood to the other, trusting in the help of the One Exalted God, and crying out: "God is great, God is greater than all who oppress and tyrannize, God is greater than all infidels who set up another deity alongside Him!" Then he recited the following lines:

> If the armies have gathered their forces against me
>> and have drawn against me their swords and their spears,
> And have all banded together encompassing my death
>> and none has spoken a word in my defense,
> And I with no spear or sword in my hand
>> and no lively steed on which to brave the battlefield,
> Alone encompassed around with my enemies,
>> unable to escape or shift my ground,
> I cry out to you: come forth and attack me,
>> surround me on the right and on the left!
> I alone with God's aid shall exterminate you
>> with the edge of my bright and burnished sword.
> I am Sayf Ben Dhi Yazan, called the bridegroom of war;
>> I shall let you have your fill of the fray.
> How many a forest have I purged of lions,
>> wild beasts who have left their dens deserted.
> My sword has no desire to seek its scabbard
>> and when I brandish it on high, it gleams.
> My sword and my spear are the staunchest of comrades,
>> my heart knows no fear at all of men.
> Here is the thick of the fighting, come and face me
>> and pay no heed to what you've heard aforetime.
> I shall make of your flesh a banquet for wild beasts
>> and a lawful provision for the carrion birds.
> I am Sayf Ben Dhi Yazan, the Yemeni,
>> sprung from mighty and honorable forebears.

When King Qamroun heard his words, he became still more incensed, crying out: "Slay him, do not suffer him to live!" And King Sayf, hearing this, and being certain now of death and destruction, began striking blows that left none standing, giving quarter to none. The sword he had taken from the chamberlain was a keen blade, hacking through skulls and joints, and making the blood flow like a gushing torrent, felling bodies in that dome, and filling it with corpses and mangled limbs. He made his enemies drink the cup of suffering, and visited woe and ruin upon them, till he reached the open air, filling the land with the bodies of the slain. They had mounted their horses and charged at him like an advancing flood; the sword was torn from his grasp and the multitude pressed in on him. Then he saw a knight approaching him with a well-balanced spear in his hand; and waiting patiently till the knight made a thrust at him, he caught hold of the spear and tugged it from his grasp, then thrust it into his enemies' breasts till he made the blood foam on the ground, crying out with a resounding voice: "Dogs, I have seized your book, and I shall destroy you and slay your king. I care nothing for any of you!"

Each time King Qamroun heard these words, he rebuked his men, calling out: "Shame on you, a man on foot, all alone, is wreaking havoc on you with sword and spear. Where is your prowess and your resolution?" Yet for all this, King Sayf would not approach a throng without hacking it to pieces, or a line of men without scattering it, till the bright day departed and the darkness of night drew near. From right and left they rushed at him, and he stopped the breath of life within them, giving their ghosts to the ground. But as he still wove a way through the throng, destroying his enemies through the length of his arm, his foot struck the head of a slain man; for the darkness of night was come, and his strength and power were exhausted. He made to rise to his feet, but the dignitaries and ministers and lieutenants gathered round him, seizing him and binding his shoulders and tying his arms and legs fast. Then they brought him before King Qamroun, saying: "King of all time, here is our enemy who has come here from a distant land to seize our book, and has wrought havoc on us, destroying our men and champions."

"Do not show me his face," replied the king. "I have no wish to view him, for I mean to give him the cup of destruction to drink. Take him to the pit that is in the mountain, the pit of doom, where no escape from death is possible. There let him perish miserably, with none to know of his end." All this while King Sayf was silent, giving no answer, uttering not a single word, certain of approaching death.

Now this pit was in the middle of a mountain, and it was called the pit of doom and terror. Eighty cubits deep it was, with a leaden cover that could not be lifted except by fifty of the strongest young men, and none had opened it for sixty years. It had been made by King Qamroun's father for those in disgrace, so that if his wrath were aroused by one of the mighty whose crimes were great, the man would be flung into its depths.

When the king commanded his men to take King Sayf to the pit and fling him in, they sprang to obey his command, binding him and setting guards over him till morning broke, while King Qamroun slept that night with an untroubled heart.

When morning came the men rose and went to seek the king's warrant, which he granted them; and they took King Sayf and proceeded with him as they had been commanded, crossing the plains and deserts. King Sayf was weeping and the tears streaming down his cheeks. Then, true Arab that he was, he recited the following words:

> Why are the days so adverse? Each day
>   afflicts me with new calamities,
> Delivering me to the spite of my foes;
>   this is an evil custom of the days.

> O time, why are you so arrogant, a traitor to me
>> when once you showed the purest favor?
> Blessed be those days that showered happiness on me,
>> but now they are hostile to me, have betrayed me.
> I was journeying in the land of Qaymar,
>> thinking that the time would be propitious
> To seek out the Book of the Nile from Qaymar;
>> but the days determined to be my inveterate foes.
> My enemies came upon me with swords and spears
>> and I fought them with what prowess I was able.
> But when my strength waned, I fell to the ground
>> and was taken hostage in chains and in dejection.
> They ordered me to be thrown into their pit
>> and doubled the chains upon me, intending to take away my life.
> I ask God on the Throne, my Host and my Creator,
>> a God on high who knows the secrets of the heart,
> Quickly to deliver me from my affliction
>> and save me from my foes and from my adversity.

His enemies took him up the mountain and brought him to the pit, guarding him close while they labored together to raise the leaden cover; and when they raised it, a cloud of black dust came out that had a foul and fetid stench. They waited for an hour, till it had ceased to rise, then made ready to fling him in.

Now while this was happening, the sorceress ʿAqila was in great distress. "What say you, sorceress of all time," King Qamroun asked then, "of our enemy being flung into that place?"

"Know, O King," replied the sorceress, "that this enemy is skilled in magic and sorcery, and can make himself invisible to the eye. Had we continued to search for him, we would have found no path to him. I only counseled you to open the dome, O King, because I knew the book would guide us to him. But for the book we should never have recognized him, and for this it was I said we should go to assure ourselves it was safe; the book, I knew, had power to work miracles and would surely guide us to our enemy. But had I made it known the book would take our enemy captive, he would not have followed us, and would not have been taken through the power of the book. O honored King, we have destroyed our enemy and our book remains with us."

When the king heard these words of the sorceress ʿAqila, he laughed and said: "Truly, daughter of a noble race, it is such as you that make the cause of justice prevail." Then the sorceress, with the king's permission, took her leave, as if to return to her home, accompanied by her servants and spurring her mule on at a trot, for she was in great haste.

But instead she made her way to the pit, where she saw the people had raised the lid. Then she said to them: "Bring him here before me, and do not yet fling him into the pit. Rather fetch ropes and bind him, so he may be let down to the bottom without injury; and there he shall remain, suffering the cruelest torment from the depth of darkness and lack of food. He shall not die except through thirst and hunger."

"You speak truly, sorceress of all time," they said. Then they brought a long rope, equal to the depth of the pit, and they bound King Sayf under his armpits and across the shoulders, and let him down till he reached the bottom. Then the sorceress said: "Let go of the rope," and they did so. Sayf, aware of the trick, descended slowly on the end of the rope till he reached the bottom. Then they closed up the pit as it had been before.

King Sayf sat alone in the darkness of that place, sure he was about to perish as though he had never been. When he saw the plight he was in, he heaved a deep sigh of dreadful anguish and, raising his eyes toward the roof of the pit, made his entreaty to the world beyond this one, offering praise and prayer to the Author of All Miracles, and reciting the following words:

> Affliction has wasted away my spirit;
>   O God, hasten to my rescue.
> My soul is in a perilous state
>   and it is for You to deliver me from peril.
> You, who have accustomed us to Your loving kindness,
>   once again do resume that mercy.
> I call upon You with an earnest heart,
>   with a voice persisting in complaint.
> O God, I am now in chains,
>   my bonds are tight and heavy.
> I am cast into a dark pit.
>   Who is there to save my troubled soul?
> I stand in entreaty at Your Gate,
>   begging for salvation out of this affliction.
> Accept my complaint and succor me
>   and generously grant me victory and freedom;
> For there is no one to have mercy upon me
>   and I have no hope save in You, O Lord!

When King Sayf had ended this prayer for deliverance, he saw a glimmer of light in the pit, though no opening was evident. He looked at the wall of that pit and saw it was dark, but a tall being emerged from it, its head close to the roof of the pit and its feet on the ground. It breathed, and King Sayf, smelling its breath, perceived it to possess the fragrance of perfume. So Sayf gave way to his imaginings, waiting impatiently and uttering not a word, only saying to himself: "I am doomed in any case, and if this being should slay me, that will be easier for me than suffering the agonies of darkness and hunger and thirst."

Then all at once this being bent down till it became like an arch and kissed the manacled hand of King Sayf and kissed his shackled feet also, saying: "King of all time, I beseech your help. Deliver me from death and destruction. I am in your hands, for I am in desperate peril and affliction, and I have none to save me but you, great King."

King Sayf was astonished that this being should so abase itself before him, though it was free and King Sayf in heavy chains and close shackles: "You there," he said. "Are you so blind you cannot see I am here in bonds and shackles, in this dark pit, doomed to certain death?"

"King of all time," replied this being, "the hour of your release from this place is not far off. But as for me, I am in the utmost torment. I shall deliver you, though, before we converse further, and after that I shall tell you of the horrors that have befallen me."

With that the being advanced and unbound King Sayf's hands and feet. Then King Sayf said: "Give me the enchanted whip I had before." And the being stretched out its hand to the wall of the pit, and lo, its hand went clean through the wall, and was withdrawn again with the whip.

"Take this whip of yours," said the being then, "but do not raise it, for if you do so, you will slay me."

"Who are you, pray," said King Sayf, "and how did you come to this place?"

"I am no male," replied the being, "but rather a female, your sister by suckling, O King; for my mother suckled you from her breast while I was a babe on her shoulder. I am 'Aqisa, daughter of the White King, from a people who believe in God, the Lord of Creation, according to the creed of Abraham, the Friend of God, father of prophets and messengers. We dwell in the Mountains of the Moon near the source of the Nile, and among us, O King, are people who are Muslims as you are, and a pious shaykh who lives with us in a hermitage, worshipping God. From him it was we learned to worship, and God guided us through his hands. But, King of all time, an infidel jinn giant came to live among us, called the One-Armed Snatcher, who worships fire rather than the All-Powerful Sovereign. And it happened once that he saw me, and his glance was followed by a thousand sighs, and he fell passionately in love with me. Then he asked my father for my hand in marriage, and my father, fearing his might, granted it him. But I hated him and would not consent he should be my husband, or I wife and kin to him. When I could endure it no longer, I went to the pious worshipper who lives amongst us in his dome and told him of my plight. 'The giant is a jinn,' he said, 'and you have no means of deliverance from his hands till the Tubba'i Himyari king comes against him, he who is ruler of Yemen and will abolish strife, the destroyer of infidels and ill-omened creatures, King Sayf Ben Dhi Yazan.' 'In what place is that king?' I asked then. 'You must ask your mother about him,' he replied, 'for she is your mother and his also.' So then I went to my mother and asked her concerning you. "Aqisa,' she replied, 'he has been flung into the pit by King Qamroun. Go to him there and deliver him from his plight, then take him with you to the Snatcher. That king is your brother, nay he is dearer to you than a brother, and his duty is to protect you.' And so I have come to you in this place, King of all time, and none but you can deliver me."

Now we spoke of this Snatcher earlier in our tale, when he came to carry off Shama, the king's daughter, when King Sayf had been with 'Atumtum, the

Piercer of Trees, and struck the Snatcher with the enchanted whip, cutting off his hand. Now this giant, when his hand was cut off and his endurance and courage extinguished, did not return to the foreign wizard, nor did he dare face Saqardyoun. Instead he fled through the wilderness till he reached the Mountains of the Moon, near the source of the Nile, where he settled down to live; and all the people, high and low, came to fear his wrath. And it happened that he passed by the palace of the White King and saw 'Aqisa, moving gracefully like a bride, with a face like the moon when it grows full on the fourteenth night. So he stood there, gazing at her as she passed by him, and his longings and imaginings grew ever stronger. Then he went to the people living nearby and asked about her—who her father was and how she was called. And they told him: "She is the daughter of the White King and her name is 'Aqisa."

When he learned who her father was, he went to the White King, dazed with passion, unable to see what was before him; and when the king saw him, he straightway rose to his feet and bade him be seated, honoring him and paying him endless compliments.

"Is there any desire of yours we may fulfill?" he asked. "For we would not withhold our very lives from you."

"I have come," replied the accursed Snatcher, "seeking marriage, for I am desirous of your daughter. Do not send me away disappointed of my request."

When the White King heard those words, he became as one under constraint: he could not but give his assent, because the Snatcher was a guest in those lands and had built a palace there in the desert regions, embellishing it till there was nothing like it in that time, and had borne off maidens too. And so the White King could say nothing to him, being rather in fear of his wrath and his tyranny over the people of the Jann; and when he asked the king for his daughter in marriage he could not rebuff him. He raised his head, saying: "You are welcome. My slaves are your slaves and we are all your slaves and servants."

"Had you failed to give your assent," the Snatcher said then, "or faltered in your response, I would have hastened your death and made this your last day, O King."

"Do not say so, Snatcher," replied the White King, "for I am yours in all that you wish and my retainers are but your slaves." So the Snatcher went off and came back straightway with a judge of the Jann, and the marriage contract was drawn up. Then the White King said: "She is now your lawful wedded wife."

When the news of this dreadful event reached 'Aqisa, she wept till she could weep no more, for the accursed wretch was ugly of countenance and vast of body, and while the White King and his retainers were Muslims, believing in the Lord of Creation, this giant worshipped fire rather than the Almighty Sovereign. She went to her father, saying: "Could you find none to give me to in marriage but the One-Armed Snatcher, an infidel who worships fire rather than the Almighty Sovereign? I will never accept him as a husband."

"What was I to say to him?" replied her father. "Through you I averted his dreadful evil from myself and my men. I feared for my people, lest they drink from the cup of death."

When 'Aqisa heard her father's words, she knew she must forgive what he had done, and that were she to remain in her land, this puffed-up infidel would bring about her shame. So she fled through the wilds and deserts, the tears streaming down her face, till she reached the pious shaykh who dwelt there among them, and whose name was 'Abd al-Salam.

"Shaykh of ours," she cried, "deliver us from this lustful infidel, who has dared to take me in marriage, though I am a believer."

"'Aqisa," he replied, "go to King Sayf, for he will destroy the Snatcher, and he alone can overcome him and bring him to nought."

"And who, sir, is King Sayf?" she asked.

"Your mother knows him," he said. "He is now in the city of Qamroun."

So she went to her mother, who told her: "Go to the pit and help him, delivering him from what has befallen him, for he is your brother and will protect you from your enemy."

Then she told her daughter how she had suckled him together with her; and thus it was that 'Aqisa came joyfully to King Sayf and told him of what had happened, saying, in conclusion: "Here I am, King of all time, come to you. My protection, and the protection of my honor and my people, is in God's hands and yours; and I shall likewise deliver you and take you to my country, where you will be my guest. There you shall live, most happy. And I too will bear you to your own country and serve you, O King, as one of your soldiers, when you have slain this giant and rid us of his evil, delivering the earth from his tyranny and cunning."

Then, drawing near and raising him up, she struck the rock so that it opened and went out the way she had come, making for the upper air. She flew with him till she alighted over the dome of Shaykh 'Abd al-Salam, then descended to the ground and was about to seek the shaykh's leave to enter, when she heard the master saying: "Enter, Sayf Ben Dhi Yazan." At that 'Aqisa took the hand of King Sayf and together they entered; and King Sayf gazed at the shaykh, and saw that his place of worship was finely embellished, and that the light shone out from between his eyes. The shaykh, seeing him, rose to his feet and welcomed him with an embrace, then kissed him on the forehead, saying: "Welcome, King Sayf, to this place."

Then 'Aqisa left him with Shaykh 'Abd al-Salam and flew off over the plains and thickets. As for Shaykh 'Abd al-Salam, he said to King Sayf: "My son, you will stay with me tonight, till morning comes, for you have been entrusted to me till 'Aqisa returns to take you to the place of the giant Snatcher."

"I hear and obey," said King Sayf. Then he sat with the shaykh in prayer and devotion till morning.

Then 'Aqisa returned, greeting King Sayf and Shaykh 'Abd al-Salam, and saying to King Sayf: "Let us be off."

"Go with her," said the shaykh, "and may God help you attain your goal."

'Aqisa journeyed for an hour, then alighted with him on the earth, saying: "King Sayf, look before you."

King Sayf looked, and said: "I see a dark shape in the distance in that plain and desert." And when she told him this was the palace of the accursed Snatcher, he said: "Take me there, so I may show you what I shall do to him with this whip of mine."

"I may not take a single step further," she replied, "in these plains and hills."

He left her accordingly and went on alone till he reached the palace but, going around it, could find neither path nor ladder by which he might enter; for the palace was high, touching the clouds. Five hundred cubits long it was, and two hundred and fifty cubits high, supported on four columns, the like of which could not be found in that time. And as King Sayf stood gazing at it, wondering how he might climb to its top, he saw an open window and people looking out from it, beckoning to him and saying: "Come, climb up to us, King of the world."

"And how may anyone climb," he asked, "when you are so high up? If you have any ropes, bring them. Then I shall tie an end around me, and you may join together to haul me up."

Now these people were maidens, and as there were many ropes in the palace, they tied one to the other till they reached the ground. King Sayf attached himself without fear to the ropes; and, when they knew the ropes held him fast, they joined together to haul him up to the top of the palace and brought him into it. When he entered he found forty young maidens there, like burnished silver, saying: "Welcome, welcome to the King of the land of Yemen, King Sayf Ben Dhi Yazan."

"Who are you?" King Sayf said then. "Who has told you my name, and why are you living here in this place?"

Then one of them, a maiden of exquisite beauty, rose, saying: "Sir, I will tell you of our plight." Then she approached him and kissed his hands. "It is," she said, "who told them all of your name and described your features."

"And what, pray, is your name?" he asked. "May it be suited to your beauty."

"I am the Princess Nahid," she replied, "daughter of the Emperor of China, and these maidens are all captives. They are the daughters of great kings, rulers of realms and dominions, and we are all virgin maidens. The Snatcher carried us off from our families' quarters, bringing us here and confining us in this place, where we have lived long in sorrow and distress. Then, one day, a voice came to me in my dreams, saying: 'Do not grieve, Nahid, for God will deliver you from your sufferings; he has decreed your release this very day at the hands of King Sayf Ben Dhi Yazan, who will slay the accursed Snatcher. This king it was who cut off the Snatcher's hand in the land of Ethiopia and the Sudan. When you wake from your dream and your sweet slumber, you will find him standing beneath the window. Haul him up then, for he it is who will slay your enemy and restore you all to your homes.' So I woke from my dream, deep in thought, and recounted what I had seen to the maidens, who told me it was mere dream and fancy. The voice brought me, too, the glad news that you will marry me and be my husband, and command me to embrace your religion and follow your creed, for I am to be your companion too in Paradise. And when I asked the voice about your religion, and what it is you worship, I was told: 'This man worships Almighty God, and there is no God but He.' Then I woke from my sleep, saying, 'There is no God but God,' and I told the maidens what I had seen. 'You speak truly,' they said then, 'without lies or shifts. We will all embrace his religion and follow his creed.' And so we all rose and opened the window and saw you standing there beneath us. 'There is the one promised to us,' I told the other maidens, 'and our afflictions will end this day.' Then we agreed together to let down the ropes and bring you up to us in the shelter of the palace; for at your hands it is that this accursed Snatcher shall die, drinking the cup of destruction. In the name of the God you worship, are you not King Sayf, the Tubba'i, the Himyari, King of Yemen the Red and its hills and lands?"

"I am indeed the King Sayf of whom you speak," he replied, "and soon now, if Almighty God wills it, I shall destroy this accursed wretch, and what God has willed shall come to pass."

"King of all time," said Princess Nahid, "stretch out your hand to me, and I will show you what our destiny shall be."

So he stretched out his hand, and she put her hand in his, saying: "I witness to you here, in truth and sincerity, that there is no God but God, and I witness that Abraham is the Friend of God. I believe in God and His angels and His Books and His Messengers and in the Day of Judgment."

When the other maidens saw what she had done, they said: "Instruct us, Princess Nahid, so we may say as you have done."

"My lord King Sayf will instruct you," she replied.

At that they went up to him, saying: "O, King, instruct us so that we also may embrace Islam."

Then King Sayf Ben Dhi Yazan instructed them how to make their declaration as the Princess Nahid had done, so that they all became Muslims at his hands; and he rejoiced that these virgin maidens had so embraced the religion of Islam and had been delivered from the worship of planets among the infidels.

"O, King," they said then, "we have become of you and for you. If you leave us now at the mercy of this giant, it will be dishonor to you."

"Daughters of kings," replied King Sayf, "if I should see him, I shall not stay my hand till I have slain him and delivered the world from the weight of his evil. Reproach me only if I delay in engaging him in combat and battle. But tell me, Nahid, of this accursed Snatcher. What does he want with these virgin maidens, and why has he assembled them here in this place?"

"Sir," she said, "he will do them no harm. Rather he will parade them before him while he drinks wine and intoxicates himself before their eyes. This he does to cause grief to the great rulers among men. Whenever he finds a maiden who is comely, he carries her off from among her kin, with the sole purpose of injuring humankind. Me he carried off from the kingdom of China; and here is the daughter of the King of India, and here the daughter of the King of Morocco, and here the daughter of the King of Zaghawa, and here the daughter of the King of Babylon, and so forth. When he seized me and brought me here, he had only a few maidens; but still he carried them off, till at last we became forty. 'Sir,' I said to him one day, 'you have parted us too long from our families. What is your purpose in gathering us here?' 'Nahid,' he replied, 'I have taken 'Aqisa, daughter of the White King, and soon I shall go in to her. Then I shall release you all and restore you to your homes.'"

"If Almighty God wills the slaying of this accursed wretch," said King Sayf, "I it is who will send you back to your people, and that which is destined shall come to pass. Where is the accursed one?"

"This, King of all times," replied Nahid, "is the hour when he comes."

No sooner had the maiden uttered these words than it grew dark and dust swirled up in the air; and the maidens, seeing these things, fled, each to her own place. "Why do you flee," asked King Sayf, "and why are you so dismayed?"

"Look to yourself, O King," they replied, "for the giant has come. He is here now, King of all time."

At that very instant the giant descended into the palace. He had legs like the masts of ships, above which smoke hung, and there he stood, a demon of hideous mien, with ears like shields, jaws gaping wide as an alleyway, nostrils like trumpets, teeth each one like a pair of pincers, and two eyes, slit open and yellow as glittering gold.

When the demon saw King Sayf, he knew him, and said: "Misbegotten wretch of humankind, you it was who cut off my hand in the land of Ethiopia and the Sudan in former days. Why have you now come to this place? Today I shall take my revenge, cutting off both your hands and leaving you with none, and so exact your debt to me."

With that the giant made to stretch out his hand to seize King Sayf; but King Sayf struck him with the enchanted whip, and the blow fell on his remaining hand, severing that also. "Misbegotten wretch of humankind," he cried then, "first you cut off one of my hands, and today you have cut off the other. Strike my neck then, and release me from my suffering; for with both hands cut off there is no life for me. Give me rest in death."

But as King Sayf was about to strike his neck, he heard a voice crying: "Step back, Sayf, do not strike again." And so King Sayf stepped back.

"Strike me, human," the giant said then.

"I do not strike anyone twice," replied Sayf. "If you have breath left in you, rise and fight me again."

Then lo, smoke came from the giant's arm, and after the smoke, sparks, and after the sparks, flames; and all the while the giant screamed in his agony, till he was consumed in the fire and only a pile of ashes remained. So it was that he perished; so his downfall was accomplished.

Then 'Aqisa came to him, saying: "King Sayf, my brother, may God give you deliverance as you have delivered me from this fearful giant. None could overcome him, neither man nor jinn, and none could strike him with the sword but you, gallant champion. May your hand never lose its cunning, and may there be none to put you to shame. Now this accursed creature is slain, brother, I shall not cease from serving you. If you have any need, tell me of it, so I may fulfill it and exert myself in your service."

"Daughter of noble lineage," replied King Sayf, "you say you are my sister; but I do not know how such kinship may be, for I am a man, and you a maiden of the jinn."

"Do not disown me," she said. "Do not turn away from me, for I am your sister, whether you wish it or not."

"My friendship you are welcome to," he replied, "and I will lay down my very life for you to drive your enemies back."

"Sir," she said, "by Him who caused the radiant light to shine and created sight and hearing, I am indeed your sister through suckling, and you my brother. My mother suckled you first when you were a baby; and after that she took you from King Afrah, and you dwelt with her till you were three years old. If you do not believe me, O King, then I will bring my mother here to you." With that she beckoned to her mother; and when she came, King Sayf said: "This is indeed my mother, for I know of no other who suckled me."

"Of a truth," said 'Aqisa, "if this is your mother, then I am her daughter."

At this King Sayf was convinced. "Sister," he said, "since your wish is to fulfill my needs, then do me the pleasure of restoring these maidens to their families."

"I hear and obey," said 'Aqisa. And with that she bore one of them off to the place she had come from, then came and took a second, asking: "From which land do you come?" And when she was told: "From Morocco," she took her back also; and each time she took one of them back, she would set her down on the roof of her family's quarters, saying: "Call out to your family, so they may come for you and you may be joined together again." Then the girl would call out, and her family would come and find her there, and 'Aqisa would say: "Here is your daughter, who was held by the One-Armed Snatcher and is delivered now at the hands of the King of the land of Yemen, King of the Tubbabi'a, King Sayf Ben Dhi Yazan. She has embraced Islam at his hands and is now a Muslim." Then they would take her in, praising the beneficence of King Sayf, wishing only that they could set eyes on him and lay down their very lives for him. And 'Aqisa continued in this fashion till all the maidens were returned, each restored to the bosom of her family, and none remained in the palace but the Princess Nahid. Her too 'Aqisa was about to take, but she would not consent. So, turning to King Sayf, she said: "What is your pleasure in this matter?"

"Return Nahid to the kingdom of China," he replied, "restoring her to her family as you did with the rest."

"My lord," said Nahid, "I am promised in marriage to you and I have professed Islam at your hands, while all my kin worship the stars. If you restore me to them, they will take me back into their creed. Do not send me back to my family now that I am one of your womenfolk. Let me rather remain by your side, for I am your wife and you my husband."

"Nahid," he said, "I have sworn an oath to marry none before Shama, daughter of King Afrah, and never to lie with any woman before her; and that is still far in the future."

"I shall wait then," she replied, "till the days of separation are past, and you meet with her again. But do not send me back to my family and sear me with the flames of parting."

"I have no place," he said, "where I can lodge you."

"O King," she replied, "I shall stay here in this palace, never leaving it till the days have gone by and what is written has come to pass."

"It is here in this palace," he replied, "that we slew the Snatcher. If you dwell in it, then the jinn will surely destroy you, and you will be bereft of me and of your family alike."

"I implore you," she said, "by Almighty God and by his prophet Abraham, and by the religion of Islam, keep me by your side, so I may serve you till the days are past. Do not, son of noble lineage, forbid me your presence and the sight of you."

"Do not bring me care on your account," he said. "I must fix my mind on attaining my goals; and were I to leave you, I should fear lest some mishap befall you."

With that he called out to 'Aqisa to bear her off and restore her to her family. But Nahid said: "I pray to Almighty God, by the sanctity of the Friend of God, to lead you to my land, King Sayf, naked and bare of head, so I may quench the fury of my heart in the sight of all, and your heart may be broken as you have broken mine."

"May God answer your prayer," replied the king, "and may you be sick and blind, and your healing be at my hands." Then, vexed, he called out again to 'Aqisa: "Bear her off and restore her to her family."

At that 'Aqisa snatched her up and bore her into the heavens, carrying her to her country and setting her down in the palace of her father, who loved her dearly, for he had not been blessed with other children; and there she was joined once more with her family. And when she invoked God against King Sayf, asking that King Sayf should marry her though a film be cast across her eyes, God responded to her prayer; and this, and how she would be healed at King Sayf's hands, and how he would marry her and return with her to the land of Ethiopia, and how Tama, daughter of the sorceress 'Aqila, would slay her, all these are matters we shall recount in the proper season; and he who loves the beauty of the Prophet will call blessings upon him.

Then 'Aqisa returned to King Sayf, saying: "Do you have any further need that I may fulfill?"

"Take me to the city of Qaymar," he replied, "so that I may visit Shaykh 'Abd al-Salam."

"I hear and obey," she replied. And with that she bore him up on her shoulders, crossing the deserts and hills, and set him down by the dome of Shaykh 'Abd al-Salam. And when King Sayf descended and asked if he might enter, the shaykh said: "Enter without fear, King Sayf." So King Sayf went in to him and kissed his hand, rejoicing at being there with him, and the shaykh greeted him in his turn and received him with honor.

"The Snatcher is slain then," said the shaykh, "and the maidens are restored to their families."

"So it is," replied King Sayf.

Then the shaykh said: "For that you will receive great recompense. But Nahid was angered, invoking God against you, as you did too against her, and the One who receives the prayer sees all. But stay with me tonight, so I may take my leave of you; for I am departing now to seek my Lord, and, if it is God's will, we shall meet again in the second Abode." And so King Sayf remained there with him, and they prayed together, praising God and begging His forgiveness till the night was past. Then Shaykh 'Abd al-Salam said: "Sayf, when I am dead, wash me from this spring. As for my shroud, it is here beneath my head; if you raise this pillow you will find it there. Place me within it, for it is one of the garments of Paradise, then stand at the door of the dome and call out: 'Prayer for the dead, and may God have mercy on you all!' And when those who respond have come to pray over me, bury me in this niche of mine."

"I hear and obey," said King Sayf. And with that Shaykh 'Abd al-Salam began humbly to pray to Almighty God, seeking His forgiveness till the dawn broke. Then he said: "I witness that there is no God but God, and that our master Abraham is the Friend of God. May God bless our master Muhammad, seal of all prophets and messengers, and praise be to God, the Lord of Creation." Then he passed over, drinking from the cup of death.

Thereupon King Sayf rose and washed him and placed him in his shroud, then went to the door of the dome, calling: "Prayer, and may God have mercy upon you." At that people came to him there in numbers known only to God, to the wonderment of King Sayf. Then King Sayf stepped forward to dig the grave as he had been instructed to do and buried him in his niche, spending the night thereafter invoking the name of God over the grave, and begging His forgiveness till the day broke; and all the while he pondered how this shaykh had lived so long, yet God had willed he should know him only at the end of his days. Then, having called down blessings on Taha the Prophet and Messenger, he recited the following lines:

> Here in the pit, I've become God's suppliant
>   in chains and ground down in the depths of the earth.
> I've bequeathed my family to the care of friends
>   and I am parted from both friend and foe.
> You who know nothing of death, don't be proud,
>   every creature must come in through this door.
> All of mankind will be under God's judgment,
>   all things will be revealed; all shall rise on the last day.
> Fie on fate which betrays and is suspicious;
>   its bliss is always followed by chastisement.
> I ask God's forgiveness and repent what I said,
>   God of the universe and the First Cause of things.

Then ʿAqisa came to King Sayf, saying: "King of all time, let me show you the world and all the wonders that are in it."

"Sister," he replied, "do as you deem fit."

So she raised him onto her shoulders and bore him apace over the plains and deserts. "How afflicted you were, brother," she said, "when I came to you in the pit." Then, when he spoke to her of the Book of the Nile, she said: "I will show you now all the things which will spring from this book." And with that she alighted with him by the side of a lofty mountain, telling him to look before him. Then King Sayf saw a distant dome in the mountains, with no man, black or white, near it.

"I see a dome in the mountain," said King Sayf.

"Approach and view it," she replied, "for you will surely have matters to attend to there."

"Go with me then," he said, "so as to instruct me in what I must do."

"Brother," she replied, "it does not lie within my power to approach it. But you are of humankind, and a king, and all things are permitted to you. Go forward then, placing your trust in God."

So King Sayf approached the dome, and lo, water was gushing out from it, whiter than milk and sweeter than honey, its scent more fragrant than heavy musk. From the four sides of the dome it came, with two rivers vanishing beneath the earth when they had once come out from the dome, and two rivers visible still. King Sayf stepped forward to perform his ablutions in one of these, then twice prostrated himself in prayer, sealing his prayer by invoking peace according to the creed of Abraham the Friend of God. Then, entering the dome, he found within a rock of red ruby whose sparkling dazzled the beholder; and he climbed onto this rock and prayed once more, prostrating himself twice and reciting from the writings of Abraham.

When he had done this, he called out to ʿAqisa to come to him there, but she called back to him, saying: "King Sayf, I cannot come one step closer; for were I to approach these waters, I should be consumed by the lightning flashing from the rock."

"Yet here am I," said King Sayf, "atop that very rock."

"Without God's special favor," she replied, "you could never have ascended it."

"Tell me," he said then, "of these rivers, and how they flow through the plains and deserts."

"The two visible rivers," she said, "are Sayhoun and Jayhoun, and they flow, by the will of Almighty God, the Eternal and Everlasting, to the lands of the Turks and Romans. As for the two that flow beneath the earth, one is called the Euphrates, and the second is the Nile, which will flow at your command, O glorious King."

"ʿAqisa," said King Sayf then, "is this not the river whose book I seek, the book Saqardyoun demanded of me as a wedding gift for Shama, daughter of King Afrah?"

"Knight of all knights, and lion of the fields," she replied, "it is the very one. But you could not wait. Rather, you entered the dome, and the book first spun round on its base, then flew out toward you, there amongst your enemies, so that King Qamroun and the people of the city assailed you all together, minded to give you the cup of death to drink."

"'Aqisa," said King Sayf, "can you tell me where the book now is?"

"Do not be troubled on that account," she said. "The sorceress has protected it with spells, till you shall come seeking it; for she wishes to give you her daughter Tama in marriage, when you have once married Shama, daughter of King Afrah. But brother, were I not anxious over home and kinsfolk, I would have shown you further wonders and marvelous things."

"Do you then know the wonders of these lands?" asked King Sayf, stepping out from the dome. "Will you not show me some of them?"

"I must first," she said, "see that all is well with my brothers and other kin. Then I shall return to show you the seven enchanted cities of that realm, each raised by one of the wizards of all time, who fashioned wonders there, of forms and colors so marvelous that all who have seen remain powerless to describe them. Seven cities there are, each girdled with a vast and sumptuous valley, with trees and rivers and birds proclaiming the Oneness of the Beloved All-Vanquishing Sovereign. This is the work of the wizards of Greece, that use both man and jinn in their arts; and they have decreed that the jinn servants may not enter the valleys, from above or from below, nor may those of humankind enter except to gaze, for they may not stretch out a hand to touch the things they see. Such is the ordinance of those who fashioned them, and they have power to do as they say."

"'Aqisa," said King Sayf Ben Dhi Yazan, "you have ravished my mind with your talk of these valleys and the wonders they hold. Since you claim me for your brother, how can you endure, now that I have heard these things, that we should return to our homelands, leaving me to dwell on these things? Take me to these valleys, so I may feast my gaze on them; for unless I do so, I shall know no joy or rest in my life, but rather live beset with endless thoughts and fancies."

"Still your anxiety, brother," said 'Aqisa, "I will accompany you wherever you wish to go, laying down my very life in your stead to keep you from harm. But, my lord, I must leave you close by the gates of each of the cities, so that you may enter; for it is not permitted to me to approach further."

"I do not ask you to enter," said King Sayf. "Only set me down close by. Then you may remain there at a distance."

"I hear and obey," she replied. Then, raising him onto her shoulders, she bore him aloft and sought out those valleys; and after an hour she alighted, saying to King Sayf: "Brother, here is the first valley. Rise now, and gaze your fill at it, according to your wish. I shall await you here."

Then King Sayf viewed there a valley spacious and abundant with grass and flowers and greenery. "Approach the valley, brother," said 'Aqisa, "for it is hard by, and you are safe from the schemes of enemies." So King Sayf walked on alone, crossing the plains and deserts till he reached the trees, and saw the rivers and palms, and the birds proclaiming the Oneness of the All-Forgiving Sovereign. It was as the poet said, after invoking blessings on the Messenger Taha:

> A valley and trees and a flowing stream
>   with gardens swaying in the eye of the beholder.
> I compare them in their motion with flocks of doves—
>   doves that are winging homeward their way,
> Flowers that are clothed in verdant dresses
>   made more beautiful with greenery.
> The boughs seem to delight in their own twigs
>   loaded with sweet, delicious fruit.
> The birds on the branches sing hymns to God,
>   declaring Him only the Omnipotent Creator.
> Water runs to refresh the branches
>   like a lover running to his beloved.
> The songs of the nightingales are echoing;
>   they sing a lament but without tears.
> But the clouds weep and their tears are the pure dews
>   while flowers smile to the blustering breezes.

Still King Sayf walked on, gazing at the valley. Then he saw, within it, a city built of white marble and red marble, with soaring walls and three hundred and sixty towers, with a lantern of brass hanging over each; and the gates of the city were of many-colored marble, the work of master architects and builders. Atop the city was a figure fashioned from silver in the perfect likeness of a man, with nails and fingers and hair, and so forth, perfectly formed, so that it lacked only the breath of life, peace be upon all. With its right hand this figure held a trumpet of silver to its mouth, and the body was inscribed all over with names and charms in Syriac lettering, written in red gold. Before the city gates were seven steeds of the finest kind, prepared for war and combat, each fitted with a harness of glittering gold, and on these were mounted seven knights, each of them like a lion or a towering mountain, or a remnant of the people of 'Ad, girded with keen swords and bearing long spears; and they conversed together in voices that resounded as if to shake the immovable mountains.

King Sayf marveled at the sight of all this; but, fixing his resolve, he approached the knights. And as he loosened his tongue to make enquiry of them, all at once they began to cry out one against the other, charging toward one another with their steeds, all dealing out blows and thrusts with the fine sword, till the blood gushed out from their bodies. Then King Sayf cried out to them, in his customary voice: "Noblest of heroes, I see you are alike in dress and mien, valiant heroes every one. You are surely brothers and kinsfolk. Why do you fight with sword and spear here in this place?"

"Welcome, noble knight," said one of them. "You are doubtless some passing traveler. We are all brothers, born of one mother and one father, and our father was a wizard named Plato, who bequeathed us a great treasure that each wants to take for himself; and so it is that we fight."

"And what is this treasure your father bequeathed you?" asked King Sayf.

"It is a cap," they replied, "which renders any who wears it invisible to man and jinn alike. The one wearing it sees both man and jinn, but they do not see him."

"And where is this cap?" asked King Sayf.

"The eldest among us has it in his keeping," they replied.

"Come down from your horses, noble men," said King Sayf then, "and I will make judgment among you; for you are brothers, and the sons of a wizard of all time, and it is a shameful thing that feuds should flare up between brothers."

They set the cap in his hands accordingly, each gazing at him. Then he said: "Bring me a bow and an arrow; and so I will make a just judgment between you and resolve this matter." Then, when they had brought them to him, he drew the bow, saying: "Tie the hems of your garments to your waistbands; for I shall shoot this arrow into the air, and you must pursue it with all your might and strength, and whoever brings me the arrow first shall gain the cap." They said to him: "We accept that." Then King Sayf shot the arrow as though from a catapult, whining and whistling into the air, and the seven youths raced after it, across the plains and fields, each hard on the heels of the other, toward the place where the arrow had fallen. And when they were far off from King Sayf, he set the cap on his own head, saying to himself: "If their words are true, then I shall be invisible to them, and I may go my way unseen."

When he had put on the cap, one of the seven approached with the arrow in his hand, running at full tilt with his brothers following close behind; and when they all arrived there, they looked to the right and to the left, saying: "Man, stranger, traveler! Noble knight, where are you?" Then King Sayf knew he was no longer visible to them and turned back, walking on till he reached the place where 'Aqisa stood awaiting his return. "I have tested its quality with men," he thought. "Let me now test it with the jinn." And with that he cried out: "'Aqisa!"

'Aqisa too looked to the right and to the left; and, seeing no trace of him, said: "King of all time, you have doubtless seized the cap fashioned by the wizard Plato, leaving his sons to grieve over its loss."

"So it is," he replied. "I have seized it, and it is now set on my head."

"Kings of the earth have died," she said, "from the desire to possess it, for no man in this time has had skill to fashion the like. But I cannot bear you up while you are wearing it. Give it to me, and I shall keep it safe for you till such time as you need it." And so he gave her the cap to keep for him, and she bore him up into the heavens, then, after an hour, descended with him to the earth, saying: "Here is the second valley, King of all time. Enter and gaze at it, and look, too, at the city. I shall sit here in this place awaiting you. But do not stay overlong."

"I hear and obey," he said, "mistress of all the maidens of the jinn." And with that he left her, walking on till he reached the valley, which he found to be full of trees and rivers and flowers and fruits and birds proclaiming the Oneness of the Beloved Almighty One. As it is said in these verses, praise be to the worker of miracles:

This garden is like a paradise,
　　how charming in it is the gentle breeze.
The chirping of the swallows around it
　　is like a balsam for the sick heart.
Friend, approach it, walk through it
　　and make yourself a dwelling there,
And drink there from the river of Eden
　　from goblets which the cupbearer proffers.
Who could look upon these branches
　　swaying and dancing and not fall in love?
The birds utter in their singing
　　the name of the High Omnipotent God.

As King Sayf viewed the place, his heart stirred within him at the name of the All-Merciful and Compassionate; and on he walked till he reached the end of the valley, where he found a great city, strongly built and fortified, secure with walls and towers, and within the walls hermitages and houses, dwellings and palaces of green whetstone, their walls built in blue and red stone, supported on arches of marble joined together, and beneath a mighty flowing stream of water. On the gates of that city was a figure fashioned from yellow brass, mounted on a horse of Chinese iron, with a horn of white polished silver in its mouth; and there too, at the gates of the city, he found a thousand knights of iron, mounted on mighty steeds, girded with long spears and keen swords, so that they looked like lions in the saddle. King Sayf Ben Dhi Yazan viewed them warily as he passed and with trepidation, ignorant of what fate had ordained for him; and when he reached the city gate and had set his right foot over the threshold, the figure stirred and screamed through the horn: "Here is a stranger, people of the city, an enemy to you! Take him to your king!" His voice resounded louder than any siren, so that all the people of the city heard him, young and old, and came running toward King Sayf, falling upon him and hemming him in on every side. When King Sayf saw how things stood, he grasped his sword, crying: "God is great!" then fought back valiantly against every assault, defending himself with the edge of his keen sword, as though he were a raging lion; solitary and alone he was, with people pressing in on him from the right and the left. Still the figure screamed and the people pressed in on King Sayf, and still he defended himself, till night drew near. Then King Sayf lost his vigor, stumbling over the bodies of the slain; he had known ordeal and affliction, and now the world had grown dark around him, and his limbs were feeble. At that the people surrounded him in still greater numbers, laying hand on him when they had overcome him at last, placing fetters on him and binding his arms and legs. And all the while 'Aqisa stood there, seeing all, but powerless to draw near him, so that she became distraught, like one bereft of her child, or as if she were ablaze. Then the soldiers led King Sayf, his hands bound, before the king of the city, who was a man of the 'Ajami named 'Aboud Khan. The king gazed at King Sayf as he stood there before him, seeing the mole and mark of beauty on his cheek (for he was a youth still, with no growth on the sides of his face), and roared out at him; but King Sayf made no tremor, either at the sight of him or at his cry.

"What white-skinned man are you?" cried 'Aboud Khan. "And what has brought you to this place?"

"I am one created by Almighty God," replied King Sayf, "a wandering stranger who has taken nothing from you at all. I do not know what crime I have committed that you should assail me in this fashion."

"Are you not the man with the green mole," asked King 'Aboud Khan, "the one who will cause the Nile to flow from Ethiopia to Egypt, turning the men of Ethiopia and the Sudan into bondsmen, and callow youths into free men?"

"When have I ever done such deeds?" asked King Sayf. "This is mere idle talk."

"The proof of it," replied the king, "is that mole on your cheek. Do not dispute further. You are surely our enemy." Then he roared out: "Bring the captain here to me." The servants hastened to obey, and when the captain came, he kissed the ground before the king; a black-skinned man he was, in middle age, with a heart like a rock, a bold and fearsome opponent, mighty for all his years. "'Abd Nar," King 'Aboud Khan said then, "take this white-skinned man, set him in a sack of canvas, and bind it up. Then hang a great stone from the mouth of the sack and another at the bottom, and sail with him out onto the lake till you reach the archways beneath the palace. Moor the boat near the mouth of the water spout, and look here, to where I shall be watching for you. When I give you the first signal with my hand, set him by the side of the boat, so that I may see him with my own eyes; and when I signal a second time with my hand, fling him into the sea, so he will be swept along amidst the rocks and stones, and the fish and the beasts of the deep will devour him. Thus we shall be rid of him and all the evil he threatens."

"I hear and obey," said the captain. And he took charge of King Sayf that very instant.

Now the reason for all this was that King 'Aboud Khan had a treasure bequeathed him, a magic ring of precious stones that had been fashioned by the king his father, whose name was Kalouth Khan. This Kalouth Khan had worshipped fire and smoke, using magic rather than the sword and the spearhead, so that he had no need of war and combat. If the ring were on his right hand, and his eye fell upon a mighty enemy, a king or a chief, then he would gesture toward him with this hand, and lo, the man's head would straightway be struck from his shoulders; so long as his soldiers were obedient, then all was well; but if they were minded to oppose him, he would stand there before them, and every man at whom he gestured with his hand would be slain, till they were forced to flee. But the spell worked only within this city, which was the second of the enchanted cities.

When Kalouth Khan died, this son, 'Aboud Khan, seized the ring and placed it on his finger, so that the people of the city, and the ministers and officers of state, gave their allegiance to him, fearing him on account of his possession of the ring. Then one day, as he was seated there among his dignitaries, he said: "Tell me, do you know if any will ever seize this ring from me?"

"King of all time," they replied, "this is a question for wizards and soothsayers, for masters of sorcery and magic. They it is who will know such a thing. Summon the wizards and ask them of this matter." And so he summoned them before him.

"Let us first consult our sciences," they said. Then, when they had done so, they said: "King of all time, we will tell you all we have seen, but first give us a pledge of safety."

"You have my absolute pledge of safety," he replied.

"A king of the Himyari Tubbabi'a will come," they told him, "a believer in the creed of Abraham, the Friend of God, who will seize the ring from you and slay you, taking possession of your kingdom thereafter, and all your soldiers will give him their allegiance. He will command the people to abandon the worship of fire and rather worship the Almighty Sovereign. King of the kings of Yemen he is, vanquisher of infidels and ill-omened persons. He is called King Sayf Ben Dhi Yazan, and he is a great king, who will come alone, without soldier or companion in arms, and slay you and seize your ring in the sight of all; and then the people of this land will serve him, and be his stay and support. And when he has conquered these lands, he will return to his homeland, safe and unscathed."

"What manner of man is this?" asked the king. "What appearance does he bear?"

"Let us first consult our sands," they replied. And when he had told them to do as they wished, they cast the sands again, and said: "He is a smooth-faced youth with no growth of hair on his cheeks, and with a green mole on the right cheek, like a disk of amber; and in the center of the mole a mark of beauty. By this you may know him clearly."

"Fashion a guardian for me," he said then, "that will know him when he comes."

"With our secret sciences," they replied, "we will fashion a sentry to be set at the city gate, who, if he sees him enter, will tell you of his coming. And then, O fortunate King, when he is once fallen into your hands, do with him as you will."

And so they fashioned the figure accordingly, setting a horn in its mouth, while the king commanded a thousand of his finest and trustiest soldiers to watch for the stranger, ready to seize him and bring him before their king. Then King Sayf, as we have described, came and fought with them, and at the last King 'Aboud Khan captured King Sayf and handed him over to his captain 'Abd Nar.

Now when 'Abd Nar (meaning, Servant of the Fire) entered his home, bringing King Sayf with him in his chains, he straightway called for the furnace to be brought; then, turning to King Sayf, he said: "Fellow, if you wish to be delivered from injury, then join with me in worshipping this fire."

"Accursed wretch," replied King Sayf, "none is to be truly worshipped but God the Almighty Sovereign, who created the night and day."

At these words 'Abd Nar fell into a fury. He bound King Sayf with four iron shackles and beat him fiercely and without let, then sat drinking strong drink till the night fell and a blue-black star rose in the heavens. Then King Sayf, in his hour of sore need, raised his eyes to the Glorious Guardian and entreated his aid, saying, with blessings upon Taha the Messenger:

> I sought the Gate of Hope while people slept
> > and all night long complained to my Master.
> I cried, "My hope in every misfortune
> > on whom I depend for succor in adversity,
> I complain to You of things You know already,
> > things which are too grievous for me to endure.
> In submission I stretch out my hand to You,
> > most Excellent to whom a man might stretch out his hand.
> Do not spurn it leaving me empty,
> > for the ocean of Your bounty satiates all who come.

When King Sayf Ben Dhi Yazan had uttered these words, directed to the Most Exalted Subject of his thoughts, lo, the captain came to King Sayf, weeping profusely and without ceasing, and kissed King Sayf's head, then cut him free from his bonds and loosened the chains from his feet; and still he kissed him and wept, making his excuses to him.

"What has happened with you, Captain?" asked King Sayf. "How is it that time has wrought such a change in you?"

"My lord," said the captain, "I witness before you here, in all truth and honesty and justice, that there is no God but God, and I witness that Muhammad is God's messenger, the Arab prophet that will be sent from the line of Mua'd Ben 'Adnan at the end of time, and I witness that Abraham is God's prophet and the Friend of the All-Merciful One, come with the holy Scriptures and truth and signs. From this day forward I believe in God and am innocent of the worship of any save Him. And I come to you now, O King, to ask your forgiveness for the things I have done, for the manner in which I abused you and transgressed against you." Then his tears streamed down again.

"Tell me then what has passed with you, 'Abd Nar," said King Sayf.

"Do not call me 'Abd Nar, O King," he replied, "for my name is now 'Abd al-Samad (meaning, Servant of the Everlasting), servant of the Almighty Sovereign, the One True God, the All-Vanquishing One. No longer do I worship fire, or invoke its power, for they who worship it are infidels."

"Brother," said King Sayf, "if your words are from the heart, then you have attained salvation. But what has happened, tell me, to deliver you from all snares?"

"My lord," replied 'Abd al-Samad, "when I beat you today, and you never flinched beneath the blows, or cried out for deliverance, a great vexation took hold of me, and I beat you ever more fiercely, so that you should beg me for mercy, saying to me: 'by your honor.' Then, when you did not do so, I was vexed once more, and beat you more fiercely yet. 'He has surely perished now,' I thought. 'I shall stay my hand till the king goes up to his palace, then set him in a sack and weigh him down with stones and fling him into the lake as King 'Aboud Khan commanded.' With that I seated myself and drank deep till slumber took hold of me. Then, as I entered the chamber where I sleep, a man blocked my way, bearing a lance of fire from which the sparks flew. 'Where are you going, enemy of God,' he cried, 'you who have transgressed against the King of Islam and beaten him, son of scoundrels that you are! Have you no fear of the All-Knowing Sovereign?' Then he grasped me by the throat, saying: 'Will you not embrace the religion of Islam, worshipping the One True God, and leave the name 'Abd Nar for the name of 'Abd al-Samad?' 'My noble lord,' I replied, 'pray tell me who you are.' 'I am al-Khader,' he replied, 'and, seeing how you have treated King Sayf, I was minded to punish you for your deed by slaying you and speeding your departure from this world. Then I heard the call of the Most Exalted One on High, saying: Do not deal with him in such summary fashion, for Almighty God shall guide him to righteousness. Rather invite him to embrace the faith of Islam; for it may be he will become a warrior in the Cause of God. And so I have stayed my hand from you. If you believe henceforth in God, and in his angels and Scriptures and messengers, you will escape vengeance. But if you stick firm in your heresy, you must be slain and go to Hell as your fate.' And so I became a Muslim at his hands, saying, as he instructed me: 'I witness there is no God but God, and that Muhammad is the messenger of God, and that he is the Arab Prophet sent from the line of Mua'd Ben 'Adnan at the end of time, appearing between Zamzam and al-Hatim, messenger of the true religion that guides to the path of righteousness, who will make manifest the religion of Abraham, the Friend of God, all peace and prayer be upon him.' Then he said: 'You are now one of the faithful, but punishment is still due to you for the pain and anguish you have caused King Sayf.' 'My lord,' I replied, 'let me be excused; for I did not know him. From this hour on I shall repent, and be one among his clan and friends, following without question where he leads, and making war, under his command, against all his enemies.' ''Abd al-Samad,' he said then, 'if he should forgive you, then you shall indeed be excused; but if he does not forgive you, then your suffering must be doubled, and none of God's creatures will have power to save you.' With that he left me, and now I come to you, recounting my story before you; for after God there is no support left me but you alone. I have been between dream and waking, O King, and the sweetness of Islam is on my lips still."

When King Sayf Ben Dhi Yazan heard these words, he sank to his knees before the All-Knowing Sovereign, rejoicing to the depths of his heart. "Tell me, 'Abd al-Samad," he said, "what will you do now? For the king has commanded you to slay me and fling me into the lake."

"By the religion of Islam, O King," said 'Abd al-Samad, "and by him who guided me to it, were the king to command me to kill you, or else die at his hands, then I shall consent to my own death, laying down my life and spirit in your stead; I would not be niggardly with my life, but lose my head ungrudgingly, for love of you and in your service. But the outcome, O King, is in the hand of God, the Ruler of Kingdoms."

Then, when he had brought him food, he went in to his family and his children, inviting every one of them to embrace Islam; and all consented, except for one white-skinned concubine whom he especially loved for her beauty, who had been presented to him by King 'Aboud Khan. When he set before her the religion and faith of Islam, she said: "This cannot be," refusing, for anything he might say, to turn away from the worship of fire. "When morning comes," she said, "I shall go to the king to tell him what you have done, how you, with your family and children, have embraced the religion of Islam. And then he will wreak swift vengeance upon you."

"Accursed wretch," he replied, "now that I have tasted faith, I care no longer for king or sultan, placing my trust in the Sovereign God, the All-Merciful and Compassionate." And with that he had the other concubines seize hold of her, and invited her a second time to embrace the Faith; then, when still she would not consent, they strangled her at his command, and placed her in a sack, leaving her feet exposed outside the sack so that King 'Aboud Khan could see their white color and so suppose the one within to be the fortunate Tubba'i king.

Going then to King Sayf, he told him of his plan concerning the concubine. "I shall fling her into the lake," he said, "in the sight of the king, so that he may be at peace, believing his enemy is dead. Then you may proceed exactly as you wish, O fortunate King."

"Do as you see fit," said King Sayf, "and may God speed you in your designs."

'Abd al-Samad ordered his serving boys to bring food, and they ate their fill, then sank into the happiest of sleeps. And when God brought forth the morning, Captain 'Abd al-Samad took the sack with the concubine inside it, and went down to his boat, while King Sayf remained on land with the captain's attendants, awaiting his return. There he watched till the boat was beneath the palace, where King 'Aboud Khan, watching also, signaled with his hand for the boat to approach the window; and when it was beneath the curve of the archway over which the palace was set, the king gave the signal to the captain that he should be flung from that spot. Then 'Abd al-Samad straightway flung in the sack, and the king, watching as it fell into the lake, saw the two white-skinned feet hanging from it, and rejoiced to the depths of his heart, clapping his hands in a very frenzy of joy. But as his hands were there outside the window, the ring fell from his right hand into the lake, King Sayf seeing this but having no notion what manner of ring it was.

When 'Abd al-Samad returned to land, he came again to King Sayf to tell him what he had done: how he had flung the concubine into the lake, with King 'Aboud Khan supposing her to be his enemy, King Sayf. "Blessed is your deed, Captain," said King Sayf. "But did you not see what I myself saw?"

"What was it you saw, King of all time?" asked 'Abd al-Samad.

"When the king gave you the signal," said King Sayf, "commanding you to fling the sack into the lake, something of dazzling luster fell from his hand into the lake."

"O King," said the captain, "that I saw too, by the sweetest of faiths."

"Surely," the king said then, "this must be the very ring that has won such fame. Now that Almighty God has seized it from him, it may perhaps fall into my hands, and so I shall attain my goal from this cursed wretch."

"I shall rise now, O King," said Captain 'Abd al-Samad, "and return in my boat to the king's palace. Then I shall cast the fishing nets and leave the matter to Almighty God. Perhaps, if the ring has fallen into the lake, it is ordained you will have your portion of it."

"If it is indeed fallen into the lake," said King Sayf, "then what help is there for us, unless God comes to our aid?"

"If we find nothing," replied 'Abd al-Samad, "we shall catch some fish and return with them. Each will attain what is destined for him."

"Rise then," said King Sayf, "with Almighty God's blessing."

With that Captain 'Abd al-Samad and King Sayf rose and went down to the lake, where they sailed till the boat was beneath the palace; and this was in darkness, during the first third of the night. Then 'Abd al-Samad raised his hand and cast the net, saying: "O blessings of Islam!" And when he drew it in, they found a young Nile fish caught in it, mightily plump, as great as a man. When the captain had pulled it into the boat, he was minded to cast the net again, placing his trust in the All-Vanquishing Sovereign; but he heard a voice call out from afar, "Sayf, the object of your desire is fallen into your hands. God has destroyed those standing against you and granted you fulfillment and joy."

"Take us back, 'Abd al-Samad," King Sayf said then. "Do not act against the wishes of the Lord of Power. Our fishing is at an end."

'Abd al-Samad returned them accordingly to the dry land, while King Sayf pondered the words he had heard called out. Then he said: "Slit open the belly of that fish, 'Abd al-Samad, for I am minded to grill it here and now, and eat from it."

"I hear and obey," said 'Abd al-Samad. And when he had come to kill the fish, and slit open its belly, lo, there was the ring within, radiant, its light sparkling into the air around it. "See here the ring of 'Aboud Khan," he cried, "with which he vaunts above all his troops and servants. Take it, my lord!"

When King Sayf saw this, he fell to his knees, prostrating himself before the Almighty and All-Bountiful One, and saying: "How great is the power of the Glorious God!"

"Here is no cause for surprise, O King," said 'Abd al-Samad, "for the fish gather always beneath the king's palace. When the king has eaten, along with his ministers of state, they shake the cloth out over the sea, and the fish always wait there to eat whatever will fall from the window; and so when the ring fell the Nile fish waiting there snatched the ring in its mouth. Yet marvelous indeed is the power of God, the Sovereign Lord, that He should so set it aside for us there, inclining us to fishing and causing no fish but that to fall into our hands. O fortunate King, this is indeed by the decree of the Lord, of the One who begins all and nurtures all."

Then King Sayf, taking the ring and placing it on his finger, found, by the power of God who cleaves the seed and the kernel, that it fitted exactly there, as though made to his express measurement. "King of all time," said 'Abd al-Samad, "I and my children and my attendants number more than a hundred in all. If you are minded to slay this king, 'Aboud Khan, then here we stand at your command, ready to wage war against any who is tyrant and infidel."

"It may be," said King Sayf, "that he too will come to belief in Almighty God, and so we shall not be obliged to fight against him; for it is better he become a Muslim, and remain here in his land, than that we should slay him and plunder his wealth. But tell me, 'Abd al-Samad, is this truly the king's ring, and does it truly have power to slay all who have displeased the wearer, if he once gestures with it toward them?"

"So it is, O King," said 'Abd al-Samad.

"Then," said King Sayf, "I shall go to this accursed 'Aboud Khan and command him to embrace Islam. If he becomes a Muslim, then I shall leave him to what destiny awards him; but if he refuses, I shall strike his head from his shoulders with my Yemeni blade."

"There is no need of that from you," said 'Abd al-Samad, "for if you once wave the ring at him, his head will fly from his shoulders with no blow from your sword."

When day broke, King Sayf went down to the shore of the lake, saying: "'Abd al-Samad, take me now to the other side."

"I hear and obey," replied 'Abd al-Samad. "Come now into the boat." Then, when they had rowed to the other shore, he said: "Now, King of peace, place your trust in the All-Knowing Sovereign."

When King Sayf had left the boat and had walked on through the city gates, the sentry cried out a second time: "Here is a stranger come!" But when the people came out to confront him, King Sayf said: "Let none here move! Take me to your king, without war or combat, then see there what deeds will be done." They told him accordingly to go before them, till they reached the palace, where the king was seated.

"Stranger," said the King, when he saw him, "did I not have you drowned yesterday? How is it that you return unscathed?"

"O King," replied King Sayf, "the Eternal God it is who delivered me. And here I am now, come to warn you if you will heed my words. Either you will embrace my religion and follow my creed, turning away from the worship of fire and consenting freely to worship the All-Merciful and Compassionate Sovereign Lord, or, if you stand out against these things, I shall strike off your head."

"So, dog!" cried the king. "With what will you strike off my head, son of scoundrels?"

"With this ring," replied King Sayf.

When the officers of state saw the enchanted ring in King Sayf's possession, knowing it to compel obedience from all over whom it was held, they turned to their king, saying: "Where is your ring, King of all time? Let us know of it."

"I have it in my coffer," he replied, "nor has any living man seen it."

"You people," said King Sayf, "how can you be so blind? Here is the ring, in my possession, and your land is now mine."

"O King," they said then, "there is the ring, on his hand, and we are counted among his followers and soldiers."

"Your words are false," he replied, "and your eyes deceive you; for I hold the ring safe, where no man knows of it."

"Here is no cause for doubt," said the ministers. "The qualities of the ring are known to all, and we are the servants of him that holds it. Fetch your ring forthwith, 'Aboud Khan, and wave it toward Sayf, giving him the cup of death to drink." Then they turned to King Sayf. "Again and again, O King," they said, "this man has reproached us with falsehood, though we are his helpers and supporters. Wave toward him with your hand, so that his head may tumble from his shoulders; and we will thereafter give our allegiance to you."

"That I shall do," he replied, "only if he refuses to embrace Islam and worship the All-Knowing Sovereign."

"Will you abjure the worship of fire," the men of state said then, "and give your allegiance to King Sayf?"

"That shall never be," replied the king. Then lo, King Sayf waved his hand toward him, and his head tumbled from off his shoulders.

When the men of state saw this, they said to King Sayf: "King of all time, we are now your servants and men."

"Turn away then from the worship of fire," he replied, "and worship God, the All-Knowing Sovereign."

"Instruct us, O King," they replied, "in what we must say."

"You must all together," he replied, "repeat these words: 'We witness that there is no God but God, and that Abraham is the Friend of God.'" And when they had all repeated this as he had taught them, King Sayf seated himself on the throne of the land, appointing 'Abd al-Samad as his chief minister, and so they continued in safety and security, King Sayf teaching them the ways of Islam for a full month, so that the people in the city and all the regions round about, men and women, old and young, became filled with the Faith; he instructed them in the writings of Abraham the Friend of God, and made known to them the Oneness of the Glorious Sovereign, till their hearts were seized by devotion, and the declaration of Islam became the sweetest of all things to them. Then he gathered the elders of state, saying: "I have attained the goal I had here in your city, to conquer it for Islam and spread abroad the declaration of the Oneness of the All-Knowing Sovereign, praise be to Him who has granted me this. I am minded now to return to my country. Choose yourselves, therefore, who shall be king over you."

"My lord," they replied, "we are subjects of the man who has the ring in his keeping. He it is who shall be king and rule over us."

"So things were," he said, "in the days when you worshipped fire. But under Islam you are not subject to this ring. Succor comes rather from the All-Knowing Sovereign. I have taken possession of the ring, and my will is that you should believe in the One True God, and may God's curse lie on any who behaves oppressively or breaks faith. I appoint my minister 'Abd al-Samad to rule over you on my behalf. Be obedient to him, and hold, all of you, to belief in God, the Lord of Creation."

"We hear and obey," they replied. Then King Sayf rose and, taking 'Abd al-Samad by the hand, seated him on the throne of the kingdom, saying: "You are to rule on my behalf, and any who stands against you is my enemy. You, the people of this city, be obedient to him, and worship God, the Lord of Creation." Then he gave into 'Abd al-Samad's keeping all the treasures of the kingdom he left behind him, saying: "These things I leave with you, in the cause of God, till such time as I ask for them." And with that King Sayf took his leave of the citizens, and of King 'Abd al-Samad, and went out from the city alone.

When he had passed through the valley in this fashion, he called out to 'Aqisa, who was seated there awaiting him. "Here I am," she replied. "How have things passed with you there? I saw how they fought against you, but had no power to go to your aid. To this very moment I have been anxious on your account." Then he recounted to her how things had passed, how after mighty struggle he had taken the ring; but there is no profit in repeating any of this, except for the invocation of God and the pious declaration of His Oneness.

"'Aqisa," he said then, "let us now go to the third realm."

"Brother," she replied, "it is as though you wished to fling your life into death's path and bring about my destruction along with yours. I shall take you to no further realms, though you give me the cup of death to drink." With that she bore him off, he thinking all the while she was journeying with him to another realm; then, all of a sudden, he saw she was descending with him over the city of Qaymar, by the side of the pit. "Brother," she said then, "from here it is that I took you, and here it is that I return you. The ring you seized is with you still, and take this cap also, for it will be of profit to you; and my peace be upon you."

"Why have you done this, 'Aqisa?" asked King Sayf.

"You are a man bold and venturesome in all things," she replied, "and I fear lest you plunge into some deep misfortune from which I cannot deliver you, as when I saw your enemies fighting against you and was powerless to come to you on account of the spells cast in those lands. And so I shall accompany you and bear you no more."

"I demand of you," he said, "that you show me the other realms."

"What is this word 'demand'?" she replied. "By God, I shall no longer, I say, go along with you. Let those who will bear their brother away to be slain. Such a thing I will never do." With that she flew off from before him, and he began to curse her; but she neither heeded him nor turned back, journeying back to her family and going in to her home. We shall have more to say of her in the proper season, and he that loves the beauty of the Prophet will call ceaseless blessings upon him.

As for King Sayf, he recalled how, if he attempted to enter, the Hidden One would cry out against him as before; and so he made his way to the tower by which he had first entered into the home of the sorceress 'Aqila and her daughter Tama.

Now of all strange things, it chanced that Tama had been enamored of King Sayf from the moment she first saw him, and could no longer endure any separation from him; and when she heard how King Qamroun had flung him into the pit, she was distressed beyond measure, saying: "Mother, how is it you say King Sayf shall take me in marriage, and yet King Qamroun has flung him into this pit? How am I to be married to him now? Rise and see what has happened with him."

The sorceress 'Aqila rose accordingly and cast the sands, saying: "King Sayf is flung into the pit." Then she cast the sands again, saying: "He is come safely out from the pit, and she that has delivered him is a jinn maiden named 'Aqisa, daughter of the White King. She has borne him to the palace of the One-Armed Snatcher, and King Sayf has fought with him and cut off his other arm, bidding the jinn maiden restore the other maidens to their families; she has borne him, too, to the seven enchanted realms. The first realm he has entered, seizing there the cap that renders invisible, and has gone on to the second realm, to be taken captive and sorely beaten, then delivered, slaying 'Aboud Khan and seizing the ring, so that the whole city has become Muslim. And now his sister 'Aqisa has borne him back to the pit and departed, leaving him there together with the cap and the ring, and he has walked to the tower. Rise therefore, Tama, and call out to the king, here beneath the tower. Tell him to enter by the city gate, fearing none."

"But will the Hidden One not warn of his coming?" asked Tama.

"I disarmed the Hidden One," she replied, "at the time when Sayf was here and all the various things came to pass, and I have kept the Book of the Nile safe till he should come for it. Tama, my daughter, this Sayf is no mean man. His standing is to be above the standing of all other kings; every ruler will lie subject to his command, humans and jinn will obey him, wizards and sorcerers will serve him. Dominion he shall have over the kings of all time. Rise now, my daughter, and bring him here, through the gates of the city, having no concern or fear for the Hidden One."

While they were thus conversing, there was suddenly a knock on the door. "Here he is come," said the sorceress 'Aqila, "without pains on our part, and sparing us the need for stratagem and shift."

With that Tama rose, saying: "Can it truly be that the king is come?" And when she went to open the door and saw King Sayf there, she ran toward him and clasped him to her breast, congratulating him on his safe return and kissing his forehead. "Are we dreaming or waking, my lord?" she cried. "God be praised for your safe return to us! How were you delivered from the pit, son of noble lineage?"

Then King Sayf began recounting the matter to her, as they went up, her hand in his, to the sorceress 'Aqila, who rose to greet him, saying: "What has happened with you, my son? How anxious, by God, I have been on your account! But God, I know, is your preserver and stay." And when King Sayf had recounted everything to her, she said: "I have knowledge already of how things passed with you, praise be to God for your safety."

Then they had food brought, and ate and drank and made merry together, with Tama all the while powerless to move her eyes from King Sayf's face, her heart suffused with love for him. And so they continued till darkness fell, and they sought rest in sleep.

When God brought forth the morning, making it radiant with His light, the sorceress 'Aqila seated herself and bade King Sayf seat himself beside her. "Sorceress 'Aqila," he said then, "I am in haste to attain my goal. How may I take the book and return to my country?"

"My son," she replied, "this is a thing which must be, and none can hold you back from it; for if any oppose you, it will be as though he opposed the destiny decreed by Our Lord, who fashions all things."

"But how is it to be done?" he said. "Am I to go in to King Qamroun bearing arms, or what other course must I take?"

"Tomorrow morning," she replied, "I shall ride to the court, and you shall have with you the cap of the wizard Plato and the ring of 'Aboud Khan, two treasures whose like is nowhere to be found. Tomorrow is the day of the new moon, and the dome will be opened. We shall ride together to King Qamroun, and perhaps the difficult will be made plain and what God has decreed shall come to pass."

When the morrow came, the sorceress 'Aqila mounted her mule and, bringing King Sayf with her, proceeded to the court. There King Qamroun rose to greet her and welcome her, and seated her alongside him, while King Sayf stood there before him wearing the cap that rendered him invisible.

"King of all time," 'Aqila said then, "let us open the dome and perform the rites of the book, then approach it and seek its protection against all who are devious and treacherous."

King Qamroun rose accordingly and went to the dome, with the sorceress accompanying him and all the men of state at his side, and the troops riding behind, till they reached the door of the temple where the book was. Then King Qamroun, stepping forward like a lion of the forest, opened the place and entered to view the book there in its place; then he fell to his knees and remained so for a long time, and all his men of state, those children of vanity and thanklessness, along with all the other citizens, knelt down also, before the book rather than the Lord of Lords. And all this King Sayf saw as he stood there with the cap on his head, invisible to all; and when he himself made to cross the threshold of the dome, lo, the chest spun round three times on its base, then slid toward King Sayf and fell there at his feet; and as all the people looked on, he stretched out his hand and took the book without fear or trepidation.

When King Qamroun saw the book spinning and sliding from its base in this fashion, he fell into a frenzy, beating his face till the very teeth rattled in his head, tearing his clothes and weeping and wailing ever louder; and all the people surged forward till the dome was full to overflowing, with a thousand feet trampling every spot. Then the king ordered his men of state to comb the city, to the right and to the left, and they did as he commanded them, going out into the plains and deserts for a full day; then, finding no trace of the book, they returned lamenting of disaster and ruin and every kind of fearful thing, telling the king that the book was nowhere to be found.

With that King Qamroun mounted his steed, and the sorceress rode alongside him, saying: "Calm yourself, King of all time. Do not so give way to alarm, for

I shall restore the book to you, wherever it may be, and bring before you the one who took it, be he man or jinn." With such words the sorceress 'Aqila continued to soothe the king, till his heart was reassured and his spirit grew calm. Then she mounted her mule and went back to her own home, where King Sayf already was, and the book with him, awaiting her return. And when she entered and saw him there, with the book grasped tight in his hand, she said: "May God grant you happiness of what He has given you. Now you have fulfilled your desires, and I wish to fulfill mine also. Now you have attained your goal, permit me to attain mine, and do not refuse my request."

"Tell me your goal," he said, "that I may help you attain it."

"It is this," she replied, "that you should take in marriage my daughter Tama, who has no peer throughout the land of Tahama, or in Yemen, or in the land of Yamama."

"I take heed of your words," he said, "nor shall I ever forget the goodness you have shown me. Your daughter Tama is the very form of loveliness, and the soul of souls, and I shall know no respite from her. But still, I say, I shall take none in marriage before Shama, daughter of King Afrah; therefore cease to speak of this, mother, and do not heap blame and rebuke on me. I have told you now how things are, peace be upon you."

"And I," said the sorceress, "shall permit you to take none in marriage before my daughter, and I have you here with me."

"This shall never be," he replied, "though I drink the cup of death."

After these words had passed between them, they went to their rest, King Sayf Ben Dhi Yazan lying down to sleep with the book and the cap set beneath his head. Now Tama had heard the words of King Sayf to her mother, and she was filled with a furious rage, her heart surging and burning within her. She stayed her hand till night came, then, in the pain of her passionate love, she stole the cap; and when King Sayf woke to find it gone, he asked the sorceress 'Aqila of it.

"My son," she replied, "it was not I, by God, that took it, nor do I know anything of it." At this he became anxious in his heart, saying: "Cast the sands for me, and find where it is, so I may strive to retrieve it."

"I have it here with me," said Tama then. "I it is who stole it, nor will I return it to you till you have married me."

"Take it then," said King Sayf, "and may God give you joy of it. I wish now you had never come to my aid and shown me courtesy in your deeds, only to set bad deed in place of good when all was mended. I have no need of the cap's aid, for the One who aids me is God, Cleaver of seed and kernel."

With that he took the book and rode out into the plains and hills, placing his trust in the One True Lord of Lords, the All-Bountiful and All-Forgiving. As for the sorceress 'Aqila, she mounted her mule, rode to the court and went in to King Qamroun, who rose to greet her, saying: "You are welcome. But what is it that has aroused such anger in your mind?"

"Know, O King," she replied, "that the one who came to our country, and has seized the Book of the History of the Nile, is now stepping the length of the plain toward the place where the sea monster is. Since yesterday I have striven to make out what had happened with him, and now I have discovered his traces. If you wish to take your enemy captive, O King, and restore your book to its former place, then make haste to the plains and dunes. And let none say that the sorceress 'Aqila abandoned you when the book was lost."

Then King Qamroun cried out, like a man crazed: "To horse, masters of the steed!" And the knights sprang astride their saddles and rode off every way, seeking the plains and the ways the whole day long. As the sun set, they seated themselves by the waterside, and ate and drank, then on they sped again; had they had wings they would have flown. As for King Sayf, he walked on alone through the plains and hills, joyful at the book he had seized; still he crossed the plains and deserts all through the day, till the sun set, and then he paused beside a stream, eating from the plants that grew there, and drinking from the water, and taking his rest, before once more rising to his feet. So it was the second day, and the third; then, as he walked on, lo, horsemen surged toward him from every side, brandishing spear and lance. "It is fruitless to seek escape in flight," they cried, "when we are all of us pursuing you. You are minded to rob us of the Book of the History of the Nile, bearing it away through the length of the plain. Prepare now to lose your life and quit this world!"

Then King Sayf, gazing at his enemies, said: "There is no power save in God." With that he began to run over the face of the great plain, as though he were a flying bird, speeding through the wilds and the abodes of beasts. And still on he ran, cutting a path through the expanse, till he saw the sun was about to set; and then he plunged in between the rocks and stones, and night concealed him with its gloomy darkness.

When his enemies, for all their searching, found no trace of him, they grew ever more wretched; all paths were blocked before them and they knew fearful things would surely befall them. Scattering on every side, they surged through all the paths and ways, while King Sayf, for his part, placed his trust in the All-Ruling and All-Vanquishing Lord of East and West.

When midnight came, King Sayf thought to himself: "The head of the sea monster is now in the east. Why should I not pursue it, while its head is still on that shore, then climb onto it, so it may bear me to the other side? If I delay now, my enemies will surely take me captive and so prevent my escape." With that he rose and went off through the night toward the lake, minded to overtake the sea monster. But his enemies too were roused and all the troops set off once more as he crossed the land that lay still between him and the shore of the lake.

He reached that shore as dawn was breaking and the sea monster was drunk still; and so he climbed up onto its back, concealing himself among the creature's scales. But when the soldiers of King Qamroun arrived, hard on the heels of King Sayf, the sea monster had woken from its stupor, and, gazing at the sun and seeing how it was already risen up beyond its reach, it cried out in a voice that made the land resound. Then the soldiers of King Qamroun, struck with terror at the cry and fearful of the destruction it betokened, stared at the creature in amazement. "Now that our enemy has approached it," they said, "he will no more escape its grasp. No doubt he took it for some mighty rock or mountain, and climbed up onto it. There it goes now, into the lake, where none of us has power to follow." And so they returned to King Qamroun with empty hands, worn out with all their exertions, and recounted to him what had passed, and all the things they had seen, and how they had at last pursued their enemy to the shore of the lake, where the sea monster had seized him. "And after that, King of all time," they said, "we know no more of him."

Then the king, ready to burst with fury, called for the sorceress 'Aqila to be brought before him. And when she had come and he had told her how the troops had returned empty-handed from their pursuit of the enemy, she said: "Be patient, O King. Let me enter my place of divination and there strive to know how things have passed. Only through me will you retrieve the book and take your enemy captive; if, that is, the sea monster has not already devoured him."

"Do as you see fit," King Qamroun said then, "for I shall not reject your counsel."

As for King Sayf, he lay there on the sea monster's back till the head of the creature reached the other shore, possessing himself still in patience till it should turn its eyes to the sun and strive to catch it in its mouth; and when, as ever, it could not reach it, and dashed its head against the earth, King Sayf descended from it, moving on toward the plains and lowlands where the home of Shaykh Jiyad was. And when he had reached it, Shaykh Jiyad rose to greet him, saying: "Welcome to you, King of all time, you who have slain the accursed One-Armed Snatcher, and restored the maidens to their families, and seized the cap and the ring. The ring, I know, remains with 'Abd al-Samad as a token of his authority, and Tama has taken the cap from you, and the book you have seized by the leave of the great Mover of All Things. As for me, my son, I have cared here for your horse, and have earned my recompense on that score, son of noble lineage." Then, when King Sayf had greeted him in his turn, the shaykh said: "Pass this night here with me. Tomorrow I must depart on the distant journey; for I am leaving this world now for the Abode of Peace. Do with me as you did with my brother 'Abd al-Salam, and so earn your recompense from the All-Knowing Sovereign. When you have washed me with your own hands, go out from the hermitage, where you will find the shroud prepared for me. Place me in it, then call for prayers from those of the Faithful who are there to hear. For this you will surely have your reward from the Lord of Creation."

And so King Sayf passed the night in Shaykh Jiyad's hermitage, each invoking the name of the All-Bountiful Sovereign, till morning broke. Then the shaykh's cheek grew pale; and laying himself down with his face toward the Qibla, he recited the two declarations of faith, then heaved a deep sigh and departed this life, praise be to the Living One who never dies. And King Sayf went to him, and washed him, and wrapped him in his shroud, then went out and called for prayers for the dead from those of the faithful who were there to hear; and the good people so chosen by the Lord of Creation came and prayed over him, then departed. As for King Sayf, he prepared a place in the midst of the niche of the hermitage, and there buried the master, reading over him some of the writings of Abraham, the Friend of God, and saying to himself:

> Bury the body in the earth.
>   There's no profit from it,
> For the secret was within the body
>   but now has ascended.
> That is the precious essence
>   which has returned to its source.

Then King Sayf rose and, having harnessed his horse, mounted into the saddle and rode out into the plains and deserts toward the city of King Afrah, rejoicing to the depths of his heart, and bearing the book with him. Still he rode on, through the night and the day, and we shall have more to say of him in the proper season.

4
Schemes & Revelations

As for Commander Saʿdoun al-Zinji, the night Wahsh al-Fala set out on his quest for the Book of the Nile, which the wizard Saqardyoun had demanded as a wedding gift for the Lady Shama, he slept as usual in his tent outside the city walls. Then, at daybreak, he rode to the city to ask after Wahsh al-Fala; and when he heard from the Head Chamberlain that Wahsh al-Fala had taken horse in the night to go out in search of the book, he was brimming with anger and resentment at King Afrah and the scoundrel Saqardyoun, and strode into the court in a furious rage, threatening to slay them one and all and to destroy their city and lay the land waste if Wahsh al-Fala did not return safe and sound.

"Here I remain," he told them, "encamped at the gates of the city, till I see how this shabby deed of yours will end. And in the name of exalted Saturn, were it not that Wahsh al-Fala might live still, and return to rebuke me, I would not leave this place, Afrah, till I had struck your head clean from your shoulders, along with the head of this Saqardyoun. But let us see how things turn out." Then he departed angrily, leaving Saqardyoun's heart ready to burst.

At that King Afrah turned to Saqardyoun, and began to blame him for all this; whereupon Saqardyoun, rising that very hour, wrote a letter to his brother Saqardis the Ill-Fated, wizard of the city of al-Dour, the seat of King Sayf Arʿad. In this letter he recounted the story of Wahsh al-Fala from first to last: how he had been adopted by King Afrah, then had asked for Shama's hand in marriage, and how he had been sent off, at last, in quest of the Book of the Nile, since Saqardyoun feared the union of Wahsh al-Fala and Shama might herald the destruction of the lands of Ethiopia and the Sudan.

"I ask you," he said, "to tell the whole story to King Sayf Ar'ad, and to describe Shama's beauty to him so that he comes to desire her and sends to ask her father for her hand in marriage. Then, if this young man should chance to return unharmed, he will have no means to claim her. But make haste."

When Saqardis received his brother's letter, he went to King Sayf Ar'ad and did as his brother bade him do; and he did indeed persuade him to seek Shama's hand in marriage. The king rose and prepared a lavish gift to be sent to King Afrah, including four necklaces of jewels, four habits of fine silk, a hundred ounces of red gold, five thousand gold dinars, ten noble steeds—each accoutered in armor, helmet, and collar and accompanied by a sword, an Ethiopian javelin and a sturdy spear—twenty Ethiopian maidens, and a thousand camels.

All these things he showed to Saqardis, saying: "I shall send this as a gift to King Afrah. And as for his daughter's dowry, I shall exempt his city and the surrounding regions from taxes for seven years."

Now, King Sayf Ar'ad had a mighty knight and defender of his realm who was known as Munatih al-Bighal (meaning, He who Butts with Mules), a champion among champions, renowned for his valor. And him it was that the king, by Saqardis's counsel, summoned and made his envoy to King Afrah, to ask for his daughter's hand. "If he agrees," King Sayf Ar'ad told him, "then present him with these gifts; and if he does not, visit severe punishment on him and bring him back to me in chains. And if Sa'doun attempts to interfere, destroy him along with all his men, and return only with your mission accomplished." Then he chose a thousand fearless champions to go with him and sent him on his way.

When Munatih al-Bighal arrived with his men at the city of al-Hadid, King Afrah came out to meet him, greeting him with splendid ceremony and leading him into the city in joyful procession. But Sa'doun, seeing this, realized some scheme was afoot and resolved to look into the matter.

King Afrah conducted Munatih al-Bighal into the court and, seating him in the place of honor, gave a great banquet for him. Then Munatih al-Bighal presented the gifts to King Afrah and handed him King Sayf Ar'ad's letter. When Afrah realized the purpose of the visit, and the gifts that accompanied it, he was at a loss what to do because of the pledge he had given to Wahsh al-Fala. Then Saqardyoun said to him: "We shall never see Wahsh al-Fala again. And even if he should return, you can tell him Shama is married to Sayf Ar'ad, who is there in the battlefield if he wants her."

No sooner were the words out of his mouth than Sa'doun strode in with his eighty men, his eyes blazing with anger; and as he entered, everyone in the court, King Afrah and the wizard Saqardyoun with them, rose to greet him—all except Munatih al-Bighal, who was puffed up at his position as King Sayf Ar'ad's envoy. When Sa'doun saw him seated still, he roared out with a voice that shook the palace.

"Who is this dog," he said to King Afrah, "who will not stand for me? Is he greater and mightier than King Afrah? Who is he and what is his business here?"

"Know, fellow," said Munatih al-Bighal, "that I am the Chamberlain of King Sayf Ar'ad, who has sent me as his proxy to seek the hand of Shama, daughter of King Afrah, in marriage. Mind your tongue, base wretch, and do not meddle in the affairs of kings."

"Have you no shame, son of scoundrels," replied Commander Sa'doun, "that you speak to me in this fashion, and that you seek the hand of the wife of my master, the gallant knight Wahsh al-Fala? By God, if you do not leave forthwith, I shall slay you with this keen sword."

Incensed at this, Munatih al-Bighal rose, unsheathed his sword and leapt at Sa'doun, who drew his own sword, and brandished it till death crept along its exquisite blade. Then he struck Munatih al-Bighal through the neck, striking his head clean from his shoulders.

When Saqardyoun saw this, he turned to King Afrah and urged him to seize Sa'doun forthwith, to forestall retribution from King Sayf Ar'ad for the slaying of his chamberlain; and he continued to press him and warn him, till at last King Afrah ordered his men to lay hold of Sa'doun. But Sa'doun fought back fiercely as King Afrah's men fell upon him, laying into them with his sword and defending his men as a lion defends its cubs; and he fought his way out of the city to the open plain, with King Afrah's men pursuing him. All that day the battle raged, and for six days more, with Sa'doun and his men valiantly battling against King Afrah's men and those of Munatih al-Bighal too. Then, on the sixth day, Sa'doun and his men found themselves pressed; their strength failing, with no escape left for them, they seemed ready to drink from the cup of death, and King Afrah began to nourish hopes of finishing them off.

Then, all of a sudden, there was a cloud of dust in the distance, which cleared to reveal a knight riding at full gallop, with a veil thrown around his face. And when the knight arrived and saw the battle, he leaned forward in his saddle and rushed into the fray, crying out to Sa'doun: "Courage, champion of all time! What is the reason for this fray?"

"And who are you to ask," said Sa'doun.

"I am your friend Wahsh al-Fala," the knight replied.

"Help me," Sa'doun said then, "against these dogs who are your own kin and people, for this fight is on account of you. I will tell you more when the fray is over."

When the knight heard this, he uttered a cry that made the very earth tremble, then called out: "God is great! I am the knight of realms, vanquisher of infidels and evil-doers; I am King of Yemen, ruler of kingdoms; I am the Tubba'i king, and my name is Sayf Ben Dhi Yazan!"

When King Afrah heard the voice of Wahsh al-Fala, and found that it was indeed he, he returned, and entering the press of battle at Sa'doun's side, cutting a swathe through his enemies, he commanded his troops to cease the fight and to put away their swords and spears. Then he rode out to meet King Sayf, minded to kiss his feet as he sat there in the saddle; but King Sayf dismounted, embraced him, and greeted him.

"How has it come," he asked King Afrah then, "that you are at war with Commander Sa'doun?"

"After you left," replied King Afrah, "it happened that King Sayf Ar'ad sent his envoy seeking Shama's hand in marriage; and I told him that she was married to Wahsh al-Fala, who had gone to bring her wedding gift. But then a quarrel broke out between Sa'doun and Munatih al-Bighal, and Sa'doun slew him; and this I could not take lightly, for it was a slight to me, happening as it did in my own court. So I took up arms against Sa'doun, and now you have come and saved us all."

"Sa'doun was in the right," King Sayf said then, "for, by God, he is the truest of friends and comrades. And is it your desire, King Afrah, to give Shama to Sayf Ar'ad?"

"In your absence, my son," said King Afrah, "I could not stand against him, or keep her from him; but now that you have come, he has no hope of gaining her. But tell me, how is it you left with the name of Wahsh al-Fala, and have now returned with the name of Sayf Ben Dhi Yazan?"

Then King Sayf told of all the things that had passed since he left them, from the first to the last, and they were filled with wonder and amazement, and with admiration for him.

When Saqardyoun saw all this, and heard the things that were said, his heart almost burst in his breast. "He left us as Wahsh al-Fala," he said to himself, "and now he has returned to us as King Sayf. He will surely bring destruction on the land of Ethiopia."

Then he left the court and summoned the remnants of the knights of Munatih al-Bighal, just three hundred and twenty men, instructing them to ride back to their city of al-Dour and tell Sayf Ar'ad that everything that had passed was by the initiative of King Afrah; and he gave them a letter to King Sayf Ar'ad, telling him to prepare a mighty army forthwith and ride out against King Afrah to destroy his land and punish him for his treachery. He also, unbeknown to King Afrah and King Sayf Ben Dhi Yazan, gave them the Book of the Nile, telling them to hand it over to his brother Saqardis for safekeeping. Then the men rode back to their city, where they handed over the letters and the Book of the Nile, as they had been instructed to do, and related matters to King Sayf Ar'ad as Saqardyoun had instructed them.

Just then, as they were seated in the court, one of King Sayf Ar'ad's chamberlains came to tell him of a man at the door requesting an audience with him. The man was accordingly summoned before the king, and it transpired he was a former chamberlain of King Dhi Yazan and had come from the city of Hamra' al-Habash to seek Sayf Ar'ad's help against Qamariyya. He told the king the story of King Dhi Yazan and how, after his death and the birth of the boy, Qamariyya had remained on the throne, allowing none to see her son from the day he was forty days old, refusing, even, to say whether he was alive or dead. She had, too, sent for troops and slaves and servants from outside the city and set them above the dignitaries and other men of King Dhi Yazan's court. "I said to Qamariyya," the man continued, "'O Queen, if the boy is still living, he will be a man now. If so, then bring him to rule over us; and if he is dead, then tell us.' 'The affairs of my son and myself are not your business,' she replied. 'If you are not content with things as they are, then depart, for I have no use for you.' And so I have come to you, O King, since Qamariyya was your concubine, to ask for your help against her."

When King Sayf Ar'ad learned that his former concubine, sent out to further his interests, had reigned for twenty years without sending him tribute, though her city lay in his land, he blazed with fury. Then he turned for counsel to his minister, Bahr Qafqan al-Rif, who advised him not to ride out against Qamariyya with his own troops; for if they were defeated, he would lose all standing because he had been overcome by a woman. He should rather pardon King Afrah for permitting Munatih al-Bighal to be slain in his court, and have him ride out, with Sa'doun al-Zinji and Wahsh al-Fala, against Qamariyya, sending word to her, at the same time, to ride out against them. In this way the two parties would make war on one another, so relieving Sayf Ar'ad of the problem of both.

Thus it was decided, and King Sayf Ar'ad forthwith sent a letter of pardon to King Afrah, giving him his pledge of safety, and asking him to go out against Qamariyya with Sa'doun and Wahsh al-Fala and seize the city of Hamra' al-Habash from her. When King Afrah received King Sayf Ar'ad's pardon and request, he was delighted and deeply relieved and led his troops out to the city of al-Dour, with Wahsh al-Fala and Sa'doun al-Zinji riding at his side.

There they were received in King Sayf Ar'ad's court, and they paid him their respects, and were seated—except for Sa'doun, who was unhappy to see King Sayf Ben Dhi Yazan in the service of King Sayf Ar'ad and was filled with misgivings. For three days they partook of King Sayf Ar'ad's hospitality, then, on the fourth day, they made ready to march. The army was fifteen thousand strong, with five thousand men belonging to King Afrah, and ten thousand to King Sayf Ar'ad, this being the number he had resolved to send to help in the fighting.

And so they set out, in their layered chain mail. At their head, like a scourge among scourges, rode King Sayf Ben Dhi Yazan, with King Afrah, ruler of the city of al-Hadid, on his right hand and Commander Sa'doun al-Zinji on his left, riding toward the city of Queen Qamariyya, resolved to topple its walls and turrets and towers and bring destruction on its citizens.

That was the city where Queen Qamariyya had ruled so many years with tyranny and injustice, having gathered around her an army of Ethiopians and

Sudanese and Arabs to do her bidding, and driven many of the former inhabitants of the land to flee. When she heard that King Sayf Ar'ad, in fury at not receiving tribute, had sent a mighty army against her, she fortified the city, prepared her troops for battle, and sent out her scouts and spies.

When her spies returned, they told her: "Queen, the dust has lifted to reveal ten thousand knights, each one a stalwart champion and a lion of resource, riding Arabian steeds and girded with Indian swords and Khatti spears."

"But how is it," she asked them, "that there are only ten thousand according to you, when I have heard from travelers on the road that they were fifteen thousand strong?"

Now, the reason for this was that as King Sayf Ben Dhi Yazan approached Qamariyya's city of Hamra' al-Habash, he turned to King Afrah, saying: "O King, we do not need so many troops to seize this city; return with your troops to al-Hadid, and I shall see to the combat against Qamariyya with Sayf Ar'ad's men." And so King Afrah had returned, with his troops, to his land and people.

When King Sayf reached the city of Hamra' al-Habash, he pitched camp outside the walls and sent a message to Queen Qamariyya. "If you come in homage and obedience," he told her, "and pay the due tribute, then all will be well. If not, I shall attack you and deal out your punishment, inflicting hardship and tribulation on you." Qamariyya, for her part, sent back word that she was ready for war and combat. And so the battle was set for the following morning.

That night, as King Sayf was engaged in prayer and devotion, a servant came to tell him of a man of dignified aspect, at the entrance to the pavilion, asking to see him; and when the "man" was ushered into the king's presence, lo, it was none other than Queen Qamariyya herself! King Sayf, thinking she had come to pledge allegiance to Sayf Ar'ad, greeted her accordingly, but after returning his greeting, she said: "King Sayf, I have heard that you are a king among knights and a matchless adversary. I have come seeking to prevent the letting of blood. Let us wrestle alone, you and I, and whoever defeats the other shall decree as he will."

When King Sayf had assented to this, Queen Qamariyya began taking off the clothes she was wearing, to reveal a body white as pure silver, and there she was in a chemise so transparent that the lightest breeze would cause it to vanish, her beauty shining through it: a form tall as a tender reed, a firm belly, a navel smooth as oil of willow, and all that was beneath it. Her intent was to snare King Sayf with her charms and her exquisite beauty.

But when King Sayf saw her thus, with her body revealed, he said: "God forbid I should wrestle with you unclothed. We will wrestle only in all our garments."

"How can that be?" said Qamariyya. "Such combat cannot be safely joined in full dress." And still she talked in this vein, till he agreed to wrestle unclothed, and rose and took off his garments, remaining only in his drawers.

As Qamariyya looked at him, she saw a necklace of jewels glittering round his neck, shining brighter than the sun and moon, the necklace she had placed beside him as a baby when she abandoned him in the valley of death; she recognized it well enough, and knew this was her son.

"Son of perdition!" she cried. "Did I cast you into the wilderness at forty days, and now you come to me seeking war and combat at twenty years?"

This she said in her native tongue. But then, turning again to the ways of trickery and deceit, she cried out to Sayf: "You are my son, and flesh of my flesh!" And with that she ran up to him, and took him in her arms and kissed him.

Sayf, supposing she was dissembling, was reluctant to believe her. So she told him how she had done it in a fit of madness, how he was in reality the son of her husband, King Dhi Yazan, and that she had witnesses who could attest to this. Then she rose and rode off into her city, returning, after an hour, with four knights of venerable aspect; these were four of King Dhi Yazan's chamberlains, whom she had summoned, to their amazement, in the middle of the night to bear out her testimony.

When these four saw him, they recognized him by the mole on his cheek, and by his perfect resemblance to his father. They fell to their knees in their joy, kissing the ground before him and saying: "This is a night like no other, for here we behold our king, come back to us. O King, we are all your father's chamberlains, and your name is King Sayf Ben Dhi Yazan, son of the Tubba'i Yemeni king, son of King Asad al-Baida', son of King Shem, who was brother to King Ham, and your grandfather was Noah, peace be upon him! And this city, O King, is your city, and this Queen is your mother, so rise and enter with your troops. There is none in it who will oppose you. Take possession of your realm, and rule over us as you will."

Then Sayf turned to his mother, saying: "How could you cast me out into the wilderness and do such evil things to me, when I am your son?"

"It all sprang," she replied, "from this madness that seizes me from time to time."

So then he told her of all the things that had happened with him since she had left him, from the first to the last. And she said: "I have known no happy day since I abandoned you. Had I only known you were alive, my son, I would have come straightway to seek you out. It was the devil who spoke to me and made me do as I did. I deserve whatever punishment you think fit for me."

And with her weeping and sobbing, King Sayf believed she was indeed happy to have him restored to her, that her show of remorse and anguish was from the heart. So he said: "I have forgiven you, mother."

"If you have truly forgiven me," she said, "then go up to your father's city, and to his throne, and take possession of them. You have the greater title to them, and take precedence over all his subjects."

"That is so," he said, "but tonight we will rest. Go back now, and tomorrow, after you have told your troops, I will come to the city."

So Qamariyya rose and rode back into the city with the four chamberlains. And the first thing she did there, under cover of darkness, was to summon one of her men and have him slay the four chamberlains who had been with her and had recognized King Sayf.

5

The Sword

Qamariyya hastened back to King Sayf under cover of darkness; and when King Sayf learned of her arrival, he asked her how it was she had returned so swiftly.

"My son," she said, "I could no longer remain in the city, or in my palace. I was minded to sleep when, suddenly, your father appeared to me in my dream. 'Know, Qamariyya,' he said, 'that the earth has claimed me, and that this is my son King Sayf, who is your son too, and flesh of your flesh. Deliver to him the castle and the city and all my wealth, and all you took from my wealth and treasures after my death. Apprise him of them and deliver them to him.' 'King of all time,' I replied, 'this is but an ignorant lad. I fear he lacks competence to rule over the kingdom.' Then King Dhi Yazan said: 'Qamariyya, this man shall be sovereign over countries East and West, and kings will submit to him near and far. All the kings of the lands will obey him, both foreigners and Arabs. He will bring the Arabs victory over the Ethiopians and the Sudanese, and the curse of God's prophet Noah, peace be upon him, shall come to pass.' And so, my son, I have resolved to give you all your father bequeathed you. Rise up, this very moment and hour, and enter into your kingdom, and I, my son, will remove to my quarters with the ladies your father specially appointed for me.

"And so that I may discharge my trust, and you may thus receive your father's monies and treasures, let me tell you now that I loaded them, after his death, onto camels and mules and horses, and went out to a desert place three days distant from the city. The wealth in gold was borne by two hundred camels mounted by two hundred sorcerers; and as for the gems, the rubies and green emeralds and yellow emeralds and diamonds, these lighter treasures were in a hundred boxes borne by fifty mules. I came, with that wealth and with these treasures, to a valley remote from the world, accompanied only (so as to have the greatest assurance of secrecy) by forty men of Ethiopia; and there I buried it in the ground, marking the place with a rock so that I could find it thereafter. Then I gathered all who had witnessed the deed and set before them food in which I had put a potent poison, so that the instant they had eaten they perished to the last man, and none remained to know the way to the king's wealth, except myself alone."

"By God," King Sayf said then, "it was wrong of you to slay men when God has forbidden us to kill."

"My son," replied Qamariyya, "I acted only by the measure of my understanding. I knew this city was built by your father, whose wife I became and by whom I conceived; and I know, too, that the King of Ethiopia and the Sudan will never, whatever may befall, be reconciled to the King of the Arabs. That was why I committed those deeds and buried the money. 'Suppose,' I said to myself, 'the King of Ethiopia should ride out against me and seize the city? His money will still remain, and I shall have knowledge of it. I have greater title to it than the King of Ethiopia. If the chance presents itself, I shall wage war against him and take my city back from him; and if none presents, I shall have my wealth to spend as I please and choose, and King Sayf Ar'ad cannot demand so much as a dinar from me.' But now that you have returned alive, Qamariyya and the soldiers and the wealth and the city are all for you to possess. Whenever it is your wish, ride out with me, and I shall guide you to the place where your father's wealth is, and I shall deliver it to you the moment you ask for it, peace be upon you."

"I must know straightway," said King Sayf, "the place where my father's wealth is. I shall not sleep till I am reassured about it."

"My son," she replied, "I thank Almighty God who has granted me to see your face, so that you may take your father's wealth and his land. Here I stand at your service. If it is your wish, I shall ride out with you this very hour, and we will neither of us enter the city till I have shown you what I buried of your father's money and treasures in the deserts and plains, to guard them from enemies and envious men."

"For my part," said King Sayf, "I have resolved to do this so as to attain my goal, and I shall not enter the city with you till you have shown me my father's treasures."

"I hear and obey," she said. "Ride out with me this very hour, my son. It is I who am the true gainer in this business."

Then Queen Qamariyya donned her habit, and when her son King Sayf had done likewise and girded himself with his sword, she took him with her.

"Is the place distant?" Sayf asked.

"No, my son," she replied, "it is not far."

So out they went into the night, none of the soldiers knowing of them. And as she rode, Queen Qamariyya spoke the most flattering words to King Sayf, telling him of the reasons for her marriage to his father; and still onward they rode.

"Is it not the natural way of things," King Sayf said to himself, "that mothers should feel compassion for their children?" He had no notion she was cunning and possessed and rode out with him so as to destroy him. But Almighty God is wise and ordains such things so that His Will may be done and His judgments carried out.

When the journey had become long and evening had fallen upon them, King Sayf said: "Mother, had I but known the place you mention was so distant, I would have brought food and drink with me. Here is the day over and gone, and still we have not arrived; and now I feel the pangs of hunger. You did not tell me of this."

"Though the road seems long to you," Qamariyya replied, "still I have only done what is wise; for if the place were near, our attendants would have found it out. But as it is, no one knows except I alone. If you are in need of food, then here, I have brought food enough for the two of us."

With that she opened the bag on her saddle and took from it food of the most nourishing kind, and King Sayf alighted by the side of the road; and Qamariyya alighted too, and they ate their fill. Then she said to him: "Arise and mount." And he mounted and rode with her through the whole night, and still they went on thus till sunset; and again she offered him food and ate with him. The accursed creature aimed to drug him, or slay him, or feed him with poison, but could not do so, so careful was he of himself. And still they went on, riding and alighting, with Qamariyya keeping him occupied and flattering him with sweet talk. When she grew tired, she would say: "My son, I am tired of riding. Pray guard me while I sleep a while." And he would reply: "Indeed, do as you wish."

For three days things passed in this fashion; then, on the fourth day, King Sayf said to her: "I am amazed, O Queen, that you thought fit to remove my father's wealth so far."

"My son," she said, "had I not done so, they would have assailed me and plundered it from me, and I would not have been able to preserve it, being a mere woman with a crooked rib and a hesitant tongue. But now here are you, with a strength and a resolution greater than mine."

Then King Sayf said: "I can ride no more in the heat of this wilderness till I have rested. There are three days and three nights now in which I have not slept; each time you sleep, I guard you; yet I fear to sleep leaving you to guard me, lest a lion or some other beast should attack you and devour you before I rise."

"Have no fear," she said. "If you are minded to sleep, then I shall sit at your head till slumber takes me. Let us halt beneath that tree."

They had come then to a great evergreen tree, able to give shade to a full hundred knights, its branches high like a canopy fixed with columns and ribbings. And King Sayf viewed that tree, which was greater than any other tree and had neither flower nor fruit, the work of the All-Exalted and Mighty One; and he marveled at the nature of the tree and the work of the All-Glorious and All-Powerful God, and knew by certain conviction that God is able to do all things. When they approached it, they found a spring of water at its foot, from which they drank; then they got down from their horses, took their bridles from them and left them to their pasture, while they rested in the shade cast by the tree.

And there Qamariyya sat, regaling him with lies and fanciful things, embellishing her speech with fine words and describing the buried wealth, telling him how they were close now to the place where it was, while King Sayf laid himself down on the sands. Then she said: "Will you not eat from these provisions?"

"I am minded to sleep," he replied, "but only after I have caught and slain a deer for you, so I may leave you to grill its meat while I sleep; and when I wake from my sleep, it will be cooked."

"My son," she said, "I have meat, cooked in its own fat and ready. If you are minded to eat, then here it is."

"I will eat," he said, "if you will eat with me."

"I have no appetite for food," she replied, "but after you have taken your rest in sleep, we shall eat together, you and I."

Then King Sayf laid himself down to sleep, having no notion of what the All-Knowing Sovereign had decreed. She, for her part, placed his head in her lap as a mark of her love for him and began to talk to him; and he listened to her words till his eyes, by the grace of the Everlasting Ruler of All, grew heavy with sleep. And she looked into his face till she saw he had sunk into slumber.

Then, lifting his head from her lap and placing it on a stone close by her, she gazed at the green mole on his cheek till bitter rancor seized her, while the sight of his face, like the moon in its fullness, gripped her heart with still greater hatred and evil.

"Son of perdition," she said, "I cast you out at forty days old, and now here you come at twenty years. Truly this is an evil happening, son of perdition, child of filth!" Then she rose to her feet, took the bridle of her horse in her left hand and, with her right, drew her sword from its scabbard, till death crept along the exquisite blade; and so, God having driven all mercy from her heart, she drew near her son and made to strike him on the head with the sword.

Now it so happened, in a fashion to amaze the keenest mind, that King Sayf moved his head from the place on the rock where Qamariyya had set it, so that it now fell from the rock, and the blow struck his forehead and the rock in equal measure. The gash to the forehead woke him, and he made to rise, but the accursed creature struck him a further blow which fell on his shoulders and cut him to the bone, then she struck him a third blow; and when King Sayf cried out with a voice like thunder, she struck him yet a fourth blow, upon his breast, and he fell unconscious. Then she struck him on the back, and the sword broke in two. When she saw him there, unconscious and with the blood gushing from him as if from the mouth of a water bottle, she supposed him to be dead; and, wiping her sword and finding it broken, she mounted her horse and sought the plains. Across the wilds and the deserts she rode, till on the fourth day she reached her city, rejoicing in her deed and sure she had attained her goal. We shall have more to relate of her in the proper season, and he that loves the beauty of the Prophet will call ceaseless blessings upon him.

As for King Sayf, he lay prostrate in his blood through all that day, till the gloomy darkness of night fell, and he woke from his faint to find himself soaked in his blood, unable to move. But since the whole world was dark, he knew night had come, and he lifted his gaze upward, saying: "O Lord God, Greatest of the Great, I pray that You, who unrolled the land and raised the sky, will keep the heavens from tumbling down upon the earth, save by Your grace; and I ask You, O Lord, in the name of Your Prophet Noah and Your Friend Abraham, those whom You have chosen, O Generous and Compassionate One, above all Your creations, by the sanctity of Your Names, the All-Merciful, All-Compassionate, You who have created me and given me form, and I recognize nothing, benevolent or baneful, in myself, You who are the most blessed Guardian and the most blessed of Stays; Dear God, if my time has come, and I am to dwell no more in the abode of this world, I ask You to make light for me every tribulation. Yet since You are All-Powerful, O Blessed God, in what You will, I pray that You will send someone to heal my wounds and make me sound again; and grant us, O Lord, succor in all tribulation and a release from all misfortune and affliction. This I pray to You, who are All-Powerful, who bring forth the living from the dead and the dead from the living, who are All-Generous, All-Kindly and All-Great, and who know all things."

When his petition and prayer were done, lo, two birds came flying from the desert wilderness and alighted on that tree, each on a different branch. Then each gazed into the other's face, and they straightway uttered the words of faith that save from perdition: "There is no God but God, alone with no other, and Abraham is His Prophet and His Godly Disciple and His Friend, may God bless him and grant him salvation." These words were uttered by the two of them together.

Then one said to the other: "Have you seen, my brother, what this accursed Qamariyya has done to her son? She has struck him with that weapon, and wounded him grievously; and we were present and witnessed this deed. What do you propose we do, my brother?"

Then the second bird said: "Do not carp, 'Abd al-Salam, against what the All-Knowing Sovereign has decreed. Know that this Qamariyya is indeed his mother, and that she will devise seven plots against him, no more and no less. The first of these was when she cast him, as a small child, into the heat of the desert. But the Guardian, the Benevolent and Resourceful One, was kind to him, sending the she-gazelle who suckled him and the female jinn who reared him; and He softened King Afrah's heart toward him, so that he too showed him kindness and brought him up at his court, concealing him from his enemies and pleading his cause against the two who opposed him. Why be surprised at the things God has worked? And now here is the second plot. She has fallen upon him with that weapon and left him here in these plains."

Then the first bird said: "You speak truly, Shaykh Jiyad. This is the deed of infidels and the willful. Yet God Almighty watches over His creatures. This accursed woman meant to hasten his destruction, accompanying him to this place and slashing him with the sword while he was in need of sleep. And herein will be his remedy, through the power of Him who created him and formed him."

Now these two birds were Shaykh 'Abd al-Salam and Shaykh Jiyad, who had met him before all these things happened, when he had made his way to the city of Qaymar and brought back the Book of the Nile. Then events passed as we have seen, and they both died, one after the other, in the care of King Sayf. He it was who laid them out and buried them, and now they were living between the two Abodes and had come this night, conversing together as we have recounted.

"My brother," said Shaykh 'Abd al-Salam then, "what is his remedy?"

"Know, my brother," Shaykh Jiyad replied, "that if a man were to take from the leaves of this tree and chew them in his teeth, they would become a paste to apply to his wounds, and would heal them that very hour, even had he been afflicted with them over many years. This is by the power of Almighty God, the Lord of all Creation. God has His reason for all things, and for this it is that King Sayf is journeying now toward Ikhmim al-Talib, to attain his final goal."

"Peace be with you, my brother," said Shaykh 'Abd al-Salam. Then they bade one another farewell, and each proceeded on his way. And all this took place as King Sayf watched and listened.

"This is indeed a marvel," thought King Sayf. "I have learned that the leaves of this tree have the power to heal wounds. And yet I cannot reach them by stretching out my hand to them. If those were my friends in life, and knew these leaves would bring me good, why did one of them not strive to supply my needs, and bring leaves for me to heal myself? But God's will be done."

He possessed himself in patience till the day broke, and his wounds began to throb. Then he raised his eyes to the heavens, saying: "My Lord and Master and my Hope, I ask You by the sanctity of Your Great, nay Greatest Name, if You know that the leaves of this tree will bring succor for my wounds, then, in Your might, summon one to bring me down some leaves, so I may heal myself. So I pray to You, who are All-Powerful, most blessed of Guardians, most blessed of Stays."

No sooner had King Sayf finished his prayer than Almighty God sent a mighty wind that descended upon that tree and, shaking it and tossing it about, cast down numbers of leaves of which many fell round about King Sayf. He took some of these and chewed them, then applied them to the wound in his thigh, and it was healed by the power of God, the Beloved Sovereign, closing there and then, as though he had never been wounded or afflicted by hurt. Then he took more, and chewed them, and applied them to his wounds till they were all healed, and he became whole, as though nothing had ever afflicted him at all. When he had sought out the places of all his wounds, and found no smallest trace of them, he knelt in thanks to Almighty God, then rose joyfully to his feet and began to walk among those valleys. And there he saw his horse still grazing, Qamariyya having left it there for fear his soldiers, seeing the horse, should ask after its rider.

Then King Sayf approached his horse, harnessed and mounted it, and then rode off, with no notion of the road he was taking; for so God had decreed it. The whole day he rode, and then he saw a spring of water and beside it a tree of lotus fruits that were ripe and had fallen. He ate his fill of these, then fed the horse till it was full of the lotus fruits, and he slept beneath the tree till morning. Then he mounted again, riding through the plains and deserts till the day's end, when he came upon a wood, with many trees and fruits; and there he dismounted and ate from the fruits and, finding the earth fertile with grass, left his horse to graze there all night long. Again he mounted in the morning and rode on, and so it continued night and day, he riding through the wilderness, eating from the plants and drinking from the rivers, till his patience began to ebb and unease grew in him. Then, raising his face toward the heavens, he besought the Greatest of the Great and, having called blessings and peace upon our master Muhammad Taha, the Prophet and Messenger, recited the following lines:

> My God, my patience is worn out, and I have no supplication
> > except to You, the sole Deliverer from danger and death.
> Come to my aid, I cannot endure what has become of me,
> > being cast away in desolation in this vast expanse.
> I have called upon You, be pleased to hear my entreaty,
> > for You have total knowledge of Your creatures.
> Who else could restore my health and relieve my sufferings
> > where the ways of escape are none, and patience is spent?
> And I, Lord, am in the extremity of affliction
> > You are the Surety for Your creatures.
> O Lord, be You my Guide, be You my Deliverer,
> > for I am weak, I am a beggar at Your door.
> I have lost my way, and I cannot cross over.
> > Be You my Guide, O Lord, through this vast expanse.
> I implore you by the Ka'ba and Zamzam
> > and by the Aqsa Mosque and by him who was transported there,
> Find a way out for me from my being hemmed in,
> > grant me the victory for which I crave,
> And protect me from the evil ones among Your creatures,
> > from the malice of Satan, and from the traducers.

This was now the sixty-first day that King Sayf had ridden through the wilderness, like some wandering madman. And when he had finished reciting that verse, he looked before him and saw two mountains, a white mountain to his right, and a red to his left; and as he rode up to them, he saw a banner set up by the side of the red mountain, and, looking to the mountain that was on his right, he saw a lofty palace. A mighty marvel it was, for the palace soared up from the earth, grazing the edges of the clouds and the mist, and between the two mountains was a teeming sea dividing them, with towering waves that astonished the eye.

He thereupon climbed the red mountain on his left, being powerless to reach the second by reason of the sea separating him from it. On the top of the mountain he descried a fortress of marble, with a column in its center twenty cubits long, inscribed with names and charms; and looking thence toward the other mountain, he saw a lofty palace in the midst of it, with a column like the one in the fortress. The two columns were close one to the other and inscribed with writing. Then King Sayf, greatly astonished at this, rode on up the mountain that had the banner till he reached the fortress.

As he drew near the gates, he cried out: "People of this place, dwellers in this fortress, peace be upon you." And he heard a voice say: "Welcome to him who has filled these lands with warmth, leaving his own land and regions in desolation! Welcome to King Sayf Ben Dhi Yazan, ruler of kingdoms and states!"

Then the door opened to him, and a man came out, tall of figure and comely of countenance, bearing the marks of piety on his face. As he approached King Sayf, he called out to him in greeting, and King Sayf answered him with greeting and a show of esteem. "Who is it told you my name," he said, "when I never saw you before this hour?"

"Sir," replied the shaykh, "my bounden obligation it is to supply your need. I have been twenty-one years in this place, King of all time, awaiting your coming so I may supply your needs and help you attain your wish. And as token of my heartfelt affection, I invite you to enter this place with me. There you may eat what I shall provide for you, and rest from the rigors of your journey and the pains of wandering."

So King Sayf went with him into the fortress; and a marvel he found it to be, built of smooth stone, soft as silk, with not so much space as to drive a needle between one stone and another, and having towers and winding passages, the work of wizards of all time, so that King Sayf wondered at it all. They entered a pleasant reception room spread with sable fur, having, in its center, a bed of glass with a mattress of wool and white woven cotton. Taking King Sayf by the hand, the master of the place conducted him to this; then, when they were seated, the shaykh clapped his hands, and lo, chairs were set and dishes were laid. Yet King Sayf saw none who carried them, and by this he knew the man was versed in magic arts.

Then the shaykh turned to him, saying: "Approach, sir, I pray you, and join me in eating these things, so that love and affection may be established between us. Eat whatever you wish to sate your hunger."

"Whoever you are," King Sayf replied, "I cannot eat unknown food. If your wish is for me to take sustenance with you so that love and affection may run pure between us, then let me first enquire of those who laid this food out for you; and let me ask you also the reason why you have awaited me these many years."

"By God," said the shaykh, "for many years, before even these twenty-one years began, there was a wizard sitting here, watching for your coming; then he drank the cup of death, and I have dwelt here in his place. We have kings and rulers that govern what we may do and what we may not, and they it is that have charged me to execute these decrees."

"And why do you await me?" King Sayf said then. "Do I have debts with you that you must retrieve, or do you have vengeance to extract from me?"

"Know, King of all time," answered the shaykh, "that King Ham, son of God's prophet Noah, peace be upon him, possessed certain treasures during his lifetime, which he bequeathed to you to hold after his death. This he did because of what he had read in the sands. He placed the treasures here, then set my father guardian over them; and I inherited the guardianship from him by virtue of the secret inscriptions, and have dwelt here all this while till the time was fulfilled and you came to this place."

"What you say bewilders the understanding," said King Sayf. "How can it be that Ham set your father as guardian, and that you inherited the guardianship from him? Did your father then see Ham?"

"No, good sir," he said. "I inherited it from my father, and my father from my grandfather, and so back from generation to generation. I myself have served only a short while."

"And you," King Sayf said, "what are you called among goodly wizards?"

"My name, O King," he replied, "is Ikhmim al-Talib, and it chances that you and I are loved ones and kin."

"And what are these treasures you mention?" said King Sayf.

"Sir," replied the shaykh, "I swear by God I have never seen them, nor do I have authority to touch them, for all things have their owner and you are owner of these. None but you has the title to enter and take them. When this night has passed, and morning has risen over us, that which the All-Conquering Sovereign performs will come to pass."

That night they spent in worship and adoration of the All-Bountiful Sovereign, till night departed on the wings of darkness and the radiance of day came in its stead. Then the wizard Ikhmim said: "Arise, King Sayf, for King Ham has left signs for you in this place. Come with me, so that doubt may give way to certainty and we may ask succor from the Lord of Creation." So King Sayf went with him till they reached the column of the tower which was in the fortress.

Then the wizard said: "See this column. The first of your signs is that you should ascend to its top."

"Wizard," said King Sayf, "that holds no difficulty for me, for I see steps coming from it, and rings; if I am minded to place my hand on one step and climb up to the next, taking hold of these rings, I may do so."

"You speak truly," said the wizard. "Others have not seen this because the Watchers have revealed it to none save you alone. Ascend as you have said, and may Almighty God take you by the hand." So King Sayf climbed to the top of that column.

"What do you see from the top of the column?" the wizard Ikhmim asked then.

"I see," he replied, "near the edges of the stone, two footprints side by side, like the imprint of human feet in sand."

"Place your feet in them," said the wizard, "then stand and look to the mountain that is before you on the other shore." So he stood there in that place.

"Wizard," he said, "I see before me a column like this column, bearing the imprint of two feet like these two feet."

Then the wizard leapt up beside King Sayf and, looking down upon his feet, smiled and said: "You are the one who bears the signs. You are King Sayf Ben Dhi Yazan, son of the Tubba'i Yemeni king, son of King Asad al-Baida', son of King

Shem who was brother to King Ham, and your grandfather is Noah, peace be upon him. This is your lineage indeed, and to you belong the treasures set in this place. May God grant you joy of what He has given you."

"O wizard," said King Sayf, "where lies the wisdom in this?"

"Come down for this night," replied the other, "and when morning comes you shall see what comes to pass, if God the All-Generous, the All-Conquering wills it."

So he returned with Ikhmim, who treated King Sayf with still more honor and deference. Then they slept, and when the night had passed, the wizard said: "Arise, King Sayf, and draw near to the column; and when the sun rises, ascend to the top of the column and place your feet in the midst of the two footprints as you did yesterday. Then strengthen your resolve and leap with all your strength from this to the other column, bringing your feet down onto the two footprints that are like these footprints, and place your feet within them."

"Wizard Ikhmim," said King Sayf, "who could ever leap such a distance, one that spans three hundred paces? Surely these words of yours are no good counsel, and I shall plunge into the sea and drown there."

"No, my lord," the wizard said, "the Watchers will help you attain the goal you seek. But you must strive, and you must be sure, above all, not to hold yourself back."

"It is all in the hands of Almighty God," King Sayf said then. "For myself I know that, were you to set me in a catapult and hurl me with all speed toward that column, I should never reach it, but rather plunge into that sea and drown, all happiness and good fortune lost. Why should I do such a thing, venturing so upon destruction and death? If the owner of these treasures wished to give them only to sink me in the depths of this sea, to die by drowning there, then of what use are the treasures to me? Do not urge me to this course."

When Ikhmim al-Talib realized King Sayf was willing to renounce those treasures rather than drink the cup of death, he softened his speech, weary of the time these things were taking.

"Have no fear," he said, "and do not be sorrowful, valiant king. No pain or hardship shall attend you in this, for the Watchers will raise you up and bring you safe to the top of the second column. No strain or fatigue shall attend you, by Him who has concealed Himself with His knowledge of the unknown."

Then King Sayf said: "I place myself in the hands of God who established the winter and the summer." With that he ascended till he stood on the top of the column; but there fear entered his heart. "Surely this is the work of jinn," he said to himself, "and I am a man. Why should a jinn guide me to these treasures? Perhaps the column is built of lead, or bears some poison within it, and when the sun rises the lead will melt, or the poison will become liquid, and I shall perish."

So he descended again, and Ikhmim said: "Why have you come down, O King?"

"My brother," said King Sayf, "I am a stranger in this land, with no friend or kinsman here, and a thought has come to me on which I seek your counsel."

"What religion do you profess?" Ikhmim asked then. "Are you an infidel or a man of the Faith?"

"Know," replied King Sayf, "that I worship the Sovereign God, Creator of men and jinn, and I follow the creed of Abraham, peace be upon him."

"Then let be the thoughts that assail you," Ikhmim said, "and place your faith in the All-Knowing Sovereign. Such is the counsel I give you, and peace be upon you."

With that King Sayf was reassured in his heart, all fear and apprehension driven from him. He ascended the column and, placing his trust in the Divine Sovereign, he set his feet within the footprints in the center of the column, strengthened his resolve, and leapt as Ikhmim al-Talib had instructed him. And no sooner had he done so than he found himself standing on the second column, his feet firmly implanted within the footsteps resembling the first, fitting into them exactly.

When King Sayf saw what had passed, he fell to his knees in thanks to the Lord of the Earth. Then, turning to his right, he found Ikhmim al-Talib standing by his side, as though he had made the leap with him.

"What have you to tell me now, Ikhmim?" King Sayf asked.

"My son," he replied, "you are he of whom the masters of wisdom and secret knowledge have told. To you belong these blessings and these things held in trust. As for me, my son, I am the servant of whosoever rules. Descend now, my son, and may God prosper you in all you seek, for you, by God, are fortunate and happy."

When King Sayf had come down from the column, Ikhmim said: "Go to the palace that stands before you, and knock on its door; and if you hear someone say, 'Who is at the door?' reply to them, 'It is I, Sayf Ben Dhi Yazan, son of the Tubba'i Yemeni king, son of King Asad al-Baida', son of King Shem who was brother to King Ham, and my grandfather is Noah, peace be upon him.' When they hear this lineage from you, they will open the door. Enter and fear nothing, reciting, in the name of God the Merciful and Compassionate, something from the writings of Abraham the Friend of God. Then go on into the midst of the palace and look to your right, where you will find a bed of pure Chinese iron that neither decays nor wears out, because it is inscribed with spells. Make your way to it, and when you are standing before it, lift the curtains that hang round the bed. There you will find a dead man lying on his back, his face upward, with seven veils on his face; do not approach his face, but observe his hands, the right hand placed on his breast and the left extended by his side. He is tall, his body the length of the whole bed. Then you shall stand on his right side and say: 'O King, you who left your treasure behind you when you passed from the Abode of Extinction to the Abode of Eternity, when your Lord chose you and you departed this world; if your soul will grant that thing you promised me, then give me the treasure.'

"If he clearly hears those words from you, he will raise his right arm. Then you shall move to his other side, and say: 'O King, when you were in the Abode of the Living, the abode of what is false, you granted me the treasure; fulfill your promise now, when you are in the Abode of Truth. Do not be niggardly of it, for I shall use it in fighting for the sake of the Lord of the Faithful, and God will grant you reward and recompense in the day of Judgment and Resurrection, the day when souls tread the path of righteousness and pass one by one before God, the day when neither wealth nor offspring will avail, if a person does not come there with his heart pure.'

"Then he will raise his other hand, the hand of his left arm. And when his two arms are raised, view his breast, where you will find a tablet of red gold on a silver chain hanging around the king's neck. Take the chain then, and unfastening the clasp, take it out from under his neck and lift the tablet from his breast, saying: 'May God reward you with Paradise.' And after that you must swiftly quit his presence. Do everything exactly as I have told you, and return to me, so I may tell you what to do with the tablet."

"Uncle," said King Sayf, "who is this dead man?"

"It is Shem," replied Ikhmim, "the son of Noah, peace be upon him."

So King Sayf went up to the gate of the palace and knocked three times at the door; and when he heard someone say, "Who is at the door?" he replied, "It is I, Sayf Ben Dhi Yazan, son of the Tubba'i Yemeni king, son of King Asad al-Baida', son of King Shem, who was brother to King Ham, and my grandfather is Noah, peace be upon him."

"Are you indeed come, King of Yemen?" the servant said then.

"I am come," he replied.

"Welcome, my Lord," said the servant. "Enter and deliver us from these tribulations."

With that he opened the door, and Sayf entered and walked up to the bed, as Ikhmim had instructed him; and when the dead man's hand was raised, he took the tablet and returned to Ikhmim al-Talib, who asked him: "What have you done?"

"I did as you said I should," said King Sayf, "and here is the tablet, which I took it as you instructed me."

"Show me the tablet," Ikhmim said then, "so that I may look on it."

"Why do you wish to take it?" said King Sayf. "Are you perhaps plotting some secret treachery against me?"

"No," replied Ikhmim, "in the name of the Almighty Lord who has knowledge of all things, I could practice no treachery on you. Do not think one such as I could be a traitor."

So King Sayf gave him the tablet, and Ikhmim fell into a faint the moment he had taken it from his hand, with no life or speech remaining in him. King Sayf was amazed and perplexed at this, fearing the servants would take the tablet back; but when he put his hand out and took it, Ikhmim al-Talib revived, saying: "There is no God but God, and Abraham is the Friend of God."

"Why did that happen with you?" asked King Sayf.

"My son," he replied, "none among the jinn can endure the names inscribed on this tablet. Had you not taken it from my hands, those names would have set my body aflame and I would surely have perished. But set the tablet here before me, and return once more to the palace, for King Shem awaits your return. You will find his right hand sunk back over his breast and the left still raised where it was before. Lift the edge of the mattress beneath his left side; there you will find a sword in its sheath. Then you shall say to him: 'O King, by your leave I shall take this sword, and strive with it in God's cause, and you will have recompense from God.' And if he does not let his arm sink, lift up the sword and gird yourself with it, and return safely to me. Do exactly as I have said, for if you go against my instructions you will perish."

"I hear and obey," said King Sayf. Then he entered the palace once more, and found the dead man's right hand sunk back over his breast and the left still raised as it had been before. So he walked forward as Ikhmim had instructed him and, raising the mattress from under the dead man's side, took the sword and girded himself with it. But when he viewed the scabbard and saw how it was eaten away by the earth and covered with rust, he said to himself: "This scabbard is of no further use. I shall take the sword and throw away its scabbard."

Then he unsheathed the sword and shook it till death crept along its exquisite blade. But when he turned to throw away the scabbard, the covering of rust fell from it to the ground and the scabbard was revealed; and lo, it was of red gold, as though it had been fashioned that very hour. Then King Sayf joyfully returned the sword to the scabbard as it had been before, and the servants in that place all cried out: "O King, do not unsheathe it again here, for it will burn us with its talismen. Take it and depart, and may God bless you in its use."

Then King Sayf realized they had no power against the bearer of that sword. He placed his hand on the sword hilt and found it to be the exact measure of his hand, no more and no less, fitting perfectly into his palm. Joy flooded through him at this, and he was minded to leave that place; but then the devil whispered in his ear. "What marvel is this?" he said to himself. "Does this dead man yet have some breath of life by which he moves? For he raised his hands so you could take the tablet, and then again so you could take this sword. Had he indeed possessed life, he would have been capable of speech; and yet if he had no life, his flesh and bone would have decayed, and I see his body there intact. I must raise the cover from his face and see if he is alive, in health and safety, but with his tongue constrained from speech; or whether he has been dead these many years, so that only sticks and bones remain of him, and these movements of his spring merely from sorcery and the secret sciences.

"And suppose, too, that I relate to any I meet, to 'Atumtum, or Sa'doun, or Afrah, or other friends, how I entered the palace of Shem, son of Noah, and took a sword and a tablet from him, perhaps one of them will say, Did you steal them, or did he give them to you? And if you then say, I stole them, you have lied; and if you say, He gave them to me, people will say Shem has been dead these many years. I shall not leave till I have looked into his face, to know if he is alive or dead."

With that he returned and drew near the bed; and he had girded himself with the sword, which was the cause of his safe escape. He lifted the first veil and the second; then, as he lifted the third veil, he was struck with awe. Yet he braced himself and lifted all the covers, every veil, wishing to gaze into the face of God's prophet Shem. Then the prophet opened his eyes, roaring with rage, and viewing Sayf with eyes like crimson blood, flames and sparks pouring from his mouth.

"Insolent man," he cried, "basest of Arabs, have you dared, in this place, to unveil the face of the sons of prophets, when they have done you kindness and charity?" Still the shrieks and cries rang out, filling every corner of the palace with tumult, so that it seemed to King Sayf as if the earth had been laid flat and the heavens plunged down upon it. Then the servants rose up at him and roared as the lions of the forest roar, so that he could no longer have stood or risen or sat, or uttered a single word, had he not girded himself with that sword; for the servants would have given him the cup of death to drink. The cries grew ever greater, and the servants and guardians of the palace dragged him off and threw him unconscious out of the palace; and he remained in his faint till the next day, at the very hour he had entered the day before.

When he woke from his faint, he said: "I witness that there is no God but God, and I witness that Abraham is the Friend of God." Then he sat up by the gates of the palace and found Ikhmim al-Talib sitting at his head, in his wraps, exclaiming in his sorrow.

"King Sayf," Ikhmim said, "have you uncovered the face of the dead man?" And King Sayf told him he had. Then Ikhmim said: "I forbade you that, warning you against these mortal dangers into which you fell. I did not leave you in ignorance. You it is who have ruined yourself, letting your good sense fail you and following the ways of ignorance. By the inscription on Solomon's ring, had I power over you, I would give you the cup of death to drink. But stay there now, where you are, till you die of sorrow, with none knowing of your death. I have counseled you, and no sin falls upon my head. Peace be upon you. I shall go my way now, for my business is completed."

"Father," King Sayf said then, "how can you hold me so light as to depart, leaving me in this place powerless to return to the first fortress?"

"My son," said Ikhmim, "I have no choice in any of these things. I am a servant, and the servant has no right to challenge the rulers. I shall prepare myself and mount; and you, if you escape, will reach the fortress in safety."

Then Ikhmim al-Talib clapped his hands, and there appeared before him a large brass jar which he mounted and struck with the whip; and it bore him up toward the heavens.

"Have patience, Uncle," said King Sayf, "and await my coming."

"And how will you come?" asked Ikhmim. "You cannot approach and ascend the column, and leap to the other column as you did before, for you no longer possess the resolution to jump. There is no escape for you from this place."

"I adjure you," King Sayf said, "in the name of the lord Solomon, and in the name of the mighty names inscribed on his ring, to remain where you are till I have tested my spirit. If my spirit holds firm, then so be it. Otherwise do as you wish."

Then Ikhmim, hearing that oath, stopped. And King Sayf ascended till he reached the top of the column and, placing his feet in their spot, prepared to summon up his resolve. But he felt his spirit waver and his limbs tremble.

"My son," said Ikhmim, "do not exhaust yourself. Be patient in the face of destiny, from which no slave has ever found escape." Then he left him, moving through the air and, after a time, vanishing from King Sayf's view.

When King Sayf found himself solitary and alone on the column, with no one at his side, he wept and made complaint, reflecting on the shifts of time and the deprivations passing nights and days bring in their train. Then he recited well-turned verses befitting his state of abasement and shame, saying, with blessings on the name of Taha, the Prophet and Messenger:

> God's covenant is absolute for His creatures
>> and is carried either openly or in secret.
> He created beings through the wonder of His craftsmanship.
>> Blessed be the Omnipotent, the Creator!
> He knows that I am one of His creatures
>> who cannot bear all this adversity.
> Life has dealt harshly with me;
>> I found no allies among men.
> I am afflicted with estrangement and dejection.
>> The Lord, my God, knows all men's secrets,
> If it be His will, He can surely save me
>> and exchange my misfortune for felicity.
> O You whose way of operation is charity
>> and in Your bounty forgive our sins,
> Whither shall I go, for I have none to pity me,
>> to have compassion on my tears and affliction?
> O Omnipotent One, O Vindicator, O You who forgive,
>> in whose hands are the greatest of things and the destiny of men,
> I entreat You, for You alone are my way,
>> the One to succor me, blessed be You, the Deliverer.

Then King Sayf came down from the column and sat oblivious to the world, passing the night in invocation of God's name, till the night was gone and the day rose; and when he woke from his sleep, he found before him a goblet of glass filled with bee's honey, clear in color, and beside it two wheaten loaves and a pitcher filled with water.

King Sayf was amazed at these things; but as he was now hungry, he first invoked the name of Almighty God, then ate and drank, wondering who it was had brought him the food. And there he sat all that day, and slept beside the column, waking in the morning to find the bee's honey and the bread and water. He ate one loaf then, and at the end of the day the other, then slept till the third day. And so he continued for three months.

Then his patience grew frayed, and his clothes and body dirty, and his nails and the hair on his head grew long. And as this state of affairs continued, he said:

"This is a thankless existence, and eating always the same food is causing my stomach to turn. I must ascend this column and leap from it. Either I shall reach the second column and return whence I came, safely crossing to reach the earth, or I shall fall into the sea and drown, so finding deliverance from this hardship. No other course lies open to me. If it is my fate to live still, then I must be saved; and if my time has come, then fruitless it is to protest against God's decree."

King Sayf rose that very hour and, drawing near the column, said: "I deliver myself into the hand of the Divine Sovereign." Then he stood on the spot where the footsteps were and, thrusting himself forward with strength and resolve, straightway found himself in the midst of the water. There he attempted to float but could not do so for the weight of his clothes. He removed them accordingly, till all that remained on his body were the drawers, and the turban, and the sword hanging around his neck, which it never entered his mind to cast away, so full was his mind of the misery of the sea, with its fierce and thrusting current. He was hurled through the water like stone from a catapult, floating now on his hands and now on his legs and now on his belly, and whenever he tried to strike out for land he could not for the strength of the water's flow; or, if he should arrive after mighty effort, he would find the land to be smooth rock, offering no place to hold or climb. Then his endurance began to grow less and his strength to ebb, and his heart grew weary, so that his soul almost passed from his body. And still he cast his eyes for a place of refuge and found none. Then, close to death, he raised his eyes to heaven and implored the Greatest of the Great, saying: "Dear Lord, if You have decreed that my death shall be in this place, then I ask You, I beseech You in the name of Islam and in the name of faith, to seize me now without pity or further hardship; but if my end is not yet, then make haste to relieve my misery. For You have power over all things."

No sooner had he finished his prayer and entreaty to his Master than a mountain appeared across his path and the current thrust him onto it, and he found an opening in the side of the mountain through which the water entered with a roar like the roar of clapping thunder; all the water was flowing through that opening, having no other outlet.

King Sayf thought to hold back, but the current pulled him whether he would or no, forcing him through the opening; and despairing of life, he said: "There is no strength, nor power, save in the Most Mighty and Exalted God." Then he stretched out his hand to the roof of the place and found it to be composed of smooth granite, on a level with the water, so that there was nowhere any space for breathing. But the current pulled him still till the roof became high, and he was able to take his breath, and he thanked Almighty God. And still the current dragged him on whether he would or no, beyond any power of his to resist, and this went on for a full day and a full night—though King Sayf had no notion whether day or night it was, or where he was going in that torrent, beseeching God the One and All-Vanquishing, as the water weighed down upon him and thrust him under many times, till he was close to death.

Then he saw, in the distance, an opening like the eye of a needle toward which the water pulled him. The closer he approached it, the lower the roof of the place grew, so that he struggled to hold himself back for fear of drowning, but could not for the force of the water. And so he continued till he was thrust right down into the water, which drove him on through the hole in a faint, and he came out into a wild spot, full of stones and rocks, where the water began to hurl him this way and that and the stones to tear at him. Then the current thrust him onto his face and pulled him forwards, before casting him up on the land like a log of wood.

When he woke from his faint he found himself in a broad valley full of trees and fruits, with a great apricot tree in whose branches he was entangled; for so it was that he had escaped the waters. Up he crawled, clinging to the branches, till he reached its top and knew in his heart that he had escaped from the water. Then he fell on his knees to Almighty God, giving thanks for his safety. Hungry now, he found apricots on the tree, each the size of a pomegranate, and of these he ate his fill.

When he had climbed down from the tree, onto rocky ground to the land side, he took off the drawers and turban which were his sole garments and laid them to dry in the sun. Then he covered his body again with these and walked through to the very end of that valley, where he found a city which was white like the whiteness of the dove. Then he said: "Thanks be to God who has delivered me from the wilderness."

And still he walked till he reached the gates of the city, which he found closed against him. But as he approached the gate, he heard a voice crying out: "Open the city and go out to him, and do not return without him, for he is our enemy and the water bore him to our land. Let us give him the cup of death to drink."

When King Sayf heard this, he said: "By God, I am the quarry of which they speak," and he turned on his heels and, returning to the tree, concealed himself among its topmost branches. Then the gates of the city opened and a man, tall of stature, rode out of it on a fine horse, accompanied by four hundred knights all fully armed and accoutered; and he led them on till they had come before the tree, and there they set up a great pavilion for him.

"Pitch your tents here," he told them, "so that we may seek out our enemy." So they set up the tents, and fixed their banners, and, in the commander's pavilion, prepared a bed of wood inlaid with gold plate, which they spread with luxurious coverings. Then the commander, seating himself on the bed, said to the soldiers: "Search the valley for him."

The whole day they searched, then returned, saying: "We have found no one."

"This cannot be," he replied, "for my father does not cast the sands falsely. His sands never fail; they show the truth, telling nothing amiss. If you see him, then bring him to me; and if you do not find him, he will surely reveal himself forthwith."

"Upon your life," they said, "we have not found him."

"Let him be," the man said then. "He will come in his own good time, for there is no escape for him from here. Bring me food now."

"We hear and obey," they replied. Then they straightway hurried off and returned to lay before him a banquet made up of every kind of food and sweetmeat and fruit, whose aroma was like heavy musk.

Then the commander sat down to eat from the food, with the men round about him, while King Sayf sat concealed among the branches in the top of the tree, maddened almost by the smell of the food wafting over him and the hunger and pain he suffered. For many days past he had eaten nothing but apricots, which added fresh hunger to the old, for fruit does not satisfy the stomach like meat and bread.

As the smell of the food wafted over him, he was minded to call out to the people and ask them to give him some of it, but drew himself back for fear they would slay him. They were, he saw, many in number, and he had no armor with which to defend himself if they pursued him. "How can I reveal myself," he thought, "when I have seen these people searching for me and know they will slay me if they should find me?"

So still he endured, overwhelmed by hunger, on and on, till they had eaten the food and had drunk, and the banquet was removed, and they all slept. This was at noontime; and when the noontime was past, the commander rose from his sleep and sat among the men attending him and once more asked for food. And again they brought it before him and laid it out in front of him, then waited expectantly around him, preparing themselves to eat. But the commander said: "None of you will eat till you have sought out our enemy and seized him, so that we may set our minds at rest."

"We hear and obey," they said. Then they all rose and scattered to the right and to the left, combing through the desert wilds. And as the smell of the food entered King Sayf's nostrils, he could endure his hunger no longer, and said: "I deliver myself into the hands of God the All-Knowing Sovereign. Perhaps He will grant me sleep." So he turned in toward the tree in whose heights he sat, and sleep took hold of him, glory be to Him who never sleeps.

When the knights had searched right and left, through the whole valley, they returned to their chief with empty hands, saying: "We have found none in this valley, either white man or black man."

"Serve the food," he said then; and they ate till they were filled, then washed their hands and slept till morning. Then their chief woke, and woke all the other men, saying: "Search through the valley. Today perhaps you will light on our enemy." Again they set off, searching for more than an hour, then returned to him unsuccessful as before. So once more he said: "Bring the food"; and they brought it before him, and the commander descended from his seat to sit down to the food, bidding them all set to with a will.

King Sayf had woken from his sleep in the morning, and as he turned his gaze on the people sitting there with the food spread out before them, ravening hunger began to gnaw at him; and with the food was apple juice, whose aroma takes the heart captive. King Sayf could not draw his attention from these things.

"Waiting for food and not partaking of it," he thought, "is the bitterest and most deadly of torments. It is sure that no man's life can be made longer if his time has come, and no fear can save him from drinking of death. I must go down to these people and ask them to give me food; and if they are minded to kill me,

I shall defend myself till they send me to dwell in my grave. They are four hundred, I know, yet if I were mounted on a horse and my stomach satisfied with food, I should dispatch them all with lance and sword, leaving not one alive. The truth is, though, that they will destroy me so long as I am hungry, for my limbs have no strength for war and combat, nor do I possess equipment to fight and confront the enemy in this place. But all this I leave to God, the Beloved Lord. I shall go down and make myself known to them; and before all else I shall eat from this food whatever befall, and satisfy my stomach. If they kill me then, at least I shall die filled and not racked by hunger."

With that King Sayf cried out at the top of his voice: "Know, people of this land, you who are surrounded by all these foods, that I am a stranger far from home and country, far from brothers and kin, sundered from loved ones and neighbors, having here no friend or companion save Almighty God, who is the Sovereign Lord. Here I have been for days past, sitting in this tree, naked, cold, and hungry. I ask you to give me food from the provisions before you."

When the people heard him call out, they left the food and ran up to the tree, saying: "Come down and deliver yourself into our hands, and we will conduct you safely to our commander. And if you stay there in the tree, we shall hack it down to the very root, then hack you to pieces with every sword we have. Surrender, and we will take you to our commander."

"I am the one," King Sayf thought, "who showed them the way to my hiding place. There is no strength or power save in the Most Mighty and Exalted God." Then he said: "You people, remain where you are. I shall come down to you, then do with me as you will, either slay me, or set me before your chief."

"Come down then," they said. "We shall all remain here."

Then King Sayf came down from the top of the tree, and they advanced toward him, then seized him and surrounded him and took him before their chief, saying: "See, here is the enemy you seek, for whom you have wearied us as we sought him out for punishment. If this is indeed he, then here he is."

When the commander heard this, he rose to his feet and looked long and hard at King Sayf. Then he said: "From what land are you, and from what tribe and lineage are you descended? Tell me the truth, or I shall strike off your head with this sword."

"Young man," said Sayf, "I am a stranger whom time has marked with hardship and suffering; and you, I see, are a person of sense, and food has been set before you. I am racked by hunger; grant me first to eat from this food, so I may allay my body's hunger, then after ask me what you will. I am in your hands, with no means of escape. Know, valiant one, that food comes before talk."

"You speak truly, son of noble lineage," said the man. "Take here all the food you want."

And so King Sayf approached the food and, setting himself down on his haunches, stretched out a hand and began to eat, like one who has relinquished all hope in this world. "Here is the meal," he said to himself, "of one who bids life farewell, and whose feet tread toward death."

He ate his fill; then, when all those present had eaten also, the bowls of food were removed and the wine and other drinks passed round. He drank with them in good will, then they washed their hands and the talk began.

"Now you have eaten," the knight said to King Sayf, "tell us who you are and what your business is that you have come to this place."

"Know, whoever you are," said King Sayf, "that I am a merchant bearing goods from one land to sell in another, seeking my livelihood and profit. Such is my custom in every land, and this year I sold a shop where I dealt in cloth and took a boat with some other merchants. For days we voyaged over the face of the sea, and when seventeen days had passed, the sea rose up against us and the winds changed. The sea raged and tossed, the waves crashed one into another, the waters frothed and foamed, and evil towered mightily over them. So it continued for three days; then, on the fourth day, we lost our bearings, having no notion where we were going. Then the sea grew calm, its tumult subsided and the waves abated, and I said to the captain, 'Look to see where we have come, and reassure us of our safety.' So the captain went up on the mast and, looking to right and left, wept and lamented. 'Captain,' I said, 'what is amiss?' 'Bid one another farewell,' he replied, 'for you have no means of escape from this place.' And when I asked him how this should be, he said, 'Our ship is nearing a mountain called the Magnet, and the ship must of necessity sink, for the mountain will draw it to itself, and take the nails from the planks, and so it will sink. Therefore bid one another farewell. If you should come safely from this, it will mean your life is long; and if you drown, then here is your end. May God on High have mercy upon me, and upon you.'

"No sooner had he spoken than the ship was drawn toward that mountain and struck it. The planks scattered in every direction, and everyone in the boat was thrust beneath the water. Every kind of thing wrought in metal flew wildly toward that mountain, and we were flung right and left over the face of the sea; and so we sank, bidding farewell to all good fortune and prosperity, clinging to the planks as we could. As for me, I climbed onto one of the planks of the ship, and the waves bore me, tossing me up and down, till fate cast me onto an island in the midst of the sea. Going up on to it, I found it to be broad, with lush pasture and foliage, and I ate from the fruits and drank from the rivers till evening overtook me. Then I feared lest one of the beasts of the wild should devour me or some sea monster swallow me up; so I climbed into the top of a tall tree and sat amid its branches, minded to sleep there. Then, all of a sudden, a bird approached and alighted on this tree, a bird five times larger than a camel; and as I began to fear for myself, lo, it placed its head beneath its arm and slept, glory to be to Him who never sleeps. Then I said to myself: 'This bird was sent by the All-Powerful Lord. I should cling on to its legs, and perhaps it will set me down in a valley where there are people among whom I may dwell.' So I slept in my place, then, in the last third of the night, woke and watched the bird till the gloomy darkness of light fled and morning rose. Then the bird woke from its sleep and moved its head; it spread its wings and gathered them again, then spread its legs and stretched itself. Fully wakened now, it made to rise up in flight, and I took hold of its legs, delivering myself into the hands of God and placing my trust in Him. When the bird felt me, it thought I was minded to seize it and rose high into the lofty heavens, while I clung still to its legs. Then, when my weight began to weary it in its flight, and its wings began to weaken, it stretched its neck toward me and opened its beak, minded to seize me in its mouth. It wanted, I knew, to bite my head from off my shoulders; so, submitting myself to Him who created the immovable mountains, and never ceasing to invoke the name of Almighty God, I loosed my hands from the bird and straightway found myself plunging into that sea. Then the water bore me up onto the land, and I came upon this orchard of yours, naked as you see me, hungry and chilled; and when night fell I feared lest some beast should discover me and devour me while I slept, or some sea monster swallow me up; so I climbed into that tree and slept there till sunrise, unable to move from place to place for the severity of my hunger. And now you have brought me before you, and I am in your land, do with me as you will."

The commander of the troops laughed heartily on hearing all this. "You have spun a long tale," he said, "unknown in any book; and whoever you may be, the story you tell is mere lies. Let me tell you why. First, you are no merchant and have not the smallest knowledge of commerce; second, the Magnetic Sea, into which you say you fell, is at the end of the world; and third, if the ship broke asunder and people died and some of them clambered up onto planks, then we should certainly know of this. Then take the bird to whose legs you clung as it rose up into the heavens. If that had truly been so, then first, the winds would have rent you apart, and second, if the bird had flown as you clung to its legs, your limbs would have trembled with fear, and you would have grown dizzy from the soaring and plummeting. Everything shows this story to be false, with no grain of truth in it, except when you say you slept hungry in that tree. Tell me the truth, for that it is that saves a man, while lies, noble sir, are a kind of slander."

King Sayf realized now that the speaker was a woman, for men's voices can be distinguished from those of women. "Whether I speak lies or the truth," he said, "why, pray, should I wish to parade lies before men, when I do not know you and have never in my life stood before you? And why should I feel bound to conceal myself from you? Do I bear blood of yours which you are minded to avenge, or do I owe a debt that you wish to claim?"

"Indeed," said the other, "you are our enemy. Never in his life did my father cast sands that spoke false, or failed to utter the very letter of the message. Why will you not admit that you entered the palace of the son of Noah, God's prophet, and took the sword from beneath his side and the tablet from his breast? Then, after he had granted you that bounty, you transgressed against him, revealing his face so as to know how he looked, which he would not endure from you; and had you not been of his progeny, he would have struck you down in his furious rage and you would never have reached the column, nor fallen into the sea, after passing so many days as the guest of the king, the son of Noah, peace be upon him. So it was that you flung yourself into the sea, and at last reached this place."

"Where did you learn of these things?" asked King Sayf.

"I shall explain all in due season," she replied. "Seize him," she cried out to her troops, "till my father comes to question him." Then, turning to those around her, she said: "One of you speed to my father and ask him to come to me in haste." And with that a rider came out from the crowd and made for the city.

Then the commander rose and said to King Sayf: "Did I not tell you I speak true? I have uttered everything as it passed."

"What proof do you have," King Sayf asked then, "that this is the truth? And how may I be assured of your knowledge?"

"I recognized you by that sign, husband of Shama and Tama," she replied, "and I shall learn too of your measure, so I may tell you of yourself. Be seated there till my father comes."

And so King Sayf seated himself, while the messenger rode off to the city and entered the presence of her father, saying: "Pray come, O King, to your daughter, for she has taken her enemy captive, and asks you to go so that she may accomplish her business, and all her interests in the matter may be revealed at your hands."

Then her father rose and lost no time in going to his daughter; and she in turn rose to receive him, then had him sit beside her, saying: "Father, here is the enemy snared and in my power, and I have brought you so you may see how I have done and endeavor to accomplish my business."

"Bring him," he said, "so that I may see him."

"He is there," she replied, "sitting in my tent." And with that she walked with her father to her tent, where he gazed at King Sayf, and his joyful laughter rang out.

"Praise be to Him," he said then, "who saved you from death, and placed you in our hands, so that we may claim our due from you."

"And what is your due from me?" the king asked.

"By the inscription on Solomon's ring," the other said, "you are none other than King Sayf Ben Dhi Yazan. Why do you disown your true name, King of all time? I praise Almighty God who delivered you from suffering and shame and brought you to this place. Here I have long sat awaiting your coming."

"And who are you, gracious sir," King Sayf said, "may God fulfill your every wish?"

"I am your friend Ikhmim al-Talib," he replied. And with that King Sayf joyfully raised his head, glad and reassured in his heart.

"Is it so that brothers behave, Ikhmim," he said, "that you, who have broken bread with me, should so betray friendship and affection? You took the tablet from me and left me desolate, mounting your jar and riding your own way, not knowing whether God would save me and bring life out of death, or destroy me and take me to Him, may He be praised. Now He has delivered me from all snares; He it is who keeps me and preserves me, for He knows how things are with me and has saved me from fearful tribulation. And now, Ikhmim, where is the tablet you took from me?"

"O King," said Ikhmim, "God forbid that I should be a traitor. Even had I no fear of the Watchers who stand in your service, protecting your mission, I should fear Almighty God who formed you and made you beautiful. By God, my son—and there is no God but the Lord of Creation—I am a man who gives you good and truthful counsel. But when I counseled you, you paid no heed, transgressing against yourself when you uncovered the face of King Shem; for in the eyes of the sons of prophets, O gallant King, this is a sin like uncovering the private parts. Had I possessed the power to save you, I should not have left you, but your salvation was not to be at my hands. Yet still I could not bear to abandon you, and so I came to my house and cast the sands, learning from their configurations what your circumstances would be from first to last. Then I returned to you once more and made arrangements for your daily food and drink, which was the bread and bee's honey, till you grew weary of dwelling alone and plunged yourself into the sea. Then all that happened to you happened, ending in your meeting with my daughter in this place; and I thank God for your safe delivery from the shifting fortunes of time. And further, my son, when it was revealed to me in the sands that you were coming to this place, I arranged for my daughter and her knights to watch for your arrival in these valleys, till at last you came, and ate, and I came to you, and we joined together again here."

When King Sayf heard this, he knew he was speaking the truth; that had Ikhmim possessed the power to save him, he would never have abandoned him. "I believe your words," he replied. "But tell me, who is it that commands these men? She is, it seems to me, a lady."

"You are right, paragon among heroes," said Ikhmim. "She is my daughter, my lovely one. Her name is al-Jiza, and in the fullness of time, you will be a spouse to her and she will be kin to you. So it was revealed to me in the sands. But all things, my son, will have their own time, through the aid and dominion of God."

At that King Sayf fell down on his knees to Almighty God for the abundant blessings with which he had endowed him. Then he said: "Where, Ikhmim, is the tablet I brought out from the palace of the son of Noah, God's prophet, peace and prayers be upon him?"

"There it is, with your wife, master of all," replied Ikhmim.

"Uncle," King Sayf said then, "how is it that I have a wife here?"

"I will show her to you, light of the eye," said Ikhmim. Then he called out, "Jiza!"

"Here I am, father," she replied, "at your service."

"Bring the tablet you have with you," he said.

"I have it here," she replied, "bound to my arm. But father, who is this you told me was our enemy; and then, when you came to him, he began to reproach you, and you to submit to him?"

"Daughter," he said, "come and stand before the knight of all time and the king of all the kings of the lands, the vanquisher of infidels and evildoers, purifier of the earth from the false and the vengeful, King Sayf Ben Dhi Yazan, son of the Tubba'i Yemeni king. He it is who entered the palace of King Shem, son of Noah, peace be upon him, and took the tablet and the sword."

"The tablet I have," she said, "but where is the sword?"

"He has it, my daughter," said Ikhmim. "Show us the tablet."

"Here it is," she replied. Then, uncovering her wrist, which seemed to King Sayf like a rod of crystal, she revealed the chain and removed the tablet, saying: "Take it, father."

King Sayf gazed as al-Jiza brought out the tablet. "Ikhmim," he said then, "this is indeed my tablet."

"You speak truly," said Ikhmim, "and you it is who brought it out from the palace of King Shem, the son of God's prophet. But be patient, O King, while I reveal to you the worth of this tablet."

With that Ikhmim took the tablet from his daughter and rubbed it with his hand, and lo, the servant of the tablet cried out: "I hear, King of all time. What is your will, O wizard?"

"What is your name?" asked the wizard Ikhmim.

"I am 'Ayrud," came the reply, "son of the Red King, servant of this tablet from the time of my lord Shem, son of Noah."

"And do you know," said Ikhmim, "who this is that stands before me?"

"This is King Sayf," said 'Ayrud, "son of King Dhi Yazan, the Himyari. His line and lineage you know, and all the deeds he has done. He it is who brought me out from the palace of my lord, Shem, son of Noah, when he took this tablet from off his breast, and he it is who will, in the fullness of time, marry your daughter, Queen Jiza. So I have told you and peace be upon you. But you it is who summoned me with this tablet. What do you wish of me?"

"I wish nothing at this time," he said. "Go your way." So 'Ayrud went his way.

"What manner of servant is this, Ikhmim?" King Sayf asked then.

"It is 'Ayrud," he replied, "son of the Red King and servant of this tablet."

When al-Jiza heard these words, she took the tablet from her father and joyfully replaced it on her wrist. "What is it you wish, Jiza?" her father asked.

"I wish nothing at all," she replied. "I have heard you say this man is my husband. Yet who told you I am in need of a husband? On my side there is neither welcome nor honor, neither happiness nor interest."

"This is your spouse," Ikhmim said then. "You are his among women, and he is yours among men, for so it was revealed to me in the sands. And here you have taken his tablet, which he toiled so bitterly to redeem, suffering the cruelest hardships on its account."

Then it was that al-Jiza became enamored of King Sayf. Yet she possessed herself in patience, concealing her unhappiness and keeping a grudging silence. "Come," she said to the men, "bring us food, for our guest is hungry." So food was brought and the men laid out the repast and stood there in attendance. Then al-Jiza turned to King Sayf, saying: "Here is food set before you. Pray eat your fill."

"Food is sweet only in company," replied King Sayf. "Either we eat together, or you must have your food removed."

"It is our custom when a guest comes to us," said al-Jiza, "that we lay the food before him, then leave him to eat from it alone. We eat only after he has eaten, rather standing in attendance on him. It is our duty to honor him so, regardless of his prestige and standing."

At that King Sayf, convinced by her words, sat down to eat, fixing his mind on the food, for he was hungry and had long been wishing for it; his appetite had grown keen, and his eyes opened at the repast before him.

Then al-Jiza rubbed the tablet and, when its servant 'Ayrud appeared, said to him: "Are you the very servant of this tablet?"

"Indeed I am, my lady," he replied.

"Who was it," she asked then, "that cast the spell on you, delivering you up into this service?"

"First," he replied, "I was the servant of King Shem, and now I shall be the servant of my lord, King Sayf Ben Dhi Yazan."

"Does this man have wives?" asked al-Jiza.

"My lady," said 'Ayrud, "this man shall wed King Afrah's daughter, Shama, and Tama, the sorceress 'Aqila's daughter, and Nahid, and you, and many more. And he shall wed Munyat al-Nufus."

At this al-Jiza became vexed. "The tablet is mine now," she said, "and you are my servant henceforth."

"Do not lose your time," he said, "for you have no power in the matter. This man is served by sorcerers and wizards and masters of the secret sciences. As for me, I am one servant among many. He has a sister, the daughter of the White King, that never leaves his side and would lay down her life for his. All who hold enmity toward him are defeated."

"And you," al-Jiza said, "have you no power to slay him?"

"How can I slay him," 'Ayrud replied, "when the sword of my lord Shem is beneath his arm?" And so she told him to be gone.

Now al-Jiza had among her servants a man whose name was Ghader (meaning, Treacherous One), a valiant and capable man, and him she instructed, through signs, that he should move around King Sayf as his mind was fixed on his food, then strike him with his sword, giving him the cup of death to drink.

"I hear and obey," he said. With that he approached King Sayf from behind, and moved around him as he was taken up with his eating, then drew his sword and struck him a shattering blow. And lo, the sword turned in its owner's hand and lit upon his own neck, striking it clean from his body, so that head and body fell together to the ground, while King Sayf, occupied with his food, did not so much as turn round.

Al-Jiza was struck dumb at this, unable to understand how such a thing had happened. But it was the work of her father, Ikhmim al-Talib, who had seen the treachery in his daughter's eyes, and how she had begun to hate King Sayf when she learned he would wed others from amongst the daughters of kings, and she to be with him like a beggar. Minded to frustrate her plans, he had summoned a servant from among the jinn, saying: "If you see any man approach King Sayf, drawing near with intent to harm him, then slay that man and do not leave him whole." And this the servant had done as Ikhmim instructed him, awaiting events till Ghader came to King Sayf and drew his sword; and the jinn was more powerful than he, driving the sword back on his own neck and striking off his head, so that he drank deep of death.

Then al-Jiza turned to her servants, and said: "Wretches that you are, why do you slay one another and commit these deeds?"

"By God, O Queen," the man said, "none of us has hastened to combat."

"Then why," she said, "has this man amongst you drunk the cup of perdition?"

"He it is," they all said, "who drew his sword in evil and injustice, so that God dealt his swift punishment. He was killed with his own sword, and no other."

"Dogs," she said, "you are here in my service. Do you seek to redress your wrongs by your own hands?"

"Such a thing cannot be permitted," Ikhmim said then. "If one of you should transgress against another, then the one wronged must bring the matter before his mistress. She it is who will redress his injury and deal vengeance on the one who wronged him." All this was trickery and stratagem on Ikhmim's part, for fear his daughter should learn of his deed and guard against such destruction in future.

"As for al-Jiza, she kept her silence, while the king still sat eating at his leisure, knowing nothing of what had passed, except that the Mighty One disposes all things as He wills. Then she turned to one of her men, saying: "'Abd al-Khayr, I wish you to approach that stranger who is eating and-take him unawares, striking him with your sword, and striking his head from his body. Do this, and I will make you chief among my servants."

"I hear and obey," the man said. With that he went to stand behind King Sayf; then, drawing his sword without fear or trepidation, struck King Sayf full on the neck with the keen blade. And lo, the head of the striker flew from off his shoulders, while the man struck knew nothing of these happenings, having no thought for anything but his food.

Then al-Jiza again became vexed, and commanded an Arab man to do as the others had done; and he was slain likewise. And so she continued, commanding one man after another, till seven had been slain in this fashion. Then al-Jiza said to the men: "Bear away your dead comrades, and may God bestow no mercy on you! This is a fortunate and protected man. Those minded to slay him have drunk the cup of perdition." And all this while King Sayf's mind was fixed on his food, and he knew nothing of these things.

When he had eaten his fill, he rose and gave praise to Almighty God for his abundant blessings, then seated himself beside Ikhmim al-Talib, while the Lady Jiza sat before them, paying them no heed at all and addressing no word to them, till the smiling day passed and the thick darkness of night drew near. Then al-Jiza rose from their midst and went to her tent, where sleep enfolded her and her spirit wandered through the heavens, glory be to Him who never sleeps and lives for ever.

Ikhmim al-Talib, too, departed to take his rest, inviting King Sayf to accompany him to his place of repose and sleep there. But the king said: "Uncle, I will sleep here in my place." So Ikhmim departed, leaving him where he was.

When King Sayf Ben Dhi Yazan was alone in that place, he said to himself: "How is it that I was guided to King Shem's palace by this Ikhmim, that I strove to bring the tablet out from there, enduring suffering and hardship for its sake, and now his daughter, this wanton al-Jiza, seizes it and all my weary effort goes for nought?" Then he set himself to a course of cunning and ingenious skill. Rising to his feet, he said: "O Concealer and Merciful One"; then, stepping over the necks of the sleepers, he entered the Lady Jiza's tent, finding her asleep on her bed. Then, praying to God to aid him in his endeavor, he stretched out his hand with nimble skill, unbound the chain of the tablet from around her neck and untied the tablet from her wrist, setting them around his own neck and wrist.

When he had returned to his place, he found himself unable to sleep, and passed the rest of the night in contentment till Almighty God brought the morning. Then Ikhmim al-Talib rose and went in to his daughter, who rose and kissed his hands, then asked him to be seated and stood there in attendance on him.

"Father," she said, "you told me I shall marry this man who is with us here. But I have learned that his wives are to be many, and if I marry him I shall be like a mere servant to him; for he is the possessor of lands and deserts."

"Jiza, my daughter," Ikhmim replied, "you have little enough sense, God knows. I am ready before all others to be a servant of this king, for he will possess lands and deserts, and the greatest wizards and masters of sorcery and magic will serve him. He will establish cities and villages and whole regions, great and small, and will compel the Nile to flow from the land of Ethiopia to the land of Egypt, and every king and every knight will bow down before him, along with every mighty wizard. Tread carefully with him, my daughter; show him obedience, and do not cross him or rouse his rage."

"I neither accept him nor desire him," said al-Jiza. "He shall never take me as his spouse, nor will I be his."

"But this is a thing foretold already," said Ikhmim. "Who can stand against the Lord of Lords?"

"I beg you, father," replied al-Jiza, "in the name of the Glorious Sovereign, do not speak to me of him, either good thing or bad, for my heart in no way inclines to him, nor do I wish to see him on any condition."

"These are words I do not wish to hear," her father said then, "for what is to happen by God's wisdom none can prevent; it is a thing that must be. If you will not take him, then give him the tablet and let him go his way."

"I shall never give up the tablet," al-Jiza said, "even were I to drink the cup of death."

"This thing cannot be," Ikhmim al-Talib said then. "How can you stand against the power of Almighty God? But if you do indeed covet the tablet and refuse to give it to him and accept him, then I shall write your marriage contract in the manner of Abraham the Friend of God, peace be upon him, whatever your own wishes are."

As they were speaking in this fashion, King Sayf came in to them and greeted them, having heard all that had been said between them. Then he said to Ikhmim al-Talib: "Father, do not vex yourself with these matters. Know that I have sworn a solemn oath to marry no woman before Shama, daughter of King Afrah. If God has decreed your daughter's lot shall lie with me, then so it must be. Do not weary yourself with any of these things."

With that Ikhmim turned to his daughter, saying: "Let him take his tablet and go his way."

"I have no tablet for him," she replied, "nor any other thing."

"My daughter," he said, "I tell you, by my life, to give this man his right and cease to be so obstinate in the matter."

So al-Jiza, laughing, stretched out her hand to take the tablet from her arm; and finding no trace of it, her heart beat faster and her cheek grew pale.

"Father," she said, "the tablet is no more there on my arm."

"And did I not give it to you," he said, "sure in my heart that you would not lose it?"

"It was on my arm when night began," she said, "and now the day has risen I find no trace of it."

When Ikhmim al-Talib heard these words, the light before his eyes turned to darkness, and he looked toward King Sayf, saying, "My son."

"Here I am," replied King Sayf.

"Upon your faith and creed," said Ikhmim, "did you take the tablet my daughter had?"

"You adjure me by the most solemn of oaths," King Sayf said then. "I did indeed take it from her while she lay deep in sleep, amid the sweetest dreams. Here it is, in my possession. Never again will I treat it lightly, but rather protect it with my life."

Then Ikhmim turned to his daughter, saying: "I swear by God, the Most Beloved and Glorious, that right is rejoined to its possessor and trust returned to its rightful owner, and I rejoice at it from the depths of my heart. What do you say now, daughter, concerning marriage with him?"

"It shall never be," she said, "even were I to drink the cup of death. If his wish is to marry, let him wish on in vain. But if his wish is to go his way, then let him give me the tablet he stole from me, along with the sword he took through your agency. He will never, believe me, go his way while they remain with him."

"Daughter," said Ikhmim, "you do him a cruel injustice in this. What do you say, King Sayf?"

"I will go in to no woman," replied King Sayf, "though she were like the morning star, before I go in to Shama, daughter of King Afrah; for I will not break my bounden oath were I to drink from the cup of perdition."

At this al-Jiza flew into a furious rage. "By God, Sayf," she cried, "you shall never leave this place before you have married me. Or, if you will not, then deliver tablet and sword and go your way."

"This can never be," said King Sayf. And with that he rose from their midst and returned to his place, sitting there in contemplation, musing on his circumstances and on what the future would hold. And so he continued till the day fled and the darkness of night drew near. Then he composed himself for sleep, but sleep would not come to him, for his mind was not calm.

As for al-Jiza, she said: "By God, I will go to King Sayf, and will not return before I have slain him." At midnight she placed in her hand a dagger sharper than the ways of destiny and sought out the place where King Sayf was, thinking to find him deep in sleep. But when she reached him, there was King Sayf squatting on his haunches. "If my heart tells rightly," he thought, "and my suspicions are well founded, al-Jiza will come here minded to slay me and take the tablet and the sword. If matters stand so, my best course is to move on toward Hamra' al-Habash."

While he sat musing in this fashion, lo, al-Jiza drew near. Then he drew out the tablet and rubbed it; and 'Ayrud said: "Here I stand at your service, King of all time, truest of protectors. What is your will, O fortunate King?"

"I wish you," he said, "to bear me straightway to the city of Hamra' al-Habash, where I left my friend Sa'doun and his troops, together with the other men and brothers."

"I hear and obey," said 'Ayrud. And with that he bore him up and cut through the airy spaces, like a flash of lightning or a raging wind. So things passed with King Sayf. And when the Lady Jiza saw King Sayf flying on 'Ayrud's shoulders, she felt bitter sorrow and hurried back to her father.

"Father," she cried, "I went at this hour to Sayf, minded to sit with him. And when he saw me, he took fright and flew off high into the heavens."

"My daughter," said Ikhmim, "do not grieve. God will rejoin you with him."

"Father," she replied, "it is not him I want, but only those treasures that are in his possession. As for him, let him go his way."

"Know," said Ikhmim, "that these treasures will all be at your disposal when the time comes. Do not be so hasty; know rather that everything comes in its due season, and that patience has a blessed reward."

Thus Ikhmim began to urge his daughter to patience and calm, and he commanded her men to take down her tents. Then he entered the city, with his daughter by his side, and sat musing on what was to come. So things passed with Ikhmim and his daughter.

6

Weddings

Now as King Sayf was flying on 'Ayrud's shoulders, he heard horns and bugles and a great tumult. So he asked 'Ayrud to seek out the cause of all this, and 'Ayrud left him on a mountainside, then returned to tell him that a great wedding feast was in progress, and that the bridegroom was the mighty King Sayf Ar'ad, ruler of Ethiopia and the Sudan, and the bride the lovely and gracious Princess Shama, daughter of King Afrah, ruler of the city of al-Hadid.

When Sayf heard this, the light before his eyes turned to darkness; he was grieved and enraged, his passions inflamed, and he told 'Ayrud to bear him to the bride's tent so that he might deliver her. Then, when 'Ayrud had set him down at the entrance to the tent, King Sayf concealed himself for a time, wishing to learn whether Shama herself wished for this marriage, or whether it was made against her will. But when he heard her lamenting her fate, and grieving for her lost love, who was Sayf himself, he entered boldly, and they fell into one another's arms with all the ardor of lovers long parted.

Things had come to this pass, Shama told him, because the two wizards, Saqardyoun and Saqardis, had assured her father Sayf had been slain, and had arranged for King Sayf Ar'ad to ask for her hand in marriage; and King Sayf Ar'ad had threatened to lay the land waste and destroy all Afrah's troops and take her by force if her father did not give her willingly. And so King Afrah had consented out of fear. Then Sayf, in his turn, told Shama of all that had happened with him up to the moment he came in to her there in the tent.

As they were conversing together, King Afrah came to his daughter's tent to prepare her for her marriage; and when King Sayf saw him, he fell into a fury and unsheathed his sword.

"Do you seek, scoundrel," he cried, "to give your daughter in marriage to another man, when you have already received her dowry and her wedding gift, the Book of the Nile, for whose sake many a noble king has died?"

At that King Afrah took fright in the face of King Sayf's anger, running straightway from the tent to King Sayf Ar'ad's tent to enlist his help; and when King Sayf Ar'ad heard what he had to say, he called to his men to attack the tent and slay King Sayf Ben Dhi Yazan and take Shama from him. Then King Sayf Ben Dhi Yazan leapt to battle in defense of his beloved, and all at once the sky darkened, and the dust swirled up, and sparks of fire flew around; there was a pelting of stones, and a clattering and a clapping of thunder, and a flashing of lightning, and shrieks and roars and thunderbolts; the earth trembled all around, and people fled in all directions. And when the storm had subsided and the darkness lifted, and the world was once more as before, King Sayf Ben Dhi Yazan and Queen Shama were nowhere to be found.

King Sayf Ar'ad, astounded at all this, summoned the wizard Saqardis to ask how such a thing could have come to pass, and Saqardis, having cast the sands, told Sayf Ar'ad that 'Ayrud had been the cause; and 'Ayrud indeed it was who had saved King Sayf and Shama, for he had watched as he had been instructed when Sayf went to Shama's tent, and when he saw Sayf Ar'ad's men pressing in upon them, he thought: "I must do as my lord commanded me." And so he had sent flames against the troops and pelted them with stones from the mountaintops; and he had then descended and borne Sayf and Shama up to the summit of the mountain, setting up a tent for them there and serving them a repast.

Now all this had come to pass because Qamariyya, having wounded Sayf grievously with her sword and leaving him as she thought for dead, made straightway for King Sayf Ar'ad's city and went in to the court, where she greeted him, kissing the ground before his feet. And when Sayf Ar'ad heard her complaints concerning the troops he had sent against her, and her protestations of goodwill and declarations of allegiance to him, and learned of what she had done with her son Sayf, his face broke into a smile.

"You tell me then," he said, "that Sayf Ben Dhi Yazan is dead."

"May you enjoy long life, O King," she replied, "nothing remains of him save his bones."

"You have done a good thing," he said then. "Truly you are the best of well-wishers, and my faith in you is well met. What are you minded to do now?"

"I ask," she said, "that you will give me a letter to the commander of the troops you sent against me, telling him to show me obedience and do my bidding. Then I will hatch a ruse to take Sa'doun captive and send him to you, so you may strike off his head and be rid of him. As for his men, I shall take care of them."

King Sayf Ar'ad consented to her plan, and straightway wrote the letter she had requested; and Qamariyya rode in haste to her city and, arriving there at night, made straight for the tent of Sayf Ar'ad's commander, so as to hand him the letter. And he, having acquainted himself with its intent, contrived with Qamariyya a plan by which they might take Sa'doun captive.

As day began to break, he sent a group of his men to tell Sa'doun he was required on some urgent business, while another group concealed themselves and lay in wait; and when Sa'doun arrived, alone, he was greeted with ceremony, then served with food and wine and entertained by the commander, till the wine began to take effect on him. Then, when the commander saw this, he clapped his hands, and his men leapt from their places of concealment, flinging themselves on Sa'doun and putting him in chains. And Qamariyya came out with them, gloating, delighted at the success of her plot.

When Sa'doun discovered she was the cause of this, and learned of what she had done to King Sayf Ben Dhi Yazan, he was enraged and sorrowful on his friend's account; but he could do nothing. Then the commander gathered his troops and set off for the city of al-Dour, taking Sa'doun captive to King Sayf Ar'ad. When Sa'doun's men woke next morning and found neither him nor the commander, they realized what had happened and, donning their armor and mounting their horses, they assailed Qamariyya; but her men were too numerous for them, and they, lacking leader and champion, and after three days of gallant combat, were forced to turn and flee. Then Qamariyya seated herself on her throne, happy in the thought that she had destroyed King Sayf Ben Dhi Yazan, and had put an end to Sa'doun's might and routed his men, so making her rule secure.

As for King Sayf Ar'ad, when Sa'doun was led in before him in chains, he roared with laughter, saying: "You are brought low, then, accursed wretch."

"It is not I who am accursed," Sa'doun retorted, "but you, who take champions by treachery when you are powerless before them in combat. What glory can you boast among kings, mocking me in this fashion when I stand in irons before you. Were I free from them, I should cleave you in two and end your life, though you hid beneath the earth."

At that King Sayf Ar'ad's fury was aroused, and he called to one of his swordsmen to strike off Sa'doun's head there and then. And so it would have been done but for the minister Bahr Qafqan al-Rif, who counseled Sayf Ar'ad against such a course, advising him rather to keep Sa'doun captive till his temper cooled, then try to win him to his side, he being a champion matchless in his time and an undaunted warrior. And so they led Sa'doun to a narrow cell within the dungeons, and left him there in his plight, seething with rage and overwhelmed with grief, with no notion of what might lie before him.

At this point it was that the wizard Saqardyoun came to visit his brother Saqardis the Ill-Fated, and together they persuaded Sayf Ar'ad to send to King Afrah again, asking for Shama's hand in marriage, and threatening retribution if his wishes in the matter were not met; for in this way the wizards aimed to ensure that Sayf Ben Dhi Yazan, with his mole, would never be joined with Shama and her mole, and Noah's curse would never come to pass. So it was that Shama was led in bridal procession to King Sayf Ar'ad's city, where King Sayf Ben Dhi Yazan found her in her tent, lamenting her bitter fate, and delivered her with 'Ayrud's help.

Now when 'Ayrud snatched King Sayf and Shama up from the tent, King Sayf Ar'ad was astounded at the event and, summoning the two wizards, took counsel with them as to what should be done. And it was agreed that they should go to Sayf and ask that he himself take up arms in knightly duel, in single combat, and that he should not seek out the help of the jinn, against whom they were powerless in fight.

Thus it was done, and King Sayf, answering their call to combat, rode out into the battlefield the following morning, on a horse black as night, girded with his sword and cased in his armor, looking like a piece hacked from the mountain, or God's judgment when it descends. Then he called out to the troops of Ethiopia arrayed before him: "Champions of the Sudan, which among you is ready for combat? He who knows me knows all that is needful, and from him who does not know me I have nothing to conceal. I am the Tubba'i Himyari king, Sayf Ben Dhi Yazan. On now to combat!"

Then King Sayf Ar'ad, in his turn, called out to his troops: "Any knight who brings him to me captive will be granted a hundred gold dinars and an Ethiopian slave girl and splendid garments of the value of a thousand royal dinars, and I will make him my minister and counselor."

The knights were thereupon chosen by lot, for all were eager to do battle; they went out one after the other to meet King Sayf Ben Dhi Yazan, and by midday he had slain thirty of them, such was his prowess and valor in the field. When the knights saw this, they became less willing, and so King Sayf Ar'ad called on them to go out ten by ten. But still King Sayf Ben Dhi Yazan acquitted himself nobly, and by that day's end, he had killed seventy more.

Next day he killed a hundred and seventy of them, and so things continued for twenty days more, with King Sayf Ar'ad growing ever more grieved and unquiet at the punishment his men were receiving, while the two wizards Saqardyoun and Saqardis seethed with vexation, their hearts ready to burst with rage and resentment. And as they debated amongst themselves whether they dare send all the troops together against Sayf Ben Dhi Yazan, and so risk assaults by the jinn, the minister Bahr Qafqan al-Rif stepped forward with a proposal: they should, he suggested, approach Sa'doun with the promise of freedom and wealth if he would go out to do battle with Sayf; for he was the only knight with power to challenge him, and he alone might slay him or lead him captive. And when the minister had persuaded Sayf Ar'ad to agree to this plan, he was sent off to speak with Sa'doun and bring his answer.

The minister went down accordingly to the dungeons where Sa'doun was held, and there found him overwhelmed by his tribulation and grief, ready to drink from the cup of death. Wishing to learn the true nature of his character and feelings, the minister seated himself and began to talk with Sa'doun, speaking of King Sayf, and of his courage and prowess and valor; and at this Sa'doun began to weep, saying: "By God, if that accursed Qamariyya had slain me in his place, I should have been happy indeed." Then the minister knew his love for King Sayf was a true love, and he leaned over and whispered to him that his lord lived still and was engaging Sayf Ar'ad's men in combat. He gave an account of the whole affair, then said he had come to release him so he could come to his king's help. He had persuaded Sayf Ar'ad, he told him, that Sa'doun could be trusted to fight on his behalf. "When you stand before Sayf Ar'ad," he continued, "humble yourself before him and speak softly to him. Tell him you agree to his request to go out and fight against King Sayf Ben Dhi Yazan and slay him; and then, when you are once in the field, do as you see fit, and aid your king in his fight. And when all is done, give him my greeting, and say my peace is upon him."

Then Sa'doun, ready to dance in his joy, said: "I hear and obey, Minister, and may God send you every good thing!"

When Sa'doun rode into the field, in full armor, he placed a veil around his face, wishing to try King Sayf's valor and prowess in the field one more time. Then he charged at him like a fearless lion, and King Sayf met him with a heart stronger than the rock, and a spirit bolder than the surging sea; they locked in mortal combat, and the dust swirled and gathered above their heads. They fell upon each other, then fell back, advanced and retreated, locked and disengaged, sallying out now to the right and now to the left, their horses galloping forward one moment then back the next, the battle raging between them like a blazing fire. And so they continued till the sun began to set.

Then Sa'doun threw down his spear, and came down from his horse, saying: "King of all time, bravest and most gallant of knights, stay your hand; for it is I, Sa'doun, your slave and servant. Forgive me for what I have done. I wished to measure myself with you in battle." And with that he removed the cover from his face.

Then, having no time as yet for talk, they cried out with one voice, "God is great!" and charged forward together against Sayf Ar'ad's men. And when Sayf Ar'ad saw this, he commanded his troops to attack the two knights all together, and the battle raged for three nights and three days, with no respite, for Sayf Ar'ad was resolved to wear them down and take them captive. Then, as the pair felt their strength waning, and were sure of drinking the cup of death, there was a thundering and tumult in the air, and 'Ayrud descended and bore them both up to safety, bearing them first to where Shama sat waiting on the mountain, then flying with them to a mountain outside the city of Hamra' al-Habash; and there Sa'doun was reunited with his men, who had fled there before Qamariyya's assault when Sa'doun was seized by trickery.

Then King Sayf Ben Dhi Yazan, and Sa'doun al-Zinji, with his men, rode against Qamariyya's city, Sa'doun bearing the aspect of red death, his eyes flashing with fire. When Qamariyya heard King Sayf's voice, crying out among the men: "God is great, He conquers and champions, He vanquishes the infidel, and blesses us with victory and triumph!" then, knowing disaster to be near, she resolved once more to employ trickery and deception. Calling out to her men to hold off from combat, she went out to King Sayf, weeping and abasing herself, and saying: "O my son, apple of my eye, I deserve that you should strike me with the keen sword, for I have transgressed against you, and none could blame you if you killed me."

Still she made a show of grief and remorse, till Sayf's heart was softened, and he said: "This was a thing decreed, mother. Praise be to God for bringing it all to good, and blessing me with great treasures from it." Then he told her how he had gained the sword and 'Ayrud's tablet, at which Qamariyya's heart was filled with chagrin and rancor and envy, but she showed none of it. Leading her son and his bride and Sa'doun into the city, she honored them there; while Sayf, having her blessing as he thought, seated himself on his father's throne, and the whole city feasted.

Then, to complete their happiness, 'Ayrud flew off and returned with King Afrah, who was about to have his head struck off by Sayf Ar'ad's executioner at the instigation of Saqardyoun and Saqardis; for these two had pinned the blame for all their misfortune on him and on his refusal, long before, to kill Sayf Ben Dhi Yazan and rid the land of him. And when King Afrah saw Sayf Ben Dhi Yazan and his daughter, and knew who had saved him, he went up to King Sayf and kissed his hands, begging his forgiveness; and Sayf forgave him for the sake of Shama and because this man it was who had reared him from childhood.

Then Sayf, reminding King Afrah that he had brought all that had been asked of him as dowry and wedding gift for Shama, requested that the wedding be held that very night. So the marriage was set for that night, with the city festively adorned; and Qamariyya gave Shama a necklace of glittering jewels, inset with fourteen stones, each with the value of a thousand dinars, and precious garments of pure silk, embroidered with threads of pure gold, and gave each of the dignitaries a splendid suit of clothes, and distributed money to all the servants. She arranged a wedding feast of seven days, in which everyone ate and drank and made merry; then, on the eighth night, the marriage contract having been made, it was time for King Sayf to go in to his bride and consummate the marriage.

As he was making his way to the bridal chamber, his mother approached him, saying: "May God bless you in this marriage, my son, and may you enjoy the bounty of wealth and happiness and offspring."

"My thanks to you, mother," he said. "All this will surely be, according to your blessings and good wishes."

"And yet," she said, "I fear for you, my son, on account of this tablet; for this is the night you will go in to your bride, and you have told me that only the pure may wear it. I fear some mishap may befall you if you wear it when you have union with your bride, as you must, and end the consummation of your marriage."

"You speak truly," he replied. Then she spoke further to him, wishing him ever more happiness and blessings, so that he believed she was truly happy for him and said to himself: "A mother's heart will always grow tender at last."

"Mother," he said, "I wish you to take this tablet and keep it for me till I have gone in to my bride." Then, taking no thought to the perils he was courting, his mind distracted by thoughts of his bride and his love, he unfastened the chain from his wrist, took out the tablet, and gave it to his mother.

Then King Sayf Ben Dhi Yazan, coming in to his bride, found her resplendent in her finery and glowing in her beauty, and he clasped her to him and took her virginity, finding her to be a pearl never before pierced; and at that moment it was, by the will of the Lord of Heaven and Earth, that the two moles came together. Then the pair spent the night in bliss, two impassioned lovers alone together, kissing and embracing and taking pleasure one from the other, before sleeping at last wrapped in one another's arms.

As for the accursed Qamariyya, she took the tablet back with her to her chamber; there, closing her door and seating herself on her bed, she rubbed the tablet with her hand, and 'Ayrud appeared, saying: "Here I am, King of Islam."

"Are you 'Ayrud?" the Queen asked.

"Indeed, my lady," he replied, "I am he."

"I wish you," she said, "to describe to me all the lands of the earth." So he described them all, among them the Valley of the Ghouls and the Valley of the Giants. Then she said: "I wish you to take my son Sayf and cast him into the Valley of the Ghouls; and as for Shama, take her and cast her into the Valley of the Giants. Do this forthwith, and then return to me." And 'Ayrud, unwilling though he was, had no choice but to obey.

So 'Ayrud bore Sayf and Shama up on his shoulders, lying there as they were deep in the sweetest of sleeps, and sped with them through the air; and they woke to find themselves hanging between earth and heaven, the wind whistling in their ears.

"'Ayrud," Sayf said, "where are you taking us, and why are you doing this thing?"

"I am to cast you into the Valley of the Ghouls," 'Ayrud replied, "and Shama into the Valley of the Giants, as your loving mother commanded me. You have only yourself to blame for trusting her and giving my tablet into her keeping."

Then King Sayf wept, saying: "Can you not, 'Ayrud, cast us into the same place together?"

"That I cannot do," he said, "lest the names on my tablet consume me with fire. Nor can you any longer speak to me, for you have taken my tablet lightly and brought me to sorrow, giving me into the keeping of a woman who speaks only falsehood." Then he cast Shama into the Valley of Giants, and, after further flight, cast Sayf into the Valley of Ghouls; and then he returned to Qamariyya.

Shama looked about her, and finding herself alone in the wilderness, with no notion of what was to become of her, she began to walk, tripping and stumbling through the rocky land, weeping and entreating God's help. Then, suddenly, twenty horsemen came riding from the mountains toward her, all exceedingly tall men. And when they saw her, they seized her and took her to their king, who commanded them to take her back and slay her on account of her small stature; for he supposed she was deformed because she had offended their god.

But as Shama was about to be dragged away, the king's daughter entered, saying: "Father, the deity creates both great and small; and since she is small, we can set her to serve the god. That would be better than slaying her." She meant, in this way, to release herself from the burden of service which had been her lot till then. Then, her father having agreed to this, she took Shama to a marble dome and opened it; and Shama went in to find a sheep there, which was their god. And there she remained in that dome, feeding the sheep and cleaning after it, collecting its dung and its urine in special bowls, for they were considered holy and used for various purposes.

And when the king's daughter had assured herself Shama was taking good care of their god, and saw how clean she kept the place, she left her to her own devices, sending her two chickens and some wheat bread each day for food, and having her slave girls gather the dung and urine of the sheep as necessary; and so Shama came to use the place as her own. So things passed with Shama.

7
Ghouls & Giants

As for what happened with King Sayf Ben Dhi Yazan, 'Ayrud cast him into the Valley of the Ghouls where he stayed till morning; and when day broke, lo, he found himself in a land of spacious gardens and spreading plants and meadows, with trees and rivers and fruit, and birds proclaiming the Oneness of the All-Forgiving Sovereign. The fragrances of the land were like heavy musk, and it bore all manner of choicest fruits. He ate from these and drank from the rivers, then began to explore every corner of the place, busying himself with this till the day departed and night drew near.

Then, knowing this to be a valley of ghouls, and fearing to sleep there, he made for a tall tree and climbed to the top of it, placing his trust in Him who created the clotted blood and gave it form; and there he remained till night had passed, now sleeping and now waking, till morning broke once more by the power of the Sovereign God. He rose then and seated himself on a branch of the tree, gazing out at the lands and deserts. And as he gazed, he saw an old man approaching the tree, hideous of countenance, his face round as a shield, his jaws and nose as great as a buffalo's, with fangs jutting out like pincers, and his ears as large as catapults; he had nails like daggers, the hair on his body was like the spines of the porcupine, and his eyes were like slits of red flame. Hideous and evil-smelling he was, his face smouldering with evil.

At this sight, King Sayf invoked God's protection, placing his trust in the All-Hearing and All-Knowing Lord, and sent entreaties to our Lord Abraham, peace be upon him, reciting some of the things he had learned from his writings. Now this creature was one of the ghouls of the valley, who had sniffed King Sayf out while he was in the tree and now came minded to devour him; but when he reached the tree, he stood there beneath it, staring for an hour, perplexed, into

King Sayf's face. Then he left him, returning by the path along which he had come, so that King Sayf praised Almighty God for his departure. But as King Sayf sat there thinking the ghoul was gone for good, lo, after an hour had passed the ghoul returned with a group of his fellows, all of them like him; and advancing steadily till they reached the foot of the tree, they placed themselves all around it, then stood there gazing at King Sayf, gazing at one another from time to time and speaking in a strange tongue no ordinary mortal could comprehend. Then they went on their way.

Again King Sayf praised God, and again his fears subsided. But then they returned a third time with an old woman, her hair white as milk and her body like plucked cotton; she approached that tree where King Sayf sat and gazed at him long and hard, then turned to her people and commanded them, in her tongue, to go their way. Then she sat beneath the tree, while King Sayf remained seated in its topmost branches, watching her till the end of the day; and when she then beckoned to him to come down to her, he replied: "I cannot come down, for any man who goes down to a ghoul perishes, either slain or devoured."

At that the ghoul woman laughed and, speaking to him in the purest Arabic, said: "Come down King Sayf, and have no fear of the ghouls; for I am their head and ruler and will protect you against them. You have a pledge of safety from me and from all the ghouls."

At this King Sayf was reassured. But still he said: "I do not believe that you, a ghoul, would give pledge of safety to a human. It is too much to hope, nor does reason induce a prudent man to place himself in danger."

"Have no fear," she said. "Here I am, sitting and waiting for you."

"I place my trust in God," said King Sayf, "in the Beloved and Mighty Sovereign, Creator of night and day."

"This tree affords you no protection," the old woman said then, "for had I been minded to devour you, I could have commanded the ghouls to stone you till you perished and fell down to them; and then they too would have devoured you, caring nothing whether you were a king among kings or a nameless wretch. Come down now, for night is upon us and you are surely hungry. Were I to leave you and return to my abode, you would no doubt be overcome by sleep and fall from the tree, and those people would devour you."

At that King Sayf climbed down, still fearful of the old woman; and when he had reached the foot of the tree, she began to walk away, instructing him to follow her. He followed her accordingly, till they reached a mountain, which she began to climb up, saying: "Come up and have no fear." So still King Sayf followed her till she came to a cave, and into this she went, saying: "Enter, King Sayf." When he had done so, she asked him to be seated and sat down herself, saying: "Are you hungry?" He told her that he was. "Remain where you are," she said then, and, rising to fetch half a dead deer, invited him to eat from it.

"Indeed, I shall not eat from this," he replied, "nor do I have any appetite for it."

"Will you eat lotus fruit?" she asked.

"Very well," he said. So she went to a lotus tree in the valley and shook it till it cast down its fruit, then gathered it up and brought it to him, for him to eat his fill. Then she herself sat down and ate the meat that was there.

"Mother," he said, "this is a great impurity. Yet I see that you understand human speech. How do you come to know who I am? Where have you come from, and what are these ghouls?"

"My lord," she replied, "the story of these ghouls is a strange one. Their father was a wizard, a man of sense and understanding, and his city was the city of Black Magic; my own father too he was, and king and ruler over this city, and his subjects were all kinsfolk, cousins, and loved ones. But quarrels and high words rose among them, and they wished to lift themselves up above him. So it was that they began to waylay people on the roads and breach the safety of the highways; and when word of this reached him, he seized a group of them, who then rose up against him in a body, minded to slay him. When he saw he had no defense against them, and that they paid him no respect and would not so much as let him live, he removed himself with his wife and his kinsfolk, journeying still till he reached this land; and here he settled, raising buildings to live in, he and his kin. Then it was decreed by the fate from which no slave has escape that his wife should be afflicted with an itch in her private parts, one which would not abate; and one day, our father, in accordance with these same decrees, set up an orchard here, planting all manner of fruit, and his wife would come each day to the orchard and sleep there to assuage her plight.

"One noonday, as she was seated there in the orchard, the affliction flared up in her private parts as it always did, and taking a dried stick, she began to scratch herself. Yet it only gnawed the more, till she was ready almost to kill herself, such affliction was she in. Then she lay down on her back and raised her legs up on to a tree, with the hem of her garment lifted, seeking relief from the coolness of the air. And a breeze blew upon her and she slept, so gaining relief from the itch.

"This became a habit with her, so that she began to come alone every day, with no men permitted there and no one to see her; for when she informed our father of this, he decreed that orchard should be for her use alone, with none but they alone to enter it. And so she continued for some while.

"Now it so happened that a he-wolf entered the orchard and looked on her while she was sleeping, then, approaching her, he joined with her and left his seed in her; she had woken while the wolf was with her, but dared not move for fear the beast should kill her. When the wolf had dismounted from her and gone off, she rose to her feet and concealed her secret; but that night, as she sat preparing food in her house, her affliction flared up from the heat of the fire, and she took a stick of wood from the front part of the fire and scratched her private parts with it, so that the smoke entered into her to lie concealed with the seed of the wolf. At that moment our father came in to her and joined with her; and so the wolf's seed and the smoke and our father's seed all combined, and, by the will of Him who unfolds the earth and raises the heavens, she conceived through them.

"When the time of her pregnancy was completed, she gave birth to two males and one female, of the form that you see, ugly of countenance and evil of smell. When my father saw that, he was minded to kill her; but, being a wizard, he cast the sands so as to uncover the matter, and he saw that the valley was promised to them and would come to bear their name, that their progeny would multiply in it till the valley was filled with them, and that their destruction would be at the hands of a man named Sayf Ben Dhi Yazan, the Himyari Tubba'i Yemeni king. This man would come because, the night he went in to his first wife, having about him a tablet possessing a servant, he would give the tablet to his mother, and she, the moment she took hold of it, would summon this servant and command him to cast her son Sayf into this place; and he it was who would cleanse the valley of ghouls.

"When he saw this, he fashioned a potent spell by which you will be empowered to destroy them, and appointed me as guardian over it. 'You, my daughter,' he said, 'will not die with them, for such is not the will of Almighty God. If this man comes, you must honor him, for God will deliver you from your condition, and your food will become purified at his hands. You will aid him in cleansing the Valley of Ghouls.' Then he fashioned for you this thing by which you will destroy them and told me your name, describing your very form to me. Many years ago it is that my father died, and I have sat waiting for you to this day, when the ghouls came to inform me—for so they have come to me from their earliest days and they obey my commands.

"When they came and saw you in the topmost branches of this tree, they were minded to break it down, then snatch you off it and devour you. But because my father had told me I should find you in its branches, I would sleep beneath it every day; and so it was that, when they caught your scent and were minded to seize you, they could not break the tree because it is my tree. Rather they came to me and told me of a human they had discovered when they were there beneath it. Then, accompanying them back, I saw you and knew you for who you were. 'This is my tree,' I told them, 'and it is not for you to break it; but nor will he, in his fear, come down to you. Leave now, and I shall sit beneath the tree till hunger and thirst conquer him and he climbs down, then take him captive and bring him for you to devour him.' They went their way as I commanded them, and I seated myself here, knowing you to be the one foretold; then I spoke with you, and you accompanied me to this place. So it came to pass, King of all time."

"And what is the spell," King Sayf asked then, "that your father fashioned for me?"

"Rise," she replied, "and ascend this staircase till you reach the top, then gaze to your right. There you will make out a great, flat wilderness with a large, round wood. Have no fear of this wood, but enter it; in it you will find a lofty dome. Keeping your back to the door of the dome, pace out sixty-one steps, then, at the end of that span, dig in the earth as deep as half your own height and descend into the hole. There you will find a round slab of marble with a copper screw, and, when you turn this three times, the slab will be raised up and you will find before you a stairway with the same number of steps as those you first ascended.

Descend these and you will discover, at the bottom, a place like a tomb surrounded by a marble balustrade, with a grave and a coffin within. When you come to the entrance of this compartment, give an account of your lineage; and when the doorway opens to admit you, enter, then twist, once and to the left, the screw you will find by the left side of the grave. At that the entrance to the grave will swing back for you, and you will find the lid of the coffin raised; and, stretching your hand into the coffin, you will find my father reclined there in death. Recite over him some of the writings of Abraham and reach beneath his head with your hand. There you will find a phial made by magic, inscribed with names and charms as thick as clustering ants; and when you take hold of this and open it before my father, you will find in it pieces of gold resembling grains of corn. Place these in your pocket and replace everything as it was, then ascend the stairway and come out, setting the marble slab as it was before and filling the hole you dug up with the earth you took before. Then climb down these stairs you first ascended and return to me here. But beware of going against the things I have told you, as you did when you took Shem's sword and wished to look into his face, with all that followed thereafter. Do exactly as I have instructed you, or you will perish. Be assured, my son, that the counsel I give you is good."

"And what is your name?" King Sayf asked then.

"I am called Ghaylouna," she replied, "because I keep company with the ghouls in this place, and have grown up with them till now."

Then King Sayf rose, and, placing his trust in God, found all those things of which Ghaylouna had spoken to be true. First he came out from the stairs and saw the dome, then he descended, beneath the ground, to the marble slab, which he raised as she had instructed him to do, and so on till he had taken the phial and opened it, looked at the grains of corn, sealed it again and placed it in his pocket. Then he returned to the old woman as he had come and showed her the phial as she had told him to do.

She was delighted when she saw this, saying: "What remains for you to do is to enter by the front of this place, where you will find a spacious area beyond the opening; and there, in the midst of that place, will be a hanging cage whose door, when you approach, you will find to be locked. Give an account of your lineage, and you will find, on the door, a screw of Chinese iron. Turn this twice to the right and the door will open; and inside the cage you will find a rooster standing with its head curled beneath its wing. Then, stretching out your right hand and invoking the name of Almighty God, draw the neck from beneath the wing and return it to its place. Hold on to it still, never ceasing to invoke the name of Almighty God, till the rooster is possessed by the spirit, and, with all its might, gives the call to prayer. The sound will be like the sound of thunder. If it so calls out the first and the second time, have no fear; but beware lest it should call out a third time, for then it will fly away and you will never again capture it, and will lose your life. If you throw him some of these grains, he will silently leave the cage, and will not cry out; and as you see it begin to pick up those grains, seize it without fear, close the door and leave the cage and everything else just as it was before, then return to me. I will tell you then how to proceed further."

"I hear and obey," King Sayf said then; and departing as she had instructed him, he returned with the rooster.

"Mother," he said, "I did everything just as you told me. What am I now to do with this?"

"My son," she replied, "you must take the rooster and go your way. When morning comes all the ghouls will find you out and pursue you, and I shall be among them, for I cannot reveal any of this to them. As they chase after you, pull a feather from the rooster and cast it toward them. The feather will fly from your hand like a lance, flaming and shooting sparks, and wherever it falls among them it will slay whoever sees it; for anyone looking on it will be struck by the fire shooting out from it and swiftly reduced to dust. But though they will flee at this, they will gather again, because they are many; they will never relent, but pursue you still, for as long as that rooster is with you. So cast another feather at them, and another, till you have traversed a distance of three days' walk; then you will pass the frontiers of the Valley of the Ghouls. But when they see you preparing to leave the valley, they will assail you all at once. Then cast the whole rooster at them, and they will all die, every one, at that very hour, with none left save me alone. And after that I shall place my trust in God."

"But why should you dwell alone in this valley," King Sayf Ben Dhi Yazan said then, "when I have become your son, and you have done me this good deed? I shall not leave you or separate myself from you. You shall remain by my side wherever I go, and we shall place our trust in the Wise and Kindly One, who will ease us in all difficult times."

"Will you then accept my company?" she said.

"Indeed I will," he replied, "even if I were to drink the cup of misfortune and affliction for you."

"I shall give you my conditions," she said. "And if you accept them, then I shall go with you."

"Make whatever conditions you will," said King Sayf.

Then she said to him: "If you sleep, I shall guard you, and if you are hungry, I shall feed you, and if you grow weary along the road, I shall bear you. If these conditions seem fitting to you, I shall go with you. If you do not accept them, then go your way as you will."

"Mother," said King Sayf, "what is there here to do me harm, when all your conditions are so much for my good? Blessed be this company and this skill, for it is pure gain with no loss in it. I shall never, by God, forget your good deed, though I should lay down my life for you."

So she agreed to go with him, as God willed and contrived it. Then she said: "We can stay here no longer. Let us go now, placing our trust in the All-Knowing Sovereign." And they departed that very instant, at the hour of midnight.

"You lack the strength to traverse this road," she said. "Come up onto my shoulders." With that she swiftly raised him up onto her shoulders and bore him on like an Arab steed; and so they continued till God brought forth the morning. Then she set him down by a spring beneath a coconut palm and, approaching the tree, broke off a branch laden with ripe nuts, and cracked open some of the nuts for him. "Eat from these now," she said, "and I shall go and find you a deer." Then she sped off like a racing camel toward the open country and, after just a short while, returned with two deer.

"My son," she said, "slay one of them in your own fashion, and leave the other for me; for I know you will not eat from my food."

"Mother," he said, "I need some wood."

"I am at your service," she replied. Then she rose to go and bring him the wood, while King Sayf slaughtered the two deer, and then skinned them both to keep his growing sleepiness at bay. When Ghaylouna returned and saw what he had done, she thought he was minded to eat the two deer himself, and said: "Do you wish me to fetch you more?"

"Mother," he said. "I should wish for some salt from God."

"This land is all salt," she replied. Then she took a piece of rock from the ground and gave it to him, and lo, it was salt.

"Light the fire," he said then.

Ghaylouna did as he instructed her, and when the wood had turned all to embers, set the two deer in among them. Then she wished to speed back to the open country to bring more deer; but finding him disposed to sleep, she said: "Sleep, and I shall prepare the food for you."

So King Sayf slept for an hour, and when he woke to find the meat cooked, he took it out, saying to Ghaylouna: "Come, mother, honor me by eating with me."

"This is your food," she replied, "since you have roasted it and toiled to prepare it. I shall go and fetch more from the wilderness for myself."

"Mother," he said, "I have no appetite for more than half a deer. Sit and eat with me, and if what we have is not sufficient, then you may go and fetch more."

So she approached, and King Sayf, taking hold of a deer, said: "In the name of God, in whom I place my trust"; and Ghaylouna repeated his words. But the two could eat no more than one deer.

"King Sayf," Ghaylouna said then, "it is as though I were sick. It is my custom to eat two deer without roasting them; yet though roast meat is the sweeter food, I could not eat even one. I think the reason for that is that I said as you did before eating."

"Mother," said King Sayf, "Almighty God has names that bring contentment down to the stomach, so that the eater will remain satisfied with food and water."

"You speak truly, King of all time," she replied.

When midmorning had come, with the sun risen over the lands, lo, a cloud of dust rose up, swirling into every corner, and the ghouls approached like the brood of jinns. This was because, on waking, they had gathered as they always did and gone as usual to Ghaylouna's dwelling, where they found neither her nor King Sayf. Then terror had entered their hearts, and going to the opening and finding the rooster gone from the cage, they were overwhelmed with chagrin at their loss. "Ghaylouna has taken the rooster and the human," they said, "and she has quit this place, minded to destroy the Valley of the Ghouls.

We must pursue her, together with that devil. Come, let us speed after them, and crush them with our fangs, then devour them till not a scrap remains." And so they proceeded, following the tracks of Ghaylouna and King Sayf till they came upon them.

Now King Sayf, as we have said, had eaten and then slept and rested; and when he saw the ghouls draw near, he placed his hand on the scabbard of his sword, the sword of King Shem, son of Noah, peace be upon him. But as he unsheathed it and prepared to attack the ghouls, Ghaylouna cried: "What is it you are doing? Where is the profit in plunging into fight with these creatures, who are so many no man can count them?"

"What then is to be done?" asked the king.

"My son," she said, "pluck a feather from the rooster's right wing and cast it at them; and prepare yourself then to see a marvel."

So King Sayf took a feather and cast it at the ghouls; and it sped from his hand like a fiery flame, coming to rest amidst the ghouls. Then flames and sparks shot out from it, slaying such numbers of the creatures as no man could count, like the numbers of the pebbles or grains of sand. When the ghouls saw this, their hearts filled with terror, and they turned on their heels and fled.

King Sayf rejoiced at this, saying to Ghaylouna: "Let us go on, mother, and cross these plains and hills."

"So we shall," she said, "with the blessing of Almighty God, the Exalted Sovereign."

And so they went on, rejoicing in their hearts, still traversing the empty wilderness, till the sun began to take its leave. And then lo, there were the ghouls streaming from every corner and pursuing them from every side, each one like a demon, with a shrieking that made the valleys shake.

"Ghaylouna," they cried, "you took the rooster, accursed traitor, and made this man your accomplice. In vain you will seek a place of safety now, with us pursuing you!"

"Sayf, my son," said Ghaylouna, "cast one of the feathers from the left wing at them, and have trust in the Beloved and All-Forgiving One."

Then King Sayf plucked a feather and cast it at the ghouls, and fiery flames shot out from it, slaying great numbers of them; and when the ghouls saw this they turned in flight, and Ghaylouna and King Sayf went on, with the terror driven from their hearts. And so they walked on till evening.

Then Ghaylouna put him down in a green and fertile place; and lo, once more yet the ghouls streamed toward them from all directions.

"King Sayf," Ghaylouna said, "throw still another feather at them, and every one that the feather touches will straightway perish."

So King Sayf began to pluck the feathers, but alternately, one from the right and one from the left, till the ghouls saw they were perishing, with only a few remaining; and again they sought flight as the tide of war turned against them.

"King Sayf," said Ghaylouna, "I am minded now to leave the valley, so that we may know peace from those ghouls. But first, my son, let us eat something." She plucked out two dry trees for him, saying: "Make a fire while I bring you some rabbits." Then she went over to a hole and, finding it to be full of rabbits, began to draw them out one after the other for King Sayf to slaughter, till he had slaughtered every one. Then Ghaylouna swiftly skinned them, and King Sayf rubbed them with salt, and she set them over the fire till they were cooked.

And so King Sayf and Ghaylouna supped, and he slept, with Ghaylouna watching by his head, till the first third of the night had passed. Then he woke and sat invoking the name of God while Ghaylouna slept by his side, till the day broke and they walked on through the wilderness. And all of a sudden there were the ghouls again, pursuing them.

Then King Sayf said: "There is no strength or power, save in the Almighty and Exalted God."

"Cast a feather at them," said Ghaylouna, "and they will perish."

"The rooster has no feathers remaining," he said, "for I have plucked out every one to cast at the ghouls, and there is now only flesh."

She asked if he had indeed cast them all, and he replied that he had. Then she said: "Cast the rooster itself at them."

"I hear and obey," he said. And with that he cast the rooster at the ghouls, and they all fell slain, with not so much as one remaining.

Then King Sayf marveled at the power of God, the Sovereign Lord. But Ghaylouna said: "Do not marvel at these deeds, King Sayf, for it is decreed that these should be their last days on earth. Let us go on our way and seek our sustenance at the hands of Him who created us."

So on they walked through the pathless wilderness, with no notion of where they were going, knowing only that God would dispose for them according to His will. And whenever Ghaylouna saw King Sayf engage himself in worship and devotion she would do as he did; and if she heard him invoke the name of Almighty God, she would repeat his words, till God changed her state, and a new health became manifest in her, and she no longer ate the flesh of beasts alone. God gave her strength and power: she walked with King Sayf, and if he slept she would guard him, and if he was hungry she would feed him, and if he was thirsty she would give him drink, and if the road grew long, and he weary, she would bear him on her shoulders. So they continued, and we shall have more to say of them in the proper season.

As for Queen Shama, she continued to dwell in the dome, tending the sheep, and began to ask each day for this or that food, because she was with child and had the cravings of all pregnant women; she would say the sheep wished to eat fruit of one kind or another, and they would bring them to her, till her time came and she went into labor. Then, by the grace of Almighty God, who answered her tears and prayers, she bore a son who was like the radiant moon, and had on his cheek a green mole like a disc of ambergris. She made him clothes from her old garments, for she had been given new ones during the time she was tending the sheep; and having dressed her baby, she named him Dummar and devoted herself to nursing him, looking always to God for succor and deliverance.

One night, as she sat nursing her baby, the candle she had lit burned
through, and she fetched another; but the old one she cast out through the
window struck some dry alfa grass, setting it ablaze. There were barrels of oil
beside them, and piles of lumber, and so the fire blazed till it engulfed the
city. The place was in an uproar as people fought the flames, and many places
were destroyed and much devastation wrought. But the dome that housed
the sheep remained untouched.

When they had put out the fire, the king asked his men if they knew of any
who had provoked the anger of the god, causing him to send the flames; and
when none could give him an answer, he rose and went to the dome to ask
the god himself, the sheep, who it was that had aroused his wrath. Now
Shama had that very minute finished removing the dung of the sheep, and in
a fit of weariness, she said: "Will the Lord never deliver me from serving you
and seeing you every day?" And with that she beat the sheep with a stick.

When the king of the giants entered and saw that, he flew into a furious
rage. "Here I set you to serve him," he cried, "and you beat him, daughter of
scoundrels, and burn our city!" Then he ordered that she be taken out and
crucified that very hour.

Now as Shama was being dragged away by the king's men, two figures were
seen approaching from afar; and so the men left Shama for the moment,
waiting to see who it was that was coming, for no strangers had ever entered
their land before, except for Shama herself, and the people feared them. And
when Sayf (for it was he and Ghaylouna who were approaching) saw a woman
being dragged to the cross, he knew in his heart that it was Shama, for he
knew from Ghaylouna that they had entered the Land of the Giants.

He came closer, fearful in his heart, and lo, Shama it was indeed; and
straightway he and Ghaylouna engaged in mortal combat with the king's
men, meting out bitter punishment on their adversaries, King Sayf with his
sword and Ghaylouna with her bare hands as she raised one man aloft and
sent him crashing against another, killing the two together. And so the battle
raged till the day began to fail, and then it happened, by God's decree, that
King Sayf stumbled over the head of a dead man and fell headlong; and
before he could rise, the men had gathered around him and put him in
chains. As for Ghaylouna, now that she was fighting alone she likewise was
seized and put in chains. Then the king said: "Set them in the dome, together
with the woman and her child, and in the morning crucify all three together."

So then King Sayf and Shama were reunited in the dome and recounted to
one another all that had befallen them since 'Ayrud seized them from their
bed; and King Sayf, going to his son, lifted him up in his arms and kissed him,
overjoyed at the sight of him. Then they blocked the door of the dome with
some granite rocks that were kept there, and ate and drank from the nuts and
almonds and sesame and water flavored with rose essence and sugar that were
reserved for the sheep's use; and taking the child with them, they ascended to
the roof of the dome and sat there to wait. When the king's men found the

door blocked next morning, the king was afraid to break down the door, for fear of arousing their god's anger. So they resolved to lay siege to them, believing they would be obliged to surrender once their food and drink were exhausted.

Twenty days the siege continued, till at last King Sayf and Shama and Ghaylouna were exhausted from hunger and thirst. Then they devised a plan: leading the sheep up onto the roof, they called out, threatening to kill the sheep and eat it unless they were provided with food and drink; whereupon the king, in his terror, supplied them with food and drink for ten days, sending them flour and dates and yoghurt and ghee, along with forty chickens and every other thing they asked for, and with water too. And after ten days had passed, the same happened again, and so things continued, with King Sayf still threatening to slaughter and eat the sheep when their food was exhausted unless they were supplied with more, and the king sending them food and drink to keep them from such a course.

After two whole months had passed in this fashion, the king, grown weary and fretful, sought the counsel of his minister, who said: "O King, what you are doing here, feeding your enemies and preserving their lives, cannot be. If they threaten to slay our god, why should that be a cause of terror to you? Our god is able to protect himself and will never let himself be slain by such as these; rather he will send out thunderbolts against them. If they still threaten in this fashion and ask you for food, give them nothing and have no fear of them."

And so it was that when King Sayf next asked for food, the king did as the minister had counseled him. "If you think," he told Sayf, "that you can slay our god, then do your worst. You will see what you receive at his hands. I shall send you no food."

At this King Sayf grew angry. "All you speak is lies," he cried. "This is a mere sheep, to be slaughtered and eaten, and the only true God, worthy of all worship, is the One God, Alone and Almighty!" And with that he slaughtered the sheep, letting its blood flow down the walls of the dome.

When the king of the giants saw this, he was beside himself, shouting to his men to attack the dome, and on they came with their swords in a veritable flood. But King Sayf and Ghaylouna stood at the door of the dome and met them as they came in, Sayf cleaving them with his sword, and Ghaylouna dashing them one against the other, till blood flowed along the ground like rainwater, and both Sayf and Ghaylouna were gravely wounded. And all the while Shama stood behind them with her son, her eyes filled with tears, entreating her Lord for deliverance and succor.

Then, as certain death faced them, a thunderbolt fell blazing from the skies, with fire and sparks and a hail of stones, and there was a clattering and rumbling and smoke and darkness; and a hand took hold of Shama's hand, and a second took hold of King Sayf's, and they were borne up, with their son, so high above the land they could hear the angels praising God in the heavenly spheres. When Ghaylouna saw them vanish in this fashion, she was struck dumb with astonishment, and a hundred swords straightway rained down on her, hacking her to pieces.

As for King Sayf, when he found his wife and himself being borne aloft in this fashion, he looked to see who had raised them and found that it was ʿAqisa. "Where have you been so long, sister?" he said. "And what brings you to me now, in my hour of greatest need?"

"Brother," she said, "when I left you there by King Qamroun's city, when you were vexed with me because I would not reveal more wonders to you, I swore not to concern myself with you further. But then my father came to me and reproached me. 'Is this how you repay King Sayf,' he said, 'after he rescued you from the One-Armed Snatcher, that you do not concern yourself with him, caring nothing for how he fares?' Then he told me how ʿAyrud had acquainted him with your mother's treachery, and how the two of you were now in the Land of the Giants, fighting to save your lives; ʿAyrud himself, he said, was powerless in the matter, for he had authority to do only what the mistress of the tablet commanded. And so I came myself to deliver you."

"May God send you rich reward, sister," said King Sayf. "Yet set us down on this mountain, for Ghaylouna is there striving against the enemy. Bring her to us, before they slay her."

So ʿAqisa set them down and went back, but found Ghaylouna dead, hacked to pieces; and so she gave her burial, then returned to Sayf and Shama and the child.

8
Kings & Magicians

After they had eaten and drunk, they remained resting in that place for three days; and then Sayf asked 'Aqisa to return him to his city of Hamra' al-Habash. But 'Aqisa reminded him that his mother was there. "If she learns of you," she said, "she will have 'Ayrud dispatch you to a still more distant land than the one where you have been. I cannot endure to see you always in this state; I wish to live with my family and friends, without fearing for your safety."

"Take me then," he said, "to a place close to my land, and go your way in peace after."

So she bore them up and flew with them all through the night, till the shining morning broke, and they alighted for rest and food. Then 'Aqisa told Sayf they were in the land of King Abu Taj, who owed allegiance to King Sayf Ar'ad, at a distance of six months from his own land.

"Leave us here then," Sayf told her, "but bring me a keen sword and a stout shield." And he enjoined her to return to him his own sword, the sword of Shem, son of Noah, which was still at that time in Qamariyya's grasp. So 'Aqisa flew off, and came back on the third day with the sword in her hand; and Sayf rejoiced to the depths of his heart, girding himself with his sword and feeling as though he were lord of the whole world, East and West. Then, when he told 'Aqisa to go her way, she would not at first because he was still so far from home; but when Sayf insisted, she told him he would find, a little beyond the mountain before them, a prosperous city in a fertile valley. Then off she flew, and Sayf and his wife and son walked till they came to a cave, where they spent the night.

Next morning, as they walked down the mountainside, they spied a group
of men on horseback being stalked by a huge and fierce lion, which growled
and roared in its fury, baring its teeth and claws; the men, in fear for their
lives, could neither advance nor retreat, for the beast would attack and kill any
who did so. When King Sayf saw this, he supposed the men to be a caravan of
travelers and, leaving Shama in a cave along with her son, went down to
where the lion was and unsheathed his sword so that death crept along its
exquisite blade. Then he stood facing the creature without fear or trepidation;
and though the king of the city and the men, King Abu Taj, cried out to him
to stay back from the lion and not expose himself to perdition, King Sayf paid
no heed, advancing on the lion sword in hand. When the lion saw him draw
near, it crouched and stretched its body for the attack, then leapt forward.
But King Sayf stood his ground and, aiming his sword straight toward the
middle of the lion's head, struck with all his might, cleaving the beast in two.

When Abu Taj saw this, he was seized with admiration for the fearless
warrior and, having his men bring Sayf before him, greeted him, then thanked
him and honored him, inviting him to share his food with him. But King Sayf
said: "I cannot now taste food, O King, for I have a wife and child awaiting
me in a cave, and I can leave them there no longer."

Then King Abu Taj asked him how such a thing could be; and on hearing
Sayf Ben Dhi Yazan's story in all its details, from first to last, he was amazed
and ordered horses. Then he led King Sayf, together with his wife Shama and
their son, with all due ceremony into his city, where he honored them,
assigning special quarters for them, with servants at their disposal, and giving
them all they needed. And the whole city rejoiced that the lion that was the
terror of wayfarers had been slain by this valiant knight.

Now it so happened, of all things, that when King Abu Taj laid eyes on
Shama he was straightway smitten by her beauty, and love for her seized his
heart. Then the devil whispered to him, causing him to imagine she was
lovelier than all the women and slave girls he had, till he could think of
nothing else. And when he discovered she was the daughter of King Afrah, he
brought two splendid sets of garments, one for Sayf and one for Shama, as a
token of his esteem for their rank and standing. Shama's garments were of the
finest silk, glittering with ribbons of red gold, so that when she was revealed
in it, its radiance was added to her own, and her beauty dazzled the eye; and
then Abu Taj felt a fire flaming within him and his passions were roused to
new heights.

He related all this to his minister, who told him: "King of all time, where is
the difficulty here? They are at your court, and you can do as you please."

"I cannot have it said," replied King Abu Taj, "that I treacherously took
my guest's wife after granting him my hospitality. Rather I wish you to go to
her when she is alone, and persuade her to grant me her favors in return for
wealth and finery."

So the minister went to the quarters of King Sayf and Shama, concealing himself there till he saw King Sayf leave to go to the court. Then he went in to Shama, who, when she saw him, angrily commanded him to leave, saying he had no place there in her husband's absence. But before he could explain his mission, King Sayf returned on some business and, finding him there, flew into a fury; whereupon the minister fled, knowing all too well how close he had been to meeting his end. And when he told King Abu Taj how things had passed, the king said: "It will be hard indeed to gain what I seek."

Then the minister gave him fresh counsel, saying: "When the court is assembled tomorrow, summon him into your presence and tell him you wish him to lend you his wife for a month, so you may enjoy her, and that you will return her to him thereafter. If he is abashed at this, and assents, then all well and good; and if he does not, then he will have brought ruin and destruction on his own head."

Next morning, King Abu Taj, having summoned King Sayf, greeted him and bade him seat himself in the most honored place, and then sat and conversed with him. Then, when King Sayf seemed contented and at his ease, Abu Taj made his request, as the minister had counseled him, in the presence of all. And when he heard what it was Abu Taj had to say, King Sayf leapt furiously to his feet and replied to him in terms of sovereign contempt. "Had we not broken bread with you," he said, "and eaten from your food, I should strike your head from your shoulders with this sword of mine." And with that he strode out and went straightway to their quarters, bidding Shama rise that very minute.

But when he had brought their horses and was about to mount and ride out, his eyes blazing in his head like live coals, he found Abu Taj's men swarming around them like locusts. "Either hand your wife over to the king and go free," the minister cried, "or prepare to meet your end." Then King Sayf, taking his stand at the door of their chambers, unsheathed his sword and shook it till death crept along its exquisite blade, and then struck out against them; and he piled their bodies high, slaying every knight who tried to come into the quarters.

At this King Abu Taj commanded that the walls be torn down and Sayf taken captive; and the men accordingly fell on the walls with axes, and hacked them down. But as they were about to close in on King Sayf, he lifted his gaze toward the heavens, entreating his Lord for aid and protection; and that very instant a mighty tumult was heard above, and King Sayf and his wife Shama and their son Dummar were snatched up into the air. 'Aqisa it was again, who had not departed, rather resolving to stay close by and assure herself that her brother and his family were safe. "When I saw your meeting with this King Abu Taj," she said, "I knew from his face that he was a hypocrite, and I was uneasy in my heart."

Then Sayf and Shama gave her their thanks, and praised God they had escaped safely; and 'Aqisa brought them fruits to eat, and afterwards two horses and provisions for the road. Then she set them on a mountain road and flew on her way.

Next morning, as they rode down the mountainside after resting and eating, they were suddenly surrounded by the horses of Abu Taj and his men; for when Abu Taj saw Shama vanish in this fashion, he was driven mad by his passion for her and, seeing her shadow cast against the mountainside, had resolved to pursue them on their way. King Sayf told Shama to conceal herself and her son in a nearby cave and, unsheathing his sword, called out: "God is great! He conquers and gives victory!" Then he leapt into the press of battle, cutting down Abu Taj's knights in twos and threes, and striking their heads from their shoulders, till the day took flight and three hundred of Abu Taj's men lay dead.

So the battle raged, between Sayf and Abu Taj's troops, for days on end, with Sayf victorious at the end of each day, whether dueling knight against knight or facing them ten at a time. And each night he would return to Shama in the cave and take a little rest, eating some of the plants Shama had managed to gather. Then King Abu Taj's troops began to fear combat with this unyielding knight, and Abu Taj himself was at his wit's end, having dueled with him in person and barely escaped with his life. And so he was minded to give the matter up and return. But his minister would not agree to this, pledging to face King Sayf in combat and personally dispatch him. And so, on the fifth day of battle, the minister rode out to meet Sayf on the battleground. And when Sayf saw him, he knew him for the man who had dared go in to Shama in his absence; and he bore down on him, harrying him and hounding him, countering every thrust and parrying every blow till, by day's end, he had quite worn him down. Then he leapt forward with a thunderous cry and struck him across his shoulders with his sword, drawing it out again glistening with his enemy's blood. And the minister fell to the earth, to chew on the bitter morsel of death.

On the sixth day, Abu Taj's knights told their king it was for him to enter combat with the valiant king confronting them; so for the second time Abu Taj rode out to meet Sayf. And as Sayf fought with King Abu Taj, he took care to draw him out onto the plain, removed from his troops, lest, if Sayf should seize him, they rush to his rescue as they had done before. Then, when they were at a good distance from them, he cried resoundingly from his saddle: "God is great, God is great!" And that very moment, as Abu Taj sat astonished and perplexed at these words, King Sayf fell on him and, seizing him by the collar, pulled him from the saddle. Then, as night had fallen, King Sayf bound him hand and foot and rode off with him toward the cave.

When they had reached the cave, Abu Taj begged Shama's forgiveness, pleading his remorse and swearing that, if they would release him alive, he would forswear his old ways and let them depart in peace and safety. And when King Sayf heard him swear by all the things sacred to the people of the Sudan, he believed him and rose to remove his bonds. Then they took one another by the hand and were joined together in good will, sitting down to talk together.

As they were thus conversing, there was a sudden thundering and tumult, and a hand was placed on King Sayf's shoulder. Then he was raised up into the air, where he heard the angels praising God in the heavenly spheres. "Who are you," King Sayf said then, "and where are you taking me?"

"I am 'Ayrud," came the answer, "and I am taking you where your loving mother bade me send you. You it is who are to blame, for you were revealed to her when she found the sword of Shem was gone. Then she summoned me and commanded me to tell her all that had passed with you; nor could I refuse, lest the names on the tablet consume me with fire."

"And where are you taking me?" King Sayf asked again.

"She bade me seize you," 'Ayrud replied, "and cast you into the land of the magicians and the gully of fire."

Then 'Ayrud flew on with King Sayf Ben Dhi Yazan, till he reached the Valley of Magicians, then set him down and flew on his way, disdainful and discontent at the plight Sayf had brought upon himself.

And now King Sayf found himself on a steep mountain, so lofty it almost touched the clouds, made all of granite rock whose edges spread out like the branches of a tree; and there was no pathway leading down from either sides or middle. And as he walked on, invoking the aid of the All-Powerful God, he saw that the mountain was a solid piece of rock on which nothing else lived or grew.

Still he walked on, growing ever more hungry and thirsty. Then he saw, in the center of the mountain, a gully so deep it seemed to have no bottom, with smoke rising from it; and he stood there marveling, gazing down into it till night fell, and the smoke was changed and flames and sparks began to shoot out from it. "God save me from this mountain wilderness," King Sayf thought then, "for from such a place escape will be hard indeed." And with that he began to pray to God for help.

While he was in this plight, he saw an old man approaching the mountain from the plain, tall and broad of shoulder, but dressed in filthy garments, and with long fingernails and teeth, an ugly countenance, and eyes red as embers. The sight of him filled King Sayf with dread, and he crouched behind a crag, praying the man would not see him, and reassured that no paths led up and down the mountain. But still the man approached, till he stood at the very foot of the mountain; then, lo, he murmured a spell and, folding and spreading his form thin, spun upwards till he stood on the mountain top! Then he walked over to the gully and, falling on his knees, began to worship the fire.

So he continued for a full hour; then, raising his head, he looked around and saw King Sayf. He gazed at him for a while, inspecting him closely, then gestured toward him, murmuring spells; and suddenly King Sayf found himself unable to move or talk, as though he had been turned to stone and become a piece of the mountain. Then the magician left King Sayf without a word, descended from the mountain, and disappeared from view.

When the next evening fell, the magician returned with eighty more like him; and as the first man had done the night before, they murmured spells, then spun upwards till they stood on the top of the mountain, then walked to the gully and knelt in adoration before the fire. At that King Sayf feared for himself, lest they slay him or place still heavier enchantment on him. And when midnight had passed, the man who had been there the night before looked up from his devotions and, finding all the others still kneeling, rose and approached King Sayf, who now began to tremble with fear.

Then the magician stood before him, saying: "Welcome, you who have left your own land desolate and brought solace to ours. Welcome, King Sayf Ben Dhi Yazan, vanquisher of infidels and evildoers."

King Sayf was reassured by these words. "Uncle," he said to the magician, "how is it that you know me and know my name? And what, pray, is your name?"

"I am Barnoukh the magician," he replied, "the head of these people. And I am a friend to you. I know you because, as I knelt here tonight, worshipping the fire as I have done all my life, a man of dread appearance, with the most hideous countenance I have ever seen, approached me with a lance of fire in his hand. He told me that all who worship the fire will burn in it at the last, and only the man who worships the All-Forgiving Sovereign will be saved. Then he said that if I did not straightway come to you and deliver you and embrace your religion, he would pierce me with his lance of fire and bring me to perdition. Then he shrieked at me so loud that I woke, finding the others in a trance; and here I now am. Tell me, in the name of God, are you not King Sayf Ben Dhi Yazan, King of Yemen?"

"I am indeed he," Sayf said then. And so, that very hour, Barnoukh became a Muslim at King Sayf's hand, and loosened the spell he had cast on him, bearing him down from the mountain and leaving the other magicians behind, still in their trance. Then Barnoukh brought two horses which they saddled and mounted, and they began to make their way out of the valley and across the plains.

Next morning, as they were continuing on their way, a cloud of dust swirled up into the air, then lifted to reveal the eighty magicians riding in hot pursuit; and the reason for this was that Barnoukh had promised they should offer up King Sayf as a sacrifice to the fire they worshipped. When they had woken from their trance to find both Barnoukh and Sayf gone, then learned that Barnoukh had embraced King Sayf's religion and borne him off with him, they pursued them; and now they engaged with Barnoukh in a war of magic, but could not prevail against him because he was the subtler magician. So then they went to ask help from the king of the land, who promised to send his troops in pursuit of them the following morning.

As for Sayf and Barnoukh, they sat together for rest and fellowship after the day's battle, and Sayf told Barnoukh his story in every detail, from his childhood up to that very moment. Then he questioned Barnoukh as to the origins of the gully of fire, and Barnoukh told him how their city was called the city of al-Ashkhas and had been ruled over by one King Ashkhas, who had a most beautiful daughter. As for the mountain, this had been the home of a king among magicians called Habis al-Wahshi (meaning, the Beast), who had a son strong as a bull to whom he had taught the science of magic and sorcery. When the boy grew up, he asked his father to find a bride for him, and his father sent to ask for the hand of King Ashkhas's daughter; but the king refused, and the magician, enraged at this, resolved to mete out a savage vengeance on him and his people. He told a group of jinn who were at his command to come and dig this gully in the center of the mountain; and they dug accordingly for a whole year, working ceaselessly, day and night. Then he forced them, for all their complaints, to dwell down in its depths, commanding them to breathe out smoke during the daytime and fire during the night. And he resolved to make this his temple, where he would worship the fire, and summoning his people, he instructed them to worship in like manner, telling them they were to make human sacrifice to the great goddess, beginning with the people of the city of Ashkhas, and so seek the goddess's favor and avert her wrath. So they attacked the city under cover of darkness, took its people captive and carried them off to the mountaintop, where they ate and drank, awaiting the appearance of the goddess so as to carry out their sacrifice. But the wine overcame them so that they slept, and King Ashkhas rose while they were in that condition and, approaching the gully, held the ropes that bound him over the flames till they were burned away; and then he freed all his people and led them to safety, leaving their captors sunk in drink.

They left the valley and rode for ten days, till they came upon the city of the magician King Shamsharone, and sought his help; and he gave them eighty magicians to ride back with them and ward off the evil of their adversaries. When they had returned to the city, the magicians fashioned human figures from mud, murmuring spells over them, then struck these figures so their heads fell from their bodies, at which the inhabitants of the mountain fell dead in their turn and the people of Ashkhas were rid of their enemies. And from that day on, the magicians who had come from the city of Shamsharone themselves embraced the worship of the fire on the mountain, coming to the gully from the city to kneel down in adoration. And so it had continued, from generation to generation, up to this very day.

Such was the story Barnoukh related to King Sayf, who was amazed at his words. And still Barnoukh conversed with King Sayf, till the darkness of night was lifted and the morning shone through, and the eighty magicians lined up before them to do combat with Barnoukh. But before any could move, a cloud of dust swirled up in the distance, then lifted to reveal the king of the city with his troops, riding in pursuit of Barnoukh and Sayf. So then Barnoukh confronted the magicians with his magic, while Sayf stood against the king and his troops with his sword, each fighting with skill and valor, meting out grievous punishment on their adversaries, till the day came to a close. Then their strength began to wane, while their enemies thronged

around them with their superior numbers, and Barnoukh and Sayf knew
death was near. Then, all of a sudden, a mighty noise descended upon them
from above, and they were snatched out of the tumult, and heard the angels
praising God in the heavenly spheres.

"Sister," said King Sayf to 'Aqisa (for she it was once more), "who told you
of my plight?"

"It was 'Ayrud, son of the Red King," she replied. "He came to tell me,
and so I came and snatched you up."

At that Barnoukh and Sayf gave 'Aqisa their thanks. Then Sayf asked her to
bear them to the city of Abu Taj, because it was there, with him, that he had
left Shama and his son.

As for Shama, when King Sayf was seized so suddenly from before her, she
sat weeping for herself, and for her husband and child. Then she reflected that
she should conceal the matter from King Abu Taj, since he was enamored of
her and, thinking her helpless and unprotected, might transgress against her
as he had attempted to do before. King Abu Taj had fainted from fear when
'Ayrud came to snatch King Sayf away, having no notion of what was happen-
ing; but when he woke to find Shama alone, he enquired after her husband,
and she told him he had returned to his city with 'Ayrud, so as to fetch his
troops and dwell in friendship with King Abu Taj thereafter, causing the land
to prosper as far as the eye could see.

At this King Abu Taj resolved to treat Shama with honor and grant her his
hospitality, lest Sayf should return with a mighty army and find his wife's
dignity besmirched and her well-being neglected; and so he led her back to
his palace and assigned her the same quarters as before, supplying her with all
she needed. Yet he could not long restrain his desire, and one day entered her
chamber and seated himself there.

"What is your wish?" asked Shama.

"If I were minded to possess you now," he said, "who is here to prevent me?"

"Beware of overweening, O King," she replied, "for the Almighty and
Exalted God it is who will stay your hand."

"Ask Him then to save you," he said, "for this very hour I must possess
you."

With that he leapt on her, meaning to ravish her, and she lifted her eyes to
the heavens, beseeching aid and salvation from God; and that very instant
God struck Abu Taj down, his organs of manhood gone and he bewildered
and filled with terror. Then Shama seated herself and began to pray.

"Are you a sorceress?" the King asked then.

"I am no sorceress," she replied. "Almighty God it is who answered my
prayer."

"I beg you then, Queen Shama," he said, "to ask Him to forgive me and
restore me; and I swear, for my part, that I shall never attempt such deeds
again."

"If your words are true and your intent sincere," she said, "then I shall ask Him." With that she raised her eyes again, asking God to forgive and restore Abu Taj. But no sooner was he whole again than he leapt on her once more; and again she called upon God, and again God answered her prayer, striking King Abu Taj with still greater affliction and pain. Once more Abu Taj begged for mercy and forgiveness, but when he was restored, he attempted yet again to possess her by force. And this time, in answer to Shama's prayer, God afflicted him with a great swelling, so that his whole body became deformed, and his skin peeled and bled, and he was ready to drink from the cup of death.

At this he begged Shama, with a sincere heart, to intercede for him, pledging to embrace the Faith and believe in God if he were restored; and Shama took pity on him, asking God to heal the king if he were truly penitent. Then Abu Taj was restored, and became a Muslim at Shama's hand, in word and heart. But his minister, who was brother to the man who had been slain by King Sayf, saw the light of Islam shining in his face, and his suspicions were roused. He approached Shama, whom he hated, asking her to be allowed to join with her as King Abu Taj had done; and she welcomed him, and invited him too to embrace Islam.

At this the minister decried his king in the court, turning his men against Abu Taj and rousing them to attack him; but he stood his ground valiantly, protecting Queen Shama and her son, and called on God to help him and grant him the victory. But the numbers were heavy against him, and his strength was beginning to wane. Then, as he saw his end approaching, there was a mighty tumult in the heavens, bearing down among them, along with flames and stones; and when they saw this the troops all fled in terror, leaving King Abu Taj and Shama alone. Yet again this was 'Aqisa, who had brought King Sayf and Barnoukh to Abu Taj's palace, and, seeing the fray, had come to their rescue.

Thus King Sayf and Shama were reunited, and they sat with Abu Taj and Barnoukh, each telling his tale, and they all rejoiced. Then 'Aqisa fetched the evil minister back, and when he refused to embrace Islam, King Sayf struck his head from his shoulders. All the people of the city thereupon became Muslims, and King Abu Taj resolved to set sail with King Sayf, and dwell with him, together with all his troops; and so they built eighty great ships and set sail one and all.

During the voyage Barnoukh the magician asked King Sayf's leave to go and strive to put an end to Qamariyya's wickedness, for he had grown bitterly angry on hearing of all the things she had done with Sayf; and King Sayf gave him leave, on condition he did not slay her but delivered her up to him to do with her as he saw fit. Then Barnoukh bade them all farewell and, stepping from the ship into the sea, instantly vanished from sight.

9
Ailments & Remedies

Now it happened that Barnoukh the magician had certain helpers and servants among the jinn, and one of these had raised him up and borne him to a mountain that stood opposite the city of Hamra' al-Habash. Barnoukh now summoned another jinn, saying: "Bring me a sheet of brass and a pen of steel." And when the jinn had brought him these things, Barnoukh told his servants to dig out a cave for him in the mountain, facing the gates of the city, and then depart; and this they did.

Then Barnoukh, entering the cave, took his steel pen and drew a picture of a woman on the sheet, then wrote on it the name "Qamariyya"; and when night fell, he took the sheet, placed it in a cylinder of lead and buried this at the city gate, appointing servants from among the jinn to have control of it, with instructions to torment Qamariyya day and night. Then he returned to the cave and concealed himself there.

When Qamariyya woke next morning, she found herself gravely afflicted, trembling like a leaf on a windy day, her heart beating apace and her head throbbing; one moment she would be blazing with heat, the next as cold as ice, so that she could no longer move or eat or drink. And, learning from 'Ayrud that this was the work of Barnoukh the magician, and that Barnoukh had been dispatched by her son after his escape from the gully of fire, she commanded 'Ayrud to go to her son. "Set him down behind the Qaf mountain," she told him, "and return straightway to me."

With that 'Ayrud sped away like a comet, descending on the king as he was sailing with Abu Taj and Shama; and King Sayf, sensing he was near, said: "Upon my life, 'Ayrud, do not shame me before everyone. I shall descend from the boat, and then you may guide me over the face of the water."

"It shall be as you wish," said 'Ayrud.

With that King Sayf rose, saying: "I am minded to walk on the face of the sea." Then he descended from the boat and walked on till he vanished from sight. But Shama knew in her heart what had happened, though she concealed the truth from all, her eyes filled with tears.

As for Qamariyya, her ailment grew ever worse, so that she felt her end approaching and rubbed the tablet in her desperation. Then 'Ayrud, feeling his body aflame, set Sayf down on an island and sped back to Qamariyya, who instructed him to bring to her the two wizards Saqardyoun and Saqardis.

"This I am powerless to do," said 'Ayrud, "on account of Barnoukh the magician. You must dispatch a special messenger to them."

So Qamariyya summoned one of her men and sent him off to the city of al-Dour, with instructions to call the two wizards to her side. Barnoukh, meanwhile, cast the sands and, learning of all these things, said to himself: "I know the perfect ruse for this." Then he summoned one of his powerful servants among the jinn. "Go to the city of al-Dour," he told him, "and there await the messenger Qamariyya has sent to Sayf Ar'ad's court. Do not allow him to enter the city till I am done with my business." And the jinn detained the messenger according to his instructions.

Then Barnoukh, by some means of enchantment, transformed himself into the exact likeness of the wizard Saqardis the Ill-Fated and walked to the city of al-Hamra'; and there he was received with joy and ceremony by Qamariyya, whose affliction was grown still more bitter. Believing him to be Saqardis, she gave an account of her ailment and told him who was behind it.

"Have no fear," he told her. "Only come with me to the mountain, and I shall reveal to you the cause of your ailment, and you may remove it with your own hand."

Rejoicing greatly at this, she rode out with him to the mountain. And when they had reached it, Barnoukh murmured a spell and, lo, the cylinder containing the enchantment was revealed. Then Qamariyya removed it with her own hands and commanded one of her men to burn it, and her health and well-being were straightway restored. Delighted now, she led Barnoukh back to the palace with her, still believing him to be Saqardis, and there she honored him and showered gifts upon him, supplying him with all his needs. And there he remained, keeping watch over all she did.

As for King Sayf, when 'Ayrud left him on the island, he walked till he came upon an underground cavern; and thinking there must be a treasure there, he went down into it. There he found a fountain of water gushing out from one corner and vanishing into another and, seated beside the water and watching its flow, a man completely naked and four times taller than King Sayf himself.

When the man saw Sayf approach, he was fearful because of his size; but King Sayf reassured him, telling him he was a man as the other was, and believed in Almighty God.

"But you," King Sayf said then, "why do you sit here, stripped of all your clothes in this fashion?"

"If I tell you," the man replied, "I fear you will ruin our livelihood, so that we can no longer carry on our business."

Then King Sayf swore that he intended no kind of harm to him, whereupon the man acquainted him with the cause. "Know, brother," he said, "that this fountain, beginning in the month of March, changes its color, going from white to red to green, and so on through ten colors; and when all this has come to pass, a crayfish with ten colors comes out from it, and here I sit waiting to catch it, then take it home to my land. And when the merchants' ships come to our land, we take the things we need from them in exchange for this crayfish. And so we gain our livelihood year by year."

"And what is the use of this crayfish?" asked King Sayf.

"If someone is blind," the man replied, "even though the blindness has lasted twenty years, let him take a piece of this crayfish, grind it up, mix it with pure, fresh rosewater and place the ointment on his eye, and his blindness will straightway be cured by Almighty God's will."

Then King Sayf resolved to take a piece of it if he could. It so happened that the day he had arrived was the seventh day of March; so he sat there for three days and, lo, the water surged and frothed and foamed, and two crayfish appeared in the midst of it.

"See, dwarfish one," the man cried. "God has sent us two of them. You shall take one and I one."

So King Sayf took one of the crayfish and tied it to the strings of his drawers. Then they rose and went to the shore, where a boat appeared with a boatman who was like the man with the crayfish but still taller. When he saw Sayf, he took fright; but his friend reassured him, and so they entered the boat and sailed off to their land.

When they reached that country, all the people there became fearful at the sight of Sayf, and, for all the assurances of their friend, they said: "Let him depart now his own livelihood is assured, lest he spoil our trade with the merchants; for this crayfish is the only means of livelihood we have." And with that they gave him the boat with its oars, and supplied him with provisions, and sent him off to sail the seas.

Seven days Sayf rowed, and at the end of this time found himself on a great expanse of water called al-Battha' (meaning, the Basin). Without limit it seemed, and its waves surged up as high as mountains and roared like thunder, playing with the boat as the raging wind plays with a leaf, so that Sayf thought his end had come. He could neither eat nor drink nor sleep, as he soared and plummeted with the waves; and so things continued for ten full days.

Then Sayf turned his gaze toward the heavens and began to pray to his Lord; and as he prayed, invoking the name of God, he spied two huge sails on the distant face of the sea. "There is my haven," he thought, and began, with great difficulty, to row toward them. Then, as he drew nearer, he saw they were fins rearing up from the back of a vast fish that lay there in the midst of the sea. When the fish saw the boat, it opened a mouth huge as the gates of a fortress and began to draw the boat down into its belly, so that Sayf found himself swiftly borne into the innards of the fish, with no hope of ever escaping thereafter. In his desperation, he leapt from the boat just in time, at the very moment the fish swallowed it; then, stripping off his clothes till only his drawers remained, and with the sword hanging around his neck, he floated that whole day on the water, still fearful of the fish, till he was cast up at last on some shore.

There he slept for a day and a night; and when he woke he was cold and hungry, weary and half-naked and afraid, and in this condition he walked on, with the crayfish still tied to his drawers. Then, on the third day, he approached a great city, around whose walls, close by the gates, he saw men's heads set in a row on the tips of sharp spears, for all to see. And when King Sayf approached a venerable-looking old man, and asked about these heads, he was told the king of that city had a lovely and exquisite daughter who had been snatched by some jinn and, returning in tears a short time thereafter, had remained weeping for some days, after which she lost her sight. Then her father had promised that anyone able to heal her should marry her and share in all the king's fortune; and men had thronged to the place, greedy for reward and position, yet none could save her; and so, in the fourth year of her ailment, the king had begun to strike the heads from the shoulders of those who failed in their claim to heal her, still promising that the man who did so should marry the princess. And still people flocked there in their greed, till now there were ninety-nine heads hanging at the city gates.

"I have come then to the right place, Uncle," Sayf said then. "I am a skilled physician and, hearing of the king's daughter, am here to heal her and so make my fortune."

"How can it be," the man replied, "that you are a skilled physician come from a distant land, when you are in this miserable state, alone and half-naked? I think you are rather some madman given to fancies. Go your way, lest you become the hundredth head upon the wall."

Then Sayf told him he had been shipwrecked on his way there with his men but had survived; and insisting on being permitted to treat the princess, he was summoned before the king. There, having consented before all the court to the king's conditions—that if he failed to cure her he should lose his head, and if he cured her he should marry her—he was ushered into the splendid palace of the princess. And there, in the center of a great hall gleaming with marble of every color and hung with silks, glowing with crystal lanterns and gold and silver, sat a maiden as lovely as the full moon, wearing garments like the garments of Balqis, with a jeweled crown on her head.

King Sayf asked for a mortar of gold, and the servants brought it to him; and he instructed them to light the fire, and this too they did. Then, seating himself and taking the crayfish, he broke a piece from it with his finger and roasted it over the flame, after which he placed it in the mortar, sprinkled some drops of pure rosewater over it and ground it to a fine powder. Then, approaching the king's daughter, he placed her head upon his knees and dabbed her eyes with the powder. At this she gave a dreadful cry and fell down in a faint, not stirring for a full hour; and when the servant in attendance saw this, he returned to the king to tell him his daughter was dead. Then the king rose and, summoning his men, went to his daughter's palace with his sword in his hand.

When King Sayf saw the maiden fall, he too believed her to be dead and began fearfully to pray to God and recall those he loved. Then, all at once, the maiden woke from her swoon with a start and rubbed her eyes, upon which a thick fluid streamed out from them. Then, opening her eyes and seeing all that was around her, her heart was filled with rejoicing, and, on seeing King Sayf, she cried out: "O, my lord!" and flung herself upon him. Then King Sayf gazed at her in his turn, and lo, it was Princess Nahid, who had prayed God to send Sayf to her naked and hungry after he had saved her from the One-Armed Snatcher. And he had prayed to God to make her blind before bringing her healing at his hands; and Sayf and Nahid rejoiced.

At that moment Nahid's father came in with his men, his sword drawn from its sheath. But when he found his daughter healed, he was filled with joy and lavished gifts and hospitality on King Sayf, welcoming him as his son. Then Nahid was married to Sayf, and the wedding feast continued for ten days; but on the eleventh day, as King Sayf was going in to his bride to consummate the marriage, lo, there was a mighty tumult above his head, and 'Ayrud appeared.

"What is your purpose here, 'Ayrud?" asked King Sayf.

"I am come," replied 'Ayrud, "to restore you to your palace and kingdom."

At this Sayf was overjoyed, unable almost to believe his ears. Then 'Ayrud raised him up onto his shoulders, and Nahid too at King Sayf's bidding, then sped back with them to the city of Hamra' al-Habash.

Now the reason for this was that Barnoukh had sat with Qamariyya after freeing her of her ailment (she still believing him to be Saqardis), and had watched and waited till she had drunk some wine and then, her heart at rest, had lain down to sleep. Then using his magic to render her so sleepy she could neither speak nor answer, he deftly took the tablet from her and departed, summoning 'Ayrud thereafter and instructing him to fetch King Sayf from whichever place he was. And away went 'Ayrud, ready to burst with joy, and found King Sayf with Nahid in the bridal chamber. And so he brought them back, and King Sayf sat on his rightful throne, with Barnoukh at his side.

When Qamariyya woke the next morning, she went to the court to seat herself on her throne—only to find, to her amazement and anguish, that her son was already seated there. Then, seeking the tablet, she found it gone and knew then that Barnoukh was the cause of it all. So once more she resolved to employ trickery, approaching her son with tears streaming down her face, begging his forgiveness for the things she had done.

"Slay me, my son," she cried, "on account of my crimes. None could blame you for it, for I it is who transgressed against you."

Then Barnoukh told Sayf to slay her and be rid of her; and when Sayf said he could not slay his own mother, Barnoukh threatened to depart there and then if he did not at least set her in prison. So then King Sayf had Qamariyya placed in shackles and imprisoned in the dungeons.

So it was that King Sayf sat upon his throne with Barnoukh at his side, to the joy of his subjects who pledged their allegiance every one. And when word of this reached Sa'doun al-Zinji and King Afrah, they joyfully assembled their troops and came to be with King Sayf; and thereafter King Abu Taj too arrived with his ships, with Shama and Dummar in them. And so old friends and loved ones came together again, and King Sayf ruled upon his throne, and happiness and contentment reigned over all.

All this time Qamariyya remained there in her cell, till at last her patience could endure no longer, and she resolved to try deceit and trickery once more. Feigning a grievous sickness, she moaned and tossed and refused all food, till the slave girl set in charge of her began to fear Qamariyya would die and that King Sayf's wrath would fall on her if he was not informed. So she went to him and told him of the matter.

When King Sayf heard this, the color drained from his face; for he was fearful his mother would die while angry with him. So he went to visit her and was deceived by her ruse, weeping tears of remorse over her and kissing her; then, saying nothing of the matter to his friends, he set her at liberty, had her bathed and dressed in finery, then placed her in special quarters close by the palace.

A short time thereafter, a messenger came to tell him the two wizards Saqardyoun and Saqardis were at the gates, and he commanded they be brought before him. The reason for their coming was that Barnoukh, when he had accomplished his designs against Qamariyya by retrieving 'Ayrud's tablet, had sent word to the jinn who had detained Qamariyya's messenger, instructing him to let the messenger go his way. And so the messenger, going to King Sayf Ar'ad, gave him Qamariyya's letter, in which she informed him of the sickness Barnoukh had placed on her and requested him to send her the two wizards. And now here they were accordingly.

When the two wizards were ushered into the court, they found not Qamariyya there but King Sayf Ben Dhi Yazan, with all his men and dignitaries, presiding over the court, and Barnoukh the magician murmuring spells, keeping guard over Sayf and his men. At this they almost fainted with shock, wishing the very earth would open and swallow them. Then Sayf, smiling, said: "Who will now deliver you from my hands?" And he straightway had them seized.

Then Barnoukh said they should be cast in prison, along with Qamariyya. But Sayf said: "I have freed my mother from prison, because she had grown sick and was ready to perish."

At this there was uproar and protest throughout the court. "King Sayf," the men said, "you have a sister who delivers you from all mishap, but we have none. If you are minded still to keep your mother at liberty, after all her scheming and evil deeds, then grant us leave to depart, to assure our own safety." Then King Sayf acceded to their wishes and had Qamariyya set in prison again, together with the two wizards.

There in the prison, Qamariyya told Saqardyoun and Saqardis of what had passed with Barnoukh, and together they hatched a ruse to regain their freedom and destroy Sayf and his men. The wizards gave Qamariyya two herbs from their bags, one green and one yellow; the green one would, if she ate it, induce a fearful sickness in her, causing her body to swell and her face to turn yellow, while the yellow herb was the antidote to this. So Qamariyya swallowed the green one and straightway became grievously sick, shrieking with pain, her joints stiff, her body swollen, and her face a sickly yellow.

Then, as before when she seemed on the point of perishing, the slave girl went fearfully to King Sayf, who had now driven all thoughts of his mother from his mind; and once more King Sayf hastened to see her, filled with remorse and fearing she would depart this world angry with him. When he saw her condition, he wept, again ordering that she should be released and accorded every care; and assigning her quarters of her own, he told no one of the matter.

That night it chanced that King Sayf removed 'Ayrud's tablet, setting it in a box placed between his pillow and the wall, and instructing Nahid to lock the door to the chamber; but Nahid was overcome by slumber, and the two of them slept. Qamariyya meanwhile, having swallowed the yellow herb and been restored to her normal condition, rose during the night and went to her son's chambers, taking care none should see her.

When she reached it, she found the door open and, entering in, found the tablet and joyfully returned with it to her room. Then she summoned 'Ayrud, instructing him first to pluck the two wizards from prison and bear them back to the city of al-Dour, then to return for her son, King Sayf, and bear him to the city of Plato, where he had stolen the cap of invisibility.

"These people," she told 'Ayrud, "are, to my knowledge, filled with hatred for my son on account of his deed, and burn for vengeance against him. When you reach the city, hover over it for a time, crying at the top of your voice and breathing out fiery flames at them, till all the people come out to see what it is you want. Then tell them you have their enemy with you, and that they should stand there with swords and spears thrust upwards to the sky, ready to hack him to pieces when you cast him down to them. Then, when they have prepared themselves accordingly, hurl him down from the heights, onto their swords and spears, so that he reaches the ground in pieces."

"I hear and obey," said 'Ayrud. Then he left her room in bitter tears and, going straightway to Sayf as he slept, leapt on him and bore him up. When Sayf woke to find himself hurtling through the cold air, he asked 'Ayrud what was happening; and 'Ayrud heaped blame and reproach on him for being once more deceived by his mother's wiles, placing his trust in one who was an infidel and had tricked him so many times before. "This time," he told Sayf, "you will not escape." And he told him where he was bearing him, and for what purpose.

Then King Sayf, lamenting bitterly, begged 'Ayrud to find some means of helping him, and prayed to God for aid and succor. "If God inspires you with some scheme to save me," he told 'Ayrud, "then I shall be forever in your debt, but if you can find nothing, then I have no cause to reproach you."

"By God," said 'Ayrud, "I must, O King, devise something to save you, if I can, in this mortal plight of yours." Then, setting Sayf down upon a mountain, he went off and returned with a walnut tree he had plucked up by the roots. He hollowed it out and tore off the branches, then placed Sayf within it and sealed the opening to it with a rock. Then off he went again, returning after an hour, smiling in his joy.

"I have settled matters for you," he said, "and you are delivered." More than this he would not say but, raising the tree with King Sayf inside it, flew on to the city of Plato and hovered over it, thundering and breathing out flames till all the people came running. There he told them exactly as Qamariyya had instructed him; then, as the people stood ready with their spears and swords thrust upwards, awaiting their enemy, 'Ayrud flew a little higher, hurled King Sayf down, and went his way.

And so King Sayf plummeted down, enclosed in the tree, spinning and tumbling through the air, thrown against its sides and against the rock till he was about two spans from the ground. Then something thrust itself beneath the tree, and seized it, and bore it up again before flying off with it. 'Aqisa it was, to whom 'Ayrud had gone with the story of Qamariyya's new treachery, distraught and begging her help; and she, following 'Ayrud to that place, had waited there till he cast Sayf down, then caught him as they had agreed.

When 'Aqisa had reached her palace, she broke the tree open to find King Sayf on the point of perishing, his body stiff as a log of wood, so that she believed him truly dead and gone. Then she began to weep and lament, crying: "Would I had been the one to die, rather than him"; and she sat there grieving.

As for Qamariyya, when 'Ayrud returned to tell her he had done her bidding, she said to herself: "There is an end of him, and good riddance." Next morning the court assembled and all the dignitaries sat in their due places awaiting King Sayf, but he did not appear; and when they found he was missing, they went to his mother, who said: "Ask no questions, but remain where you are. Any who thinks to threaten me will die, for this is my kingdom. Let no man oppose me."

At that King Afrah and Sa'doun al-Zinji hastened to Barnoukh, asking him to cast the sands and see what had happened with King Sayf; and Barnoukh told them to remain where they were and preserve the city against King Sayf's return, pledging to deal himself with Qamariyya.

As for 'Aqisa, she endeavored to revive King Sayf, shaking his limbs till she felt his heart begin to beat. Then she wiped his face and hands with water till the night had passed and she was weary, raising her eyes to the heavens and praying to Almighty God for help. And God straightway answered her prayer, sending a wizard of human kind who came to her riding on a brass casket with wings of brass set on it. Floating down alongside 'Aqisa, he said: "Do not weep, 'Aqisa, for he will be blessed with long life. Here I bring his remedy. Take these three phials, then rub his body with ointment from the first, and place the contents of the second in his mouth and put drops from the third in his ear. And my peace be upon you."

"Who are you pray, good sir?" 'Aqisa asked then.

"Do not ask now," he replied. "You will know in the proper season."

And so he departed, and 'Aqisa went to Sayf, rubbing his body with the ointment from the first phial, and placing drops from the second in his mouth and drops from the third in his ear, so that a copious yellow liquid poured out from it. At that King Sayf's limbs began to stir and the life to flow once more in his veins; then, coming to himself with a start, he said: "God be praised!" and opening his eyes, he found 'Aqisa seated there beside him, weeping and sorrowful. He asked her where he was and what had happened with him; and she told him the whole story, from the moment 'Ayrud had called on her to go and save her brother up to that moment when he himself had opened his eyes there in her palace.

Then Sayf asked her to return him to his city; but this she would not do, insisting he should remain ninety days with her, so she might enjoy his company and attend to his needs; and try as he might, he could not persuade her otherwise. So Sayf agreed then to pass that length of time with her if she would go to Hamra' al-Habash and gather news of his friends and loved ones.

This she did, returning joyful and laughing. "Have no fear," she said. "All is well. Things stand ill with your mother, for God is punishing her for all she has done."

"How is that?" he asked.

"Know," she replied, "that when your friends and your men woke to find you gone, they went to Barnoukh the magician to know what had happened with you. And when he cast the sands and learned of all your mother had done, he was angry, and so were your men. 'Leave me to deal with her,' he said. Then, taking a piece of paper, he wrote down names and charms in black ink, held the paper in his left hand, and murmured incantations over it till it flew from his hand and soared upwards to the top of the palace where Qamariyya was. There it began, little by little, to swell, till at last it became like a black dome over the palace, hanging over its four corners, encircling the palace completely. And so the palace was plunged into pitch darkness, above and below, and Qamariyya, stunned at this, began to imagine every kind of happening and see all manner of things before her. Then, if she stepped outside, she seemed to see jinn in the shapes of eagles and other birds, so that she trembled with fear and returned to crouch in her palace, ready to lose her mind. Knowing this to be Barnoukh's work, she would reach out her hand to the tablet, but always it would be too heavy to move. And Barnoukh himself went to King Afrah, saying: 'Your son-in-law is absent on a certain business. Take his place on the throne, and have his son Dummar seated beside you, so that all may know Sayf Ben Dhi Yazan has a rightful heir. The rest of us will aid you and support you.' With that he mounted a casket of brass and flew off to the treasures of the Greeks, where he took three enchanted phials and brought them here so that I might heal you. Then he returned to his place in the court, informing no one of the matter."

When King Sayf heard all these things, and knew all was well with his family and kingdom, his face shone with joy. "May God reward you, sister," he cried, "for all you have done for me, and for setting my heart at rest." Then he sat with her in her palace, eating and drinking and making merry, till the ninety days agreed on had passed.

10
The Garden of Delights

"'Aqisa," he said then, "the days have passed, and my patience is exhausted. I can stay no longer. Take me back now to my land, and to my wife and mother and children."

"And how can I take you back," she replied, "to her who every hour seeks to harm you?"

"Sister," he said, "do me this service, for I can no longer endure to be parted from them."

"I hear and obey," said 'Aqisa. Then she rose and, lifting him onto her shoulders, soared up with him into the lofty heavens; and as they flew, all of a sudden there was a sweet and lovely fragrance.

"'Aqisa," he said.

"Here I am at your service," she replied.

"What is this fragrance?" he asked.

"Brother," she said, "do not question me on these matters, but let me rather deliver you to your home and abode." Then, when still he insisted, she said: "This is the fragrance of the valley set aside for the enchanted Garden of Delights, fashioned, through their wisdom and secret sciences, by the masters of sorcery and magic. It is called now the Garden of the Wizards, and none may enter it; for the wizards have made it for the use of their daughters, as a place for their recreation, where others may not wander. Should any but the offspring of great kings enter it, the servants bear him off into the wilds and hills and destroy him, causing him to drink the cup of death."

Now 'Aqisa uttered these words to strike fear into King Sayf Ben Dhi Yazan, so that he would enquire no further, and would not ask her to descend into that garden and tarry there. But King Sayf said: "'Aqisa, my sister, I desire to view this garden, to see what plants and trees it has, and what are their flowers and fruits and colors."

"Brother," she replied, "hear my words and do not, in your obstinacy, disregard my advice. You have no need of this. Follow my counsel and cease to insist, and let me rather deliver you to your land. I seek only your good, and I fear harm and evil will befall you."

Then folly tightened its grip on the king, and he said: "I will not listen to advice in this matter, nor will I heed your counsel. I must see this garden and gaze on the beauty of the people of this time. I enjoin you by the inscription on Solomon's ring, and by the great temple presiding over all the jinn; for should I return to my family and people and tell them I passed over the Garden of Delights, they will say: 'Tell us what it is you saw there,' and if I do not describe it, they will mock me. Nor would it be right to invent an account, for falsehood dishonors a man."

"Is it for this," she asked, "that you wish to view it?"

"Indeed, sister," he replied. "And so it must be."

"I hear and obey," she said then; and with that she bore him down to the ground, he being ready to faint from the sweet fragrance.

"Brother," 'Aqisa said then, "permit me, in God's name, to counsel you; for, by God, though caution has no power against destiny, I do not hold you lightly, now that God's pledge stands between the two of us."

"'Aqisa," said King Sayf Ben Dhi Yazan, "of what do you wish to warn me?"

"I must warn you," she replied, "on two accounts. First, there is in this garden a building fashioned and made firm by the secret sciences. Should you encounter it, do not draw near or view it, for so you will find more ample fortune. And do not, in the second place, remain more than two or three hours, for should you stay longer, you will drink the cup of death. Such is my counsel to you. And do not, either, approach the trees, or seek to pick any of the fruits whose fragrance is sweet like allspice, for all this was made by sorcery and enchantment. Be doubly cautious, brother, and do not go against my counsel, lest you destroy yourself. I myself have no power to come to your aid, for the servants would destroy me."

"I hear and obey," said King Sayf.

"Go then with the blessing of Almighty God," she said, "and since neither I nor others can enter, I shall sit here awaiting you, brother, till you have viewed the place and return in safety. Now I have told you. Do not cause me anxiety on your account."

Then King Sayf Ben Dhi Yazan, placing his trust in Almighty God, walked up to the gate of the garden, and he saw that it was open, and fragrances like ambergris issued from it; and when, filled with wonder, he entered, he saw channels and wheels, plants and trellises, the wheels turning of their own accord with none to attend them. The plants of the garden were two of each kind, some identical and some not, such plants as plums, and pomegranates, and apricots, and almonds, and walnuts, and hazelnuts, and peanuts, all of good variety, together with succulent apples, and figs, and firm grapes, and golden quinces, and lemons on the branch, apricots from Hama and Khorasan, narcissus and jasmines, roses and nisreen, myrtle and sweet basil and anemones. He saw, too, birds on the branches praising the Sovereign Lord in all languages with their different tongues and words. The turtle dove would give praise to God, and the sparrow would answer and the lapwing lilt, and then the thrush would warble back in rhyme; all the birds giving praise to God, the All-Forgiving Sovereign, and invoking the name of Him who is One and Almighty, to whom alone all things return. Such a garden it was as has been said:

> O man of resolute will, do not be hesitant,
>   arise and gaze upon the garden's beauty.
> Enter the gate and see the ripening fruits
>   and take enjoyment of their lovely hues,
> While the soft breeze is sporting with the waters
>   and the linnet repeating his melodious tunes,
> And branches are proud of the fruits which they bear
>   and the lovely forms of maidens are swaying.
> Come, gaze upon the roses and the flowers,
>   on the jasmine and on the chrysanthemums.
> Praised be my God, the Painter of all creatures;
>   May the Founder of the universe be exalted.

Then King Sayf Ben Dhi Yazan began to walk round that garden, looking right and left, forward and back, to see the wheels turning, and the fountains spurting, and the birds flying among the branches; and so he continued till he came to the building 'Aqisa had warned him not to approach. As he drew near to it he saw that it was a feast for the eye and a joy for him who sought delight, a thing to bewilder the minds of the knowledgeable, mounted on forty columns of silver, and between each column and its neighbor, a window of yellow brass with frames of red gold. Round about it, within the single platform of brass, half a fathom high and four cubits wide, that circled it from door to door, were many cabinets for storing necessities, all in marble and upholstered with silk furnishings fashioned by magic so that no dust could settle on them, and they could be neither folded nor lifted from the floor; and there were chairs too, inlaid with red gold and studded with gems. Forty chairs there were, each facing a cabinet beneath the platform and having behind it a sign in gold to show that each who had a chair had one of the cabinets also. The sight filled King Sayf with longing and wonder, and when he opened the door of a cabinet, lo, inside it was upholstered, the whole made from yellow brass, and its walls lined with silk. Within was a set of clothing woven from gold and silver thread, its buttons made from gemstones, such a thing as only a king and lord of castles and villages and cities might possess; and the clothing was stored within in a bundle of silk. Then King Sayf opened all the cabinets, finding each to be like the first, and he knew that 'Aqisa had spoken truly, that these garments belonged to the daughters of kings who came to this place borne on the shoulders of the jinn. Wishing to know whether each set of garments had its separate owner or whether all belonged to the one owning the building for the use of whoever might come there, he examined them and found that every set of seven outfits was of the same exact colors.

"To what end is this search?" the king said then. "And who can tell what such people are minded to do? The garments I have seen, but what is the aspect of those that wear them? Surely those possessing such garments are unmatched in this world. I shall not leave this place till they have come, so that I may see them with my own eyes, to know whether they are human or jinn. Yet if 'Aqisa warned me not to approach this building, it was because something here would do me injury." With that he drew back from the building, till he reached a spot with tall and dense foliage, and there he sat watching the building.

Now as he was seated there, some birds came flying from the open country, winging their way toward that garden, and they hovered, then descended till they alighted before him on the roof of the building, then slid down it, flocking together and using small ledges specially contrived for their descent and ascent.

"What a size these birds are," thought King Sayf as he viewed all this. And as he still marveled at the sight, one of the birds descended to the ground and began to look right and left, forward and back. Then, raising its head, it said to its companions: "Come down now, for we are safe here. There is none from outside." When the birds heard this, they all flew down alongside the first, as doves fly down beside doves, following it into the building. Then each bird stood before one of the chairs, undoing the buttons that were beneath their arms; the holes for these buttons were rimmed with gold thread and the buttons were of gold, spread from beneath their arms to the very tips of their wings. Then, when they had finished undoing their buttons, they took off the feather robes and set them down on the chairs, and there were revealed maidens like radiant stars, or like the full moon when it rises. They all of them acted in this fashion, save for one who flew up over the dome and alighted on the ledge, refusing to descend with the other maidens and disport herself with them. The others then took the feather robes from off their bodies and each, opening one of the cabinets in the building, took a silk wrap and enveloped herself within it.

Now set in the midst of the building was a marble fountain, filled with water like bars of silver, over which wheels turned. All the maidens now seated themselves on the edge of this fountain, and began to move their hands and dangle their legs in the water; and all the while King Sayf Ben Dhi Yazan remained concealed in the foliage, watching them and seeing all they did. Then they all went out to the middle of the fountain, their hair spread on the face of the water, and began swimming together, diving and frolicking and laughing, swaying around one other; and so things continued for an hour.

All this time the one maiden had remained on the ledge of the building, disinclined to come down with the others and take off her robes. At last one of the girls raised her head, saying: "Queen Munyat al-Nufus, why have you not come down with us and taken off your garments as we have? If the Queen does not seek to cheer her spirits, what is to become of the attendants in her service?

The wise course, O Queen, would be to descend with us, and take off all your garments, responding to your companions and rejoicing in your youth."

"As for me," the queen replied, "my spirit has been cast down and my breast filled with foreboding since I descended into this garden, for my heart tells me there is a man here."

"What is this you say, O Queen?" said the maiden. "How is a man to come to this place? Had one come the sentry of the place would have destroyed him, for it is set aside for maidens alone, with no place for a man to alight." And still she spoke such words, till at last the queen descended from her ledge and came to stand before her chair, which was the greatest of them all, encrusted with gems and inlaid with red gold. Then she undid her buttons as her companions had done, and like them stripped off all her garments and enveloped herself in a wrap of silk, yellow and red and green. Then she approached the fountain, minded to enter it like her companions; and she was as the poet described it, when he said:

> A beautiful girl stood there with loosened garments
>> and I asked her, "Wherefore have you painted your fingers?"
> She said, "I wiped with them my lips of honey."
>> I said, "That's true enough, but why are your lips so honeyed?"
> She said, "A bee visited them, mistaking them for its hive."
>> I said, "That's true enough, but why does your hair hang loose?"
> She said, "My nurse is coming presently to comb me."
>> I said, "That's true enough, but why are your eyes darkened with kohl?"
> She said, "Some black eyes have been gazing upon us."
>> I said, "That's true enough, but why are your roses withered?"
> She said, "The morning breeze withered them for jealousy."
>> I said, "That's true enough, but why is your neck so slender?"
> She said, "From the weight of the necklaces I wear."
>> I said, "That's true enough, but why are your breasts showing?"
> She said, "From the tightness of the buttons which I use."
>> I said, "That's true enough, but why is your waist so slim and small?"
> She said, "From the weight of my belts and tunics."
>> I said, "That's true enough, but why are your pantaloons so loose?"
> She said, "I tripped over the girdle and it broke."
>> I said, "That's true enough, but why is your pussy wet?"
> She said, "I have my monthlies just like your women do."
>> I said, "You're a fibber, I won't take that excuse!"
> She said, "You've asked about something that's not your property,
>> to me you are a brainless nincompoop.
> How can your sort ever gain one like me
>> without the risk of death and of spilling blood?"
> Alas for me, how can I have any hope
>> of ever gaining possession of such a girl?
> I ask God's pardon for all I say and do,
>> from every misdeed of which I am guilty!
> And may God's blessings rest on the purest of men,
>> Muhammad, who delivered the eloquence of the Quran.

Now as King Sayf gazed on her, he was seized with imaginings, becoming ever more possessed, transported from one state to another. As for Queen Munyat al-Nufus, she went down into the fountain with the maidens and began to disport herself with them, and they with her, all making merry together, with none to keep watch over them. They began to embrace as a lover embraces his beloved, their perfumes wafting out from them, so that the garden was filled with musk and scent. At that King Sayf sensed fire and flame kindling in his loins, and was seized with torment; unable to endure, he was ready almost to lose his mind, afflicted by love's ailment over which no physician has power. "This is a plight indeed into which I am fallen," he thought, "a thing from which I find no refuge or escape. Here I am now, trapped like a bird in the cage; for if I should come out and these maidens see me, it may be they will join together against me and destroy me, and I without power to lay so much as a hand on them. Were they to strive against me, I should lack all strength to withstand them in war and combat, so comely and lovely are they, above all this Munyat al-Nufus, to whom all dreams and hopes return. Were she to seize me, with her right hand or her left, my limbs would lose their vigor. She would consume me, striking me with the cutting swords of her glances, casting arrows into my soul from the bows of her eyes. Such a thing, by God, I never expected to find. In such affliction and tribulation none can aid me save God, the Exalted and Generous One. I shall return to 'Aqisa and recount to her what has passed."

All this while the maidens remained together in the water, mingling in joy and delight, and performing the strangest of deeds; each would spread her two palms for another, to aid her in floating on the face of the water, and they would tumble and turn across one another's hands, and so it continued for a long time, until the sun began to set. Then King Sayf left them, contriving to make a way out of that garden and hasting between hills and mounts to where 'Aqisa stood awaiting him.

When she saw the distress he was in, that he had departed from her sound of body and had returned sick and ailing, she said: "What has passed with you? Tell me what has occurred to afflict you in this fashion." But he had no power to speak, for sorrow had overwhelmed him, and he fell into a fit of anguish, sobbing and sighing and moaning, in such a daze he could utter not a word, his soul ailing and his heart heavy with love.

It was hardship for 'Aqisa to be parted even for an hour from King Sayf, so tenderly did she love him; and seeing him now in this condition, weeping and lamenting and stammering in his speech, she said once more: "What has passed with you?" And when he told her of the things he had seen, she beat her face, saying: "Did I not warn you, brother, on no account to enter the building? Yet you paid no heed. This is a distant hope, hard indeed to attain. To this garden it is that the daughters of kings come to disport themselves, borne there by the jinn, and some have garments fashioned by sorcery, through which they have power to fly. Did you discover the name of her you saw?"

"Her name," he replied, "is Munyat al-Nufus."

When 'Aqisa heard this, she once more beat her face, weeping so that the tears streamed down.

"I weep from love and passion," King Sayf said then. "But for what reason do you weep, daughter of noble lineage?"

"Brother," she said, "it is for the passion that has afflicted you. This is an ailment that has no remedy, for this Munyat al-Nufus you have named has a father called Qasim al-'Abous, who is the ruler of the Diamond Isle, an enchanted island lying at the end of the world, at a distance of thirty-four years from us. He is an obdurate and mighty king, full of malice, with troops more numerous than the pebbles or grains of sand. Over forty realms he rules in that island, each with its cities and fortresses and villages and regions and lesser provinces, not one of them lacking a king of its own, with troops and men and warriors and elephants and wizards and sorcerers. As for his own city, where he himself holds sway, it has a full four million troops, set one and all in readiness for war and combat. They have no wives, nor do they possess crafts or houses of merchandise, nor do they have any kind of work to do; rather they await war and combat, prepared to enter the tumult and tribulation of battle. He has, too, three hundred and sixty wizards, one for each of the days of the year, and each day one of them appears before him. All the kingdoms stand in utmost awe of his might; China and all its followers send him tribute and fear his unrelenting wrath. Sagacious in such weighty matters, he has made for his daughter and her companions enchanted feather robes, as though they were birds, and when a maiden puts one on, she takes on the very likeness of a bird, able to fly whenever she wishes and go anywhere as she desires; for in a single hour of daylight she will traverse the span of a full year's journey. All the world is theirs; the lands with their cities and valleys and plains and seas are like a mere quarter in which they move swiftly from house to house, and the road does not stretch out long before them as it does for the traveler. If such, brother, is the condition of your beloved, how are you to meet with her unless Almighty God, the All-Generous and Exalted One, should will it?"

"For what reason," King Sayf asked then, "did they come and alight in that garden?"

"Brother," she replied, "it is their custom to come every year to that place for recreation and repose. There they dwell for seven days, in prosperity and joy and laughter, eating and drinking wine; and then, when the seven days have passed, they depart in safety. Such is their custom, son of noble lineage. Deliver yourself therefore from the burdens of love and passion, for they will bring you only misery and sickness. I counseled you against the course you took, and you paid no heed, and now this is the affliction and punishment into which you have fallen. The wise course is to let me bear you back safe to your land, where you may comfort yourself with your wives and children, and all your troops may have sight of you."

"Sister," said King Sayf, "I will not, by God, hear such talk from you or any other. I will not listen to the chider's reproof, nor will I turn back from this queen till I have attained my hope with her, and lain in union with her; or else I shall perish beneath the hooves of high-stepping horses, my breath choked from me by the blades of well-tempered swords and the spikes of tapering lances."

"Will you dwell in a land that is not your own," asked 'Aqisa, "and forgo all your family and children and troops?"

"Sister," said Sayf, "I have neither children, nor family, nor kinsfolk, nor friends, nor loved ones. I will heed nothing and brook no question. My beloved I must have, by craft or through war and combat."

"And how will you come to meet her?" asked 'Aqisa.

At that the king wept, the turmoil within him growing ever fiercer. "Sister," he said, "my patience and endurance are at an end and the fire of passion burns in my body. If you have power to help me, then help me; and if you lack such power, sister, then you stand excused and may go about your business. As for me, I shall not move from this place till I have possession of this queen, Munyat al-Nufus, though I were to drink the cup of bitterest death."

When 'Aqisa saw how King Sayf Ben Dhi Yazan was fallen into the net of love and passion, and that wise counsel would be all to no avail, she wept for him, the tears of compassion streaming down her cheeks. "Brother," she said, "I have, by God, no power to come to her country, nor am I able to enter the building where she is."

"'Aqisa, my sister," he replied, "I do not ask you to bear me to her country. There she is in the garden. How could I bear to wait till she flies on her way, leaving me to dwell here after her, ablaze in the scorching fire?" Then he sang out the following words:

O 'Aqīsa, cease to blame me.   My heart is ground down with love,
     my ears complain of the din of words
        and they are intolerable to me.
 I have seen in this place   the sister of celestial nymphs.
     She had my heart drink deep of love
     O 'Aqīsa, what shall I do?   I have seen Munyat al-Nufus,
Her beauty's greater than the sun's,   and I want her to be my bride.
My heart burns in the fire of longing.   My body and my patience are spent.
There's no escape from the spilling of blood
     until I reach the fulfillment of my hope,

for now I have nothing left but tears.

King Sayf Ben Dhi Yazan it was who recited these verses, the tears streaming down his cheeks, while 'Aqisa listened, her heart ready to break with sorrow on his account. And when she knew that he was fallen into the trap from which there was no escape, she said: "By God, brother, if such is your condition, I will come to your aid, striving for you to have possession of this maiden, though my soul should perish and I be torn from all my family and kin. But so that I may know rest and reassurance, recount to me everything that passed. When you entered the garden, did you view them there, or did they come to it after you reached it?"

"Sister," he said, "when first I entered, I viewed the whole garden, and then I went into the building, where I saw the chairs and cushions and furnishings but no living being, human or jinn. Then, seeing the foliage, I sat on the ground in the midst of it, finding its scent sweet. So it was that things began, and before I knew it these birds were descending and all that happened, happened. Then, when my heart grew heavy, I came to you and told you of what had passed. Such is my tale, sister, and peace be upon you."

With that King Sayf wept, the tears streaming down, he being rent by love and passion as the mighty had been before him. Then 'Aqisa said: "The day is at an end. Rise now, so that I may bring you food, then rest your heart with sleep; and after that return to them under cover of darkness, and strive to steal the feather robe. If you are able to take it, place it beneath your clothes, then conceal yourself beneath the water wheel. They will search all through the garden for you, everywhere except that place, for they have acquired the nature of birds, and birds will not venture to approach a thing that spins round. When they have searched for it and do not find you, she will tell them to go and bring her another robe like the first. Then, when they leave her and she remains there alone, reveal yourself to her and show her the robe, saying: 'This is yours.' At that she will rise and hurl herself upon you, and you must run full tilt in your turn, not stopping till you are forty feet beyond the garden. Return then and seize her. I will be with you when you do so and keep hold of her for you."

"And what, sister," said King Sayf Ben Dhi Yazan, "if she should send some of the birds only, keeping the rest in her company?"

"Brother," said 'Aqisa, "that would be your evil fortune. But things will not pass so, because the country is a distant one and only the whole group may journey to it. When you have taken the robe, conceal yourself, as I said, beneath the water wheel. She will not come out before the end of the day, and when she sees that the robe is not on the chair, she will think one of the maidens is playing a prank on her. 'Maidens,' she will say then, 'which of you has taken my enchanted feather robe?' Then they will say: 'By God, O Queen, we have no knowledge of it.' Then she will be filled with anger, crying out at them furiously, saying: 'Woe to you! Search the garden and see who has come here to this place.' They will conduct their search with fear and foreboding, but will not venture near the water wheel. Then, when they have searched the whole garden and failed to find it, they will say to her: 'O Queen, we have not found it, and do not know who has dared take it.' And she will say: 'It may be that its servant has taken it and fled, but I will stay here in this place, which is enchanted as you know, and you I command to go to my country and bring me another robe. But hasten back to me, lest harm befall me from some enemy.' When they see her vexed, they will all rush off, putting on their clothes and departing straightway for their country, leaving her there. And know, brother, that, even traveling with all dispatch, through daylight and darkness, it will take them a full three days to reach their country, and three days more to return in full haste. Know too that she rules over the Island of Maidens and everyone in it, and that her soldiers number a hundred thousand; bold and resolute she is, one of the great and mighty. When you see, brother, that the maidens have departed for their land and she remains alone in the garden, come out as I told you and reveal yourself to her. And if she says: 'Who brought you to this place?' tell her: 'The power of God the Sovereign Lord brought me here.' Then she will say: 'Leave this place.' 'And you,' you shall say then, 'why do you remain here without your people?' She will say: 'On account of something that has been lost.' Say to her: 'No doubt it is this feather robe.' Then, keeping your distance from her, take a single feather from your collar. When she sees this in your possession, she will spring at you, and you must take care to keep yourself from her, running always ahead of her. She will pursue you with the swiftness of the ostrich, and you must take heed she does not catch you while you are there in the garden, for there she will destroy you were you the most accomplished knight on earth, and give you the cup of destruction to drink. Run still ahead of her till you are forty feet beyond the garden, then return to her, as I said. There she will be humbled at your hands, for when you take hold of her braid, she will submit, saying: 'Take pity on your captive.' But pay no heed to her words, drawing her on to me by the ends of her hair, and then I will tell you what you should do. All this is if you succeed in taking hold of her. If you do not, then be patient for a further year."

When Sayf heard these words, he rose and walked on to the gate of the garden, placing his trust in God the Almighty Sovereign. Then he entered beneath the cover of the trees, treading lighter than the dust of the air, till he reached the building where the maidens were. There he found them still as they had been before, within the fountain, tumbling and turning in the water like glittering stars; and there was Munyat al-Nufus amongst them, like the moon amidst the stars.

"Praise be to Him," King Sayf said then, "who created you and gave you form, the One True God, the Eternal and Everlasting." Still the girls were lost in their sport and song, looking like the flowers of the field. Then King Sayf said: "O Compassionate, All-Concealing One, who are Yourself shrouded in mystery, conceal me from all eyes and turn all glances from me, Almighty and All-Forgiving One." And God answered his prayer, hiding him from all eyes by virtue of that which had lain within the knowledge of Almighty God since ancient times, which had been writ by destiny on the brow; and the thing that had been concealed became manifest.

Then King Sayf Ben Dhi Yazan reached out and took the feather robe, placing it within his garments, while the All-Compassionate and All-Concealing One kept him hidden; and he made his way back from the shelter of the trees till he reached the place beneath the wheel, his tongue never ceasing or forgetting all the while to invoke the Lord of Lords who had aided him in seizing that robe. It seemed to him then that he possessed the world and all that was in it. So things passed with King Sayf.

As for Queen Munyat al-Nufus, she left the water, together with all the maidens, and each maiden, going to her chair, began to take her clothes and put them on. Then, when they had done so, they put on their feather robes, all except Munyat al-Nufus. When she did not find her feather robe, she felt the world closing in on her; she no longer knew what was before her, her eyes rolling upward and mind and reason gone. "Woe to you!" she said to the maidens then. "Who, wishing to jest with me, has taken my feather robe? Come, bring it here to me."

"Mistress," they replied, "of what robe do you speak? None of us, by God, left the water before you."

"It is my feather robe I mean," she said. "The one who has done this surely wishes my death. Come, bring it here and put aside this dissembling; for since I came to this place, I have felt my heart hold back and my mind fail me. Some enemy, I think, lies in wait for us in the heart of this garden. If you have not taken the robe, then search this place."

"Mistress," they replied, "this garden is enchanted and none may enter it." But they began to search through the garden, till they had combed every spot and place of concealment, except beneath the wheel, for it creaked as it turned, and the maidens could not endure to draw near it. When she had lost all hope of recovering her robe, she turned to her companions in sport, saying: "I cannot leave this garden except by flight, for the way is too long to pass on foot; and now flight is lost to me. I shall remain here in this place while you strive to traverse the valleys and bring me my other robe from my palace. Make all shift with this, or enemies will overcome me."

"We hear and obey," the maidens replied. And with that they flew off toward their country, leaving Queen Munyat al-Nufus in the garden. Entering the building, she sat there deep in thought; while the king, viewing her solitary state from the shelter of the trees, knew that he had attained all he could ever desire or hope for. Then his face sparkled with light, and he approached the door of the building, full of joy at the course things had taken.

"Why do you remain here in this building?" he asked. "Why have your friends flown off, yet you have not flown with them?"

"Who are you," she replied, "and how have you come into this place? Are you man or jinn? You I believe it was who stole my robe and took away my joy, leaving me in the condition I am."

"It was indeed I," he replied, "who took the robe, to attain my goal and desire from you. Here it is now, comfort of my heart." With that he took a feather from within his garments as a sign that this was indeed the robe; and when she knew he had taken it, the light before her eyes turned to darkness.

"What has drawn you to such a deed," she said, "by which you have cast yourself into the way of destruction and the worst of snares? By God who is great, you are now come to an evil pass." With that Queen Munyat al-Nufus sprang toward Sayf like a lion, pouncing on him like punishment itself, and he ran from before her, making for the gate without once looking back, summoning all his resolve as she threatened to catch him. Once he stumbled over the roots of some tree, almost falling onto his face; but then he steadied himself, and still he raced on, while Munyat al-Nufus, knowing now that her robe was with him, pursued him in her turn till he had gone out of the garden. Still she followed wherever he went, till two miles or so separated King Sayf from the garden, and he had left the whole enchanted land around forty feet behind him. Then, as she bore down on him, he turned back toward her like a lion and pulled her by the ends of her hair, hardly able to believe his good fortune.

Then Munyat al-Nufus felt sure of drinking from the cup of destruction, knowing there was no longer any release or escape from his hands. Then, her distress growing ever stronger, her heart ready to break, she said: "Sir, now that you have attained your goal, take pity on your captive." But he gave her no answer or any speech at all, still holding her by the hair till he had brought her to 'Aqisa, who was there awaiting his arrival.

'Aqisa approached Queen Munyat al-Nufus and greeted her, saying: "Queen of all time, mistress of maidens and women, know that you have attained what none attained before you; for this is the king of the kings of all time, the most accomplished of all knights."

"'Aqisa," Munyat al-Nufus said then, "is it come to this, that you bring humans to our land, permitting them to enter our garden and view our dress and appearance, and that you spur this scoundrel on to take hold of the daughters of kings? Who now, when my father learns of this, will deliver the two of you from his hands? He will surely give you both the cup of destruction to drink, and will lay waste the lands of Qamar and the source of the Nile, destroying all that live there, and sparing none."

"Mistress," said 'Aqisa, "this is no scoundrel, but indeed the highest of kings, who has soldiers and helpers among man and jinn alike, whose hand commands wizards and sorcerers and sages and masters of the secret sciences, commanders and supporters. You alone have no knowledge of him, acting according to the common saying, that he who knows not the falcon roasts him. But I shall tell you now, O Queen, who he is. This is the king of the kings of Yemen, the vanquisher of infidels and evildoers; this is King Sayf, son of King Dhi Yazan, son of King Tubba' the Yemeni, who is matchless among kings, with none to approach his measure. My brother he is by suckling, a valiant hero and indomitable foe. But do not suppose he has taken you captive; rather you have made a captive of him, taking him hostage with your beauty."

"And why," asked Munyat al-Nufus, "has he come to this place, entering the garden never approached by man or jinn. This place is protected by charms and spells, the skilled work of the wizards of other days."

"Know, O Queen," said 'Aqisa, "that, after staying some days at my palace, he asked to be borne to Hamra' al-Habash; and then, as we chanced to pass over this place, he asked me to set him down so that he could relieve himself. I descended with him accordingly, and he, leaving me, went on to look into the building. Then love which humbles the mighty cast him toward you; able to endure no longer, he ventured to steal your robe, and all that happened, happened. This is a thing foreknown by God, the Mighty and All-Powerful, Lord of this world and the hereafter. Do not fret at this, O Queen, for he that possesses you well knows your worth and status, and with him you will be honored above all your followers and dependents."

Still 'Aqisa spoke such honeyed words to her, beguiling her with pleasant smiles, till at last Munyat al-Nufus relented and smiled in her turn, knowing no escape was left to her, that she remained solitary and powerless whatever she might say. "'Aqisa," she said then, "why do we not enter the garden, where we can sit and eat and drink and make merry?"

"I have no power to enter, O Queen," said 'Aqisa. "Rather I shall seat you in a palace better than the garden." With that she set the two of them on her shoulders and sought the lofty heavens, continuing thus till she bore them down over the palace of the One-Armed Snatcher, whom King Sayf Ben Dhi Yazan had slain before, when 'Aqisa sought his aid earlier in this tale. This palace had furnishings of the finest jeweled satin and beds of wood, inlaid with sheets of red gold; and there she seated Queen Munyat al-Nufus on a bed, and King Sayf on another like it, saying: "Converse together while I make arrangements for you to be served."

With that she called out to the servants and attendants of the palace, commanding them to prepare food to bring health to the body. Then they labored to produce pigeons and hudari and quail, slaying the birds and setting them in the pots. Then 'Aqisa asked for drinks, too, and sweetmeats, and served King Sayf and Queen Munyat al-Nufus with fare to smooth away all frowns. And 'Aqisa began to mollify Queen Munyat al-Nufus, saying: "Queen, you are mistress of this place, my brother Sayf Ben Dhi Yazan and myself your mere servants and attendants. Cast off all care now and be happy. Know that all that happens to a person is ordained from ancient times, and that goals are attained only through hazard and endeavor. Had King Sayf Ben Dhi Yazan not been decreed fortune and success by God, he could never have viewed you, never seen your shadow. You, O Queen, have taken possession of his heart and overwhelmed his innermost soul. You are meant only for him and he only for you; for you are endowed with loveliness and worth, splendor and perfection, and he too takes pride in his valor and prowess over heroes, his steadfastness in war and combat, his kingdom and sovereignty over cities, regions and districts, villages, castles and domains."

Still 'Aqisa spoke such words to Queen Munyat al-Nufus, till she ate with the gallant King Sayf Ben Dhi Yazan, and they ranged wide in their converse, the queen laughing and smiling. Then 'Aqisa was happy and, placing their hands one in the other's, she said: "Join hands now, and make your marriage contract according to the creed of Our Master Abraham, the Friend of God." And lawful contract was accordingly made between them.

King Sayf Ben Dhi Yazan, knowing then what he should do, did it to the utmost of his strength, according to the law of those days. 'Aqisa departed from them for a time, then returned with a garment in which she clothed Queen Munyat al-Nufus, so as to make her a bride for King Sayf, and set on her crown and necklace, little as she needed such things; and she became resplendent

beyond the sun and moon, as though the riches of the world had been bestowed
on the poor. Then 'Aqisa, gazing at her, said to herself: "Truly, there is beauty
in humans and jinn, praise be to Him who created all by two, the One True
Sovereign God." For Munyat al-Nufus was as some have described her in the
following verses:

> Over her cheek she has an amber speck
> who stole my mind and robbed me of my patience,
> who sways with a graceful form that rends my heart,
> who pierces my soul with glances like spears.
> Her mouth smiles and her ruby lips display
> a treasure house of perfect diamonds.
> She strikes with the sword which is her eyes
> and pierces spearlike with her beautiful form.
> She makes assault with her exquisite looks
> and assails with the sultan of her loveliness.
> It is as if gardens embellished her cheeks,
> as if the hand of genius illuminated her profile.
> There is no beauty like her face rich with jewels
> or like her crimson lips kissed by sweetness.
> Her face is bright like the full moon in its splendor
> shining from the vault of the star-studded sky.
> From every eyelash she lets slip an arrow
> and from each pupil she wounds us with a dagger.
> If I should die of longing for her face,
> in the way of love it's not accounted sin.
> If she should bargain for the moments of union
> I would purchase them with my soul and treasures.

Then, when they had eaten the food and Munyat al-Nufus had found her
spirits again, 'Aqisa brought the drinks, together with fruit from the bushes
and palm trees, fit to preserve health and be a remedy for the ailing. She
released, too, the vapors of incense and ambergris, and brought dressers for the
hair who adorned Munyat al-Nufus, and jinn singers who sang of the joy of that
day. And all this while King Sayf Ben Dhi Yazan became ever more filled with
passion, his sister entertaining him, till the day fled and night came with the
gloom of darkness. Then 'Aqisa, knowing that their remaining together would
be followed by union, locked the palace with the two of them inside, and said:
"Take your fill now of one another. I shall remain apart from you." Then King
Sayf, feeling himself secure against all evil things, approached his beloved and
sipped from the dark beauty of her lips, then placed his breast against hers, and
his waist upon hers, and his organ of manhood entered deep into her, bringing
her to instant fulfillment. So it was that he took her virginity in delightful
union; so he attained the goal of his hopes, and they embraced one another.
Now King Sayf Ben Dhi Yazan was able to hug and embrace and kiss his
beloved, his misery falling away from him; he found her to be a pearl never

before pierced, a mare never mounted by another. So he passed the night, in embracing and the act of love, and Queen Munyat al-Nufus, by the power of the All-Conquering, All-Generous One, conceived a boy child, of whom there will be much to tell in due season; and he that loves the beauty of the Prophet will call ceaseless blessings on him.

When Queen Munyat al-Nufus rose the next morning and opened the gates of the palace, 'Aqisa came and greeted them, congratulating them and sitting with them. Then King Sayf said: "'Aqisa, my sister, I am resolved to remain here in this palace till all gloom and anxiety have fled from me, and I ask you to take charge of our food and drink as loved ones do for each other."

"You have no need of me, son of noble lineage," she replied, "for the servants of this palace will bring all the food and drink you desire, though you were to stay among them for a thousand years."

Then King Sayf Ben Dhi Yazan remained a while in that palace with Queen Munyat al-Nufus, lost in his love for her, forgetting Hamra' al-Habash, and his kingdom, and his fortune, and all else, till one day Queen Munyat al-Nufus said to him: "My Lord, I have often heard you tell of your soldiers and supporters. What now holds us back from your land, from dwelling with all your troops? By God, my heart is not at ease that we remain here."

"I too," he replied, "long for my family and my land, to have power to bring joy to my friends and vex my enemies." Then, turning to 'Aqisa, who all this time had not left him, he said: "Sister, bear the two of us to Hamra' al-Habash, so that I may see what has passed there."

"Be seated on the bed," 'Aqisa said then, "both you and your wife, so that God's will may be carried out." And when they were so seated, 'Aqisa placed herself beneath the bed and bore it up into the lofty heavens, where they could hear the angels singing God's praises in the starry spheres: "You who believe in the One that made you, invoke His name, He who never forgets you." But when she had heard these things, and soared high, and wished then to descend, a tremor seized her limbs, and she said to her brother King Sayf Ben Dhi Yazan: "Brother, I have no more power to move so much as a step, for I smell the odor of enchantment over a land of great expanse here in this place; and this, I know, is the work of Estokan, a wizard of ancient times and one of the greatest sorcerers. There is no means of warding off its power. I have no strength now to reach your land or remain in this place any longer; rather I must return to the palace where you were, to set you down and stay with you there."

"Sister," he said, "there is no need for you to return. Set us down now in this place."

"There is no land beneath us, brother," she replied, "but only sea. I have no notion, by God, what I should do."

"Seek out an island for us," King Sayf Ben Dhi Yazan said then.

"I hear and obey," she replied. And with that she descended and set them down with the bed; and lo, they were on an island with trees and rivers and birds praising God the Almighty and All-Forgiving One. As King Sayf gazed around him, he saw a coconut tree, each nut having the size of a large watermelon, and so many in number as to suffice for thousands. Any coming to this island and breaking some of them open would find a kind of milk within them, its taste like honey, sufficing for food and drink alike, and with an aroma to drive weariness from the heart; and should any have bread with him, he might dip the bread in the milk and eat. But if a man lacked bread, still he would find, breaking open the nut, that it was like condensed halva, with a taste sweeter than honey, more delightful than almonds and sugar, more fragrant than heavy musk and incense and ambergris; and all this by the power of God who creates and gives form.

Then 'Aqisa said to King Sayf: "Is there anything you have need of?"

"Indeed," he replied, "I wish for some wild beasts or other beasts that can be eaten."

"I hear and obey," she replied. Then, having departed for a while, she returned with a fat wild cow, which the king slew and skinned, taking the meat from off the bone; then, when 'Aqisa had brought some logs, he kindled a fire in that place and roasted the meat, of which he and Munyat al-Nufus ate their fill. After this they found a pool of water, purer than snow and sweeter than honey, and of this they drank.

"Brother," 'Aqisa said then, "what more do you wish of me?"

"And you," he said, "what are you minded to do?"

"My wish," she replied, "is to return now to my country, for I have stayed long with you in the Snatcher's palace, and do not know how things have passed with my family."

"Go, then," said King Sayf, "but return to us in a short while."

After three days 'Aqisa departed accordingly, while the king stayed in that place with Munyat al-Nufus till they had eaten all the meat from the beast they had, then ate for some days from the nuts that were on the island, still remaining there day and night; and then they walked along the seashore till they had left the part with the coconut trees far behind them. Still King Sayf supposed that 'Aqisa would come to him, and he waited accordingly. Then, when she did not come, he said: "If only we had remained where we were before, eating from the coconut trees till God should dispose for us and send us our sustenance."

So they continued till they were two days' distance from the place with the trees. Then Queen Munyat al-Nufus said: "Let me contrive a trap to catch something. Give me your sword, and I shall dig a pit in the ground and lie in wait there. Then, if a deer should chance to pass over me, I shall seize it and strike it."

"Do as you see fit," replied King Sayf.

She was happy at that, and setting her trap as we have mentioned, she lay in wait there till, to her joy, she seized a male deer. Then they gathered wood and roasted the meat and ate their fill, voraciously, to appease their hunger; but as it was a day of scorching heat, with the land blazing around them, their thirst grew intense, till they began to despair of their lives. King Sayf would dip his body in the salt sea, and this parched him still more. Then, when they were sure their end had come, King Sayf began lamenting his state and the state of Queen Munyat al-Nufus, longing to redeem her with his very soul, though he should descend into the grave. Turning right and left, gazing forward and back, he found no stay or support save the Faithful and Everlasting Lord, no friend but the steadfast All-Knowing Sovereign; and, relinquishing all hope of meeting living creature, he lifted his gaze to the heavens and made his supplication to Almighty God. "O Lord," he said, "Mightiest of the mighty, You who have raised this sky and spread this land over the current of the waters, You who taught Adam to name all things, deliver us from the misery of thirst." Then he recited as follows: "Praise be to the most splendid in beauty. Be kind to us, Thou on High, in what you ordain; Everlasting, Eternal One, the Steadfast, the One True God, Sovereign who promises eternity; You who without how and wherefore sit upon the Throne; You who are our pattern for wisdom, the First, the Final, the Manifest All-Mysterious One, Giver of hope and Hope Itself; You who grasp and unfold, Bequeather of the wealth of creation, Living and Eternal; You who are present like no other, beyond all likenesses and images, You who are loving and kind to Your creatures. We are forever bereft of endurance, we are unworthy of Your pardon; You who are All-Worthy, above error, You toward whom all faces bend, You with whose Light the lanterns of eyes are lit. The times have gone stale and we lack all urge to restore them because of a rottenness in ourselves, where misery now dwells. Refuge of the anxious, when there is no refuge save Your Grace, what You know has come to pass, and You are for me the most blessed Refuge from the turmoil within my breast. Answer then my prayer, my Lord, and protect me from the evil of the time and the happenings of this age of mine. Restore to us that in which our happiness lay; and order our affairs anew, for the trouble is great. Blessings now on the Prophet Muhammad, noblest of creatures, at the end and the beginning."

When King Sayf Ben Dhi Yazan had uttered these words, the sea began of a sudden to toss, frothing and foaming, the waves churning one against the other. Then, by the will of God the All-Vanquishing Sovereign, it cleared to reveal ships like piercing meteors heading from all sides for the island, seeking refuge from the raging weather. When they reached the land, they moored their ships, then came down every one onto the island; and when they saw King Sayf there, with his wife Munyat al-Nufus, fear seized them, for they supposed no human could be in such a place.

"Where have you come from," they asked, "and who brought you to this place? Are you human or jinn?"

Then King Sayf, seeing the fear the people had of them, said: "Indeed, I am human as you are. There is no need for such terror."

At that they drew near, walking around him and asking why it was he had come to that place. Then the eldest among them came forward in great haste, and, looking closely at King Sayf, cried out: "My Lord, set aside all anxiety. I am your servant King Abu Taj, and these here are my ships and my men. But what has brought you to this place? What has cast you onto this island where none dwell?"

"I have remained here," said King Sayf, "only to await you. Praise be to God for your safety, for I have longed to see you. And now God has rejoined us with those we love."

"But how did you know, O King," said King Abu Taj, "that I would visit this island where you came to await me?"

"Brother," said King Sayf, "the believer sees with the light of Islam, and his heart guides him in such matters. Should it speak to him of a thing, that thing must needs be true." Thus said King Sayf, but revealed nothing of what had passed with him; and there they sat conversing together. Then King Abu Taj ordered that food be brought from the ships, and the serving boys strode forward accordingly. Abu Taj and King Sayf ate, and Queen Munyat al-Nufus was served with the choicest foods, and they made merry together, praising their Lord for what He had given them. Then King Sayf Ben Dhi Yazan ordered some of the men to take a ship and go from that shore to the part where the coconut trees were; and, making their way there accordingly, they filled the ship with them and returned.

Then King Sayf said to King Abu Taj: "See, O King, here is a strange thing indeed, one to perplex any mind."

"How should that be, O King?" asked King Abu Taj.

"Because," replied King Sayf, "if you take some bread, then break open one of these nuts, you will find a thing like milk within, and you may eat from it with the bread. Yet if you have no bread, still all will be well, for what is inside is like condensed halva. Such is the work of Almighty God."

When Abu Taj heard these words, he became surer yet of the truth of Islam. Then, when they had broken open some of the nuts and eaten from them, they boarded the ships, clearing, on the vessel reserved for King Abu Taj, a place for Queen Munyat al-Nufus; and King Sayf thereafter spent his days with King Abu Taj, and his nights with Queen Munyat al-Nufus. Spreading their sails, they journeyed night and day, with no notion what way to pursue or toward what coast they should head. Day after day King Abu Taj would say to the lookout: "Climb the mast and spy out land for us. It may be we shall find deliverance by the will of the Almighty and All-Merciful One." Then the lookout would mount and descend again, saying: "There is nothing save sea and sky."

Still they sailed on, with Almighty God disposing for them and easing their path in every way; truly He is able to do all He wishes, is all-knowing and merciful to His subjects. Then, as they continued still, the lookout climbed to the top of the mast, and said to King Sayf: "King of all time, I see land and desert drawing near; and I see far off the walls of Hamra' al-Habash."

"By God, captain," King Sayf said then, "if this be true, the reward for good tidings is yours." So they went on till all the ships sailed safe into the harbor, the soldiers filled with joy at these best of tidings, and the kings and troops coming down to congratulate one another. Then the drums were beaten, and the horns blown, the tents were set up on the plains and domains, through the length and breadth of the land; and there they remained for three days, taking their rest from the rigors of the sea.

Then King Sayf Ben Dhi Yazan turned to King Abu Taj, saying: "It is my wish now to mount and ride toward Hamra' al-Habash. Prepare your troops and noble men accordingly, and let none remain on foot."

"I hear and obey," said King Abu Taj. And with that he sent to the city and had horses brought to them, and King Sayf Ben Dhi Yazan mounted along with his troops, while for Queen Munyat al-Nufus they prepared a sheet of wood like a bed and had her ride in it; and so they proceeded toward Hamra' al-Habash, the city of King Sayf Ben Dhi Yazan. There will be more to tell of them in the proper season, and he that loves the beauty of the Prophet will call ceaseless blessings upon him.

Then King Sayf turned to Abu Taj, saying: "Brother, what has happened with my wife Queen Shama, daughter of King Afrah; for I left her with you, then departed and have had no word."

"Know," replied Abu Taj, "that Shama was with me when I reached your city of Hamra' al-Habash with my troops, when you also, O King, were present with us. Then the Lady Shama went up to her quarters, and dwelt there as was her custom, while we remained in your service. Then, when we woke and did not find you, we asked Barnoukh the magician why you had not come to the court, and he replied: 'His mother it is who has prevented him, and we shall surely suffer fearful trial and conflict on her account.'"

He was silent then, saying no more, and King Sayf was reassured in his heart concerning his wife and son. And so they moved on, as we have said.

11
The Great Battle

As for Barnoukh the magician and King Sayf's other men, when King Sayf did not appear and Qamariyya came to seat herself on the throne, Barnoukh, as we told before, threw a spell of darkness around her palace to prevent her from leaving it; and if ever she wished to stretch out her hand to take 'Ayrud's tablet, she would lack all power to do so, finding her arms as stiff as wood. So then she wrote a letter to King Sayf Ar'ad, informing him how she had rid herself of her son and of what Barnoukh the magician had done to her, and begging him to send her wizards to help lift the darkness from her palace. This letter she sent by one of her trusted servants, under cover of night.

When Sayf Ar'ad received it, he turned to the wizards Saqardyoun and Saqardis, instructing them to ride to Qamariyya's aid; whereupon the two wizards told him that if he wished to be sure of victory, he should send, along with them, some of his boldest knights and champions, who could confront the troops of Sa'doun al-Zinji and King Sayf while they dealt with Barnoukh. And they asked for two of the most renowned warriors in all the land, Sabik al-Thalath and Daminhour al-Wahsh. The first of these had been so named for his ability to bend three lances at once, then bend them back again, without snapping them, and the second because he had been reared in the forests and mountains, where he would wrestle with lions and tigers, and eat from the beasts of the wild and drink from the rivers. And Sayf Ar'ad agreed to send for them.

Then his minister counseled him to send also for a warrior named Maymoun al-Hajjam, who was the terror of the land because he would rob caravans and kill all who went to fight him. This man lived in the Forest of Lions, refusing allegiance to any. So tall was he that when he sat, men thought he was standing, and when he walked he walked as high as the tallest tree; and so mighty was he of body that no horse could bear him in combat, and he fought only on elephants.

King Sayf Ar'ad thereupon sent for Sabik al-Thalath and Daminhour al-
Wahsh, who answered his summons forthwith; and he dispatched a letter to
Maymoun al-Hajjam containing a pledge of safe conduct and promises of
wealth and position and the hand of his daughter in marriage if he would rid
him of Sa'doun al-Zinji for good and all. This he sent, together with a
caravan of splendid gifts, by the hand of the two wizards Saqardyoun and
Saqardis, who rode out to the Forest of Lions in fear and trembling; and they
delivered the letter and the gifts to Maymoun al-Hajjam, persuading this
feared and fearless warrior to ride out against Sa'doun al-Zinji on King Sayf
Ar'ad's behalf.

And so Maymoun al-Hajjam returned with the two wizards to King Sayf
Ar'ad's court, where the king had him sit by his side on a chair of Indian ivory,
lavishing great honor and hospitality on him. And it was decided that the two
wizards and the three warriors would ride out, together with Sayf Ar'ad's
troops, to the city of Hamra' al-Habash, where the wizards would confront
Barnoukh the magician while the warriors dealt with Sa'doun al-Zinji.

But as they were eating and drinking in the court, and conversing of the
battle to come, lo, there descended from the ceiling, spinning and clattering
to the ground, a man of hideous countenance, his hair and nails long and his
teeth jutting out, bearing an evil smell and dressed in filthy garments, appear-
ing like the progeny of the jinn.

"Who are you," asked the king, "and what is your business here?"

"I am sent by my people," he replied, "who are magicians and sorcerers
from the mountain of fire and the great gully; eighty of us there are, who
worship the fire. Some time back a man short of stature came among us, and
our intention was to offer him as a sacrifice to our goddess; but our chief
protected him and embraced his religion, then fought against us on his
behalf, so that both escaped. I have come in search of them and have heard
they dwell in your land."

Now the reason for this was strange indeed. When Barnoukh and Sayf had
been snatched up by 'Aqisa, and so delivered from the eighty magicians
together with their king and his troops, these magicians had gone in to their
king next morning to find him slain. Now this king had a son called 'Abd
Lahab (meaning, Servant of the Flame). "Who could have killed my father,"
he said, "except those two who fought against us yesterday?" And he had his
troops go out in search of them, but they found no trace. The true reason for
the king's slaying was that 'Abd Lahab had become enamored of the
minister's daughter, who loved him in return, and had endeavored to arrange
a meeting to satisfy his desire for her; and the minister, learning of this, but
powerless to prevent 'Abd Lahab communicating with his daughter, had
summoned one of his slaves and promised him his daughter's hand in mar-
riage if he would kill the king's son. That night the slave entered the royal
chambers and, finding the king asleep before the fire to which he had been
kneeling in worship, and taking him for 'Abd Lahab, had approached from

behind and dispatched him with his dagger, then returned to inform the minister. At this the minister, greeting him with profuse thanks, bade him sit and called for food; but no sooner had the slave taken his first mouthful than he cried out and fell in death, and his body was cast into the wilderness. Then, next morning, when the king's son discovered his father slain and could find no trace of Sayf and Barnoukh, whom he supposed to be the culprits, he summoned his magicians; and after consultation they resolved to seek out the pair and deal them a grievous death. Thus it was that the messenger had been dispatched to comb the lands for them.

When King Sayf Ar'ad learned the cause of the magician's coming, his face became wreathed in smiles. "Know," he said, "that I too seek this pair. Sayf Ben Dhi Yazan, though, is dead, and Barnoukh is there with Sa'doun al-Zinji. Those we are preparing to vanquish in war."

Then he told the messenger to fetch the rest of the eighty magicians so as to join in the battle. The messenger vanished and was gone for three days; then, on the fourth, he returned with the others, who all came whirling down into the court. The king and his dignitaries, together with the two wizards and the eighty magicians, feasted and made preparation for three further days. Then King Sayf Ar'ad gave each of the three warriors command over four thousand men, and the troops and commanders and magicians, along with the wizards Saqardyoun and Saqardis, set out toward Hamra' al-Habash.

As for Barnoukh the magician and King Afrah and Commander Sa'doun al-Zinji, they were seated in their usual fashion when a cloud of dust swirled up to block the view, then, in less than the space of an hour, cleared to reveal galloping horses and coats of armor and banners and the glitter of helmets and the sharp tips of lances, too many to count, and a flashing that stretched into the distance, the neighing of horses, the beating of drums and the blowing of pipes and horns, the tumult of men and the snorting of she-camels and he-camels, the cries of champions and a procession of phalanxes like the gushing flood, or like a shadow sideways cast; all the ominous signs of armies bent on war and combat. So they advanced still, till they reached the city walls; and there they pitched the tents and fixed the banners and flags, continuing in this way till the smiling day fled and night brought up the armies of darkness. Then they lit their fires and sat in their tents, joyful and full of good cheer, waiting for day to break.

When Barnoukh the magician had closely surveyed these troops, he dispatched a scout to learn more of them; and after a short while the man returned to inform him that the three commanders of King Sayf Ar'ad, King of the Sudan, were there, along with eighty soothsaying sorcerers and the two accursed wizards, Saqardis and his brother Saqardyoun. Then fire blazed from Barnoukh's eyes, and rising straightway to his feet, he entered his chambers and summoned King Afrah and Commander Sa'doun al-Zinji to inform them to whom the troops belonged. "Make ready to meet them," he said, "and to face them in war and combat when morning comes."

Then Sa'doun, filled with rage, cried: "I am minded to go out to them this very hour and deal them evil recompense."

"Stay your hand, valiant one," said Barnoukh, "for the day is fled now, and night draws near. In the morning the matter will lie in God's hands. Leave them tonight to pitch their tents; wait in patience till morning breaks, then do all as you see fit."

"I hear and obey," Sa'doun said then.

So they agreed not to act till the All-Bountiful God brought in the morning, shining on the land with His luminous star. But the accursed Saqardis, rising from his sleep, said to Commander Maymoun: "Champion of all times, my counsel is to ride out this very hour and advance on the city, thrusting with the sword against any who stand in our way, sparing neither young nor old; and then let the engineers be instructed to breach the wall and bring down the outer defenses. Then, when daylight comes, we may enter the city and strike with the keen blade, hacking down slave and freeman, capturing that son of perdition Sa'doun al-Zinji and wreaking destruction on all the debased slaves that are with him."

"That is wise counsel," Saqardyoun said in his turn, "with which no man could find fault; for in this fashion we shall spare the blood of the troops."

"Do as you see fit," replied Maymoun al-Hajjam. "I shall not reject your advice."

Then, mounting their horses, girding themselves with their blades, and taking up their steepling lances, they spread themselves across the length and breadth of the land and advanced like lions of the forest, minded to tear asunder the gates of Hamra' al-Yaman. On toward the walls they rode like flaming torches, till they drew near the city; and there, lo, they saw a broad and teeming sea round about it, surging with waves, and ships moving across its face with sails spread wide, and fishing boats too, so that they were perplexed and dumbfounded at the sight.

"When we came here yesterday," they said one to another, "there was no sea here, but only dry desolate land. Where did this sea come from that we see now, standing between us and the attainment of our hopes?"

"By exalted Saturn," the wizard Saqardis said then, "and by the stars and him who made them, this is the work of Barnoukh the magician. He alone is capable of this, placing such an obstacle between us and the city. What are we now to do?"

"We have eighty magicians with us," replied Saqardyoun, "as well as the two of us. Let us not fret at such deeds. We shall surely attain our goal."

So then they summoned the magicians and, when all were assembled, Saqardis said: "My brother and I will bring this sorcery to nought while you remove the darkness that lies over Qamariyya; or else my brother and I will remove the darkness from her, and you remove this sea and the obstacle it presents."

"We will remove the darkness," they said then, "and you remove this sea." Thus it was agreed, and they departed then, musing on Barnoukh's deeds, and on how, in the space of an hour, he had created a surging sea against them through his secret knowledge.

Returned to their tents, they summoned the commanders. "We are minded to enter our place of divination," they told them, "and are resolved not to come out from it till we have attained our goal, bringing to nought the work of Barnoukh the magician, who created this sea and these boats to hold us back from entering the city. Be watchful, on your part, in keeping yourselves and your men safe, and we shall return to you when we have broken these spells."

"We hear and obey," the commanders said, "and here we stand ready for war from this very hour."

And so the eighty magicians entered their place of divination, remaining there all that day and night; then, on the second day they came out with their enchantment set down on a piece of white paper inscribed with charms and Syriac names and Hebrew writings, and murmured their spells over this till it soared up in the air, rising still till it reached at last to the top of the palace in which Qamariyya lay. Then it spread itself, growing ever larger till it covered the very turrets of the palace, and folding down its edges all around, it descended to the earth; and every spot of the darkness rose to the upper side of the paper, leaving none remaining within the palace. Then the paper itself rose up, so that the darkness wrought by Barnoukh was lifted, and light returned to the palace just as before, and Queen Qamariyya was afflicted no more.

So things passed with the magicians. As for Saqardis and his brother Saqardyoun, they fashioned, through their magic arts, cylinders of lead and copper on which they inscribed names and charms thick as clustering ants; and taking these, they approached the sea that was around the city and set a cylinder in each of the four corners. Then they seated themselves and, as they recited certain incantations known to them, the mouths of the cylinders opened like great chasms, and the water gushed down into them with a roar like a thunder-clap, so that in the space of an hour every last drop was gone as though it had never been; and the boats too entered into the cylinders, to reveal land and sand that became dry desolate plains, and the city walls straightway appeared.

Barnoukh the magician, seeing this, was amazed, saying: "There is no strength or power except in the Exalted and All-Powerful God. In the name of Abraham, the Friend of God, had I known they would remove these hazards, I would have devised others."

Then Commander Sa'doun al-Zinji, seeing how he boiled there with fury, like water in a cauldron set above the fire, said: "Barnoukh, my brother, let magic be now, and let us rather strike the enemy with the keen sword. See how they stand there all around us, and we are no nearer our goal with them. You shall see now the work of your servant Sa'doun, how I shall plague our enemies till they are humbled and dumbfounded!"

Then Commander Sa'doun rose straightway to his feet and hastened furiously to case himself in iron, donning his armor and girding himself with shield and weapons of combat till he became a sight none could match, like a piece hewn from a mountain, or God's judgment when it descends; and forth he went, at the head of his men massed likewise to the right and the left behind him, crying at the top of his voice: "Open the city gates!" Thereupon the men approached the gates and opened them, and came out from the city of Hamra' al-Yaman like raging lions.

Then King Afrah, seeing Commander Sa'doun as he rode, was spurred on to ride out in his turn; and mounting his horse and girding himself in the panoply of war, his soldiers mounted behind him, he raced headlong after Commander Sa'doun, fearful lest he drink the cup of death and suffer at the evil hands of Saqardis and Saqardyoun and the rest of the infidels and heretics; for this Sa'doun was the defender of the armies of Islam and the most valiant champion among them.

The Ethiopian troops, for their part, were like the brimming sea; and when the wizard Saqardis saw the soldiers coming out from Hamra' al-Yaman, seeking war and the press of battle, he ordered them to attack. The men mounted accordingly, and the champions made themselves ready, and then the columns were assembled, with men arraying themselves in their hundreds and thousands, till at last the two armies stood face to face, to the right and to the left, in the center and on the flanks.

The first to ride into the battlefield and invite war and combat was Commander Sa'doun al-Zinji, riding on a slender golden-brown steed taller than other horses. Back and forth he rode, riding straight up on his horse, his head held high, and crying: "Let any who will come now to duel and combat against me. Now is the day the earth trembles; let not the feeble and impotent come forward. He who knows me knows enough, and to him who does not know me I shall make myself known. I am Commander Sa'doun. Come, dogs of Ethiopia and the Sudan, onward to the fury of war, and learn from me what combat is. Come out now, and taste downfall and death at my hands, knight against knight, or ten knights against one, or a hundred against one, or if you will, bear down on me one and all; for I am equal to the whole pack of you, and shall utterly destroy you all and lay your lands waste!" Then, with blessings on Taha the Prophet and Messenger, he recited the following lines:

> If the market of destruction be set up
>   and bodies smart from the point of my spear,
> Let me charge gleefully at champions,
>   my sharp sword cleaving the limbs from the ribs.
> The point of my spear when I brandish it
>   sways to and fro as a serpent sways.
> I have a steed who, kicking up dust,
>   charges with the speed of the lightning flash.
> I wade through seas of death without fear
>   when death is greedy in time of war.
> My name is Sa'doun and the champions know me;
>   I fill the hearts of my enemies with terror.

When Commander Sa'doun had uttered these words, Saqardis, seeing how he bore himself, cried out to the Ethiopian troops: "Woe to you, go out to this base slave who has abandoned the religion of Saturn to follow other faiths!" And straightway a mighty knight sallied out to meet Saʿdoun, all girded with iron and heavy chain mail, and advanced to the center of the field, swaying from side to side as though drunk with wine.

At that Saʿdoun al-Zinji cried out: "Woe to you, son of scoundrels! What evil wretch are you that come to be my first adversary in the combat?"

"Woe to you Saʿdoun!" the knight cried in his turn. "You do not know me, it seems. I am Maymoun al-Hajjam, whose fame spreads far through the hills and highlands. The King of Ethiopia sent for me on your account, to rid him of the threat of you and hasten your journey to the grave; and now here I am, horned demon, come to cleanse Ethiopia and the Sudan of your presence."

"Maymoun," Saʿdoun said, "if, tempted by the Devil, you have come seeking me at Sayf Arʿad's behest, then here I am ready to take you in combat." With that they bore down each on the other, Commander Maymoun on an elephant and Saʿdoun al- Zinji riding his noble steed, careering to and fro and letting out such cries as to make the horses prick up their ears and send a shudder through the body of every knight.

Then Saʿdoun, looking full at Commander Maymoun, said: "You are minded, I know, to protect yourself from my fury with that elephant of yours; for my horse will never consent to wheel round such a beast. Either ride a thoroughbred steed, doing battle with me in the manner of champions, or let the two of us rather fight on foot till the victor is known from the vanquished, and each finds the end to which he is destined."

"Saʿdoun," Maymoun said then, "I have no horse able to bear my weight in combat, to do you justice in the field."

"Cease to bandy words," said Saʿdoun. "If you will not do as I have said, I shall thrust my lance through the elephant's eyes and kill him, so that you fall down from his back; nor will you have cause to blame me. You would be well counseled to come down this instant, and cease to set your mind on foul play, which is the undoing of men."

As the exchange between the two grew ever more prolonged, the wizard Saqardis approached Commander Maymoun, saying: "Battle cannot be done this day, for we must abide by the rules of combat."

"Of what are you speaking?" Maymoun asked.

"We must take our rest for three days," replied Saqardis, "before engaging our foes. Then, after that, you shall exchange messages in the manner of noble rulers, and war and combat will go on thereafter with spear and sword." And so Commander Maymoun withdrew from his confrontation with Commander Saʿdoun, without attaining the goal he desired.

When they returned to their tents, they summoned the eighty magicians; and when all were assembled, the wizards said: "We have done our part. Now it remains for the troops and commanders to engage in arms."

"I went out into the field today," Commander Maymoun said then, "minded to engage in combat, but Saʿdoun al-Zinji stayed me on a pretext. 'It cannot be,' he said, 'that I should fight against you riding on your elephant. We shall fight only mounted on thoroughbred steeds.'"

"Commander Maymoun," said Saqardis, "how can such a thing be as that you have done today? It is the custom of warfare that soldiers go out and acquaint themselves with one another. It is not worthy of you to go into the field, the first day, to do combat with Sa'doun al-Zinji, nor does it strike fear in your enemies. The wiser course is to stay your hand for a day, and so you will be acquitted of all rebuke."

"My goal," Maymoun said then, "is to accomplish our business and fulfill the needs of King Sayf Ar'ad; and I care nothing how it is done."

"Every man among us wishes for these things," said Saqardis. "But if you were to go out into the field and slay him or take him captive, then the soldiers would say: 'We too, with our own hands, could have slain Sa'doun and given him the cup of death to drink.' And then, Commander Maymoun, you would have nothing of which to boast. But if the knights were to go out into the field and fail to match Sa'doun in combat, bearing witness to their own impotence and downfall at his hands; and if you then rode out into battle and he chanced to defeat you, you would not be vanquished, for he would be known for a mighty knight; and if you chanced to defeat him and take him captive, you would gain thereby great glory over all."

"The wizard speaks truly," the commanders Daminhour al-Wahsh and Sabik al-Thalath said then; and on this note they slept. When the next day came the masters of war bestirred themselves to battle, and the first to challenge to combat was Commander Sa'doun al-Zinji. Out he rode for the fray, holding his head up high. "Men of Ethiopia," he cried, "and sons of the Sudan, come into the field if you proclaim yourselves valiant knights!"

No sooner had he spoken than a knight of the Sudan rode out like a demon to meet him, closing on Sa'doun and thrusting his spear at him without further ceremony; but Commander Sa'doun parried the blow, and now each closed in on the other, coursing far and wide. The knight's name was Abu Sinan, and a champion he was indeed, but Commander Sa'doun gave him no respite; he harassed him and pressed him and closed all paths of escape to him, then struck him across the shoulder with his sword and drew it out again glistening with his blood.

When the wizard Saqardis saw this, he cried out to Commander Sa'doun: "May your fingers lose their power and your limbs be rent asunder!" But Sa'doun paid him no heed, still coursing to and fro.

Then the slain man's brother rode out into the field. "Prepare to meet your end, slave of perdition," he said. "I it is, and no other, who will slay you today." But Commander Sa'doun, disdaining to reply, fell on him with his sword and dealt him a blow that struck his head from his shoulders. Then a third man rode out to meet him, and him too he dispatched in the twinkling of an eye, piercing him through with his lance and leaving him writhing on the ground. Then a fourth he sent by the same path, and a fifth, and a sixth; and still he went on, slaying all who rode into the field to confront him, till, when the day departed, ninety men of the Sudan had perished at his hands and he had taken twenty-two captive.

Then the drums of disengagement were beaten, and all combat ceased; and Commander Sa'doun returned to the assembled horsemen. Then King Afrah and Barnoukh the magician came to meet him, saying: "A man of your stamp, Commander Sa'doun, gladdens the heart." And his men, seeing him to be like the purple anemone from the blood of knights, took his soiled coat of armor from him and dressed again in a clean one.

"By God," King Afrah said then, "you have satisfied the heart's desire with your deeds, and won the approval of the Glorious Sovereign." When they had taken some food, Sa'doun was minded to take his place on guard, but King Afrah said: "That is not fitting; since you engaged in combat alone, the duty of watching falls to me."

Then Barnoukh the magician placed a cap on Commander Sa'doun's head, saying: "Wear this at all times, and you shall never be wounded, nor taken prisoner, nor brought low."

"I have placed my trust," said Sa'doun, "in Him who is Invisible to the eye, in Almighty God whom no mortal man can conceive." And with that they slept, filled with joy and praising God.

When the men of the Sudan returned, Saqardyoun came forward with Saqardis, both of them ready to choke with fury, their hearts bursting and their souls full of sorrow. "Do you see, Commander," they said, "what Sa'doun al-Zinji has done?"

"Saqardis," replied Maymoun, "I was minded to rid you of him the moment I rode out, and you it was who held me back. Now, in the name of the house of 'Asatin, I swear I shall enter no combat with Sa'doun till he has first slain all the men of Ethiopia and Sudan; and then I shall fight him alone, thrusting my Yemeni sword deep in his body. You told me, Saqardis, that his was the greater shame, and so I stayed my hand to spare you any disgrace; and now he has utterly destroyed King Sayf Ar'ad's men before your very eyes. All this has come about through your meddling."

"If the war continues so," said the magicians, "we shall come to lack troops and champions."

"Commander Maymoun," said Saqardis, "in the name of Saturn, I swear I held you back only out of consideration and good counsel, because you are a man of rank, and it is not fitting you should initiate war and combat."

"Your reasons are wise," the troops and the wizards said then, "and no man can find fault with them." And on that note they slept.

As for Commander Sa'doun and his friends, when they had returned and settled themselves in their places, they began to exchange counsel and strategy. "Commander Sa'doun," said the princes, "we it is who should go out to meet them tomorrow morning and take our satisfaction from these scoundrels. This day you have satisfied the heart's desire and won the pleasure of the All-Glorious Sovereign; tomorrow you shall rest, and we shall assume the duty of combat."

"In the name of Islam," said Commander Sa'doun, "I swear none of you shall go out into the field till the hooves of the horses have thundered over my head, and my last breath is drawn, and I dwell in my grave."

"You are our protector," they said then, "and the commander of our army. If such a thing were to befall—may God avert it!—we should be like sheep without a shepherd, and our enemies would strike out at us like serpents."

"Nothing but good can come of this," rejoined Sa'doun, "if such be God's will. If they duel with us on fair and proper terms, then I am equal to them. But I have seen among them a knight called Maymoun, whose like no eye ever beheld. I pray to God he might become one of our party and embrace the religion of Islam; and I say that tomorrow he will ride out into the field so that the victor may be known from the vanquished. If they should mass against us with their armies, then all of you charge forward behind me, and God will champion whomsoever he wishes." And so they slept, till God brought the morning.

Then the warriors set themselves astride their saddles, and Commander Sa'doun mounted his horse, and his men arrayed themselves for warfare. And all the champions of Islam mounted, with King Afrah at their forefront, cased in their armor and bearing their lances aloft, placing themselves and their lives at the service of the All-Vanquishing Sovereign.

And when Saqardyoun saw the champions of Islam riding out to do battle, he began to reproach the Ethiopian troops for their failure the day before. "Woe to you," he cried. "What will you say to King Sayf Ar'ad if we are powerless to vanquish such a paltry band as this? I swear, in the name of Saturn, if you do not fight to good purpose today, I shall send to King Sayf Ar'ad to tell him you have no stomach to fight the enemy and are feeble in this battle."

"Wizard of all time," they replied, "do not admonish us in this fashion. Know that this Sa'doun al-Zinji is more than our equal, many times over. He has brought death to our troops and utterly destroyed our champions. But for him those men would never have stood firm before us, or borne our advance. You it is who stayed Commander Maymoun when he was minded to ride out and meet him, though no other man could withstand him. Let him ride out to meet him now, and tear the heart out from between his ribs. If Sa'doun should perish, then all combat thereafter would be easy. You could command us to attack, and we would charge at them all together, hacking into them with the keen sword till no trace of them remained. But while Sa'doun al-Zinji is still of their number, they will care nothing whether we assail them."

"In the name of Saturn," said Saqardis, "every word you speak is the truth." Then he turned to Commander Maymoun, saying: "Knight of all time, the moment has come. Our need is for you to enter the field to kill this devil's offspring Sa'doun, and make him taste the cup of shame at your hand."

"Are you raving, wizard," said Maymoun al-Hajjam, "or are you bewitched, that you speak of him in this fashion? What is the measure of this Sa'doun that he should stand against me in the field, matching me in war and combat? A mere base wretch he is, and if I ride out to meet him, I shall give him the cup of perdition to drink."

"First among champions," the wizards said, "if you are minded to send him to his grave, then take these two champions with you, for they are the most valiant of knights."

"Cease this idle talk," said Maymoun. "I care nothing for champions, be they few or many." With that he rose to his feet, fire blazing in his eyes and, leaving his elephant to one side, mounted a steed of the finest breeding so that Sa'doun could not reproach him as he had done before.

But as he made to go into the field, a knight of the Ethiopians rode out on a horse black as the night when it falls, girded with keen sword and bearing a dark lance, and cavorted to and fro challenging to war and combat. The troops of Islam, viewing this, were minded to engage him, but Commander Sa'doun was there before all of them, wheeling his horse toward the knight like a madman, then charging at him with a heart firmer than the rock and a soul stronger than the current of the sea when it swells.

"Who are you, son of perdition," he cried, in a voice that made the very mountains ring, "that you should ride out at the start of the combat, when I had made myself ready for Maymoun?"

"And what is your measure," retorted the Ethiopian, "that Maymoun should ride out to meet you? This is the battlefield of knights, from which only the cowardly hold back. If you come seeking war and combat, then whoever rides out to meet you is your opponent; either you slay him or he lays you low. You are not reserved for Maymoun to bring down in death. Prepare yourself for combat if you are indeed a champion."

"You speak truly," said Sa'doun. "And I see you have a comely face and an eloquent tongue. What pray is your name?"

"I was first called Abu Nab," said the Ethiopian, "but now I am known as Mulakim al-Rih (meaning, He who Punches at the Wind), and my fame has spread far and wide, through all the Sudan. Prepare now for combat."

Then they crashed and clashed, each against the other, the battle growing ever more fiery between them, so that their eyes were smeared with the kohl of the other world and they were ready to drink from death's bitter cup, the dust of their combat hanging between the earth and the heavens. Then Commander Sa'doun leapt on his foe, harassing him and pressing him close, shutting every means of escape against him, while Mulakim al-Rih, for his part, lunged, spear in hand, at Sa'doun; but Sa'doun struck the spear, shearing it through to cut off the head, then raised himself high in the saddle and charged at his foe, leaping on him with all his strength and striking him across the neck with his sword, so that the knight's head was struck from his shoulders, and God swiftly bore off his soul to torment and hellfire.

When the Ethiopians and Sudanese saw these fearful things, each man felt certain death grip him. But Saqardis cried out to the Ethiopians: "Forward to the battle!"

At that Commander Sa'doun cried in his turn: "Come then, infidels, forward to the combat, to the thrust of the spear, and the blows of swords!" Then he began to range over the field, riding its whole length and breadth, till a second knight rode out to meet him and was slain, and a third, who was left writhing on the earth, and a fourth, who ended weltering in his blood, and a fifth, who was swiftly laid low in his turn; and so it continued till he had slain ten and taken four prisoner, and the knights would no longer draw near him. And when he saw how they held back, he wheeled to the right and killed two, then to the left and killed a further two, then toward the center and killed three, then returned to the field, crying: "How is it, dogs of the Sudan, that you stand there neither fighting nor retreating? Is this the counsel of Saqardis and Saqardyoun?"

At that the champions rode swiftly out to him in the field, albeit against their will, and there he stayed the breath of life in their bodies and dashed their bodies to the ground. The more the wizards witnessed his deeds the greater their anguish grew; and so things continued till evening fell and they returned to their tents. And so it was too on the third day, and on the fourth.

Then, when he returned, King Afrah and Barnoukh the magician congratulated him on his safe issue, and King Afrah said: "Commander Sa'doun, permit us now to replace you in combat, so you may rest awhile from the rigors of the field."

But he, thanking them, said: "King Afrah, so long as they do combat with me, I shall let none of you weary yourselves in fighting, unless they treacherously rally their numbers against us. If that should happen, then you must join the attack and protect my rear, according to how I charge or withdraw." And with that they slept for the night.

As for the wizards, the world seemed to close in around them; and Maymoun now began to mock them, saying to Sabik al-Thalath and Daminhour al-Wahsh: "These accursed wizards dispense decisions and commands and injunctions to all the troops. Yet what good have we seen from them, and what have they wrought to merit our thanks? I hear from them mere words, of no use to any man. They command the Sudanese and the Ethiopians to assail Sa'doun, staying the hand of Commander Maymoun. That, truly, is the beginning of madness."

But the magicians said: "Commanders of the Sudan, do not forsake war and combat out of anger against the wizards; for if you do, the enemy will hack us to pieces." Then, turning to the wizards, they said: "What strategy is this that brings such destruction in its wake?"

"Our wish," said the wizards, "is for a straight and honest attack, in which none will flee from the battlefield, with the commanders in the forefront, so that the hearts of the champions will stand fast, tearing into the enemy in their fury."

"That is a wise course," the commanders said then. "No man can find fault with it." Then they slept for the night, each taking his turn to watch; and when the day broke, the knights mounted their horses, each bearing his piercing lance aloft and girding himself with a keen-edged sword. So it was that the champions arrayed themselves for battle, surging in their hundreds and their thousands, with beating of drums and blowing of horns.

The troops of Islam mounted too, loudly proclaiming the Oneness of the All-Knowing Sovereign, and saying: "Righteous is the creed of Abraham the Friend of God, peace be upon him!" Then Commander Sa'doun rode out at the forefront of the troops of Islam, with King Afrah on his right hand and Barnoukh the magician on his left, all of them giving thanks and praise to God.

The men of the Sudan and Ethiopia likewise set themselves in formation, with the commanders Sabik al-Thalath and Daminhour al-Wahsh and Maymoun al-Hajjam advancing at the head, and the champions of the Sudan following behind, each one a valiant champion and lion-hearted knight. Then Sa'doun al-Zinji, gazing at the gleam of armor and the glitter of helmets, grew eager for the fray, burning to confront the trials of war and bristling with armor; and he flung himself into battle, daubing the infidels with the pencils of blindness and visiting on them every kind of shame and confusion. There limbs were struck from bodies, and blood gushed and flowed, and Commander Sa'doun blazed and raged in battle like a man possessed, causing heads to fall like fruit from the trees. All the while his men protected his rear, each man among them the equal of many champions together; and when they reached the midst of the throng, they raised their voices in hallelujahs and chants of "God is Great!" sending up their prayers to the All-Powerful Sovereign.

King Afrah attacked, followed by his knights, worthy champions one and all, and the troops of Hamra' al-Yaman attacked, those followers of King Sayf Ben Dhi Yazan at present under his command. Followers of Islam they were, and the deadly sword struck in their hands, meting out judgment and fierce decree. As for Commander Sa'doun himself, he was roused to the highest pitch, and stormed every way, jubilant at the clouds of dust swirling that day, striking down the knights in ones and twos. And his brave men did likewise, wreaking carnage on them and pitching great numbers from their horses, hurling them to the ground in their fives and in their tens, each possessing the force of ten, so that the bold grew pale at the sight of them.

Through all this the three enemy commanders, Daminhour al-Wahsh and Sabik al-Thalath and Maymoun, fought on without stint, as though each were the fiercest of lions. And all the while Barnoukh the magician stayed at the heels of Sa'doun al-Zinji, fearful lest the magicians should slay him under cover of the dust. As for King Afrah, that flower of knightly valor, he gave his sword its due and the beasts their sustenance from the dead. And Barnoukh cast a spell over the weapons of the infidel, to keep them from harming God-fearing Muslims, striving side by side with Commander Sa'doun.

A day of fearful trials it was in that battle, and one of those witnessing it, who was called Bakhit Ben Sa'd, after praying and giving peace in the name of the worker of wonders, recited the following lines on the things he saw:

> Black warriors came arrayed, presuming to conquer
> God-committed souls, embracers of Islam.
> They charged on the Muslims with swords and spears,
> But the God of mankind has more knowledge of men.
> Foremost among them were three captains,
> each a lion in his ferocity and strength.

First of the three was the knight Maymoun,
    called Master of the Charge, fierce captain of the cavalry.
Next to him comes Daminhour, Son of the Beast;
    war is given a banquet at his hands.
The third is Sabik al-Thalath, Fate's final decree
    when he plunges furiously into battle.
He charges at the Muslims, infidel that he is,
    with undaunted heart, as solid as rock.
Following after come fourscore priests,
    each of them versed in necromantic arts;
And these are followed by a countless hoard
    expertly trained in all the arts of war.
They are without peer, and when they attack
    even a little child turns grey with terror.
Saqardyoun and Saqardis devise their stratagems,
    both are misguided and full of deceit.
They attack Islam meaning to demolish it
    But by God's grace, Islam stands firm and noble.
Islam meets them with the cry of "Allah Akbar!"
    declaring that the manifest God is One.
King Afrah led the right flank of the army
    and on the left was Barnoukh, priest and teacher.
Sa'doūn the Zinji was prince of their hoard,
    who welled up like a flood to meet our army.
They bestirred themselves in the ocean of war,
    ready to drink a draught from the cup of death.
How many a leader, after he was mounted,
    lay prone on the ground dumb with shame;
And how many a right arm was bereft of the left arm,
    and how many a finger and wrist were severed;
And how many confederates waged the battle united
    and were soon scattered by the thrust of spears!
They were drunken and stupefied with the wine of death.
    Their cup was the sword, the wine was their own blood.

So matters continued, and none did greater wonders in the field, where the spearheads struck at their breasts, than Commander Sa'doun al-Zinji, the sword-wielding knight, and King Afrah and his fearless men. Unsparing they were with their swords, cleaving heads and shattering bones, till the day fled and night let fall its darkness.

They were minded to disengage then, but this the accursed Saqardyoun would not permit. He approached Maymoun al-Hajjam, saying: "My son, you will never find a better hour than this, when death itself has shed its mask." At that the three commanders bore down on the noble band of Muslims, striking shrewdly with their cleaving swords and thrusting with their vanquishing lances; and so they fought the whole night long, holding off all attack against themselves. But the soldiers of Islam bore the blows of the sword patiently, obedient to the All-Knowing Sovereign, till at last the numbers grew heavy against them and they were ready to drink the cup of death.

Then Commander Sa'doun al-Zinji, seeing downfall and death surely approaching, plunged into this raging torrent, flinging himself into the tumult of battle, seized by fury and hacking off limbs and heads, his mouth foaming, so that he tasted a bitter taste on his lips and utter destruction awaited him. The enemy hemmed him in on every side, blocking every path to safety; and all this while he was slaughtering his enemies and pitching great numbers of them from their horses, till at last he grew weary, his strength waned more and more, and his end drew near. His hopes faded then, and he saw too how the knights of Hamra' al-Yaman had fallen back, on the point of downfall and death; all saw the Angel of Death looking into their faces, making ready to claim their bodies.

Then Commander Sa'doun, raising his eyes to the heavens, said: "Dear God, Greatest of the Great, You who taught Adam all things, who set the land above the surging waters, who teach the ant to crawl through the black darkness, whose power raised up the heavens, I beseech You in Your Name, the All-Great, and in the name of Your Prophet, Abraham the Friend, and in the name of the verses of the Quran and the Scriptures and the Torah and the Bible to succor us in our trial and deliver us safe. This I pray, O Lord, to You who have power over all things, who are King and know what is fitting for Your subjects."

Then Almighty God straightway answered Commander Sa'doun's prayer. In the heart of the plain a cloud of dust swirled and billowed, so that the land became turbid with it. Then, after an hour, it dispersed to reveal the gleam of broad swords and the glitter of spearheads, and whole regiments of knights came into view; and at their head was King Sayf Ben Dhi Yazan of the Tubbabi'a, destroyer of infidels and evildoers, with King Abu Taj and his forces on his right hand and Queen Munyat al-Nufus on his left. With them were champions filling the plain like the gushing flood or the shadow sideways cast, with mighty chants of "God is One!" and "God is Great!" shaking the land with their tumult.

Then King Sayf Ben Dhi Yazan heard the voice of Commander Sa'doun and knew the affliction he was in; and Arab that he was, honor and gallantry flared up within him, and the two charged forward at the head of all their troops. King Sayf was wearing armor of blue steel, dipped in red gold of most radiant luster, and King Abu Taj bore such another. They were girded with Indian swords whose blades were swifter than death itself, and bore stout spears each with a head like the serpent's tongue.

Then the two knights attacked, and all their soldiers with them, roaring in voices like thunder, piercing limbs and hearts with their spearheads; they bore down on their enemies like the mountains of Wadi Zurud, destroying every infidel and unbeliever and idolater. King Sayf Ben Dhi Yazan, battling furiously, cried out: "God is Great! God conquers and gives victory! He upholds us with victory and triumph, and He has shamed, dogs of the Sudan, all who profane Him!" And on his right hand, King Abu Taj cast heads around him like balls and hands like the leaves of trees. King Sayf plunged into the tumult, straightway hurling his enemies from their horses and camels, hacking the men of renown and companions in battle with his sword, and plucking out hearts with the point of his well-balanced spear.

There the men of Ethiopia and the Sudan saw such battle and field as they had never dreamed of, knowing punishment and pain indeed. Most scattered in flight, some tasting death with the sundering sword, and the press fell back from Commander Sa'doun and King Afrah, so that their hearts were filled with sudden joy. Then the field opened up for Sa'doun, and he was able to strike with the sundering sword and pierce with the fine, well-balanced spear; he gave the sword its due and the beasts of the field their sustenance from the flesh of the dead, slaking his thirst for vengeance against his enemies and dealing out punishment indeed to his enemies. As for King Sayf, when he tasted the sweetness of surging battle, his Arab soul swelled and he joyfully recited the following lines:

> When dust is stirred up it soars high in the air,
>   and every lion-warrior is scattered like sand.
> War summons me and I am at the ready
>   with a zeal that never slackens in combat.
> I am Sayf Ben Dhi Yazan, my blood is noble,
>   long is the lineage of my ancestors.
> I trace my descent from my father's fathers,
>   and do not trace it from my mother's brothers.
> I was born an iron man, my heart without fear,
>   my dauntless will can shatter the mountains.
> Come, you miscreant dogs, toward me,
>   to join battle with you is my delight.
> Your battalions count as nothing with me,
>   and in my sight they are all as nought.
> God has supported me with victory,
>   decreeing misbelief be wiped out of my lands.
> He has inspired me to walk in the straight path
>   with the faith of truth that comes from God Almighty.
> How many nights have I journeyed over the land,
>   wandering at large in the vast wilderness,
> With no companions, none to answer my call
>   except for the lions who purposed to devour me.
> Now my enemies will really know me
>   when the long course of the day is spent.
> I will strew the ground with the bodies of the slain
>   and quench the thirst of the earth with their blood.

Then King Sayf, gathering all his mighty strength, struck as the lightning bolt does from the heavens, daubing the eyes of his enemies with the pencils of blindness, and afflicting them with all manner of anguish and confusion. The hacking blade sang out there, so that the forces of the enemy grew fewer, and the coward was lost in amazement, and the base man fled, stupefied. Then King Abu Taj too was moved to verse, and recited the following lines:

In the ranks of war, lions and warriors fear me.
Their flesh creeps through terror of my might.
I buy souls cheaply in war's market
when the guts of men are constricted with fear.
O you who have never beheld death's image,
come to me, for I am that terror, death.

Then King Abu Taj, in his turn, struck and lunged like the lightning bolt falling from the heavens, daubing the eyes of his enemies with the pencils of blindness, while his troops stormed forward every one, roused as he-camels are roused, and made the blood of the enemy flow like the gushing torrent.

When Commander Sa'doun al-Zinji heard the voice of King Sayf Ben Dhi Yazan issuing from the swirling dust, his heart filled with joy and he blessed the day this had come to pass. Then he charged forward in fashion fit to shake the immovable mountains, his resolve soaring above former adversity, sure now of redeeming himself from death. His was an hour like no other, as he bore down on the enemy from every side, falling on them like the flood, afflicting them with war and misfortune and heaping ceaseless vengeance on them. Still the sword did its work, still blood was spilt and men slain, till the sun began to set and the infidels turned to flee, yet found all paths blocked before their faces. Then, when darkness fell, all roads became dim to the eye; and the sword ceased to strike, and they returned to their tents.

But Sa'doun al-Zinji, in his joy, went not to his own tent but to that of King Sayf Ben Dhi Yazan, standing there before him, then kissing his hands and feet.

"My lord," he said, "can it really be that you are in the abode of this world, or is this a dream? Surely, by God, I am in the midst of a dream!"

For his part, King Sayf was like the purple anemone with all the blood of knights that had flowed over him, and so too was King Abu Taj and all the soldiers with him. Then King Sayf Ben Dhi Yazan sat in the tents with his followers, and King Afrah instructed his servants to make shift and bring them food. And when they had eaten and drunk and made merry, King Sayf Ben Dhi Yazan inquired as to the cause of the wars.

"By God, O King," King Afrah and Sa'doun al-Zinji said then, "we know of no reason for them. We were sitting here, when, with no warning, we saw horses approaching and knights seeking war and combat."

"And you, Wizard Barnoukh," said the king, "do you not know the cause of these wars?"

"How can I not know their cause," Barnoukh said, "when I am their father and mother? What passed was this: your mother, by means of 'Ayrud, dispatched you to the land of Plato, and we woke here in the morning to find you gone; so then I cast the sands to learn what had happened with you, and set to work on 'Ayrud, who then went to inform 'Aqisa. Then she, lying in wait, seized you from beneath 'Ayrud, and I, learning of the hardship that had befallen you, went to 'Aqisa bearing the phials with your medicine from the treasure of Greece. There I left you, returning to the city of al-Hamra' to cast a spell of darkness over the palace of your mother; and so I left her for a long while. I knew you would marry

Queen Munyat al-Nufus, and so I left you to yourself to complete your business, remaining here in the city and awaiting the works of Almighty God and the destiny He decrees. But the accursed Qamariyya, catching us unawares, sent to the King of Ethiopia to tell him of what had passed; and he then sent her these three commanders, so that God's decrees should come to pass, and they should become people of the Faith. If you prevail over one of them, do not slay him, but rather take him captive, for it may be that Almighty God will ordain their happiness at your hands. But how, O King, did things pass with you?"

"What happened with me you know," said King Sayf Ben Dhi Yazan. Then he recounted all that had befallen him, which it is needless to repeat here. And they were full of wonder at what they heard, thanking God for his deliverance and his safe return to them; and King Abu Taj too rejoiced at the turn events had taken. Then King Sayf, because he was so enamored of Queen Munyat al-Nufus, took it upon himself to keep watch over all the troops.

"Know, O Queen," he said, "that you hold sway over this land, and I too will be under your command. Do not therefore permit yourself feelings of sadness."

"Here I am," she said, "a stranger and alone. You it is who disposes. Do with me as you will."

"By God," he said then, "you shall receive only love and honor from me; and as for the women of this city, they are all your slaves, every one."

Then she thanked him for his words, comforted in her heart when she learned that he was a king whose command was obeyed, possessing soldiers and servants and followers.

Next day the troops stood in their columns ready for the fray, then moved off in their hundreds and their thousands; and King Sayf Ben Dhi Yazan watched the meeting of the armies, leaping between the two lines and proclaiming himself to the two camps, riding to and fro in the field, till the path of his horse led him to the commanders of Ethiopia and the Sudan.

"Commanders of the troops and regiments," he cried, "noble heads of these tribes and multitudes, is there a vigorous knight among you that will come out to do battle and submit to the trial of heroes? Here I stand, concealing nothing. Whoever knows me knows enough, and to him who does not know me I shall make myself known. Know that I am that man poor in the presence of God, King Sayf Ben Dhi Yazan, ruler of the city of Hamra' al-Yaman, destroyer of infidels and evildoers. Make haste now to battle and the trial of heroes."

When the wizards Saqardis and Saqardyoun saw this, madness took them in its grip, and they stared each at the other. "Here we are," they said, "rid of Commander Sa'doun, and now here is Sayf Ben Dhi Yazan come to cap our own relentlessness with relentlessness and injury of his own. Here he is come seeking war and combat."

Then Commander Sabik al-Thalath turned, saying: "Why are you so over-wrought, wizards, at what has happened here? Why are you struck with such abject terror? A knight has come out into the field, a white-skinned man. For my part, if a thousand white-skinned men were to join in arms against me, I should send them to their death with sword and spear. By the house of 'Asatin and its long march from East to West, I must ride into the field and strike out at this devilish knight; and I shall prove his better in the fray and endow him with a suit made crimson by his own blood. I care nothing for him, nor for a thousand like him."

He was minded to mount then. But Daminhour al-Wahsh counseled against it, saying: "Be seated and let combat alone."

"Be seated both of you," said Maymoun al-Hajjam. "I it is who will take over the fighting in these coming days."

"I have sworn by the House of 'Asatin," replied Sabik al-Thalath, "and I cannot break my oath."

"Cease to quarrel among yourselves," the wizard Saqardyoun said then. "If you are truly bent on combat, if you must perforce ride out into the field, then I shall cast lots here in this very place, and he to whom the lot falls shall go out into the battlefield." And the three commanders accepted this.

When the casting was done, the lot fell on Sabik al-Thalath; then, when they repeated it a second time, and a third, still the lot would fall only on him. And so, donning his armor, he rode his horse out into the field and confronted King Sayf Ben Dhi Yazan.

"On guard for battle," he cried, "if you are truly a champion!" Then he rode to and fro through all the field, thrusting with his quivering spear so that all the assembled champions were stunned at the sight. Then he made his stand in the field and, pointing his fingers toward King Sayf, recited the following lines:

> You who come to war, to the battlefield,
>   face the piercing thrust of our spears!
> You shall see marvels making war against us
>   in the dust stirred up when two armies meet.
> You will be cast to the ground and covered with earth
>   and daubed crimson with your own blood
> From the sword of Sabik al-Thalath when you meet him,
>   a champion, fully armed, a knight leading his peers.
> Keep away from the market of war, young warriors,
>   when you witness the furious charge of the cavalry.
> If you knew who I was you have to encounter,
>   and witnessed my war deeds and my prowess,
> You would not dare to come out and fight willingly,
>   you tyro in war and in martial arts.
> Here I am! I have come out ready for the combat—
>   never have I been a weakling or coward.
> I am the horseman of war, a noble adversary,
>   my peers are cast down by thrusts of my sword.
> I was never scared by any warrior in battle,
>   for I fought him and overcame him with my spear.
> You will be abandoned, slain in the dust,
>   food for the ghouls and the wild beasts.

When King Sayf Ben Dhi Yazan heard this, he said to Sabik al-Thalath: "May God slay you and bring you to the dust, for you have courted downfall and utter destruction, praising yourself with your ravings and your twittering tongue. Abject coward, basest of the men of the Sudan, you have embraced vanity and falsehood, angering the Sovereign God, who has made you a desolate wretch in the life to come, in the layers of hellfire with the Garden of Eden forbidden you. The truth of this you shall see with your own eyes. But let me answer those verses of yours." Then he responded in like vein:

> Cast aside your lying and your false boasting,
>   you unclean Ethiopian blacks!
> You who worship a false god,
>   you are thrust forth from the Almighty's gate.
> Foolishness has possessed your minds,
>   you come to the battlefield full of conceit.
> May your hand be lopped off, for you have joined
>   ignorance to misbelief and likewise to tyranny.
> You've come to face me, get a taste of the spear
>   from the hands of one who worships the Almighty,
> Who has borne witness that God is Truth,
>   may He be revered who created me from nothing!
> I am one who accepts Abraham as true prophet.
>   Blessed be he, he testified for God.
> Here is war! Now you will taste my thrusts
>   and fall blood-stained and full of remorse.
> I am the annihilator of evil, the sword of Himyar,
>   I come from the company of Islam and the true faith.
> I will not slacken in fighting any knight
>   until he confesses the Oneness of God,
> And returns from straying in the path of error
>   to the true religion, changing falsehood for faith;
> Or else he shall take a draught from my sword's cup,
>   death is the edge of my Yemeni sword.
> He will be slain and cast upon the earth,
>   food for wild beasts and carrion birds alike.

When Commander Sabik al-Thalath heard these words, the light before his eyes turned to darkness and he charged furiously at King Sayf Ben Dhi Yazan, scowling and knitting his brows. Each made stern trial of his opponent, the combat growing ever fiercer. Each struck ceaselessly with the honed sword, each thrust ceaselessly with the well-balanced spear; then they closed in on one another like mountains round a gully, fighting with firm hand, the fires of the furnace blazing in their hearts, each filled with fury and rancor against the other.

Then they disengaged like the mountains of Wadi Zurud, each sure he was lost. And so the war and combat continued long between them; long did the Yemeni sword strike and the light, well-balanced spear thrust. Sabik al-Thalath was like the dumb rock, unyielding to any mortal—except on that day. For he saw King Sayf Ben Dhi Yazan, saw how in truth the king dazzled the eyes, and was sure of perishing through either sword or spear. He had sought greater things, but had fallen short of his goal, losing now all hope of life, with all refuge from death denied him.

All this while King Sayf was harrying him and engaging him, till he had utterly wearied him and worn him down. And when King Sayf saw that Sabik al-Thalath was growing ever more confused, and sensed, from his own deep knowledge of war, the exhaustion of the commander's horse, he drew alongside him till knee rubbed against knee; then, crying out in a voice which made the land and hills ring, he stretched a hand out to his opponent's throat, seized hold of his collar and squeezed on the jawbones till his eyes started almost from their sockets. In the name of Islam he cried out and, like the thunderbolt in his power and resolution, plucked his enemy (no more bragging and blustering now) clean from his saddle and dashed him down onto the earth. Then he called out to Sa'doun al-Zinji, who bound him hand and foot and gave him into the charge of a group of Muslim champions; and they carried him off to the tents.

At this the wizards struck their faces in their anguish. "Are you minded to accept this?" they cried out to the soldiers of Ethiopia. "Will you permit a white-skinned man to bear away Commander Sabik al-Thalath, one of the greatest commanders of the Sudan, before your very eyes? Make haste to assail this devil."

Then all the troops charged and pressed together, closing in on King Sayf Ben Dhi Yazan. And he met them with a heart firmer than the rock, and a spirit bolder than the surging sea, striking at them with the manly sword, sending their heads flying like balls, and their hands like leaves of the trees; while, at his side, Commander Sa'doun heaped blackest death on the enemy, displaying the arts of combat in matchless fashion. And when King Abu Taj saw this, he too was moved to charge into this raging sea, his soldiers following him in wave after wave; and he cast the enemy down in their ones and their twos, the dust swirling in clouds, till day became like darkest night. The fray grew ever more fierce, the trials ever more somber. Lives that had been long grew short now, the mountains shook and the earth quaked, the sundering sword sang out between the two camps, the heads of spears pierced men's breasts, and the fires of war burned more fiercely yet. Truth prevailed there and the hateful perished; the lion-hearted knight strove still that day, while the coward sought flight from the punishment and trial he witnessed. And so the two camps fought on till the day departed by Almighty God's leave, and approaching night brought the disen-gagement. Then the two armies turned from combat, leaving the slain lying there on the sandy plains.

When the troops had seated themselves in their tents, and the servants had brought them food to eat, they lit the fires and in their turn stood guard against thieves and demons. They sent out too to learn who among the troops of the Sudan had been laid low on that day of mighty tribulation; and they found that five thousand six hundred and seventy lay slain there on the plain, to say nothing of those who were gravely wounded. Then the wizards struck their faces in their anguish, while the magicians were at their wit's end as to what should be done. "Victory seemed ours," they said, "and all our hopes about to be fulfilled at the enemy's hands. And now this white- skinned man, King Sayf Ben Dhi Yazan, has dealt grief and misfortune on us and on all the troops. Truly Saturn was not with us; for had he been, he would have given us victory against the enemy."

"Wizard," Commander Daminhour al-Wahsh said then, "all this has happened through your own ill-starred strategy, because you shrieked out to the men to charge all together. Because the troops are not versed in the methods of combat, our enemies destroyed them, bringing down on them punishment indeed. I believe your only purpose in accompanying us was to bring utter destruction on our troops."

"And how do you expect war to be?" retorted Saqardyoun. "Is it not in the nature of war that there should be a victor and a vanquished?"

"So it is," said Daminhour. "Yet the combat of knight with knight holds no surprises, for none rides out to fight except the man who knows how to fight. For my part, I counsel we fight only in single combat till we see the outcome of the disengagement." So it was with the Ethiopians and the Sudanese; and with that they slept.

As for King Sayf Ben Dhi Yazan and Sa'doun al-Zinji and King Afrah and King Abu Taj, when they had disengaged from battle, and returned to their tents and eaten their food, and when they had given praise to God the All-Knowing Sovereign, King Afrah said to his soldiers: "Make a count of the numbers slain today."

"Of our own troops," they told him, "ninety men have been killed, and of Sa'doun al-Zinji's soldiers, two have been killed, and of King Abu Taj's soldiers, thirty, and of the troops of Hamra' al-Yaman, eighty-five."

Then Commander Sa'doun said: "If they should wish, tomorrow morning, to engage us in single combat, I have a strategy in mind which I believe to be sound."

"Tell me what your idea is," said King Sayf.

"My lord," he said, "when morning comes, I and my men will assemble on the right side, and King Abu Taj with his troops on the left, and King Afrah on the right flank, and Barnoukh the magician, with the troops of Hamra' al-Yaman, will take command of the left flank, and you, O King, will take the center, making ready there to thrust and strike; then we will advance against them, and our numbers are sufficient should they mount an attack against us. But if they engage us in single combat, then I shall ride out first into the battlefield, and give them the cup of mortification to drink. And any man of Ethiopia and the Sudan who fights with me I shall pierce with the head of my spear, and there will be an end of him. But I adjure you, O King, by the name of Abraham, the Friend of God, not to stay me in the battlefield and hold me back from combat; for it may be this dog Maymoun will ride out to meet me, and I long, by God, to meet him. Let my heart attain its desire in this, for I have long heard tell of his courage."

They slept till morning came, and then the men of the two camps mounted their fleet horses, girding themselves with their broad swords and grasping the hafts of their spears; and when Commander Sa'doun saw the troops of Ethiopia lining up before him, to left and right, in the center and on the two flanks, he knew they were minded for single combat.

"O King," he said then, "here is my wish fulfilled."

"If so you will have it," said King Sayf, "then ride out; and if you find yourself unable to withstand your enemies, here am I to preserve and protect you, destroying all who stand against you."

While they were thus conversing, a knight rode out from amongst the troops of Sudan as though he were a son of the jinn, in all his panoply, protected by a mighty shield, with a gilded coat of armor on him, and, on his breast, a mirror of gemstones and other wonders, riding a steed as noble as knight ever rode, and bearing a Yemeni sword that gleamed like lightning. So he rode till he reached the center of the field; and then he called out: "If any champion among you is minded to engage me in war and combat, let him hasten to his grievous trial. But let none ride out to meet me save your white-skinned king, whose name is Sayf Ben Dhi Yazan, so I may meet him before you all in the field. If he defeats me, he may do with me as he will, and I shall serve him as a slave serves his master; and if I take him captive or defeat him, then I shall do with him as I desire. But if I am victorious, I shall not harm him or harass him in any way. Rather, he shall release Sabik al-Thalath into my hands, and I shall restore him to liberty."

At this Commander Sa'doun was minded to ride out into the battlefield and strike the knight. But King Sayf said: "Remain where you are. None has sought help from you. I it is who am summoned, and it is not fitting, if someone challenges me, that you should go in my stead."

Then King Sayf Ben Dhi Yazan leapt into the midst of the field and, approaching the knight, said: "Here I am then, steadfast knight, come to you as you wish." Then they closed each on the other, without further ceremony; each unsheathed his sword and fell upon his opponent forthwith, and they fought sternly, locked together in mortal combat, parrying and driving back, advancing and retreating, moving now to the left and now to the right, now urging their horses forward, now galloping back. This Daminhour al-Wahsh—for he it was— was the scourge of all scourges, the misfortune of all misfortunes, and he fought on with King Sayf Ben Dhi Yazan in that battle, each striving to mete out a bitter downfall to the other, till the two were ready to drink from the cup of death; and Sa'doun al-Zinji advanced, and King Afrah and King Abu Taj too approached the tumult, their eyes fixed on the field.

Daminhour al-Wahsh was stunned and dazzled at what he saw from King Sayf, so that his heart, so firm before, grew less staunch, and he began to regret riding out into the field. But regret was fruitless there. Even were he to seek deliverance in flight, all paths would be blocked to him, and so he had perforce to conceal his fury and distress, and show steadfast endurance. At last he sensed his horse grow exhausted, and King Sayf, knowledgeable in the arts of war, knew it too. Then

King Sayf stood erect in his stirrups and, stretching himself to his full height and shrieking out against him, reached out his hand to his opponent's armor, then, his hand firm with the steadfastness of faith and piety, took his foot from the stirrup and kicked his opponent's horse to the flat plain beneath him; and Daminhour al-Wahsh was left hanging from King Sayf Ben Dhi Yazan's hand like a tattered garment. Then, when his enemy wriggled in his grasp, striving to free himself, King Sayf lifted him up, holding his armor by the neck, then dashed him to the ground, shaking every bone in his body. And no sooner had the knight struck the ground than Commander Sa'doun was there like a man crazed, straddling his chest like a millstone, remorselessly crushing his shoulders and driving his arms back by main force. Then he bound him fast, hand and foot, dragging him away and giving him into the charge of two bold knights. "Chain him up," he told them, "alongside his friend Sabik al-Thalath."

When Saqardyoun and Saqardis witnessed the capture of Daminhour al-Wahsh, all patience and forbearance left them; their hearts were ready to burst, their throats grew dry, and a bitter taste entered their mouths. They struck their faces till the blood flowed from the nose, crying out to the troops: "Forward now against those who have taken your commanders captive and brought your fortunes low; make haste to attack, let none hold back from the valiant-hearted charge!"

At this the champions surged forward one and all; but King Sayf Ben Dhi Yazan, the lion-hearted knight, met them, and worked amongst them with his sundering sword, sending their heads spinning over the face of the sandy plains; and Commander Sa'doun followed him, and so did King Afrah and King Abu Taj, each charging headlong into the field and flinging down the corpses in their ones and twos. Such a marvel, by God, was King Sayf Ben Dhi Yazan on that day! He assured the safety of the battlefield for his troops, destroying the men of Ethiopia and the Sudan and piling their bodies high on the ground. As for King Afrah, he seized the breath of life from the enemy and hacked their bodies to pieces, giving them a cup of purest death to drink, striking them with the broad sword and roaring and crying out against the enemy, so that all their valorous knights perished.

As for Commander Sa'doun, he was not to be outdone this day, as he turned the wheels of war like a mill, piercing the breasts and eyes of the enemy with his spearhead and passing round the cup of death for the men of Ethiopia to drink; near beside himself he was, slashing with his sword at the backs and sides and bellies of his adversaries. The dust swirled in clouds, and hearts burst, and the keen-edged sword sang, and the head of the spear sank deep, and the bold and steadfast champion was known on that day. The grave gaped for many a man, and many a horse fell; the blood boiled in countless veins, countless heads were cleft and hearts confounded. A mighty battle it was indeed, in which the Supreme Sovereign, the All-Powerful and All-Vanquishing, was truly revealed. There the Faithful stood and saw their hopes crowned, while the infidels lay crushed in defeat, stupefied and cast down; and so they remained till the day fled and the darkness of night descended. Then the drums signaled the disengagement and the fighting ceased.

When the soldiers of Islam returned to their tents and had eaten the food provided for them and lit the fires, Barnoukh the magician rose, saying: "I shall take on the watch till morning, so that you may all take repose."

"We are in your debt, wizard," King Sayf replied then.

As for the infidel troops, they returned to their tents, with Saqardis and his brother Saqardyoun and the other magicians among them, dumbfounded one and all at the deeds they had witnessed; and when they counted the dead for the day and found they numbered two thousand and more, the counselors struck their faces and plucked out their beards with their own hands. "Our troops have been put to shame," they said, "before kings and before all men, rich or poor. We had eighty thousand troops, they will say, and three commanders, each with a whole tribe at his command, together with eighty magicians and two wizards; and all these were bested in combat by a paltry band. King Sayf Ben Dhi Yazan vanquished them and poured out shame and misfortune upon them, giving them a drink bitter to the taste and destroying them utterly, his troops numbering a mere four thousand."

Then Maymoun, turning to the wizards, said: "Just what have we witnessed from you magicians? And when have you fought alongside us?"

"We are wizards," they replied, "and straightway, when we came here, we lifted the darkness contrived by Barnoukh the magician and so delivered Qamariyya; and then you brought the magic to an end. Had we seen Barnoukh the magician cast new spells, we would have broken them; but we fear ourselves to perform things Barnoukh the magician would bring to nothing, for he sits there ready for whatever we can do, watching for us as a cat watches for a mouse. Barnoukh is no light thing; we have to beware of him and his magic wiles."

"You admit then," said Maymoun al-Hajjam, "that the only course is to pursue this battle through the blows of the keen-edged sword; and that had Sa'doun al-Zinji not been with the troops we should have overcome them. I myself saw him yesterday, returning from the field like a raging lion, and tomorrow morning I am minded to challenge him to single combat. Let him come, and I shall embroider his armor with his own blood, laying him low once and for all; and should Sayf Ben Dhi Yazan come out after him, I shall rid these realms of him, and the whole earth too. If these two are slain, we shall account for all his troops and champions, caring nothing for all the lion-hearted heroes in the world."

"Do that," the wizards said then, "and we pledge we will prevail on King Sayf Ar'ad to give you his daughter in marriage and make you a partaker in his good fortune. You shall become his minister, the governor of his realm and the swordsman of his wrath; your word will be like his in the kingdom, and he will show you favor above all the dignitaries of his state."

"Let there be no more talk," he said, "till the darkness is past and the smiling day returns."

So matters were disposed there. As for King Sayf Ben Dhi Yazan, he made enquiry as to the number slain among his troops. "O King," they said, "ninety have been slain from among our numbers, and four of the slaves."

At this King Sayf wept, saying: "I swear each and every believer fighting in God's cause is dearer in my eyes than King Sayf Ar'ad's kingdom, with all the money and treasure and horses and men it contains. Had I known things would pass so, I should not have permitted a man among you to go out to battle."

"O fortunate King," they replied, "we know each man who dies here is a martyr, and each who lives is blessed. What better lot than that the people of Islam should stand between blessings and martyrdom? Why did we march alongside you, O King, with all our men and knights, except with a mind to lay down our lives for you, together with all we own, lives, men and all."

Then King Sayf Ben Dhi Yazan thanked them for their words. "By God," he said, "you have satisfied the desire of the heart, and done all manner of good deeds, and won the pleasure of God, the Glorious Sovereign. And now, what are we to do with this small band of ours, so as to finish this business without delay?"

"Know, O King," replied Commander Sa'doun, "that the men of the enemy will hold fast only behind Maymoun. If we take Maymoun captive, those other troops there will flounder. Either they will scatter, or, should any hold his ground, he will drink the cup of death."

Then King Sayf Ben Dhi Yazan ordered food to be brought, and they ate and drank, praising and giving thanks to their God. Then King Sayf said: "I fear, Sa'doun, lest the Ethiopians seek to deliver their captives from among us, bringing all our endeavors to nought. I am minded to summon them before me and invite them to embrace Islam. Should they become Muslims, they will then be of our camp; and if they do not, I shall strike their necks and ease my heart of their charge. What is your counsel on this?"

"Do as you are minded to do," they all replied, "for we are all of us more obedient than slaves and will follow where your own counsel takes you." And so King Sayf Ben Dhi Yazan commanded Sa'doun to bring them before him.

"I hear and obey," replied Sa'doun. Then he went and returned with them, bound as fast as could be. And when they were set before him, King Sayf said: "Commanders, this long I have kept you here in my charge. Is it your wish I should deliver you from captivity, permitting you to go your way or do as you are otherwise minded? When I first took you captive my intent was to strike your necks. Yet I had hopes of you, and, hesitating as to the proper course to follow, I have summoned you before me now to ease myself of your charge. Either you shall become Muslims and join yourselves to the camp of Islam, winning martyrdom should death overtake you and blessing should you live on; or else you shall be slain forthwith. Say now which of these you find fitting, and make haste with your reply."

When the pair were silent, neither having a word to say for himself, King Sayf said: "Since you hold yourself, it seems, above the religion of Islam, nothing remains for you but the cup of death. Arise, Commander Sa'doun, and strike their necks, bringing them swiftly to death." And Commander Sa'doun rose accordingly and unsheathed his sword.

"What is it, O King, that you wish of us?" Sabik al-Thalath asked then.

"My wish," he replied, "is that you should leave the worship of Saturn and rather worship the Mighty and Glorious God; for this Saturn is a mere star among the stars, and none is to be rightly worshipped except God, the Eternal and Everlasting Sovereign."

"And where is your God that you worship?" asked Sabik al-Thalath. "Reveal Him to us, so that we may worship Him with you, and, seeing Him, may do your bidding and follow you."

"My God," said King Sayf, "sees and is unseen. He is in the highest realm, and no time passes over Him, nor does any place contain Him. His throne is in the heavens and His power on the earth. He is the One True God, Sole and Unshakeable; none shares with Him, nor is any comparable to Him or in His likeness, nor does He have mate or offspring. He is not to be seen and He has no abode. Whoever links another with Him is a heretic, and his lot will be hellfire on the Day of Doom."

When Sabik al-Thalath heard these words, a shudder ran through him and he fell dumbstruck to the earth, awe seizing him at the name of Almighty God. Then he straightway said: "You speak truly, King of all time, and your words proclaim the truth. Only teach me how it is that a man enters your religion. How does he follow your faith?"

"Place your thumb and three fingers together," said King Sayf, "raising your index finger, then say as Moses did in his petition: 'O Restorer and Mighty Teacher, instruct me, so that I may be exalted.' God told Moses: 'The best thing my servant can say is: There is no God but God, a declaration light on the tongue, and Muhammad is God's messenger, through whom faith is fulfilled.' This proclamation of God's Oneness is balm to the heart, bringing blessing to the believer. Better it is than words of weightier measure, light to repeat on the tongue; and if all the deeds in the world were set in a scale, and all the plains and the mountains too, it would surely outweigh them to say: There is no God but God, and Muhammad is his messenger."

When Sabik al-Thalath and Daminhour al-Wahsh heard these words, their hearts were opened up to Islam. "In truth, King Sayf," said Daminhour al-Wahsh, "I have heard men tell how God is One, Alone and Unshakeable, how He cannot be seen, nor has any abode or resting place. Yet you speak of Muhammad as God's messenger, though the Faithful say Abraham is the Friend of God."

"You speak truly," King Sayf said then. "He of whom I speak is the Prophet of the end of time, who will come with Divine Proofs and with the Quran. He is the highest prophet and the seal of the messengers, of the line of Abraham, God's blessing and peace be on him, and on his kin and his noble companions."

When Daminhour al-Wahsh and Sabik al-Thalath heard these words, they submitted in their hearts to the creed of Islam. Then they said to King Sayf Ben

Dhi Yazan: "If we should now become Muslims, will God accept us when we, in our blindness, worshipped Saturn so many long years? Will He not rather turn us from His gate, shut out from aspiring to know His Glory?"

"If you truly believe in Almighty God," said King Sayf, "and are done with the past, God will be bountiful to you in His pardon and acceptance and approval."

"We are now become believers in God," they said then, "and in His Prophet and his angels and his Scriptures."

Then Sabik al-Thalath was the first to say: "I witness there is no God but God, and that Muhammad is His messenger, and that Abraham is the Friend of God, and the prophet of this our time."

"You have attained Paradise," said Sayf Ben Dhi Yazan, "and are now written amongst the camp of the All-Merciful."

After him, Daminhour al-Wahsh too became a Muslim; and blessings and good fortune were ordained for them both. Then King Sayf Ben Dhi Yazan, rejoicing at their entry to Islam, went to them and released them from their bonds, kissing them on the forehead and bringing garments which he bestowed on them, saying: "You have won blessings." Then he ordered food to be brought, and they ate and drank with King Sayf and all the men who were present, passing the night in contentment and joy.

And through all that night King Sayf instructed them in the ways of piety and the principles of Islam, rejoicing with them till Almighty God, the All-Generous One, brought forth the morning, illuminating the world with His light. Then the mart of war and struggle was assembled, and the columns set up, men arraying themselves in their hundreds and their thousands, then standing there face to face.

This very night it was that Commander Maymoun had vowed to Saqardis and Saqardyoun to ride out into the battlefield and fight with Commander Sa'doun, either taking him captive with his own hands or giving him the cup of death to drink, and then, in his triumph, to deliver Sabik al-Thalath and Daminhour al-Wahsh. And so he slept till morning, having no notion that the two champions had left wayward paths to follow the path of righteousness and success, that He who paves all roads had opened up their way to them.

When that day came, Commander Maymoun rode out into the midst of the field, mounted on an elephant taller than any steed. On his back was a coat of armor made by God's prophet David, peace be upon him, so close knit the links were like the eyes of the locust and the keen Indian sword was powerless to pierce it, and on his head he had an ordinary iron helmet, round and polished like pure silver, and likewise impenetrable; in his hand he bore a broad Indian sword with the messenger of death written on its blade, and on his shoulder an East Arabian spear writhing like a snake, with a head like the head of a scorpion.

Then, spurring his elephant on into the field of combat, he called out in his thunderous voice, so that all men near and far heard it: "Let any who will, come try me in war and combat! Know, men of Hamra' al-Yaman, that I come here into the battlefield, the ground of the keen and thrusting sword. You are all servants, with not a king or sultan among you; rather you are followers of Saʿdoun al-Zinji and his troops, and Saʿdoun, from what I hear tell, is a follower of King Sayf, the white-skinned man. Here I am, come into the battlefield minded to attain our ends and finish this business; and so it is that I have held the troops back from war and combat, for it is not knightly chivalry to permit the troops to fight one band against another while we sit watching for the outcome. Rather let King Sayf Ben Dhi Yazan, who has destroyed infidels and evil-doers with his sword, ride out into the field. If he should take me captive, then let him set me with Sabik al-Thalath and Daminhour al-Wahsh whom he took captive yesterday, and we shall all be captives awaiting what he ordains for us; and if I should take him captive, I shall require those two prisoners in his stead. But if, being a king with servants and subjects, he disdains to ride out and face me, saying it is not fit for a man of his standing, then let one who is my peer come to face me; I mean Commander Saʿdoun al-Zinji. Then, if he should defeat me, I shall be a servant and slave to him; and if I defeat him, then he shall perform whatever I ask of him."

When Sabik al-Thalath and Daminhour al-Wahsh saw all this, they wished to ride out and confront him. But King Sayf Ben Dhi Yazan said: "Remain where you are, and do not violate your sanctuary by contact with that devil." He was minded to ride out himself to face Maymoun, but Saʿdoun al-Zinji, taking hold of his reins, said: "King of all time, permit me, in the name of Almighty God, to go out against this demon."

"Commander Saʿdoun," said King Sayf, "I do not forbid you to confront him, but it is my purpose to take him captive; for God may perhaps guide him to the Faith, and then, being as he is a knight of renown and a famous champion, he would be of use to us in our holy warfare and help us attain the ends we desire. Ride out then to meet him, I shall not stay your hand; but if you worst him in combat, take care not to slay him but to take him captive, as I said, in the hope that God will guide him to the Faith, and he will join the camp of the All-Merciful."

At that Commander Saʿdoun set off, riding out into the field till he was there before Commander Maymoun. "Make ready for battle," he cried, "if you are indeed a knight who strikes and thrusts."

"What youth are you?" said Maymoun. "Are you King Sayf Ben Dhi Yazan, who holds himself so bold and mighty and skilled in combat?"

"Are you grown mad, Maymoun?" retorted Saʿdoun. "This king of whom you speak is one of the greatest of kings, having under his command countless such as you and I: leaders of armies, commanders and kings, and every manner of man both rich and poor. How can it be that the king should ride out to fight with the likes of you in the field where swords thrust and strike? So many more there are of your kind, that claim to possess the arts of chivalry and are minded to strive toward their goals, and yet the days cast them back, shamed and brought low! You and I, together with thousands like us, are not equal to a drop among his surging waters, nor to a spark or a puff of smoke from his fire. If indeed you hold yourself a knight among knights, then here is the field, and here the combat."

With that Sa'doun al-Zinji struck Maymoun al-Hajjam like a fearless lion and engaged him in battle. Then the dust and darkness gathered over their heads; reproach and rebuke ceased, and the words became few between them. Without respite they thrust each at the other with well-balanced spear, struck each at the other with deadly sword, still galloping to and fro, approaching and retreating, attacking and exchanging blows, till disaster and the blindness of death drew near. God preserve us from the rage of the Sudanese, who are like the offspring of the jinn! The eye grew dizzy following their course, as the spear snapped and the sword broke, each striving to give his adversary the cup of death and shame to drink. And so they continued, parrying and thrusting one at the other, till the virtue was gone from the arms they bore, the swords and spears all rent in pieces. Then they threw down their weapons and flung themselves into a clinch, furious rage growing ever fiercer between them.

"Will you wrestle with me, youth?" said Commander Sa'doun. "Let us, you and I, essay the strength of our wrists and make trial to see which of us is bold, with no terror of war. If you have any skill, then make ready for the struggle. And if you are not versed in the arts of wrestling, then let us carry on as before in war and combat."

"Youth," Maymoun said then, "wrestling is my craft, in which I was reared from childhood amongst my people and kinsfolk and loved ones. How should I not know how, when I am mother and father to it?"

Now Commander Sa'doun had only proposed this because Maymoun al-Hajjam was, as we have said, mounted on an elephant, while Sa'doun rode a noble steed. Sa'doun's goal was to have him dismount and join him there on the earth, so as to gain the better of him; for he had sensed the exhaustion of his horse, whereas the elephant was like a huge and lofty mountain. Eager for the fray, Sa'doun flung himself at him the moment he came down, assailing him with all his vigor. Then they tugged each at the other, harassing and assailing and punching till the blood flowed from their noses and disaster and the blindness of death drew near. And as the ground there was strewn with rocks and with stones both great and small, they began to pelt each other with these till their feet dug out pits like graves. And so they continued till the day fled and the darkness of night descended in its place; and then the drums of disengagement beat, and they departed from the fray, each scowling at the other, to return to their tents.

When Commander Sa'doun returned from the field, King Sayf Ben Dhi Yazan met him and congratulated him on his safe return, rejoicing to see him there. And Sabik al-Thalath also greeted him, saying: "By God, a bold champion and a stout adversary you are! God has approved your struggle in His cause, and granted you all you are minded to achieve." He thanked them for what they had said, and then King Sayf Ben Dhi Yazan, seating himself and commanding Sa'doun al-Zinji to be seated also, had food brought to them, and they ate and drank and made merry together.

"Commander Sa'doun," said King Sayf Ben Dhi Yazan, "how was your adversary today?"

"He is truly a mighty knight and matchless warrior, O King," replied Sa'doun, "and burning for the fray. By God, I have known no assaults like his assaults, and no leaps like his leaps, nor any like him at all, except for my master King Sayf Ben Dhi Yazan, lord of the Kings of Yemen. But tomorrow morning, King of all time, I shall, if Almighty God grants the victory for me, bring him down to the dust and lead him captive. Let it be as God wills and ordains." So it happened here.

As for Commander Maymoun, when he came back from the field to the place where his tents were pitched, Saqardis met him, congratulating him on his safe return, and saying: "How did you find your adversary, knight of all time?"

"By exalted Saturn," said Maymoun, "by the star and that which made it, he is, wizard of all time, a matchless knight, without peer for steadfastness in war and combat. But tomorrow morning I shall bring him down to the dust and lead him captive."

"Knight of your age," said Saqardis, "know that Saturn is with you and will grant you victory over your opponent." And so Maymoun retired to his rest.

As for Sabik al-Thalath and Daminhour al-Wahsh, they had stood watching what passed in the field, and borne witness how Sa'doun and Maymoun had risen above all other knights in prowess. And as the wheels of converse turned, Daminhour al-Wahsh said: "Commander, I have never, through all my life, seen a man perform in battle what you and Maymoun have done."

"By God," said Sa'doun, "he is truly a gallant knight and a fearless champion, matchless in these times, and I pray that Almighty God will guide him to the religion of Islam, so he may be of our camp in the struggle against base unbelievers."

"You speak truly, bold-hearted knight," replied Sabik al-Thalath. "An unconquerable lion he is indeed. We have witnessed how King Sayf Ar'ad feared him; and we make truce with him to assuage him and guard against his wrath. Maymoun struck terror in him by his valor and strength and prowess."

"Commanders," King Sayf said then, "in the name of the All-Knowing Sovereign, Lord of Zamzam and the Holy Shrine, and by every noble sentiment, I must ride out tomorrow morning to meet him in combat and there pluck him from his very saddle, as the bird of prey seizes the pigeon, and invite him to embrace Islam; and if he does not become a Muslim, I shall strike his head from his shoulders with my sword."

When they heard him utter these words, they all fell silent. Then Commander Sa'doun said: "My lord, who can gainsay your valor? There is none like you, either among the bedouin or those dwelling in towns." And with that they slept till the Almighty and All-Bountiful God brought forth the morning, illuminating the world with His glittering star.

Then the knights mounted their splendid steeds and the columns assembled, arrayed to the right and to the left in their hundreds and thousands. And the first to enter the round of combat was Commander Maymoun al-Hajjam, riding out into the midst of the field and flourishing his spear in a manner to astonish the knights.

"Come now to combat," he called out. "Make haste to the battlefield, and let none ride out to meet me save King Sayf Ben Dhi Yazan, whose fame is spread far through the lands and realms, who is reputed to do battle with man and jinn alike, and who has dealt punishment to all kings and knights with his sword."

No sooner had he uttered these words than King Sayf leapt onto his horse and rode out to confront him. Sa'doun al-Zinji and Sabik al-Thalath and Daminhour al-Wahsh had wished one and all to go out to meet him, even if the one to go should be chosen by lot, but this King Sayf would not permit, saying: "My purpose is to attain our goals and prolong the combat no longer." And then he rode out, as we have said.

"Know Commander Maymoun," King Sayf told him then, "that your friends have embraced the religion of Islam, joining themselves with the people of the Faith and the camp of the All-Merciful. I give you this choice now: either you shall believe in Almighty God and yourself enter into the religion of Islam, or, by God who is the only God, I shall make you a byword with all people by striking your head from your shoulders with the edge of my sword."

When Maymoun heard King Sayf utter these words, the light before his eyes turned to darkness. "Who are you," he said, "that you speak to me so, in words that will have bitter harvest? Tell me your name forthwith, lest you live to regret it."

"I am the leader of these troops," King Sayf said then, "and the ruler of this city; and I it is that you have called out to combat. Bandy no more words. Either profess belief in God Exalted on High, or else make ready for combat, if you are indeed a champion."

"Look rather to yourself," said Maymoun, "for this day you shall sink down to your grave, and all your present shall be exchanged for past."

"Hold your tongue," cried King Sayf, "dog of the Sudan and Ethiopia!" Then he rode full tilt against him, roaring with all his strength, and combat was engaged. Now they drew close and now they drew off, and theirs was indeed an hour to make men quake, and to make the solid rock melt with its heat. Like lions they fought, closing in like the mountains round a gully and cleaving apart like the valley of Wadi Zurud, each believing himself lost; an hour it was at whose trials the hair of the newborn babe turned grey. Then two mighty blows fell between them. Maymoun's blow, coming down wide of the mark, hit the breast of King Sayf's horse, so that it fell dead forthwith; and when King Sayf saw that, fury seized him, and he struck the elephant, letting the sword fall in the middle of its head and striking it clean off from its neck, so that only the mangled carcass remained.

Then Maymoun, cut to the quick, flung himself at King Sayf like a madman, his eyes ready to start out of his head. But King Sayf Ben Dhi Yazan met him, and they battled on for an hour sufficient to sow feud and misfortune, grappling with arms and wrists, through every kind of harsh ordeal, till the day drew to a close. Then Maymoun grew weary, his courage beginning to ebb and fall away; and King Sayf Ben Dhi Yazan, expert in the arts of war, knew this and leapt on him with all his might, besting him with his resolution. With his right hand he seized

Maymoun's belt, and with his left he grasped his coat of armor; then, holding him in a grip almost to send him mad, he raised him up like a bird in the claw of the venturesome hawk and dashed him against the ground, shaking every bone in his body. And there was Sa'doun standing ready to take him captive, seating himself upon his chest and thrusting back his arms, shackling him with chains and binding him hand and foot. And so he was led to the tents.

There King Abu Taj and King Afrah and Daminhour al-Wahsh and Sabik al-Thalath, along with Sa'doun al-Zinji, received King Sayf; and when they had seated themselves, and the servants had brought in the food at his command, he ate together with all the commanders and noble kings present, then called for Maymoun to be brought before him.

"And now, knight of all time," he said, "what have you to say concerning Islam? Can it really be, by God, that a man of your stamp should, through upholding infidelity and tyranny, be among those destined for hellfire?"

"I am in your hands, O King," said Maymoun. "Do with me as you will. Never have I seen a man take another captive, then honor him as you, fortunate King, have done."

Then King Sayf ordered that he be delivered from his bonds and shackles and bade him be seated. "My wish, Maymoun," he said, "is to give you good counsel, so that you may embrace Islam and be henceforth a soldier in the cause of God the All-Knowing Sovereign. So you will become like your brothers here, Daminhour al-Wahsh and Sabik al-Thalath, and like Commander Sa'doun. Here they stand, with the light of Islam shining from their faces. But I can counsel you three times only; after that I shall strike your neck and leave your loved ones to grieve for you. If your heart desires to accept Islam, make haste to do so, and peace be upon you; and if, in your vanity, you remain immovably wayward and depraved, then you shall see where the ways of injustice will lead you."

"Teach me," Maymoun said then, "to say the words through which I may enter Islam, as you taught them to these noble commanders."

King Sayf Ben Dhi Yazan replied: "Say, I witness there is no God but God, and I witness that Abraham is the Friend of God, and His prophet and messenger." And Maymoun became a Muslim in word and in heart.

Then King Sayf, commanding the four of them, Sa'doun and Maymoun and Sabik al-Thalath and Daminhour al-Wahsh, to come together there and bear witness all together, ordained that they should enter a pledge of brotherhood among themselves, so that none should part from the other by joining himself to infidelity, and that each should be like one hand helping another against all their enemies. And when they had done as he commanded, chairs were set up for them in the pavilion around King Sayf, and thenceforth, when he seated himself, King Afrah would be seated on his right side and King Abu Taj on his left, while, as for the commanders, he placed Sa'doun and Maymoun on the right and Daminhour al-Wahsh and Sabik al-Thalath on the left; and so the king's pavilion became like the Garden of Eden, he there seated like a lion among lions. Thus was arrayed the court of King Sayf Ben Dhi Yazan, king of the Tubba'i kings of the land of Yemen.

As for Saqardis and Saqardyoun, when they learned King Sayf Ben Dhi Yazan had taken Maymoun captive, a burning fever descended on them, and they struck their faces, dumbfounded by what had occurred. Then, summoning the magicians before them, they said: "You have journeyed to us here from a distant land, with the goal of taking Barnoukh the magician captive, along with the one who caused him to depart your country and repair here. Here you came in pursuit of him, and when you stood before King Sayf Ar'ad, King of Ethiopia and the Sudan, he did not send you away empty-handed, but rather supplied you with troops and dispatched you to where your adversary was; and we too have accompanied you. What is it then that has held you back from the end you desire? Why do you not endeavor to accomplish your business, and seize Barnoukh the magician, who is your enemy?"

"Rejoice now," they replied. "For by the fire and its sparks, you shall now witness such magic from us as shall amaze him that sees it."

"Do this," said the wizards, "and you shall have pride of place among knights and champions."

So they were agreed, and each of the eighty made trial of his powers. The first to make trial was their chief, whose name was 'Abd Nar, a man of high skills who, on account of his wisdom, had been appointed leader over them after Barnoukh's departure.

"Before all else," he said, "we shall cast a spell of immobility over the kings who are there with King Sayf. King Sayf himself is girded with the sword of King Shem, son of Noah, and this I believe protects him against enchantment, along with Barnoukh."

"Let us wait then," they replied, "till all the court is assembled, and then we shall cast the spell over them all. If a man falls beneath the enchantment, then so he is destined. And after that we will try our strength against Barnoukh, for he alone will remain, with none there to lend him aid, and so we may triumph over him should he resist us."

They laid their plans accordingly, devising the spell of immobility; and then their chief 'Abd Nar rode to the court on a casket of brass and stood there above the court, bearing the spell. And as each king seated himself in his place, and the other followers seated themselves or remained standing according to their custom, he cast the spell of immobility over them all. Now this spell was contained in a bowl filled with purified water, over which they had recited incantations known to them; and as 'Abd Nar sprinkled the people from the bowl, they all grew stiff, becoming like stone, their eyes starting out and none able to move from his place.

As for the troops of Islam, when the day rose they mounted and rode out into the battlefield as usual. There the columns assembled, arraying themselves in their hundreds and their thousands, and awaited King Sayf Ben Dhi Yazan, and Sa'doun al-Zinji, and King Afrah, and King Abu Taj, and Maymoun al-Hajjam, and Daminhour al-Wahsh, and Sabik al-Thalath, rejoicing one and all that the splendid champions had embraced Islam and would henceforth lend their aid in war and combat. But when they did not appear, a number of the troops went off to the court, and seeing them there in that condition, cried out in terror at what had passed. "The magicians alone," they said, "could have done these things to our kings."

When word of this reached a group of the womenfolk, they went in to Shama, saying: "Rise and look to your father and husband, for the magicians have bewitched them, turning them to stone, with their eyes starting out." Then Shama ran out frantic, like a slave girl and, coming to the court and seeing the condition of her father and her husband and all that were with them, cried out to announce the news, weeping and wailing ever more bitterly.

Then she commanded the servants and soldiers who were present to bring Barnoukh the magician before her; and men ran swiftly to Barnoukh, saying: "Make haste to the kings, for they are utterly undone."

When he had reached the court, Shama said: "See, wizard of all time, what the sorcerers and magicians have done to the Muslims."

"Have no fear," replied Barnoukh. "The magicians have indeed cast the spell of immobility over our kings, but I it is that will hound the magicians."

With that he brought a bowl of brass and filled it with fresh water, reading over it certain incantations known to him till the water began to boil over as though in a cauldron and a sudden tumult rose outside the building, filling every corner of the desert.

"Shama," Barnoukh said then, "take this bowl with you, and then, when the water ceases to seethe, sprinkle it over each of them and they will surely return to themselves. For my part I am going to do combat with those infidel magicians, awaiting the victory Almighty God will grant me."

Then he left the tent, and lo, there were the eighty magicians in the midst of the battlefield, each one like a demon. They had stayed the hands of the Ethiopians and all the ranks of the Sudanese, saying: "Remain there in your places, till we have prevailed over Barnoukh the magician and destroyed him among the troops; for he it is that is the mainstay of the Muslims." Each infidel among them had summoned up a particular kind of magic and sorcery, no kind being like another; and when Barnoukh walked out into the field, some conjured up a lance and struck him with it, and some sent a serpent against him, and some a lion, and some cast a spell of transformation over him, and some a spell of deafness, and some a spell of blindness, and some fashioned an arrow of steel; there was not one of the eighty but hurled against him some spell he had contrived. And when Barnoukh saw this, he began to undo the work of all these sorceries one by one; but still the magicians wrought on, and no sooner would he deliver himself from the eighty sorceries cast against him than they would conjure up yet others for him, from which he escaped only with the gravest hardship. And still he defended himself, repelling their sorceries, till at last they sent out against him a hail of stones with tongues of fire. Had Barnoukh not been a master among magicians he could never have survived that day; but versed as he was in all the kinds of magic, and stronger and more vigorous too through embracing the religion of Islam, he said: "No harm shall touch me at all, by the grace of al-Khader Ilyas."

Saqardis and Saqardyoun, seeing all the things that were passing, left the magicians to deal with Barnoukh and returned to their troops. "Know," they said, "that the kings and commanders of the troops of Islam are turned to stone through our magic, none remaining with power to move his left arm or his right. Never will you find a more favorable chance than this. Go now and assail the troops of Sayf Ben Dhi Yazan and all who are in Hamra' al-Yaman, plunging the sword in them till you have wiped them out to a man. Then their wealth will be yours to plunder, and their women free for all to seize as booty. Show them no mercy, but give them over to destruction."

At that the men mounted their horses and sped off toward the city, none of the troops opposing them, for they were like sheep without a shepherd; and Barnoukh, watching what had passed, and seeing the people of Islam were ready thereby to drink from the cup of tribulation, knew his only course was to raise his eyes to the heavens above this world, toward the haven of prayer. And so he began to recount his woe, abasing himself humbly and beseeching Almighty God with reverence and a flood of tears. "O God, Lord of Lords," he said, "You know how I spent so many years of my life worshipping the fire, till You alone guided me to the path of righteousness, and I joined myself with your camp; do not lay defeat on me now, and do not grant the infidels and workers of tyranny victory over me. Do not put me to the test, for I am a slave seeking favor and charity. An infidel in darkness I was; do not make me a vanquished believer. Cast back from me Your enemies, whose deeds are idolatry and pride, who speak abominable words and falsehoods. I am frail, so lend me strength, O God, and deliver me from the plight into which I am fallen; for You have power to do all things." In his severe pass, his Arab soul asserted itself, and he uttered these words of supplication:

> O Thou who canst descry the heart's secrets,
>> beneath my ribs it's crying out to Thee.
> O Thou alone art able to discern
>> its falsehood or its true fidelity.
>
> For I was drowned deep in a sea of error,
>> far off from harmony and righteousness,
> Until Thou didst open up my heart to guidance
>> with Thy compassion and Thy tenderness.
>
> I testify that Thou alone art God.
>> Thou art my way, Thou also art my goal.
> I follow Abraham who was Thy Prophet,
>> the friend of God, a man who had no guile.
>
> I am afflicted by an evil race
>> who know no justice, for their whole desire

Is following the religion of the Magian—
  their hearts are set upon the cult of fire.

I am their prisoner, they will have no mercy
  even though they give my body to the flame.
There's none will save me, I in my dejection
  knock on Thy door and call upon Thy name.

Open a way from all that hems us round
  and lift the weight of things that might confound.

When Barnoukh the magician had uttered these words from the depths of a seared and wounded heart, Almighty God accepted his prayer and granted him victory over his enemies; for God does not turn away from those who call on Him, or destroy the hope of any man. Suddenly a cloud of dust rose up into the air, floating over the land like a mist and swirling around an indomitable knight and fearless champion, mounted on a steed as black as night that seemed to fly almost, so swiftly did it pace. The knight had a veil set over his face, beneath which the light of his brow surpassed that of the crescent moon, a silk banner was unfurled across his shoulder, and before him was an old woman riding on a casket of brass. When they reached the pavilion where King Sayf Ben Dhi Yazan was, and all the kings with him, bewitched every one, the knight saw Queen Shama at the entrance with the sword unsheathed in her hand.

"May no harm befall you," said the old woman, "but only good and righteous things. Are you not Shama, daughter of King Afrah?"

"I am indeed she, lady," replied Shama, "and here are my husband and my father, and all those who follow the leaders of the Faithful, bewitched, as you see, every one."

Her aspect filled Shama with awe and fear, and she feared too when she saw the casket that could travel great distances with its every movement, and how she rode it, as though she were come as a scourge.

"Shama," she said, "which is King Sayf Ben Dhi Yazan?"

"Here he sits," she replied, "bewitched, at the front of the pavilion, with all these things come to pass upon him."

"Rejoice, Shama," the old woman said then, "for this very moment he shall be restored to health and safety, by the will of the Creator who surpasses all His creatures."

While they were conversing in this fashion, the rider approached, saying to the old woman: "Mother, who is this woman with whom you are speaking?"

"This is Shama," she replied, "and her husband is King Sayf Ben Dhi Yazan."

When the knight heard these words, his whole aspect changed. "Stand back from her," he cried, "so I may strike her head from her shoulders, stopping her breath and leaving her kinsfolk to grieve for her!'"

Now this rider was not indeed a man, but Tama, daughter of the sorceress 'Aqila, who, as we told before, had vowed to slay any wife of King Sayf Ben Dhi

Yazan should she meet her. But her mother said: "Leave this madness, Tama. She is the wife of King Sayf Ben Dhi Yazan, and you have no business with her. Let be your obstinacy, and know, rather, that we have important matters at hand. We have come here to deliver the people of Islam from their distress."

"Mother," she replied, "I have sworn that every wife of King Sayf Ben Dhi Yazan I meet I shall slay, and here is the first of them. Slay her I must, and so fulfill my oath; lies and falsehood must not be my mates."

When Queen Shama heard those words, the light before her eyes turned to darkness. "What is this you have sworn, wanton wretch?" she cried. "Am I your freed slave that you can slay me?" With that she drew her sword and advanced on Tama, who unsheathed her sword and advanced in her turn.

But the sorceress 'Aqila, laughing at the pair, ordered the servants to keep them one from another. Then, turning to her daughter, she said: "Are you not ashamed? Here we are come to mend this state of affairs, and you, for the sake of your passion, are minded to bring this man's life to destruction when he is afflicted with such miseries and hardships." Then, turning, she sought to assuage Shama. "Stay your anger, daughter," she said, "for she is your sister and my daughter, and you are still dearer to me than she is." And so the sorceress continued till she had mended matters between the two of them.

"And you, Aunt," Queen Shama said then, "who, pray, are you? What has brought you to these lands, and how do you come to know that King Sayf has been enchanted in the midst of war and combat?"

"By God," the sorceress replied, "you shall indeed hear the reason for my coming. When King Sayf came to me in his quest for the Book of the History of the Nile, I aided and delivered him. He had with him there the cap of the wizard Plato, and this it was that he used to take the book. When he had attained his goal, I wished to give him my daughter, Tama here, in marriage, but he said he would take no wife before Queen Shama. So we took the cap from him and gave him the book, and he departed from us to return to you; but as the days passed, he never asked after us, nor did we see him. And when things passed so, my daughter Tama asked: 'Mother, where is King Sayf, who promised to return to us and take me in marriage? Now that he has attained his goal, he cares only for his own affairs, asking after neither of us. You it is who delivered up the Book of the Nile to him and let him depart from us, and still he has not returned as it was settled he should.' 'Daughter,' I said, 'there is surely good reason why he has not come to us. Let me discover what is happening with him.' So then I cast the sands, and said: 'Know, Tama, that your husband is beset by eighty magicians who have fixed him in stone, and two kings and four bold commanders with him; and though Barnoukh fights on still, he too is harried by the magicians, in the direst straits. For your sake, my daughter, I shall rise and go to deliver them all, so that you may swiftly enter in on your husband.' Then I commanded one of the helpers of the jinn to conjure up a horse for Tama to ride, I myself riding on my casket; and so we proceeded till we came to rest here by the pavilion of King Sayf."

Then 'Aqila, gazing at the bowl, said: "Shama, who is it that wrought this?"
And when she was told Barnoukh the magician had wrought it, she took the
bowl and recited spells over it, intoning till the water ceased to seethe and
became still. Then she sprinkled King Sayf with it, and after him King Afrah, and
then, in turn, King Abu Taj and Sa'doun al-Zinji and Maymoun and Daminhour
al-Wahsh and Sabik al-Thalath, so that they were restored one and all to their
former state. "I praise God for your safety, King of Islam," she said to King Sayf;
and then she recited the following lines:

> Letters have ceased, and I am now become
>   like dwellers among tombs in my despair.
> No news from my beloved—I'm no bird,
>   nor have I wings to fly upon the air.

"Pray who are you, mother?" King Sayf said then.

"I am 'Aqila," she replied, "and my daughter is Tama, who has suffered trials,
on your account, like the trials of the Day of Doom. You are promised to her, yet
you have withheld yourself from her; and such a thing we do not expect, for
when kings once give their promise, they do not break it."

"And where is Tama?" asked King Sayf. "By God, for my part I am enamored
of her too, and burn for her; for she is the delight of my eye and of the heart that
beats between my ribs."

When Tama heard these words and knew that he loved her, the rage in her
heart cooled and she came to him and kissed his hands. Then, turning to her
mother, she said: "Here we are now after our journey, joined with King Sayf in
his pavilion. Truly it may be said of us:

> Of torments that I suffer, this is the worst:
>   not to be with my beloved yet so near;
> Like camels in the desert dying of thirst
>   though on their backs the water skins they bear."

"Tama," said King Sayf, "by the glory of my Lord, all that holds me back from
marrying you is the time to shake off these troubles. When that is done, banquet
for victory and wedding shall be held the same day."

"As for me," said the sorceress 'Aqila, "I shall deal with those eighty magicians
that confront Barnoukh." With that she entered King Sayf's tent and concealed
herself amongst the people there, and, summoning a servant from among the
jinn, instructed him to give her the names of the eighty magicians. Then she cut
out pieces of paper in the shape of human figures, to the number of eighty, on
which she penned certain magical inscriptions, writing on each one the name of
one of the magicians; and, mounting her casket, she made her way to the
battlefield.

At that moment Barnoukh was close to destruction, sure now that no escape
was left him from death, and was, as we told, praying to God and uttering the

verses we set out before. Then lo, the sorceress 'Aqila approached, her hair flying loose over her shoulders. She descended on those eighty magicians, coming between them and Barnoukh, then released the eighty figures from her hand, so that they soared up into the air and hovered in the heavens; and each figure among them took on the aspect of a fiery flame plunging down on the earth, entering the breast of one of the magicians and issuing from his back, so that all the eighty straightway dropped down like the hollow stumps of palm trees, with no life remaining in them. And all this while Barnoukh marveled at her deeds, rejoicing in his escape and his enemies' destruction at her hands, as God swiftly bore their souls to the torment of hellfire.

"Come with me now, Barnoukh," the sorceress said, "for it may be that the Exalted Lord, may He be praised, will bring good at our hands. It is my wish to marry my daughter Tama to King Sayf Ben Dhi Yazan, for she is one of his women and he is one of her men; but it has been too long now, brother, for you know no woman can be settled except in marriage, and I am beside myself for my daughter, who is dearer to me than my own life. I ask you to take my part with King Sayf; and if it be that he can marry my daughter only after settling this turbulent business and cannot fight all those people alone, then I shall scatter them through the power of secret knowledge, leaving neither rulers nor servants among them."

"You speak truly, sorceress," said Barnoukh. Then he accompanied her, and they went in to King Sayf and greeted him; and when King Sayf saw them, he rose and ordered seats to be brought for them; and they seated themselves, honored and joyful.

"King Sayf, my son," said the sorceress, "hear from me these two verses:

> You gave your promise to us;
>   we stretch forth our hand.
> Keep that promise youth!
>   The white flag is in the wind."

Then the sorceress turned to her daughter, saying: "Tama, where is the cap you took?" And when she had taken it from her, she said: "King of our time, here is the cap. Do not say I took it from you because I am powerless to fashion one like it, for I have fashioned you a girdle of stained leather which is, God knows, better than the cap. The cap has power only to conceal its wearer from the eyes of others, but if you don the girdle, then no troops, be they few or many, will ever have strength to resist you or prevail against you; when you enter the thick of the fray, to assail those who stand there against you, their steadfast courage will desert them."

With that the sorceress 'Aqila brought out a deerskin girdle inscribed with names and charms in Greek, and presented it to King Sayf, saying: "Do not delay, but gird yourself straightway with this, and then fall on those enemies of yours and thrust them through with the sword till you have scattered them into the wilds and hills; or else permit me to accomplish the business, and I shall, within this hour, lay them out lifeless on the ground; for warfare by secret knowledge, O King, is swifter than the blows of spear and sword." So it is that she who is wise has uttered these comfortable words in verse:

> A hero's sword that lopped ten peaks:
> that is a thing we have not known.
> But we have known a drop of ink
> that could a thousand flags haul down.

"If it is your pleasure, O King, to command me to slay those troops for you, then concern yourself no further. I shall scatter them through the wastelands and deserts, and cover the face of these highlands with their bodies."

Then King Sayf called to the whole encampment, commanding them to ride out; and they mounted one and all, King Afrah, and King Abu Taj, and Commander Sa'doun al-Zinji, and the commanders Maymoun and Sabik al-Thalath and Daminhour al-Wahsh. And when they were seated on their horses, with the troops of Islam mounted behind them, King Sayf cried out: "God is great, with all sway over the oppressor and tyrant, and over those who commit idolatry against Him!" Then he recited the following lines:

> When the dark spears are raised
> and the bright swords are unsheathed,
> Let me brave the fire of battle,
> mounted on a brisk, lean steed.
> I am Sayf Ben Dhi Yazan who is called
> the bridegroom of war on the day of Jihad.
> If one day the millstone of war revolved
> and the claws of death gripped the enemy,
> I would hear the clanging of my sword's strokes
> on the skulls and upon wrist bones.
> So summon me and I shall be at hand
> with a heart perdurable as hard granite.
> My spear has been my comrade since my childhood
> and my sword's an heirloom from the times of 'Ad.
> How many a battalion have I faced in combat
> when they brought forth my stubbornness of temper,
> And led them captive with the edge of my sword,
> razing their towns and villages to the ground,
> Gave them their fill of the thrusts of my sword,
> led away their horses, my sword being the drover.
> I am of the blood of Tubba' the Yemeni,
> my fame redounds throughout the whole wide world.
> The heroes of battle when they beheld me
> chose me for their support and for their stay.
> With them I charge against the infidel host
> in hope that God should grant me victory.

Then King Sayf bore down on the base and depraved infidels, charging into a sea of darkness and swirling dust, thrusting with the well-balanced spear and striking with the deadly sword, trimming off hands and heads, while Commander Sa'doun al-Zinji cried out behind him, and Maymoun al-Hajjam too followed him, and the valiant knight Daminhour al-Wahsh, and Sabik al-Thalath, seasoned in combat, charged forward, all visiting punishment and tribulation on their foes, striking with the noble sword and thrusting with the stout spear; and theirs was one of the greatest battles recounted in any tale. Behind them the knights of Islam charged, dealing blows with the sword and thrusts with the well-balanced spear, so that heads were cleft and bones shattered and the dead piled high on the ground; the dust and darkness gathered, and the tide of battle turned fierce against the infidels, so that they were ready to drink from the cup of death.

When the wizards Saqardis and Saqardyoun saw how events were turning, and knew death and destruction were near, each said to the other: "See, brother, how eighty magicians have been slain in a single hour; how all has turned against them, their bodies consumed beneath the hooves of lithe-bodied horses. All our effort, all we have done, has been brought to nothing, and if we fall into the hands of the Muslims, we shall drink deep from the cup of death. The wise course now is to flee, for if Sayf Ben Dhi Yazan should seize hold of us, he will glory in striking our heads from our shoulders with the keen-edged sword, and this day will be the last of our lives. Most fitting it is then, brother, that we seek safety in flight; for though a thousand shames should attach to us, shame and scandal are better than the loss of life. See now how the men of Ethiopia have perished before our eyes, their tents and encampments seized! All who venture out against these enemies fall slain, powerless to escape before death and destruction strike."

So they agreed, and, all paths closed before them in the face of such dangers, they forthwith sought safety in flight. As for the troops, when they saw the commanders had embraced Islam and the magicians were utterly destroyed and the wizards in flight, they were desolate and lost all heart. Throwing down all they had in the way of garments and other goods, they abandoned their encampments, and turned the heads of their horses, scattering into the wilds and hills to seek safety there. But the people of Islam pursued them for four full parasangs, striking their backs with the sword, and ceasing only after they had destroyed them in atonement for their deeds; no more, it is said, than a quarter survived from those regiments, the rest perishing like combed cotton on the edge of the sword.

Then King Sayf Ben Dhi Yazan, with all those alongside him from the camp of Islam, returned and seized all the Sudanese and base Ethiopians had left behind them, horses and weapons and money and other wealth, and returned successful and triumphant, rejoicing in their victory and praising God the Lord of Creation. King Sayf thereupon seated himself in his pavilion with the rich booty spread out before him. A third he reserved for himself; a third he divided as he deemed fit, one half for King Abu Taj and King Afrah, and the other for the four commanders, Sa'doun al-Zinji and Daminhour al-Wahsh and Sabik al-Thalath and Maymoun al-Hajjam; and the final third he divided, as he deemed fit, amongst the troops, two parts each to the cavalry and one part each to the infantry. And a mighty recompense it was, for the forces of King Sayf Ar'ad had been eighty thousand men with eighty magicians, and the magicians had concealed in their caskets gemstones and jewels the like of which surpassed all power to describe.

All this was seized by the people of Islam, so that they became prosperous beyond all fear of poverty, their hearts cheered and their minds at peace. As for those who were martyred fighting in God's cause, King Sayf summoned their wives and such offspring as remained, giving them what was due to their fathers and husbands. And so the people were joyful and reassured in their hearts, and took their rest in contentment.

12
Retribution

Now all this while none gave thought to Queen Qamariyya, or enquired after her. But the darkness had been lifted from her, and she remained restless for news, till at last she heard her son had been victorious and sat on his throne in peace. Then she rubbed ʿAyrud's tablet and, when ʿAyrud answered her call, commanded him to go that very instant to the place where her son was seated, then grasp him by the neck and choke the life from him, or else bring him to her so she might slay him herself, since all other means had failed. ʿAyrud went out accordingly, weeping in his sorrow and, making his way to where King Sayf was, was about to go in to him as usual; but he was assailed by the odors from the deerskin the king was wearing.

"So be it, O King," ʿAyrud said then. "You are under protection, and that is indeed the best of fortune." Then, returning to Qamariyya, he told her he was powerless to draw near Sayf on account of the enchanted deerskin girdle that had been fashioned by the sorceress ʿAqila and inscribed with charms for his protection. At this Qamariyya was furiously angry and dismissed ʿAyrud.

After a while Qamariyya's patience would endure no longer, and summoning one of the foremost jewelers of the city, she commanded him to make a tablet identical to ʿAyrud's tablet that was in her possession, and to engrave it with exactly the same inscriptions. Then, when he had completed his work, providing her with a tablet that was the perfect likeness of the original, she poisoned him along with the servant who had accompanied him there and herself took their bodies out into the wilderness.

When she returned, she concealed the true tablet and took the false one to her son. "Here is your tablet, my son," she said, weeping all the while, "forgive me for all those deeds of mine. The devil it was that tempted me to such mad courses." Then she told him how his father had appeared to her in a dream, reproaching her and enjoining her to repent, to go to her son and profess Islam at his hands, so that she might join him in the world to come.

"My son," she said to King Sayf, "teach me what I should say to become a Muslim, and so have the blindness removed from my heart."

Then King Sayf, overjoyed at this still more than at the restoration of his tablet, took it on himself to teach her what she should say; but none among his friends and dignitaries was taken in by all this. As for Qamariyya, she sat plotting and awaiting the chance to rid herself of her son or steal the deerskin from him. Again and again they warned him, but he paid no heed to them.

Meanwhile, his three new commanders, Sabik al-Thalath and Daminhour al-Wahsh and Maymoun al-Hajjam, asked his leave to return for a time to their homes, to visit their kinsfolk and friends, and to return with any who would accompany them; and this was granted, and they departed.

When Sabik al-Thalath returned, he came in to the king and kissed his hand, then said: "My lord, I have a gift which I beg you to accept."

"What is this gift?" asked King Sayf. "Whatever it is, I accept it without question."

"It is my daughter, Um al-Haya'," replied Sabik, "whom I offer to you in marriage, if she may be so fortunate."

It so happened that Sabik, when he returned to his home, had told his family of how he had embraced Islam, and of King Sayf and all the things that had happened, and had invited them to become Muslims too and return with him. He had a daughter, lovely and fair of speech, who had straightway joined him in the faith, and he had resolved to make her one of King Sayf Ben Dhi Yazan's wives. When King Sayf now heard of this, he straightway gave Sabik ten thousand dinars for her bride price, and that very day the marriage contract was written, the wedding feast held, and quarters set aside for Um al-Haya', so that all that now remained was to consummate the marriage.

Next morning, when the court was in session, Tama, the daughter of the sorceress 'Aqila entered, saying: "King of all time, it is as though you had forgotten me and your pledge to me, even though I became a Muslim at your hands. In the name of Him who guided me to Islam, I swear I shall kill any woman you now marry before you marry me. Keep your word now, or let her blood be on your hands."

King Sayf smiled at this, for he loved her and owed her mother much. "I swear by God, Tama," he said, "that I have not forgotten you, and that I love you with all that is in me. But everything has its time, and I have sworn not to take you in marriage till you restore the cap you seized from me. Give me the cap and so release me from my oath. Then I may become your spouse, and you my kin."

"And I for my part," said Tama, "have sworn never to give you the cap till you have taken me in marriage. You shall see who will be the winner in this." With that she flounced out, leaving King Sayf fearful of what she might do to his wives, especially Munyat al-Nufus, who was the one he loved most dearly. Accordingly he kept Munyat al-Nufus from her sight and watched over her; and so things remained for a time, with King Sayf believing he had possession of 'Ayrud's tablet, and dwelling in happy contentment.

Then, one day, a servant came to tell King Sayf a man of venerable aspect was at the door; and when the man was brought in before him, who should it be but Ikhmim al-Talib? King Sayf rose to greet him, embracing and kissing him, then had him seated beside him and was about to ask for food.

"I have no desire for food," said Ikhmim. "I come rather on behalf of my daughter. I promised her she should marry you when your business was accomplished, but though she waited, you never returned, and now her patience is at an end. She vowed to take her life if I did not bring her to you, so here I have brought her; and I ask you, my son, to marry her and heal her heart."

King Sayf, smiling at this, honored Ikhmim al-Talib and set aside quarters for him and his daughter, supplying all their needs. Then, three days later, he summoned a judge, saying to his court: "You know, all of you, that Tama, daughter of the sorceress 'Aqila, has sworn to slay any woman I take in marriage before her. I, for my part, have taken an oath not to marry her till she gives me the enchanted cap, while she has sworn, she says, to withhold it till the marriage; and we both of us wish to fulfill our oaths. Know too that the wizard Ikhmim al-Talib here saved my life and helped me gain possession of the tablet and the sword, the like of which have never been possessed by any other man. I have promised to take his daughter in marriage, and now here he is come for the fulfillment of that promise. How do you counsel me to proceed?"

At that the wizard Ikhmim al-Talib said: "I release you from your promise, O King."

"Have no fear of my daughter," the sorceress 'Aqila said in her turn, "for the wizard is our friend and neighbor. His daughter shall not be slain, nor need he fear for his daughter on account of mine. I shall stay Tama's hand, O King, admonishing her both for your sake and for his."

Then Tama spoke out in the court. "What are these words of the King?" she said. "Is he minded to hold back from marrying my cousin, seeking, in this fashion, to resolve the whole business? I call you all to witness that I shall harm no woman he has married up to now—I mean Shama, Munyat al-Nufus, Um al-Haya', and al-Jiza, daughter of the wizard Ikhmim al-Talib; in the name of Islam, I say, I shall do them no injury. But let him not take another in marriage before me."

"May you be well recompensed," they all replied. Then the judge came forward to make the contract between King Sayf and al-Jiza, and wedding celebrations were held for seven days; and then King Sayf went in to the two maidens, Um al-Haya' and al-Jiza, and consummated the two marriages in a single night, and a night of great joy it was.

All this while Qamariyya was watching and waiting and plotting, growing ever more rancorous and discontented as she saw him marry the two maidens and become still more secure and happy in his court. At last she rose and went to Nahid, daughter of the Emperor of China, who rose to meet her and joyfully returned her greetings, saying: "Welcome, mother. God has sent you to me, and you will perhaps find some means of relieving my distress." And when Qamariyya asked her what it was she meant by this, Nahid told her that since Sayf had brought her from her country he had neglected her, never touching her when he came to visit her, but rather spending the night in prayer and devotion, and that of late she had seen nothing at all of him.

At that Qamariyya promised her son should spend that very night with Nahid, persuading her, in return, to steal the deerskin from beneath her husband's pillow and bring it to Qamariyya. She needed it, she claimed, as a remedy for an ailment, and promised she would prevail on Sayf to spend all his nights with Nahid thereafter. And Nahid, believing her, promised to help her.

Then Qamariyya went to her son in the court and reproached him for neglecting Nahid in favor of others, telling him of Nahid's unhappiness and asking him, for his mother's sake, to spend that night with her.

"I hear and obey," said King Sayf. "Tonight I shall go to her." And Qamariyya bore the good news to Nahid, delighted at the success of her scheme and reminding Nahid of her promise concerning the deerskin.

When King Sayf came that night to Nahid's chambers, she met him joyously and had him sit down, serving him with the best food and entertaining him. Then, after talking and drinking together, they began to embrace and kiss, and King Sayf rose and took off his clothes, including the magic deerskin which the sorceress 'Aqila had fashioned for him, which he placed under his pillow; then, having enjoyed union with Nahid and taken his pleasure with her, he laid his head down on the pillow and fell into a deep slumber.

When Nahid knew from his aspect that he was sleeping, she rose and stretched out her hand to take the deerskin from beneath his pillow, not knowing what fate had in store for her; and as Qamariyya had told her she would be waiting by the door, she went swiftly out to deliver the skin as she had promised. Then, lo, a sword blazed and gleamed with a light greater than the lightning flash, and, falling on Nahid's neck, struck her head from her shoulders, sending her lifeless to the floor with the deerskin in her hand. And when the accursed Qamariyya saw this, she was struck with panic lest the same punishment should befall her and she fled in terror.

Now when the sword struck Nahid, she had uttered a terrible cry which woke King Sayf; and when he found Nahid no longer by his side, and ran out to find her weltering in her blood, he was filled with a great sorrow and grief, for she alone of all his women was a stranger in the land, with no kinsfolk there. Then, having wept and lamented over her, he said to himself: "This surely is the handiwork of Tama, who, in her passion, has betrayed her promise." And as he stood there, Tama herself came to him.

"Tama," he said then, "who is it that slew Nahid?"

"I myself it was," she said, "with this keen-edged sword."

"And why Tama," he asked, "did you break your oath and kill a woman who was guiltless?"

"As for breaking my oath," she replied, "I did no such thing, for the four I swore to leave untouched are still alive and with you. And as for her being guiltless, how far that is from the truth! She took the enchanted deerskin from beneath your head while you slept and was minded to give it to your mother, who would have destroyed you when she once had that and 'Ayrud's tablet."

Full of anger at this, and believing Tama's words to be false, he rubbed the tablet so as to summon 'Ayrud and learn the truth; but nothing happened. Then, when he had rubbed it twice more to no avail, he realized his mother had tricked him, and that Tama it was who had watched over his well-being and delivered him. But when he rose and went in haste to Qamariyya's palace, he found she had fled.

Next morning, when all those present in the court heard how Nahid had been slain by Tama on account of Qamariyya's treachery and evil, they rebuked King Sayf for paying no heed to their counsel, rather pardoning his mother constantly and affording her chances to work her menace; and every man there swore to hack Qamariyya to pieces with his sword if he should meet her.

As they were talking, 'Aqisa flew in and greeted them, to King Sayf's great joy; and when King Sayf told her what had passed with Nahid and Qamariyya, she turned to him, saying: "Brother, if I search her out and bring her, will you give me leave to slay her in atonement for her deed?"

"Only bring her," he replied, "and you will see what I shall do."

"As I know you," 'Aqisa said then, "you will have me strive to bring her, then stay my hand once more from giving her her due. But by the inscription on Solomon's ring, this time I shall not let her be, say what you will." Then she said to the company: "I shall seek her out and bring her, but on that condition only." And with that she flew off.

A few days later she returned, and King Sayf said: "Do you have news of her?"

"Indeed," she replied, "after weary effort. But I ask your leave to do with her as I will."

"I have delivered her fate into your hands," he said, "should you gain hold of her."

"Then," she replied, "I have news of her."

Now when Qamariyya saw Nahid was dead, and that Sayf had awoken, she fled terrified to her palace and there rubbed 'Ayrud's tablet; and when he appeared, she instructed him to take her to Nahid's father, whose name was al-Sammsaam, and who was a mighty ruler and sovereign over all the lands of China. So 'Ayrud set her down on the top of the king's palace; and as the king was sitting in the palace amidst his attendants, Qamariyya entered in to him, resplendent in her finest robes and jewels and exquisite in her loveliness, so that he was instantly smitten with her.

When he asked her who she was, she told him she had journeyed from the land of Yemen with sad news of his daughter, who had been slain by that

same Sayf Ben Dhi Yazan who had cured her of her blindness. King Sayf had
striven to slay her too, she told him, when she rebuked him for killing Nahid,
so here she had fled in fear for her life. The king was aggrieved over his
daughter, but so enamored too at the sight of Qamariyya that his first inten-
tion, before all else, was to make her his bride; and so he asked her to em-
brace his religion, which was the worship of fire, and when she had done this
they were married according to the custom of the place, and he went in to her
and joined with her and slept beside her. At this point it was that 'Aqisa
discovered them after seeking Qamariyya far and wide; and she returned with
her news to King Sayf.

At that King Sayf, furiously angry with his mother, asked 'Aqisa why she
had not brought her back.

"I cannot approach her while she has the tablet," replied 'Aqisa, "nor can
any jinn."

"I will go to China with 'Aqisa," Barnoukh the magician said then. "It may
be, O King, I shall contrive a way of stealing the tablet from her."

With that Barnoukh mounted his brass casket and flew beside 'Aqisa, and
they alighted on the palace of al-Sammsaam in the early part of the night; and
Barnoukh, creeping down alongside the window of the palace, found them
drunk, and Qamariyya saying to the king: "How long must you wait before
avenging your daughter's death?"

"In the name of the fire," he said, "I shall indeed ride to the land of
Yemen, leaving no one there alive."

"And I," she said, "will come to your aid with an army raised from the
King of Ethiopia."

After a while sleep took hold of them, and Barnoukh, entering and creep-
ing up to Qamariyya like a venomous snake, invoking God's name all the
while, stretched out his hand and unfastened the tablet from her arm. When
he had it safe, he felt as though the whole world were his, and returning
through the window to his casket, he said: "Let us return to King Sayf."

King Sayf was waiting for him, and when Barnoukh handed him the tablet
he was filled with joy. Then, turning to 'Aqisa, he said: "'Aqisa, where is my
mother?"

"I will bring her to you straightway," she said, "but only on the condition
we agreed before." Then off she flew, returning in a short time.

By this time morning had broken and the court was full. Then 'Aqisa
approached, bearing Qamariyya aloft, high above the palace, and crying out
in ringing tones: "Know, King of all time, that this is Qamariyya, who
contrived so many plots against you. Now I shall fling her from my hands and
send her lifeless to the ground; and so you will be rid of her evil and menace."

"'Aqisa," the king said, "bring her down to me here."

"Never," said 'Aqisa then. "Never shall you see her living again." And with
that she flung Qamariyya up into the higher air, and, when she fell, caught
her and flung her up again. Then Tama unsheathed her sword, minded to go

out and slay her before she reached the ground; but ʻAqisa, snatching the sword from her hand, dashed Qamariyya upon it, cleaving her through the middle of the body, and so again and again, till she fell to the ground hacked to pieces; and then ʻAqisa flung the head into King Sayf Ben Dhi Yazan's lap.

"May your hands cease to grasp, accursed one!" cried King Sayf. "So I shall render you, jinn outcast, if you fall into my hands!"

Then she said to King Sayf: "Brother, you will not see me again, nor I you; but now I shall fear for you no more, for she it was who time and again brought you low, may peace be upon you." And with that she left him and flew her way.

As for King Sayf, he grieved and wept over his mother, burying her remains himself, and observed a period of mourning, dispensing charity and holding memorial banquets. And when the period was over, he sat joyful and content on his throne. And now it was that messengers came to him with the glad news that his wife al-Jiza, daughter of Ikhmim al-Talib, had given birth to a son lovelier than the full moon. Then King Sayf rose and, going to his wife's chambers, named his son Nasr (meaning, Victory), and there was joy and feasting as everyone rejoiced at the newborn baby. And so the days passed.

13
The City of Maidens

As the days passed and still King Sayf did not wed Tama, she grew fretful and angry, threatening to slay his dearly loved wife Munyat al-Nufus; and so King Sayf called upon his notables and men of state to help resolve the problem of the oaths he and Tama had taken. Their counsel was that he should make the marriage contract, upon which Tama could give him the cap, and only then, when she had given it to him, would he go in to her and consummate the marriage. The custom was that two fat cows should be slaughtered and their meat distributed when an oath was redeemed, but King Sayf pledged to slaughter seven. So it was done that very day, and he proclaimed Tama's bride price to be ten thousand gold dinars.

When King Sayf asked Tama if this was acceptable to her, she replied: "King of all time, though you wish to take me, still more do I wish to take you, and the price is acceptable. But my Lord, I ask you to grant me a wish at such time as I may ask it." He granted this request, and the marriage contract was thereupon written and a wedding feast held that lasted seven days.

Now as King Sayf's wives feasted together, eating and drinking and making merry, they began to dance. The first to dance was Um al-Haya', and all the women admired her; and then al-Jiza rose to dance, and then Shama. But each time one of them danced, Munyat al-Nufus would say their movements were clumsy and not like the dancing she knew in her own land. Upon that they insisted she dance and show them, for, as she was the loveliest among them and King Sayf was passionately enamored of her, they all esteemed her and wished to please her. At first she would not, being with child, but finally she rose to her feet and began dancing for them, swaying like a shoot of jasmine, weaving and moving her body till they were all dumbfounded at the sight.

Tama had never, she thought, seen anyone like her. "My lady Munyat al-Nufus," she said, "is it so that people dance in your land?"

"This is nothing," replied Munyat al-Nufus, "compared to the way I dance in my feather robe, for that is enchanted. Had I the robe here with me, I would show you."

"Does King Sayf have the robe?" she asked. And when she was told this was indeed so, Tama resolved to ask the king for it.

That night Queen Munyat al-Nufus gave birth to a son; and when the king heard of this, he went to her chambers to see the child, whom he named Masr. This boy, he was told, would be blessed and fortunate; and he would build a great city named after his own name, through which the Nile would flow. And King Sayf Ben Dhi Yazan rejoiced greatly at this.

That same night King Sayf went in to Tama and consummated their marriage. Then Tama told him her wish, which was that he should permit her to see the robe of feathers belonging to Munyat al-Nufus; and when she had promised to take all care of it (for he feared lest Munyat al-Nufus should take it back and return to her land and family), he gave it her to look at.

So the days passed. Then one day, when King Sayf had gone hunting with his men, Tama invited Munyat al-Nufus to her quarters, having singers and food and drink brought before them, and they passed the night in merry making. Then, when Munyat al-Nufus danced, Tama turned to her, saying: "It would please me to see you in your feather robes."

"If such is your wish," replied Munyat al-Nufus, "then bring it to me here."

"I fear," said Tama, "that you will put it on and fly away to your land."

"If your heart is uneasy," said Munyat al-Nufus, "then do not give it me." Thus she feigned indifference, as she had done since the first mention of the robe; but in truth her heart was aflame.

"Promise me," Tama said then, "that if I bring it, you will return it to me." And when Munyat al-Nufus promised accordingly, Tama rose and fetched it, then gave it to Munyat al-Nufus where she was sitting with her child in her lap. The sight of it filled Munyat al-Nufus with delight, and, donning the enchanted robe of feathers, she fastened it and fluttered with her wings, flying round and about to the amazement of all the women who saw her. Then she descended and, taking her child and cradling him securely to her breast with a silk kerchief, up she flew once more and hovered in the air, before alighting on the ledge of the palace and standing there gazing at them.

"Sister," said Tama, "descend and keep us company here."

"Sister," replied Munyat al-Nufus, "it is long since I wore it, and here it is come to me without pain or endeavor." With that she burst into peals of laughter, and Tama, knowing she had been tricked, felt her heart ready to burst. Try as she would, and her mother the sorceress 'Aqila too, nothing would persuade Munyat al-Nufus to descend. "I have recalled my home and family," she told the sorceress, "and I long to see them and be with them. I shall not descend. If King Sayf should come and enquire after me, tell him this: 'I have returned with my son to my own country, for the peace of my heart and soul. Neither you nor any other king shall keep possession of Munyat al-Nufus, daughter of King Qasim al-'Abous, for the daughters of kings cannot be taken by theft. You seized me first, then afflicted me with grief and deserted me to take other women. But what has been has been. If you have any valor and resolve, and if you truly love me, then pursue me to the City of Maidens in the islands of Waq al-Waq.' With that she clasped her son beneath the garment at her breast and vanished through the air, leaving Tama and the sorceress 'Aqila distraught and fearful of the king's wrath.

Then the sorceress devised a plan. Summoning a carpenter, she had him fashion a wooden figure in the likeness of Munyat al-Nufus, which she then painted to appear real, lacking only the spirit. Then she took this to Munyat al-Nufus's palace and, setting it on her bed there, called her slave maidens and told them: "Your lady is dead." At that they wailed and bemoaned her fate, and word spread through the city that Munyat al-Nufus and her son had died, with none knowing the truth save Tama and her mother.

When King Sayf returned from the hunt, he saw Munyat al-Nufus's palace shuttered up, with cobwebs hanging in its corners; and he cried out, as though thunderstruck, in a voice that shook the palace: "What has happened here? Where is my wife Munyat al-Nufus?" Then they told him she had died while eating and drinking with Tama and that they had buried her.

At this news the light before King Sayf's eyes turned to darkness, and he moaned and lamented, weeping floods of tears. Then he went to enquire of Tama and, hearing the same story from her, he fainted; and when he rose once more and remembered Munyat al-Nufus, he struck his face and tore at his clothes, like a man beside himself. Then he went to seat himself beside the grave, grieving and wailing, unable either to sleep or eat or drink; and so it remained for twenty full days, till he was on the edge of death.

When the sorceress 'Aqila saw to what state the bitterness of his grief had brought him, she said: "Torment yourself no more, King of all time, for Munyat al-Nufus is not dead but alive. I shall tell you truly all that passed." And when she had told him the story from first to last, King Sayf's face became radiant, and he smiled, reproaching the sorceress for not relating this sooner, and so subjecting him to the anguish he had endured. Then he changed his garments and bathed, and spent the first night thereafter with Tama, refusing to reproach her. "He who aspires to a precious thing," he told her, "must risk a precious thing, and so long as she is alive I shall not despair of being rejoined with her." Then, having spent a night in turn with each of his wives, Shama and al-Jiza and Um al-Haya', he resolved to go in pursuit of Munyat al-Nufus.

Now it so chanced that his sister 'Aqisa came to visit him for the first time since Qamariyya's death; and when they had conversed together and had become reconciled, King Sayf asked her about the City of Maidens, requesting that she bear him there. She realized then that Munyat al-Nufus had departed but counseled him not to try to pursue her, for the road there was hazardous and difficult, and even should he arrive he could not pass through the gates, as the Watcher would cry out against him and the maidens come out and slay him; for no male was ever allowed to enter the place.

"And why," King Sayf asked 'Aqisa, "does this city have only maidens? Why are there no men there?"

"The reason for that is strange indeed," replied 'Aqisa. "The island is called the island of Waq al-Waq, and it was ruled by a king called Kafur, who had two sons, one named 'Asim and the other Qasim. So he built two cities, called after the names of his sons, and told them that, were he to die, they should each inherit a city and be as one, without any strife or envy between them. Then he married them, on the same night, to the daughters of his minister, and the wives conceived; and after King Kafur's death, each son took his own city and lived in it with his wife. First Qasim's wife gave birth to a daughter, then 'Asim's wife to a son; and when they were grown up, 'Asim wrote to his brother asking his daughter's hand in marriage for his son. This did not please Qasim, but he asked his daughter even so; then, when she expressed unwillingness, he sent back word to his brother that his daughter did not wish to marry. Thereupon 'Asim, furiously angry at this, resolved to take vengeance on his brother for withholding his daughter in marriage, and, summoning his wizards and magicians, asked them to devise some enchantment by which all the maidens in his brother's city would come to his. Accordingly they made a statue of a maiden in white wax and chanted spells over it, so that all the maidens straightway left Qasim's city and sped to 'Asim's, standing there before him captive in mind and body. Then the wizards devised further enchantments to prevent any male from entering the city, placing Watchers on the wall to warn of any man trying to enter, and so contrived things that the maidens should all be warriors, versed in the arts of chivalry and horsemanship.

When Qasim learned of what had happened, he summoned his wizards, who were forty in number, instructing them to devise a means by which all the males in his brother's city should come to his; and this they did, setting Watchers and sentries to cry out or to capture any maiden who tried to enter the city. But wishing to see his daughter Munyat al-Nufus, who was now in the other city, he asked his wizards to devise a way to achieve this, and they accordingly fashioned for her a robe of feathers which she could don to fly and visit her father; and when she asked for forty chosen attendants to fly with her and keep her company, her father had robes made for them also. Then, when 'Asim died, Munyat al-Nufus became ruler of the city, and her father Qasim had the wizards build a palace for his daughter at a distance of three days' flight, surrounded by a garden for her recreation and pleasure. There she would go every year with her forty companions to disport herself for a while, till the day came when she fell into your hands."

"'Aqisa," said King Sayf, when she had finished recounting all this, "if my wife has plunged into the sea, then take me into the depths in pursuit of her. And if she has ascended into the heavens, then let me cling to the tails of her garment and ascend with her. Were I to drink the cup of death, I must pursue her, for I can bear her absence no longer."

When 'Aqisa at last agreed, King Sayf assembled all his dignitaries and men in the court and set his son Dummar in his place, asking them to lend him their aid. Then he took his farewell of all and departed. 'Aqisa, who had also taken farewell of her family in the meantime, then asked him if all his affairs were set in order, and if he had with him all his special treasures, the tablet and the sword and the cap and the whip. "Indeed, sister," he said, "I have them here."

"Summon 'Ayrud," she said then, "for I have need of him."

So King Sayf rubbed the tablet and 'Ayrud appeared, saying: "What is your pleasure, King of all time?" Then 'Aqisa told him where they were heading, and for what purpose, assuring him that the king could not be dissuaded.

"What say you to this, 'Ayrud?" she asked.

"Wherever he commands me to go," 'Ayrud replied, "there I shall repair, placing my trust in the All-Powerful God."

Then King Sayf, gazing at his palace and court, began to recite verses telling of his sorrow and longing for his wife and son, and of his resolve to pursue them:

> O my palace, look upon my departure;
>   I go to her who reigns over my sinking heart.
> O my palace, I had left my son in your keeping,
>   a lad still in the ignorance of youth.
> I've come to know what my wife, al-'Abous's daughter,
>   has done to me, which left me bereft of words.
> That dress which was in Tama's keeping she got hold of
>   by stealth, so that she could make her escape.
> She thought I would be unable to track her down,
>   but at her heels I cleave the dark unknown.
> O 'Aqisa, you have knowledge of my story;
>   come help me, therefore, to traverse the hills.
> O Masr, my son, you have deserted me
>   and left me burning among live embers.
> You followed your mother, and both unleashed my anguish,
>   leaving me in torture from your alienation.
> Separation from you has scorched my heart;
>   my once tranquil life is now full of rage.
> O Munyat al-Nufus, why this estrangement?
>   My heart turns on a spit in the fire of anguish.
> I come to your country in the cause of honor;
>   I come to your islands with an urgent quest
> To rescue you with the edge of the sword
>   and with the point of a sharp Samhari spear,

> And make him who seeks to prevent your return
>   taste of the cup of death from my sword blade.
> And I will break the enchantment of your lands
>   and you shall witness great and marvelous deeds;
> And I shall gather two lines of your girls
>   and of your young men and arrange their marriages,
> And establish the religion of God among you,
>   the great and righteous truth which pure hearts love.

Then King Sayf Ben Dhi Yazan said to 'Ayrud: "Raise me up, son of the Red One, and, you, 'Aqisa, accompany us as we have agreed."

"I hear and obey brother," said 'Aqisa. Then 'Ayrud, laying hand upon him, raised him onto his shoulders and they began their journey through the wastelands, 'Aqisa following behind; and soon they had vanished from sight, delving deep into the wilds and hills. When evening fell, King Sayf Ben Dhi Yazan asked 'Aqisa to provide supper for them, and she brought the means to satisfy his hunger; then she held him firm on 'Ayrud's shoulder, and he slept as they flew on through the night. Then, when morning broke, 'Aqisa bore him up in her turn, saying to 'Ayrud: "Bring him some roast venison to eat." 'Ayrud thereupon brought her a gazelle which they prepared as they journeyed, and King Sayf ate.

So it was in the evening and for a further five days, when they alighted for a day's rest, then on for five more days; and if 'Ayrud bore him, 'Aqisa would supply all his needs of food and drink, and if 'Aqisa bore him, 'Ayrud would provide these things for him, and so things continued for two whole months, day and night, as they traversed a distance of a hundred years for ordinary mortals. At last they drew near to a lofty mountain, soaring so high into the air that it brushed the clouds. There they set him down and, as it was evening time, brought him food and drink and remained there till morning.

"Brother," 'Aqisa said then, "look there straight ahead of you, in the midst of the land."

"I see only a dark form," he replied.

"That," she said, "is the beginning of the islands you seek. They do not lie within our compass, and we have no power to take so much as a step into them; it is because of the spells laid upon them that we have set you down here in this place. Know, too, that the jinn of those lands are our enemies, and we have no power of entry against them."

"May God prosper you," said King Sayf. "I have set my fate in the hands of Him who raised the heavens and taught the names to Adam. Only await me here till I return to you, or till you hear of my death."

"Have no fear, brother," said 'Aqisa. "All shall turn to good."

Then they brought him down from the mountain as he instructed them and, bidding him farewell, returned to their places, while he moved on toward the dark form they had pointed out to him. As he walked on, the shape turned to yellow, and he discovered before him a city, where, as evening had fallen, he slept solitary and alone at the gates, placing his trust in the good and glorious God.

When day broke, King Sayf woke from his sleep and, gazing to right and left, saw a man sitting at his head in the attitude of the pious. King Sayf was abashed at the sight of him but, teaching firmness to his heart, approached him and kissed his hands, saying: "Sir, who pray are you?"

"King of all time," replied the man, "I am one of your brothers living alone here in this place, your brother in faith and honor, and our shaykh it was who sent me expressly to meet you."

"And who is our shaykh, sir?" asked King Sayf.

"Our shaykh al-Khader, peace be upon him," said the man. "He has sent me, saying: 'Go to King Sayf and help him attain his goal.' And now I am come, O King, in obedience to his command. Tell me of yourself, and what it is you seek here in this land."

"Know, brother," said King Sayf Ben Dhi Yazan, "that I passed through the Garden of Delights by the side of the sources of the Nile, where I saw their birds of humankind, and when I gained the robe of the eldest by trickery, God guided her to Islam and I married her. But when, in due season, she had given birth, she took me unawares, seizing the enchanted robe; and, setting her son at her breast, she flew back to these lands. Now I have pursued her here, seeking the restoration of my wife and child, for whose sake my very heart is shattered. Such is my wish and purpose."

When the shaykh heard these words, he began to laugh and smile, saying: "All shall be eased by the will of the All-Knowing Sovereign."

"Sir," said King Sayf, "if you are able to aid me in some way, make haste to do it, for by God I am in a wretched state."

"I hear and obey," said the man. "Wait here till I return to you."

With that the shaykh departed, returning after an hour with a bundle embroidered with all manner of silver and gold thread.

"Take this bundle and open it," he said. "Within you will see marvels. Know this bundle is yours, for it is promised to you, and my shaykh has commanded me to deliver it up to you with all its contents."

King Sayf took the bundle accordingly and opened it, and lo, there was a suit of clothes revealed, of satin embroidered with all manner of precious metals, the garments of women and not of men.

"Of what use is this bundle to me?" asked King Sayf.

"Sir," replied the shaykh, "it will be of the greatest use to you. And here is yet more." And with that he handed him an emerald, saying: "Take another gift." Then he said: "This goblet too is a useful possession." So King Sayf took the various gifts, saying to himself: "Of what use are these things?" And still the shaykh said: "Take this ball, brother," and when King Sayf took it, he said: "Take this mallet."

So he took them all, then said: "Of what use are all those possessions to me?"

"Brother," said the shaykh, "each of these things has a secret, which is a secret of Almighty God. As for the suit of clothes in the bundle, you will be entering the City of Maidens, where no man lives. These garments are like theirs, and if you don them none will cry out against you, for your master has secretly brought them to you, along with the rest of the items, from the treasure of Kush Ben Can'an. It is the work of the wizard A'la Trous, God have mercy upon him, who was one of the wizards of Greece, and died in the Faith. You, brother, will be entering the City of Maidens, and between you and that city are the Islands of Waq al-Waq. When you enter those islands, don these garments and carry with you this emerald, which will guard you against the chill that assails you in the high places, so that no freezing air will harm your ears, or cold overwhelm you; and if you are in the heat, the sun will not harm you. It has other great uses besides: if you are minded to sleep, move it to the right and you will find bedding, and you will sleep by the Power; but the servant bearing you will not know this, and if he is minded to speak to you while you are sleeping, then the servant of the Power will answer in your place. As for the goblet, it is enchanted, and will straightway bring you all the food and drink you ask; while the ball and mallet will be useful to you in sports you encounter. You will come to see the truth of my words. This is what your shaykh has instructed me to pass on to you, and may peace be upon you. And I too wish to make you a gift, brother, for you are surely a stranger in these regions, unacquainted with these lands and deserts."

"May God send you rich reward," said King Sayf. "What is it you have for me?"

"Now welcome to you," replied the other. "I have long awaited you, and I have knowledge of the enchantments governing these lands. I shall make you a gift the like of which no man has ever seen."

Then the shaykh rose and, walking over to a cave, returned bearing a tablet of red gold with a chain of white silver, on which were inscribed names and charms and figures and tracings, different from those on 'Ayrud's tablet.

"Brother," he said, "take this tablet, which commands a giant who is one of the servants among the jinn. He is called al-Khayraqan and is of matchless might, before any other jinn. He it is who will aid you, bearing you through the islands of Waq al-Waq; if you rub the tablet, the servant will come just as your servant 'Ayrud would were he able to enter these lands. This is my gift to you. But I enjoin you, O King, when this servant has once borne you where you wish to be, and when you have once accomplished your business, that you then give him his tablet and release him to go his way, for so I have promised him. And indeed he would be of no use to you thereafter, for he has no power in your country."

"Sir," said King Sayf, "I hear and obey."

"Put on the suit of clothes," said the shaykh, "and depart with God's blessing, taking these other items with you and placing your trust in Him."

At that King Sayf Ben Dhi Yazan thanked him, saying: "May God send you rich reward." And he asked him to pray for him.

"God will swiftly meet your needs," replied the other, "but should any mischance befall you, then call on me, and I shall come to your aid."

"And what, pray, is your name?" asked King Sayf Ben Dhi Yazan.

"I am called Abu 'l-Nur al-Zaytouni," he said.

And so they took their leave one of the other, and when King Sayf had walked on some distance, he took the tablet and rubbed it lightly, and lo, a servant appeared like the mist, saying: "Ask what you will of me, King of the Arabs, then release me as kings free slaves."

"Accomplish my business for me," said the king, "and I shall indeed release you and restore your tablet to you."

"You are King Sayf Ben Dhi Yazan, are you not?" he said. And when told that it was indeed he, he asked: "What is your will?"

"That you should take me," replied King Sayf, "to the islands of Waq al-Waq."

"I hear and obey," said the giant. Then, raising King Sayf up onto his shoulders, he ascended with him into the upper heavens, flying on with him still till noonday drew near; and a great distance he had borne him, for he was a mighty giant. Then he set him down on the ground to rest, saying: "See, this is the first of the seven islands."

Then King Sayf looked and saw a vast meadow and a teeming sea; and on one shore of the sea a mortar of yellow brass over which stood a column of Chinese iron.

"What is this sea, giant," he asked, "and what is this mortar?"

"My lord," he replied, "this is the first of the islands of Waq al-Waq, and these are old spells that have lost their power. Here is the first of the lands you seek. If you are minded to cast your eye around it, I shall show it you, and if you wish to journey further, I shall journey with you to the place you seek."

"Here is a land," said King Sayf Ben Dhi Yazan, "where I never in all my life set foot. I should wish to pass a day viewing it."

"Let it be as you wish," said the giant.

Then the king brought out the goblet he had with him and, covering it with a white napkin as Shaykh Abu 'l-Nur had instructed him, placed his right hand over it, and said: "In the name of God, bring me a dish of tharid forthwith, with roast venison." No sooner had he uttered these words than the goblet grew hot and smoke came from it; and when King Sayf raised the napkin, he saw the goblet was full of tharid, yoghurt, and rice, with roast venison on top of them.

"By God," said King Sayf, "this goblet is the best of possessions, bringing food without labor or endeavor. A marvel among marvels it is." Having eaten and given praise to Almighty God, he rose to view the island, then, returning to the place he had started from, said to the giant: "I wish to move on to the next island. But let our path lie close to the ground, so that I may see what it holds."

"O King," said the giant, "from here to the next island is only mountains and seas. The marvels to stun the beholder are in the islands themselves."

"When shall we reach the second island?" asked King Sayf. And when he was told, by morning, he said: "Travel on as you wish."

Then the king placed the emerald beneath his head and slept through the night, while the giant flew on till the light of dawn gleamed. Then the giant said: "My lord, here is the second island."

"Bear us close to the ground," said King Sayf, "so that I may view it."

"I hear and obey," said the giant. Then King Sayf, viewing round about him from the air, saw the island lay between two seas, vast in extent, with two lofty mountains of granite, and tall trees stretching as far as the eye could see, whose leaves amazed the beholder; for they had the form of lovely maidens hanging by their hair from the branches, the winds swinging them right and left.

At that King Sayf Ben Dhi Yazan said: "There is no power or strength except in the Exalted and All-Powerful God. Surely, giant, the king of this place is a tyrant to do such things to these people. What deeds have they committed that he should bind them to the trees in this fashion?"

"O King," the giant replied, laughing, "the king of this vast and fruitful land is the King of this world and the hereafter, that is God, the All-Vanquishing Sovereign, who rolls the night back on the day, and transforms hearts and visions. He it is who created these trees and made their fruit as you see them, in the likeness of humankind, fruit of which both travelers and those who live here may eat night or day. And when darkness falls, and the sky of night shines forthwith, each of them utters cries and shouts and shrieks, and in their speech they say, Praise be to the Sovereign Creator. This they repeat a second time, and a third, in unison, and should one of them drop to the ground, it lives for three days and dies thereafter; and this is the work of the Everlasting One who never dies. Some, here, have the likeness of males, young and old, and here are others in the likeness of women, comely virgin maidens lovely as the moon."

When King Sayf heard this, he was filled with wonder at the things so ordained and his heart more filled with desire for the religion of Islam. "Blessed be God," he said, "the Almighty and All-Knowing, Creator of light and darkness." Then he said: "Giant, I wish to alight and pass the night here, so that I may hear their words with my own ears; for in all my life I never saw or heard the like of what you recount, and I should wish to view these divine secrets."

"Let it be as you wish," said the giant. And there they remained on that island, with the mind of King Sayf Ben Dhi Yazan much exercised with these things, till the day departed and the gloomy darkness of night drew near. Still they possessed themselves in patience, till the first third of the night had passed; then a breeze blew over them such as would restore the sick to health, and lo, God made the fruit, as they hung from their trees in that fashion, utter praises in unison to Him, the One True and All-Vanquishing Sovereign, saying: "Praise be to the Sovereign Creator!" And so it happened a second time, and a third, and still they cried out, till night took its appointed leave and the beams of morning appeared.

When King Sayf Ben Dhi Yazan heard these words, he began to praise the All-Powerful and All-Knowing Sovereign; his heart responded to the call of Islam, and he shed copious tears in his awe of the splendor and beneficence of God, saying with a true heart: "I witness that there is no God but God, and I witness that Abraham is the Friend of God, and that Muhammad is the messenger of God, who will be revealed at the end of time to enjoin good deeds and proscribe evil deeds. Happy the man who sees his coming, and believes in him, and is one of his friends and helpers." Then he said: "Giant, in the name of God the All-Merciful and Compassionate, these fruits are the work of the Sovereign Lord."

"Let us, O King," said the giant, "journey together to the third island, which is greater in extent than this one, with every kind of form and color."

"We should go on indeed," replied King Sayf Ben Dhi Yazan, "if such be the will of the All-Powerful God." But first, bringing out the goblet, he covered it, and said: "I wish to eat a loaf of bread with yoghurt." And when he uncovered the goblet, there was revealed the thing he had asked for, and he ate his fill. Then the giant bore him up and they journeyed together for a day and a night, till at last he set him down between four mountains that stretched up into the heights, lofty and soaring, with tall trees between them from which hung fruits in the likeness of maidens, their cries like those of the men on the first island; but a great difference there was between the voices of the men and of the women, for the men's voices were deep and those of the women melodious. At that King Sayf was filled with wonder at the power of the Almighty and Compassionate God. They had, he saw, long hair like ingots of pure gold, by which they hung from the trees, and when night came, they cried out with their cry.

"Praise be to Him," said King Sayf Ben Dhi Yazan, "who, if He wills something should be, says be, and it is." Then he said to the giant, "I wish for something to eat."

"And what better food in the whole world, O King," said the giant, "than these maidens here, for nothing has a finer taste?"

"Can they then be eaten?" asked King Sayf.

"Indeed they can," replied the giant. "If it is your wish to eat, I shall bring one for you."

"Yet it has a human likeness," said King Sayf. "None but a ghoul would eat such a thing."

"One would think," said the giant, "that you doubt their nature as fruit. Do you not know that God has power to make all things? Was it not He who created the Universe?"

And so King Sayf Ben Dhi Yazan asked the giant to bring him one. "I hear and obey," said the giant; then, approaching a tall tree, he seized a maiden by the hair, plucked her from the branch where she was, and brought her to King Sayf, saying: "Take it, my lord."

King Sayf contemplated her hands and her feet and the green-black color of her eyes, and said: "Praise be to the One who shaped her and gave her being."

Then the giant advanced and, taking her in his hands, broke her in two pieces, then removed the peel from the sides, so that a fragrance rose from her sweeter than heavy musk; and he saw that the inner part was laid out in segments like an orange, each the full length of the body, like the ribs of a human being, and that her right arm was like jasmine and her left likewise. And when King Sayf Ben Dhi Yazan ate from it, he found the taste to be like the taste of tender walnut, and sweeter than honey, finer than all other foods. "Arise, giant," he said then, "and let us journey to another island."

"I hear and obey," said the giant. Then, raising him up onto his shoulders, he bore him along and set him down in a land vast in extent, with teeming rivers, lush with foliage and blooming flowers; and he found there a great river from which streams flowed that no man could count or measure and, by its banks, a mortar of bronze, with a column on which were inscribed names and charms like clustering ants.

"What is this mortar and column?" King Sayf asked the giant.

"Know," replied the giant, "that these islands are all enchanted, each of the seven, with such a column and such a mortar. Formerly, before their powers were brought to nought, the Watchers assigned to these columns would cry out against any stranger passing through the lands, giving the alarm against the approaching adversary."

"Who fashioned these Watchers, giant?" King Sayf asked. "Who set them over the land, and who has brought them to nought?"

"Know, King of all time," replied the giant, "that their beginnings were strange." Then he recounted the following tale:

There was once a sorcerer named 'Abid al-Najm (meaning, Worshipper of the Star), and this man had a son who was the greatest scoundrel of his time, sparing no maiden or woman he saw in the land, but rather taking her aside and possessing her forcibly, against the wishes of her family or any other set as guardian over her. Should her husband or any of her people venture to resist him, he would slay them, dashing them to the ground amid their own blood; and if she were to hold back from him, still he would take her by force, fulfilling his desire with her, then slaying her and shedding her blood.

Now this king had a minister whose name was Kiwan, and he had a daughter of exquisite loveliness, finer than any other in her form. And one day the son of King 'Abid al-Najm chanced to see her as she walked in the garden, and his heart becoming fixed on her, he was minded to take her then and there, coming in from the road. But the servants told him: "Master, this is the minister's daughter." And so he held back from her, out of cunning and fear of his father.

When the maiden went back into the house, she told her father: "The king's son was minded to come in from the road and take me by force."

"I must inform his father," he replied; and rising there and then, he went in to King 'Abid al-Najm, greeting him and kissing the ground between his hands. Then, when the king asked him what news he brought, he said: "King of all time, your son Prince Shahouta made to accost my daughter Jaljala as he passed, and I know that if he wishes to accost a maiden or a woman, then none of her family can hold him back; any that ventures to oppose him he slays, and if she herself resists he ravishes her, then slays her when he has had his way with her. I know, too, that the people of this land fear him only on account of your sorcery and magic, and your rank over them, and that you, O King, are unaware of these things. Now here I have informed you of his doings."

When 'Abid al-Najm heard this, he was displeased and ordered that his son

Shahouta be summoned to his presence forthwith, dispatching after him seven messengers who found him wandering round about the houses as was his custom. And they told him: "You are to attend on your father, 'Abid al-Najm."

"Why has my father summoned me?" he asked.

"The minister has recounted to him," they replied, "how you were minded to accost his daughter as you passed."

Then Shahouta, fearing his father, said to the messengers: "Return and tell him you could not find me."

"How can that be," they replied, "when he knows the secret sciences, and the hosts of giants and jinn servants will tell him of it? Return with us now, and do not expose us to harm at his hands."

"I shall not come," he said, "for I am sitting here now in wait for a woman with whom to divert myself, or a maiden with whom to take my pleasure."

"Indeed you must come with us," they answered, "for we cannot disobey the king."

"This shall not be!" he cried. And still they insisted and still he refused, till at last they took him against his will, dragging him along into his father's presence.

"Shahouta," his father said, when he saw him, "what leads you on to act in this depraved fashion?"

"Father," he replied, "I love women and maidens and cannot hold myself back from them. If I chance to see a maiden or a woman, then I speak softly to her, and if she accedes to me, then I do her no harm; but if she resists, then I take her by force to fulfill my desire, then slay her after on account of her own sin. Nor have I done a vicious deed then, for I have slain none who was guiltless."

"And why," his father said, "were you minded to accost the daughter of my minister?"

"I did not know," he replied, "that she was the minister's daughter. When they told me of it, when I learned she was Jaljala, daughter of the minister, my arms fell abashed."

Then the king said to his minister: "If you see this boy again approach your daughter Jaljala, do not consult me in the matter, but rather speed his death forthwith, giving him the cup of shame to drink." These things the king said by way of warning, to appease the minister and strike fear in Shahouta.

"I hear and obey," said the minister. And so their interchange ended.

As for Shahouta, when he left his father's presence his love and passion grew still fiercer; consumed he was with fiery longing, all his desires now fixed on the minister's daughter. And at last his steps took him to Jaljala, where she lay asleep in her bed, and he woke her with a strong heart and a bold spirit. When she woke to find the king's son there before her, she was afraid, knowing that if she were to withhold herself from him he would slay her; so she resigned herself, and he climbed onto the bed with her and they kissed and wound around one another, and then he took off the clothes he was wearing and instructed her to do likewise; and when her body was revealed, it surpassed the light of candles. Then he joined in union with her, taking her virginity, and he had relations with her after consuming drink, in which she took great pleasure, so that she was moved by an overmastering love for him. Then, after their union, he took her onto his lap, placing his arm on her arm and his breast on her breast, and they embraced together and slept, their breathing sounding out.

Now it happened that night that the minister entered his daughter Jaljala's quarters, and there he found her asleep with the king's son sleeping beside her, their arms twined around one another in the manner of spouses or lovers, each pressed tight against the other, lover and beloved together. Then, shocked and enraged at the sight, his anguish growing ever fiercer, he jabbed at the king's son with his spear, and the son awoke from his sleep in terror, to find the minister standing by his head.

"Woe to you!" cried the minister. "Who gave you leave to come into these quarters and do these things? Do you take my daughter for a woman like those you see in base men's houses?"

"Minister of all time," said Shahouta, "nothing has passed between us to require such words. Now I am here, may I not leave your house in safety, as I entered it?"

"How can that be," said the minister, "when you have pierced a way into the furnace and made it a home for men?"

"That is no shame," he replied, "for she is a minister's daughter and I am the son of the mighty king."

"If I give you leave to depart safely," said the minister then, "give me your word never to do this again."

"How can that be," replied the king's son, "when I am afflicted with love for your daughter?"

"Go your way now," said the minister. "If you return a second time, I shall dash you to the ground in death. You have no power to hold back from any woman, and for that it is that I keep you from her. You are known as a depraved and adulterous man; for if a man not yet of age has relations with seventy women, we magicians, in our religion, consider him an adulterer. As for the mature man, no adultery attaches to him, for he knows his business better than you."

"Minister," said Shahouta, "there is no inequality between him who is of age and him who is not."

"I have given you fair warning," said the minister, "never to return to my house and not to draw near my daughter."

"That can by no means be," replied Shahouta, "even were I given the cup of death to drink."

When the minister heard this, the light before his eyes turned to darkness, and he bethought himself of 'Abid al-Najm's words when he said: "If he approaches your daughter, do not consult me in the matter, but rather slay him." And at that, growing ever more enraged at the young man's obstinacy, he set his hand on the hilt of his sword and drew it till death crept along its exquisite blade; then he struck the king's son's neck with the edge of the sword, striking his head from his shoulders, so that he fell dead to the ground, chewing on bitterness and blood. Then he ordered that the body be cast out into the wilderness, and the servants flung him out on the hills; but the minister concealed his secret, suppressing all knowledge of what passed.

As for King 'Abid al-Najm, he was seated next day on his throne when the doors of the court opened and four men entered, tall as palm trees, greeting the ruler and kissing the ground before him.

"What news do you bring?" asked the king. "Who are you and from where have you come?"

"Know, King of all time," they replied, "that we four are hunters who hunt beasts in the wild, and catch rabbits in the open spaces, and also hyenas and tigers and deer. Such has been our custom always. And it chanced that on this day, as we journeyed from our place of abode to the hunting grounds, we saw vultures and other birds of prey moving back and forth. 'Such birds,' one of us said, 'hover only over a corpse. Let us see whether a wolf has killed a sheep.' So we went to the place, and there we found a man slain and flung down there, his head hacked off and his body stained with blood and earth; and when we looked more closely, we found it to be your son Prince Shahouta, cast down on the ground in two pieces. Had we not discovered him, the beasts of the wild would have devoured him."

When the magician 'Abid al-Najm heard these things, his heart was filled with pain and wild imaginings, till he foamed and frothed in the frenzy that seized him. "O my star!" he cried, then struck his face and head, and tore at his hair and beard, roaring, old man though he was, in a thunderous voice. And when he had made them repeat their story, he knew this was surely the work of his minister, and he turned on him in a rage, saying: "Who slew my son Shahouta and brought down shame upon him?"

"I it was who did it, King of all time," replied the minister, "and you it was who instructed me in that course. I told you before of what he had done; and yet when you said to me I should slay him, I did not do so, but rather admonished him, saying: 'Prince Shahouta, do not approach my daughter, and so oblige me to act in my defense. Let my daughter be, for you will bring no happiness in this.' But, consumed as he was by vanity, he paid no heed to my words. He went in to my daughter in the darkness of night, thrusting with his rod into the fiery furnace and making an opening beneath the lid, so that it became a dwelling for men. I admonished him, but he would not be admonished, following only his desires."

When King 'Abid al-Najm heard these words, the light before his eyes turned to darkness. He snorted and raged and cursed the sun and moon, saying: "What is there of justice and equity in this? Because he pierced a way into your daughter's furnace, you bring him low in death? You are a minister, are you not? Your duty was to honor him for my sake, knowing him to be my son and the life of my heart. But though you have slain him, I shall not slay you in your turn, dealing with you as you yourself have dealt; for I fear the blame of those who would say, King 'Abid al-Najm slew his minister Kiwan after so many years of service. But, by the shining stars and circling planets, you shall not live in my land, neither you nor your daughter nor your womenfolk. Leave my sight forthwith, you and all the throng who follow you."

"I hear and obey, O King," said the minister. Then, knowing harm would befall him if he remained there, he rose forthwith and left the king's presence, taking his womenfolk and his daughter and his wealth and his family, and journeyed toward the wilderness and plains, with no notion of where he should go.

As for King 'Abid al-Najm, when the minister had left his presence, he said to himself: "The minister Kiwan will find it hard to quit these regions. Perhaps he will take refuge with one of the great kings, rulers of broad lands, and come to us with troops numerous as the teeming seas. I must surely strive to discover his intentions." So he cast the sands, and through these it was revealed to him that the minister Kiwan had, after his departure, met with four magicians skilled in the secret sciences, making complaint to these concerning his affairs and inducing them, with promises of wealth, to come to the king's land to work their magic. Then, having agreed with them on these matters, he left them that very hour and journeyed with his daughter and other womenfolk to the realms of a king called Haris, who was ruler of the islands of Arwiqa, throwing himself on his protection and requesting his help; then, receiving assurances on this score, he brought his womenfolk into the city of Arwiqa and began to prepare his troops for war and combat. Matchless were the men gathered around him, with honed swords and tapering spears and high-stepping steeds prepared for confrontation and duel. The minister Kiwan disbursed great sums on the troops set apart for the affair.

When these evil tidings were revealed to King 'Abid al-Najm in the sands, and he knew his minister was striving in full enmity against him, he said: "My only course now is to defend my land, repel the enemy with my soldiers, and protect my womenfolk and children; for unless I perform mightier deeds than they, especially those four base and cunning sorcerers, they will blot out all trace of me and lay my land waste."

With that he rose and, entering his place of divination, fashioned these seven columns of brass and iron, placing these mortars beside them; and he entrusted them to Watchers as a means of preserving his islands and all the lands they contained from magicians and willful men, so that the magicians, should they come, would find the land protected and its people ready for battle, and would be powerless in the presence of the precautions 'Abid al-Najm had taken. Then he erected walls with catapults and stones set up on top of them and fortified his land to the utmost, so bringing comfort to his heart and assuaging his terror.

For their part the four magicians left their places of divination and met with the minister; and then the troops made ready and advanced all together to attack the islands of Waq al-Waq, along with the minister and King Haris and all their companions, meeting the four magicians by agreement along the way. As King 'Abid al-Najm looked, he saw the dust swirl high into the air, blocking the view, then clear, then rise up again into the sky, growing till it concealed all that lay between earth and heaven. Then, after an hour, the dust cleared once more to reveal a long line of troops, like the flood or a shadow sideways cast, approaching the islands from every side. At that the Watchers shrieked out ever more fiercely against them, and sent out thunder and lightning together with hails of stones and fiery flames, thrusting them two parasangs back. All who approached the city they cried out against in this way, so that none could draw nearer; and if a man stood his ground, then the people of the land would come to bring him down in death.

Then King Haris approached the minister Kiwan, saying: "We can endure no longer. Men we know how to fight against, but not the jinn." And so the minister summoned the magicians and sorcerers to request their help in destroying the enemy; but though they exercised their skills, working all manner of magic and spells, they could gain not the smallest hold over the situation, nor could the minister Kiwan in any way prevail against the resistance of the Watchers.

When two full months had passed, and still all their efforts had been in vain, the other magicians went to their chief, saying: "Where is the use of all this striving that attains nothing? Here we stand, powerless, who learned all these sciences from you alone. If the magician 'Abid al-Najm is stronger in these sciences than you, why did you not tell us, so we might enter his service and learn from him to our profit?"

"Only remain where you are," he replied, "and I shall stay your adversaries' hands." And with that, rising to his feet and entering his place of divination, he began to murmur spells. Being of high standing among magicians, he was resolved to perform something of note when he saw his men so powerless; and so he forcibly summoned the Humar of the earth, reciting names and incantations both secretly and openly till they appeared before him, saying: "Tell us your wish, magician of all time, so that we may serve you accordingly."

"Lay open to me," he said, "all that 'Abid al-Najm has worked with his Watchers."

"He has cast a spell on the seven islands," they replied, "and has set seventy jinn servants over each column and seventy giants over each mortar, with power to thrust back all who pass and draw near; and so he has preserved the land so that none can approach it."

"If such are the enchantments," he said, "tell me how they may be brought to an end."

"Magician," they said, "we have not told you what it is he did, and how he wrought his deeds to their end."

"I adjure you," he said, "in the name of what is written on the ring of Solomon son of David, peace be upon him, to tell me any way you know of redressing the evil and bringing the spells to nought."

"Know, O magician," they said, "that he wrought it all on a tablet of yellow brass inscribed with names and charms, which he bound round the neck of a raging lion as great as a bull or greater, fashioned out of red leather; and he set this lion at the very end of the last of the islands, with seventy giants of the mighty jinn standing guard over it. If this lion were to be destroyed, all the spells would be broken and the enchantments removed from the islands."

"And what power will destroy it?" he asked.

"Know, magician of all time," they replied, "that in the treasure of King Kush Ben Can'an is something to destroy all those works and all the enchantments they contain; if you only had that, you would be saved, and all the men with you, and no champions or deeds could hold you back."

"I enjoin you," he said, "by the mighty names inscribed on the ring of Solomon, peace be upon him: fetch me the thing to bring those spells to nought."

When they heard these words, they flew off through the air and were gone a full hour. Then they returned, saying: "Know, magician of all time, that we went to the treasure of Kush Ben Can'an; but when we wished to draw near, the jinn servants forestalled us, and we have no power to enter without their permission."

Then the magician, rising to his feet forthwith, said: "Bear me to the place and I myself will accomplish the business." So they bore him up till they had brought him to the gates of the place where the treasure of Kush Ben Can'an was; and there he knocked, and the servants asked him what his business was.

"It is my wish," he said, "to break the spells cast over the islands, and the power of all the columns and mortars 'Abid al-Najm set there, and of the wall, and to rid the place of the jinn servants."

"So Kush Ben Can'an has commanded us," they replied. Then, opening the gates of the place where the treasure was, they said: "Take that which breaks the spells, and restore it to us after you have accomplished your business."

"You have my word on it," he replied.

With that they handed him a bag full of fine sand, and a second bag, and a bow, saying: "Take these things and accomplish your business with them as you wish, then return them to their place."

"I hear and obey," he replied. But not knowing what he should do with the things he had taken, he summoned a jinn servant to ask him.

"As for the bag of sand," the jinn said, "if you sprinkle sand from it onto a column, the helpers will flee from it never to return, and it will fall into ruin never to be restored, and so too with the mortars. As for this bow, in the second bag are three arrows. Aim the first arrow at the lion, and if it strikes home the power of the lion will cease; but if it does not strike home, the ground will swallow you up to your knees. In that case shoot the second; and if that does not strike home, then the ground will swallow you up to your loins. In that case shoot the third arrow. If that strikes home, the power of the lion will be at an end; and if it does not, then the ground will swallow you up and you will go the way others have gone before you. But one of the arrows must strike home, for the arrows are designed for this lion only."

Then the magician, taking these things, returned to the islands; and when he reached the edge of them, he straightway took the yellow sand as the giant had instructed him and sprinkled it over the columns and the mortars, causing all the jinn servants around them to depart. Then, approaching the lion, he shot the first arrow at it but missed the mark, and the ground swallowed him up to his knees.

When he saw that, he shot the second arrow, and this too missed, so that the ground swallowed him up to his loins. Then he wept over his plight, saying: "Were it not that the ground held me in its grip, I should now repent of my purpose." And he began to regret he had ever assailed the Watchers. "Magician of all time," the other magicians said then, "shoot the third arrow."

"I fear to shoot," he said, "lest the ground swallow up the rest of my body and I die this very hour."

"You must do it," they replied, "for you have no other means of salvation."

Then he said: "You speak truly. I shall shoot the third arrow, and either I shall strike home on the lion or perish in misery and wretchedness." And with that he grasped the third arrow and, murmuring spells and crying out against the lion, he shot the arrow and struck home in the breast; and the lion tumbled to the earth like a log of wood and lay there bereft of movement. And the spells were broken, and the troops, crying out and surging forward, entered the islands.

Then such a battle there was between 'Abid al-Najm and the minister Kiwan as to make the hair of babies turn white. The troops fell upon one another, and the time of all men drew near, as the crow of separation shrieked over them and hands and feet were lopped off; and at the close of the day, the chief of the magicians encountered King 'Abid al-Najm and fought with him. But 'Abid al-Najm overcame the chief of the magicians. And the seven islands of Waq al-Waq remained empty as you see them now, barren and arid, with none to speak or listen in them. Such, O King, were the things that passed here.

"And so this land," said King Sayf Ben Dhi Yazan, "is empty of Almighty God's creatures."

"At this hour, O King," said the giant, "it contains no man but you alone; for its king was slain by his enemies through the agency of the minister, and those enemies were themselves destroyed by the servants of King Kush Ben Can'an's treasure."

"Since matters stand so," said King Sayf, "bear me to another island."

"I hear and obey," said the giant. Then, raising him onto his shoulders, he bore him up into the heavens, and, after two hours had passed, said: "Master, here you are at an island with trees and rivers and birds proclaiming the Oneness of the Almighty and Forgiving One; and the fruit of the trees is once more in the likeness of women exquisite in their loveliness and form and radiance and proportion, hanging from the trees by their hair."

"Praise be to Him," King Sayf said then, "who makes perfect all His works. All-Powerful He is indeed." Then he said: "Giant, the road has been long, and I am minded to set you at liberty and restore your tablet to you, so you may go your way."

"King of all time," replied the giant, "we have traversed the islands in safety and have entered the last of them now. If it is your wish, as you say, to restore my sovereignty over my soul, then pray do so." It was the giant's goal, in this fashion, to spare himself hardship and tribulation.

"Base jinn," said King Sayf, "how do you speak of traversing these lands when I know the last of the islands is the seventh, and we are now only in the fourth? Your intent is only trickery and deceit and falsehood, and you are using lies and fine words with me. By the name of Him who created the loftiest mountains, who knows the numbers of the pebbles and the grains of sand, if you do not bear me through the three islands that remain, I swear I shall burn your tablet in the fire. Three islands I have seen, and now here is the fourth; and yet you claim we have traversed seven. Had that been so, we should have entered the Islands of the Maidens and seen the fulfillment of our wishes."

When the giant heard these words, he knew King Sayf Ben Dhi Yazan was not ignorant of the ways of service, having been served by 'Ayrud, son of the Red King; and his only course now was to abase himself before him.

"My lord," he said, "I beg you not to do so and to pardon me for the words I uttered and the course I proposed to take. I had forgotten the three islands; but now I have recalled them to mind, I shall bear you through them. I uttered those words to you only from joy over my deliverance."

"By God, giant," said King Sayf, "if you are intent on deceit, then know deceit rebounds only on the one that essays it. I came to those lands and highlands trusting only in the Lord of Lords. Beware deceit, giant, and do not be deceived by the temptations of the devil."

"Master," he said, "I acknowledge my fault." Then he approached King Sayf and, kissing his hands, begged his forgiveness, which was granted him. Then the giant said: "Know, O King, that the maidens of this island are not like other maidens, for they are good too for the act of love; more delightful in this, indeed, than human women are."

"Giant," said King Sayf, "these creatures are surely for food."

"My lord," he replied, "this is fruit which Almighty God set here for His creatures when these islands were full of people, before they were destroyed in the fashion I recounted. People would pluck these fruits from the trees, and some would eat them as they are, and some would cook them, and some would salt them and place them in jars to eat out of season, and some would have relations with them. There is no sin in that, for they have the status of bound slaves."

"Bring me one of them," said King Sayf, "so that I may see how they are." And so the giant went off to fetch him one, then set it before him and went off again; and King Sayf, understanding his intent in this, looked at the maiden. He had been some time absent from his womenfolk, and it is said by some that he joined with her forthwith, as the Sovereign Lord decreed; but others say he declined to do so out of decency before God the Ruler of All Realms.

When the giant returned, King Sayf said: "Take her far from me." Then he rose and went to the river, where some say he performed his ablutions and recited as much as he was able from the writings of Abraham, the Friend of God. Then he said to the giant: "Could you find no better means of appeasing me, base jinn, than through playing the pimp? Do you not know that is a sin for which there is no forgiveness?"

"What is to be done, O King?" the giant asked.

"Beg forgiveness of God," said King Sayf, "the Almighty and Glorious One."

"O King," replied the giant, "I did this thing only to make you well disposed to me after your anger."

"Jinn dog," said King Sayf, "if you do the like again, or make any mention of these matters, I shall burn your tablet in the fire."

Then the giant, abashed, understood he had been guilty of pimping after a fashion, and in his shame said to King Sayf Ben Dhi Yazan: "My lord, I pray you will teach me the way of repentance so I may beg forgiveness of Almighty God and return to His ways. Then it may be He will cover past faults and forgive me the hateful sins I have committed." And so King Sayf taught him the way of repentance, and he desisted from pimping ever after.

"Bear me up," King Sayf said then, "and journey with me to the fifth island."

"I hear and obey, King of all time," said the giant. Then, raising him up onto his shoulders, he made for the clouds and the upper heavens. Still they traversed valleys till evening came, and then they alighted on the fifth island, and the giant set him down from his shoulders, congratulating him on their safe arrival.

"I wish you to bring me some lamb's meat," King Sayf said then, "for a meal of fruit has no substance in it."

"My lord," replied the giant, "there are no sheep to be found in these lands."

"Then," said King Sayf, "praise be to God, I shall feed myself, for Almighty God gives me no need of you for my food. You think only to appease me through playing the pimp."

"I see, my lord," said the giant, "that your heart is set against me still. I pray you will forgive me my sin."

"Giant," said King Sayf, "I have no power in the matter, either to command or to admonish, for this is a sin Almighty God alone can forgive. But be patient awhile, and I will show you how, by God's power, I may have the cooked lamb's meat you told me is not to be found."

With that King Sayf Ben Dhi Yazan set the goblet before him, covering it with the white napkin as Shaykh Abu 'l-Nur had taught him, and said: "I wish, by the power of Almighty God who created all passing things, to have tharid of pure bread and well-cooked lamb's meat." Then he lifted the cover and a small cooked lamb was revealed, perfect in its form.

"See, giant," said King Sayf, "the bounty of Almighty God and the charity He has bestowed upon me."

"My lord," said the giant, "how did you come by all this?"

"By placing my faith in Almighty God," replied King Sayf, "for he is the Seeker-Out and the Vanquisher, Lord of East and West."

Then King Sayf asked the giant: "Does this island have the same fruits as the ones before it?"

"My lord," replied the giant, "the fruit of the trees here is of two kinds: the first like those you saw before, and the second like the heads of humankind, resembling them in every way, in their eyes and ears and nose and lips and hair and neck; but they have no bodies, being heads alone. They praise Almighty God, but they are fruits too, and men come here to this island to buy them when they are at their sweetest (for they have their special season), and eat only them. As for the inhabitants of the island, before destruction overtook them they would take more than they needed for their provision and bear them to the most distant lands, exchanging them for cloth to make their garments. Such was their custom."

"Giant," said King Sayf, "for each question I pose you have an answer. Where did you gain such knowledge?"

"King of all time," replied the giant, "though I am the son of a king among the jinn, I love to hear songs and take pleasure in merry making and amusement and pleasure and music. The great magicians would summon me to their service, commanding me to bear them to this realm; and when they had attained their ends, doing all the things I told you of, they would instruct me to return them to their country."

"And why," asked King Sayf, "was it their custom to come here?"

"My lord," he replied, "it was their wish to take these fruits and eat them when they entered their places of divination, for once engaged in such matters they would touch no other food."

"You speak truly, giant," said King Sayf.

They passed the night there on the fifth island, and next morning King Sayf, having risen and performed his ablutions, and uttered the prayer prescribed by the creed of our master Abraham, peace be upon him, said: "Giant, bear us to another."

"I hear and obey," replied the giant. Then, raising him onto his shoulders, he bore him through the spaces to the sixth island, and set him down there. And King Sayf, gazing around him, saw a single river watering the whole island, and a column and mortar like the ones before, and tall trees with leaves wide and round like a tray, spacious enough for a man to seat himself in, and bearing a sweet fragrance; as for the fruit of these trees, it was formed, on one side, like a human face in all its kinds, dark or white or red, while the other side resembled legs of a color inclined to red, like the hue of the grape. But some of the fruit, too, was like the upper body of a lion, in many colors, praised be He who transcends all resemblance.

When King Sayf Ben Dhi Yazan saw this, he was filled with wonder, saying to himself: "Praised be He who is able to do all things. None has His knowledge, for He is All-Powerful." "Giant," he said then, "these forms have no peer."

"Know, King of all time," said the giant, "that the fruits of these trees are the sweetest of all food; and their language is the best of all language, for they praise God continually, without ceasing. If a man takes one of these fruits to eat, and bites into it and eats it, it remains full of joy still, feeling no pain and touched by no anger or distress; and should anything remain of it after the man has eaten, then it reforms itself in the air, becoming once more as it was. Then, when evening falls, a bird comes and raises it up to its old place, where, by God's power, it is rejoined to its branch and passes the night in its place, as though no one had plucked it or eaten from it."

"There is no God but God the Mighty and Exalted," King Sayf Ben Dhi Yazan said then, "and of Him, the Great and Forgiving and Compassionate, I ask forgiveness. But giant, I cannot believe this till I have seen it with my own eyes. Bring me one of them."

And so the giant rose and fetched him one, and King Sayf ate some of it, leaving the rest. Then the giant asked him if he had eaten his fill; and when he replied that he had, lo, it was transformed before King Sayf's eyes, becoming whole as it had been before.

"And will you now," King Sayf said to it, "return to the place where you were?"

"Indeed I shall," it replied, "when the Jammal bird comes to set me back there."

"Giant," King Sayf said then, "bear me away from this place, for by the Sovereign and Exalted God I fear for my mind."

And so the giant bore him to the sixth island, where he found a great river. "This, O King," said the giant, "is the Island of Lions, and it too has its column and its mortar."

"Why, giant, is it called the Island of Lions?" asked King Sayf.

"Because," replied the giant, "the fruit of the trees here resembles lions, some having the face of a man and the body of a lion, and some the contrary."

"Truly God creates what He wills," said King Sayf Ben Dhi Yazan. "And are they all fruit?"

"Indeed they are," replied the giant. "Some, too, have the front portion of an ostrich, and all of them, one like the other, say, 'Praise be to the Sovereign Creator.' Know, King of all time, ruler of men and jinn, that this is the sixth island, here exactly as you see it, and all that now remains is the seventh island, which is the Island of Frost. That island no creature can enter, either man or jinn, for the Watchers are entrenched there, assailing none and assailed by none; and there are no marvels there at all, for the inhabitants worship the Watchers themselves, knowing nothing of the Creator of humankind. They do not leave it, nor does any stranger enter it; for should a stranger essay to enter, then the fire consumes him, and for this it is called the Island of Frost."

"And after that island," said King Sayf, "what is there then?"

"After that," replied the giant, "there is nothing except for the island you seek, the island of King Kafur, where you will see the City of Maidens on the right hand, and the City of Men on the left."

"And are there no dangers or difficulties in our way thereafter?" asked King Sayf.

"O King," replied the giant, "the hard is made easy by the will of God the All-Powerful Sovereign."

"Bear us," said King Sayf, "to the entrance to the Island of Maidens, for we have no business on this island.'"

At that the giant joyfully raised him up and, journeying with him like an arrow shot from the heart of the bow, soared up with him into the heavens. "O King," he said, "plug your ears now with cotton."

"Have no fear," replied King Sayf, "but journey on with Almighty God's blessings."

So on he flew, through the first day and night, and through the second day till noon. Then the giant descended with him, saying: "Here, O King, is the entrance to the Island of Maidens." And with that he set him down on the ground and said: "Take these things, my lord, which were given you, the ball and the mallet and the garments and the goblet. All speed to you in your business, O King, and my peace be upon you."

"Ha, giant," said King Sayf, "and why are you giving me these things? Are you not my companion whether we travel or stay? If you hold back from my service, then your tablet will remain in my keeping."

"My lord," said the giant, "if you wish to keep me in your service all my life long, there is none to prevent you. But this land you are entering now is one where I cannot follow you. Each land, O King, has its own decrees; and even if each land a man enters could be entered too by a jinn, here my lady 'Aqisa, and 'Ayrud, the son of the Red One, would have better title to serve you and keep you company than I. But here I shall sit, King of all time, awaiting your return, so that I may bear you back to my master Shaykh Abu 'l-Nur."

Then King Sayf, seeing there was no dissembling in his excuses, said: "Where is the way to the place?"

"Here is your way, on the right-hand side," said the giant, "and may God be your Champion and Helper."

With that King Sayf Ben Dhi Yazan took his leave of the giant and, removing the clothes he was wearing, donned the garments he had with him, becoming like a woman. Then he took the enchanted goblet, and the ball and mallet, and the green emerald, and all the other aids of which we spoke before and, saying: "I place my trust in God, Creator of the empty places," walked into the midst of the wilderness and crossed the wilds and deserts, his lips never ceasing to repeat the name of God the All-Powerful Sovereign. On he walked, through the first day and the second and the third; and when he was hungry he would ask for food from the goblet, and when he was thirsty he would place the emerald in his mouth, and so he continued many days together. And when evening fell at the end of each day, he would sleep only after invoking protection in the names of Almighty God, the All-Knowing Sovereign.

At last he came upon a green meadow with trees and a river whose water was unlike other water, being yellow like cow's milk. And on the other side of the river, beyond the meadow, there soared a lofty white mountain, and on the banks of the river were trees and shrubs in whose branches birds invoked the Oneness of the All-Forgiving Sovereign; but gazing at the world around him, he found, to his surprise, no other person to bear him company; and he stood there in that spot, deep in thought.

Now this was the river we spoke of before, which had been fashioned by the magicians between the two cities, to which the maidens would generally come to disport themselves on its banks. And when King Sayf Ben Dhi Yazan saw all this, he ascended the mountain and found, beyond it, a lofty mountain like the one on which he stood, with a path like the one on which he was traveling, and he saw, too, meadows and islands and rivers; but these he left, making his way to a cave where he began to offer up his worship to Almighty God, beseeching Him and uttering prayers to Him, till morning broke as the All-Bountiful One brightened the world with His light. Then King Sayf rose to his feet, and having performed the due prayers, descended the mountain, and walked through the meadow to the water, where he seated himself to contemplate the works of Almighty God.

And as he was so seated, suddenly the maidens approached, descending the path into the valley and turning toward the water, dressed in their women's garments; and King Sayf, seeing their garments to be unlike his own, left them and busied himself with his devotions. Still the maidens approached, disporting themselves together, and still King Sayf watched them. And as he was so engaged, a second group of maidens approached, wearing garments neither like those of the first group nor having any resemblance to his, so that he grew uneasy, at a loss as to what he should do in the matter. As for the maidens, again they began to disport among themselves, while he dared not draw any nearer, for fear they should see him and decry him on account of his strange garments. Then a further group came, wearing clothes different from those of the first two groups and unlike his also; and this added to his unease, so that he held himself back from them. And still groups of maidens came, till the valley was filled with maidens, with no one group resembling another, but each group rather having its own mode of dress. And when King Sayf saw that his garments were still like none of theirs, he grew close to despair, with no notion of what he could do in the matter, his soul ready to leave his body, such was the turmoil within him.

With matters come to this desperate pass, he raised his eyes toward the haven of prayer, to the heaven that is above this world, and began to beseech the aid of the Lord of Earth and Heaven, saying: "O God, You who know what lies hidden in the breast, You who are called Almighty, the All-Forgiving, I beseech You, in the name of the Sura of al-Tur and the Book inscribed in unsealed leather and the Fortunate House, to show me kindness in all Your ordinances. This I pray to You, Almighty, All-Forgiving One, to whom all things return." Then, after invoking blessings and peace upon the most beautiful, he recited the following lines:

> I implore you, O most Merciful, You who hear man's prayers,
>> Succor me, for I seek guidance so that I shall not go astray.
> O God, your servant stands humbled before You.
>> My sin is great, forgive me, O my Lord.
> I am a stranger in the mountains and the wilderness,
>> I am pierced by anguish for I do not see my beloved.
> You are my strength, my refuge and my help.
>> Rescue me, You who know the promptings of the heart.

If my God will not give ease to my grief,
on whom else in my weakness should I call?
I have endured as I could the absence of my love,
but when my patience was spent, once more I complained.
I came to the door of the All-Bountiful humbly
and cried, "O God, Reliever of calamities,
Hope of the downcast, it was by Your grace
that manna was showered upon Moses' people.
I charge You, by the books You've sent to men,
and by the prophets who guided them to faith,
And by the Ka'ba, and Zamzam and al-Safa,
and by the two holy cities safe from destruction,
And by the Aqsa mosque and by Mount Arafat,
on which evil ways were abrogated,
Be my ally, grant victory and defend me
from my adversaries, and from reprobate souls."

No sooner had King Sayf completed his prayer of entreaty to his Lord than a cloud of dust swirled up in the air, then cleared to reveal a group of maidens, equal in size to all the groups that had come before; and as he gazed at them, he saw they were all wearing garments resembling his, to the last detail. At this his heart was cheered and his spirit calmed, and he knelt in thanks to God, saying: "Praise be to God, who has plucked all unease from my heart and relieved me from my fears. Truly He is able to perform all things that He wishes."

So where before King Sayf had withdrawn from the maidens through the field, now he began, little by little, to approach this group, till finally he was in their midst, mingling with them and walking in their company. And when they reached the maidens who had come before them, they greeted one another, disporting themselves joyfully; and when they revealed what it was they held in their hands, lo, each had a ball and a mallet like the ones he himself held.

When all the maidens were assembled in the meadow, and King Sayf there among them gazing at their doings, a call went out among them: "Maidens, three times the queen who is sovereign over you says you shall seat yourselves to eat; then, after the meal, you shall disport yourselves together and be joyful here in this place."

When the maidens heard this, they seated themselves to the right and the left, some before and some behind, just as they were bid, then a cloth was spread and the dishes laid out. Eleven groups there were, each installed in its own place and moving forward in its turn to take the food; and they ate and drank and made merry, then washed their hands and the dishes were removed. After the sweetmeats and the drinks, they were minded to disport themselves, and ten maidens charged with giving the commands called out as before: "Maidens, it is the queen's pleasure you should divert and disport yourselves; but she charges you to shun all uncivil behavior, for that will bring you to harm and destruction, and the queen's wrath will fall upon you."

"We hear and obey," said the maidens. And they rose forthwith to remove some of their clothing and so make themselves freer for the sport. Then one of them rose to request from the queen a ball of red gold, with which it was the maidens' custom to play; and when this was thrown to her, she took it and began to roll it, and the other maidens with her. At that King Sayf too approached to disport himself with them, for he was like them and they like him in their dress.

Then one of them struck the ball, and it rolled along the ground till it reached his feet; and he, summoning up all his resolve, and all his skill and strength, gave it a mighty blow with an arm made strong by faith and piety, so that it shot forward like a comet, far across the meadow, and the maidens could have caught it only after a half mile, and that after much weary chasing. But King Sayf, swifter than they, reached it before them and struck it again, still further than the first time; and when the maidens again raced in pursuit, so as to have their turn of striking, again he was there before them, striking it yet a third time. As often as they essayed to come to it and strike it with their mallets, so often would he divert its course and race off in pursuit, reaching it before them, till at last the maidens grew weary and began to perspire, unable to endure further; and they were furiously angry, too, at these doings, flinging the balls and mallets down onto the ground. "We shall no longer disport ourselves," they said, "till we have made complaint to our queen. Let her see who this maiden is, who is so uncivil to us, spoiling our sport. On account of her, wearying our hearts and pushing and pursuing the ball alone, we have been constrained to end our game."

"But we do not know," some of them said then, "what maiden she is, or of which group."

"Maidens," others said, "approach and disport yourselves together, so that she cannot come to the ball, and excuse her for her fault. Then, if she begins once more to be so uncivil, let us tell our queen of her behavior from first to last and exact our due from her at the queen's hands."

"This is wise counsel," the others said then, "with which none can find fault."

When King Sayf heard how the maidens had resolved, he said to himself: "I must not act so again, for I have spoiled their sport, forgetting their strength and endurance are not as mine are." And so, when the maidens picked their mallets up from the ground and began to strike the ball with them, he played along with them at their own level, drawing no attention to himself.

At length they wearied of disporting themselves with the ball and, flinging it down, seated themselves on the ground to rest; and after an hour the criers called out: "Maidens, do not hold yourselves back from the custom the queen has permitted to you."

"We hear and obey," the maidens said. But King Sayf was bewildered, for he did not know of which custom they spoke. Then the maidens rose, each clasping another like her, embracing one another in pairs, then rolling together through the meadow, each riding on the other's breasts; and King Sayf could not throw himself onto one of them and do the like. "By God," he said to himself, "this is a custom without peer. But what if one of them should cling to me and desire should grow strong in me? Should I disport myself with them, I must guard against that, and may Almighty God, in His exalted mercy, grant me the grace of concealment!"

While he was so reflecting, one of them drew him aside, clinging vigorously to him and engaging herself with him. She was one of the loveliest of face among them, and when she said, "Why are you so lazy and do not disport yourself?" her words seemed sweeter to him than pure water to the heart of a thirsty man. And straightway King Sayf Ben Dhi Yazan seized hold of her, clasping her as she had clasped him, and drawing her to him as she had drawn him to her, and clinging to her as she had done to him; and so each pressed close against the other, doing as the other did. Each time his hand passed across her buttocks she would quiver beneath it like a soft fish, and this would renew King Sayf's desire, so that his limbs grew weak and his reason began to falter. Then the maiden became still bolder and more vigorous, and still she disported herself with him and he with her, till at last they were grappling together, tugging at one another with both arms, and King Sayf, getting the better of her, flung her to the ground and sat astride her breast. Then his body grew heated and his passion strong; and as for the member bestowed on him, its desire was aroused and its vigor grew fierce. In vain King Sayf endeavored to lay it to rest: it rather leapt out from its cover, forcing his clothing upward, revealing all things as clearly as a guide in the market place.

When the maiden sensed his condition, she knew this was no maiden with her but one of the male sex. "Woe to you," she cried, "basest of men and vilest of champions! Why are you, a man, come to these lands wearing the garments of a woman? Why have you mingled with the maidens and disported yourself with them when you are not like them, and your form does not resemble their form? Now you are here among us, it is our right to tear your soul from your body, to blot out your joy and destroy the breath of life in you. But rather than hack you to pieces forthwith, I shall say a man has entered our city and seen the condition decreed for us."

With that she was minded to call out, but King Sayf, placing his hand over her mouth, said: "I beg for mercy and sanctuary here with you, and here place myself in your charge, becoming your attendant boy and slave and servant. Do not betray my secret, for I have thrown myself on your mercy."

"From what country have you come," she asked, "and how did you reach these realms?"

"I will tell you my story truthfully," he replied. "But first you must pledge me safety of body and soul."

"I grant it," she said. "Cast aside all fear, for you are under my protection and have my pledge of safety in the name of the Sovereign God. But tell me now how you come to face such perils, from which no way to safety remains open to you."

"My lady," said King Sayf, "I am a stranger from another land, and I come on account of my wife. She came first from these regions, and fled my land to return here, bringing my son with her. It is for her sake alone, and that of my son, that I am here; and as yet I do not know where she is."

"Young man," she said then, "had you fallen into the hands of another of these maidens, she would not have kept your secret; for had the maidens known you for what you are they would have hacked you to pieces with their swords. But had the queen discovered you, she would not have permitted one drop of your blood to fall to the ground; and as I, young man, am under the queen's command, and all these maidens are under my command, I shall help you achieve your goal. But should you find your wife, how, tell me, will you remove her from this place? How will you bear her away, and how can you converse with her, while you are amongst these maidens? Still, I shall help you, young man; it may be that Almighty God, may His name be praised, will ordain that you be rejoined with your wife and son."

When King Sayf Ben Dhi Yazan heard these words, he thanked the maiden from his heart. "Sister," he said then, "what is your name?"

"I am called Murjana," she replied.

"And what is your rank," asked King Sayf, "with the queen?"

"I am her minister," she said, "and the governor of her kingdom. These maidens are under my command one and all, and I am under her command."

"Let me lie under your protection," he said then. "Do not leave me to the queen or to the maidens, for they will do away with me."

"Have no fear," she replied, "you are now safe from such disaster and I shall accomplish your business for you, joining you again with your wife and child. But your account amazes me. These maidens are all virgins, knowing nothing of men and untouched by them, and yet you say your wife has a child. What, pray, is her name?"

"She is called Munyat al-Nufus," he said, "and my name is Sayf Ben Dhi Yazan."

"If you should find your wife," she said then, "still you have small hope of returning with her to your land."

"By God, lady," King Sayf said then, "it is true I have come to this land only with the greatest hardship, but let God still do with me as He will." Then the passion rose in King Sayf's heart, and a burning fire kindled within him as he recited the following lines:

> My heart melts away with longing and with fire;
> those whom I love have departed far away.
> Slumber does not lie upon my eyelids
> and in bitter floods the tears gush forth.
> Grief and her remoteness have kept me in anguish
> and I was certain that I was abandoned.
> Those whom I love do not know me any more,
> even my own people, and I can find no friends.
> Life had accustomed me to love and generosity,
> but all has been changed utterly to false-seeming.
> It has taught Munyat al-Nufus to abandon me,
> she without peer in loveliness and form.

I lost the sight of her beauty, my palace is darkened,
 and the world has become a narrow, empty place.
Prithee, Murjana, come you to my aid;
 to be parted from her is bitter to the taste.
How can I be patient? She's gone and my son with her.
 My heart is bound to them with strong links.
Both of them are now distant from my sight,
 I cannot unloosen the chains that bind me.
May my greetings reach them at all times,
 so long as the camel caller leads his caravan.

As Murjana heard these verses of the king, and saw how he wept, she felt her
heart ready to break. "Truly, young man," she said, "your wife is dear to you and
a fervent passion has seized your soul; for unless you loved her dearly, you would
not so have come from a distant land to face such perils."

"Sister," said King Sayf Ben Dhi Yazan, "my wife is worthy of that; and if I
were to be slain for her sake, I could not call myself wronged, for she merits
redemption through wealth and through soul and heart and eyes."

"By God," she said then, "I shall not rest till I see you rejoined with her
forthwith, if indeed she is here and such is your fortune." Then, leading him
some way from the other maidens for fear they should hear their talk, she said:
"I shall conduct you among all the maidens, summoning before you each who
is called Munyat al-Nufus, so you may discover your wife and delight your eyes
with sight of her. If it is indeed she, do not speak with her, but rather silently
incline your head; and if it is not she, make a sign to me, then turn from her and
walk on."

"I hear and obey," he replied. Then, telling him to await the end of the sport
the queen had decreed for the maidens, she continued with King Sayf in mirth
and gaiety till all was over and they made to leave. Then all the maidens made
their way to the queen, Murjana with them with King Sayf at her side, and once
more the cloth was spread and the dishes laid out, filled with various foods and
syrups, with greens and sweetmeats and other things. Each group of maidens ate
according to custom, with King Sayf and Murjana looking on, and when they
had taken their fill of food and washed their hands clean, the minister, having
taught him the signal between them, mounted her steed and rode toward the
river, while King Sayf remained there with the maidens.

Then each group swam in turn in the midst of the water, the maidens having
first removed their garments to reveal bodies shining like crystal and let their hair
fall down over their shoulders and backs; and Murjana, mounted on her steed,
rode up to one of the groups and called out: "Munyat al-Nufus!" At that a
maiden from the group approached to know her pleasure, and Murjana said: "I
did not see you today, daughter, among the maidens, and so it was that I
enquired after you." Then she turned to King Sayf and made enquiry with her
eyes to know whether this was his wife; and he made sign to her that it was not.

She moved on accordingly to another group, calling out: "Munyat!" And
when three maidens came out toward her to know her pleasure, she said: "Ah,

you are indeed there!" But when she turned once more toward King Sayf Ben Dhi Yazan, he again made sign to show she was not among them. So Murjana said to the maidens: "The queen instructs you not to stay long in the water, for it is cold, and she fears it will do you some injury." And so they told her they would leave the water.

With that she left them, moving on to one group after the other, till she had been round them all; and then she made sign to the king to tell him there were no more maidens called Munyat al-Nufus. "Young man," she said, "the only ones remaining are those in the court, around the queen's throne. Accompany me there, and I shall show you those as I have shown you these."

So then she proceeded, followed by King Sayf, to the court, where all those assembled rose to greet her; and when she had seated herself in her place, all the other maidens of lower rank, together with King Sayf, stood there with their arms crossed, ready to serve her and awaiting her command. Then, when the queen had greeted Murjana and Murjana had returned her greeting, the minister began to tease those maidens who were called Munyat al-Nufus, talking with them and looking toward King Sayf, and he would make sign to her; and so things continued till she had made the full round of the maidens.

Then she said to the queen: "My lady Munyat al-Nufus, I wish your name were still so, as it was before, without any kind of change." At that the queen laughed, while Murjana made sign to King Sayf that none was left by the name of Munyat al-Nufus except this one alone; and King Sayf inclined his head.

At that Murjana rose laughing, and left the court with King Sayf following behind her. "This Munyat al-Nufus who rules over them," he said, "she it is who is my wife."

"Know, King of kings," replied the minister Murjana, "that her name is not Munyat al-Nufus, for I called her that only by way of jest. Her true name is Nour al-Houda."

"Minister," he replied, "this and no other is my wife, beyond all doubt."

When Murjana heard this, she inclined her head, saying: "King of all time, are you he who is called King Sayf Ben Dhi Yazan, the Tubba'i Yemeni?"

"I am indeed he," he replied.

"And what," she pursued, "brings you here from your own land, a land so distant, by such hard and arduous paths?"

"None other," he replied, "than that business I told you of, and you alone it is I ask to accomplish that business, for I am now under your charge and protection, and you have given me your assurances."

"You speak truly, King of all time," said Murjana. "But know this queen is not the one of whom you speak; her name is rather Nour al-Houda. But her sister is in truth Munyat al-Nufus, daughter of King Qasim al-'Abous, and a while back she came here from your land and is now held captive, suffering bitter injury and wretchedness. If you will follow my counsel, return to your own land and rejoin your family and your troops; leave her be and find another to marry, for there is assuredly no escape for her from the confines of the dungeon. Return to your land, O King, and so keep your life and dignity safe."

"And how could I ever desert her to marry another," replied King Sayf, "when she is my wife and my stay, the soul by which I live? If reason, minister, were my only guide, I should follow your counsel; but she has possessed my heart and my mind; my soul and my sight and my hearing are all with her, and even when she is absent from me, thought of her fills every corner of my being. Having journeyed here now, to the place where she is so close, I cannot return to my land without her. Were my breath of life to be snuffed out, I should accept it; and any suffering I should endure for the sake of her suffering." At that passion and anguish seized hold of him, and calling to mind the days of harmony and love and union, he recited the following lines:

> I long for a gazelle who's heir of all loveliness,
>   nourished by all things fair in beauty's garden.
> I cannot bear at all being parted from her,
>   even the traducer takes pity on my state.
> This gazelle, as she sways and addresses me,
>   seems born as if armed with fatal arrows.
> People said when she swayed her body and turned her head,
>   God has not created a plenilune like her for nothing!
> Blessed be God, how lovely is this gazelle,
>   how the sword of her glances has ravished my heart!
> By God and, yet again, by God, I love her countenance,
>   she has kindled a fire within my soul!
> Even should she die I'll not forget her love
>   though she stayed a thousand years in the grave.
> Patience has abandoned me since she departed,
>   longing and anguish harbor in my heart.
> If a lover should swear that all of his heart
>   were possessed by that gazelle, he'd be no perjurer.

When King Sayf had uttered these verses, he said: "Minister of all time, I ask you, as you are a person of honor, to make shift that I may have sight of her in some place; and then I will leave her in her sorrowful distress, to suffer abasement and shame, returning to my own country and leaving her in the land of the enemy. So that my heart and soul may find peace, I shall tell myself she has died, leaving her here in her anguish and downfall. Let her know that all this has passed because she broke the faith and covenant."

"By God, King of all time," said Murjana, "matchless in this age, Queen Munyat al-Nufus has never one moment forgotten you. Each time I go in to her, she says: 'Murjana, what has befallen me is for the wrong I did King Sayf, for I indeed betrayed him.' And she said, among other things, that she longed for her eyes to see you once before she died. Know that she yearns for the sight of you, reproaching only herself for your separation."

"Who set her in prison," asked King Sayf, "and what is the cause of her captivity?"

"Her imprisonment, O King," said Murjana, "has a strange cause indeed. But now is not the time for words. My first wish, son of noble lineage, is to bring you to see your wife, and after I shall tell you. But know this city of ours cannot be entered by any man, and there in the city it is that Queen Munyat al-Nufus is held captive. I can conceive no way of bringing you to her."

"And why," asked King Sayf, "may men not enter?"

"In the beginning," she replied, "this city was built by the magicians with spells and with Watchers set over it, and on that account only maidens may enter it." Then she told him, with all its twists and turns, the story 'Aqisa and 'Ayrud and the giant had recounted to him before, and of how the two Watchers at the gate of the city would cry out against any stranger who entered, calling: "People of the city, such a person has entered your city and is now amongst you, a man, no less." Then the maidens would come to destroy him with their swords. "Likewise," she said, "if a maiden enters the city of men, the same will happen to her. Should you enter by the gate of the city, I fear the two Watchers will shriek out against you, and I shall not lightly expose you to danger, because you are the king of all time, and because, too, I have given you protection and pledge of safety. If you will heed my counsel, return to your own land and so preserve your life. Do not suffer destruction among those who are not of your kind, and so sink into your grave."

At these words all King Sayf's resolve returned. "I shall never quit this land," he said, "though I should drink from the cup of death, till I have seen her; and I cannot come to sight of her except through you, under whose charge and protection I am. Here am I at your mercy. Do with me as you deem fit." Then he wept and made complaint, and, after invoking peace and prayer on the maker of miracles, recited the following lines:

> Thinking of you night and morning I face anguish,
>   for your love I have abandoned children and kinsfolk.
> Tears scald my cheeks, you being absent from me,
>   and sleeplessness is a comrade of my eyelids.
> And my body has dwindled and wasted away,
>   the last resources of my patience are spent.
> Tears have scorched my eyelids and burned me away;
>   what a wonder to behold a sea of flaming fire!
> My heart complains for the absence of its tenant;
>   if she be absent, there still is her dwelling place.
> There's nothing in my body but the intangible soul
>   which I ceded to her who has wasted my body.
> O Murjana, be generous, have pity upon me;
>   all who behold me weep for my condition.
> I am parted from my kin, from home and from kingdom,
>   after being exalted, I find grief and humiliation.
> Until I see my Munyat again and bring her back,
>   all things on earth for her sake are nothing.

For the love of God, grant me a meeting with her,
and tomorrow you will be richly recompensed.

When King Sayf had uttered these verses, Murjana knew that King Sayf loved Munyat al-Nufus with a matchless love. "Do not weep or be sorrowful," she said. "I shall bring you into the city though I perish on your account. You shall stay in my own house, and I will not break my trust. I must be the means of bringing you to your wife, though I should spill my own life's blood for yours. But hear, King of all time, what I now say to you: when the maidens enter their city, as they will this very hour, do not enter with them through the city gate, causing the Watchers to cry out against you. Rather leave the other maidens, once you have accompanied them to the gates, and walk beside the walls as far as the turreted tower; then sit beneath this tower till Suhayl's star rises toward you and all eyes close in sleep. Then I shall come to you from the tower and let down a rope with which to bind yourself; so I may raise you up into the tower, and you perhaps cross the wall without the Watchers crying out. Then I shall bring you into the city, to your wife Munyat al-Nufus; you may satisfy your longing for her, seeing her with your own eyes, and then I shall let you down once more from the tower, leaving you to go your way. Such is the plan I have conceived. Take good heed of my counsel, King Sayf."

"You speak truly, Murjana," said King Sayf. "This plan has no equal." And so it was agreed. Then the minister Murjana, bidding King Sayf farewell as he stood there in his female garments, mounted her horse and shouted to the maidens: "Murjana commands you all to come out from the river." With that they came out, donned their clothes once more and made their way toward the city, with the minister at the head of them and King Sayf in their midst, continuing so till they reached the gates of the city. Then, as the maidens began to flock in with their various groups, King Sayf separated himself from them and walked beside the wall till he reached the tower we spoke of before; and there he concealed himself as Murjana had instructed him. And meanwhile the maidens, having entered the city, went on to their various homes, while the queen and Murjana likewise returned to their abodes.

At midnight, the minister Murjana went out onto the top of the tower and, gazing down from its turrets, saw King Sayf there beneath it as they had agreed together; and she let down the rope and shook it. So it was that the king, seated there awaiting her, suddenly saw the rope dangling, with a basket fastened to its end, and he rose and seated himself in the basket and pulled on the rope. Then Murjana, together with her slave maidens, pulled the basket up toward the turrets, saying: "Hurry, so that no one sees us." Together they worked the rope till King Sayf, to his great delight, had been brought up to them; and when they had set him down, Murjana commanded the slave maidens to bring food, and they ate with him and drank and praised Almighty God.

When they had finished, Murjana said to King Sayf: "Come, let us go now to Munyat al-Nufus."

"I hear and obey," said King Sayf. Then he walked on behind her, God giving them concealment, till they reached the gates of the prison where Queen Munyat al-Nufus was; and on these gates King Sayf saw a lantern of white crystal, lit with almond oil, and at their side a slave maiden, whom he knew to be the keeper of the prison, sitting on a bed of Indian ivory.

Murjana approached this maiden, saying: "Kawkab!"

"Here I am, minister of all time," replied the maiden. "Know that Queen Munyat al-Nufus was just now speaking of you. 'Kawkab,' she said, 'if only the minister would visit me here, and see the anguish and abasement to which I have sunk, I might perhaps find some relief at her hands, for none has shown me greater compassion than she.' And with that she began to weep and express repentance for what she had done."

"I wish my eyes had lost their sight, Kawkab," the minister said then, "rather than see her in this plight. But open the prison door so I may see her."

"I hear and obey," replied Kawkab. "But who, O minister, is this maiden with you?"

"This Kawkab," she said, "is one who loves Munyat al-Nufus, one of my slave maidens, who has asked leave to see her."

"I hear and obey," said Kawkab. Then she rose to open the door of the prison, and Kawkab and Murjana entered, Murjana saying to King Sayf: "Maiden, go in to see Munyat al-Nufus and the misfortune that has befallen her."

But as King Sayf was about to step forward, Kawkab said: "Minister of all time, I have no warranty to permit any but you alone to go in to Queen Munyat al-Nufus. I fear this thing will bring disaster on me."

"Have no fear, Kawkab," the minister Murjana said then, "for my maiden here is no stranger, having once been slave maiden to Queen Munyat al-Nufus. That is why, in her desire to see her mistress, she begged this favor of me. We shall keep the matter secret, be assured of that. None will know of it at any time, nor is there any stranger among us."

"You speak truly, minister of all time," said Kawkab. But when she approached King Sayf and raised the veil, there was revealed a face unlike that of a woman, for a man's face is evident from the signs of his beard and mustache. Furious now, the keeper of the prison said to the minister Murjana: "Is this a way to act, minister of all time? Here is no woman but a very man."

"And how would a man come to us, Kawkab," said Murjana, "when we live in an enchanted city, bound by spells? Do you not know that a man, had he entered the city, would never have come so far? The Watchers would have cried out against him as one."

"I am astonished, lady," said Kawkab, "at so strange a happening; for I see him with beard and mustache, having an appearance like no woman's, and I fear injury and grief."

"This is the seal of the Lord of Heaven and Earth," said Murjana.

"If we are truly women among ourselves," said Kawkab, "then let her remove her garments. So we may see her bosom and what lies beneath."

When the minister heard this, she knew her situation had grown desperate; and as for King Sayf, he stood rooted to the spot like one of the dead, saying to himself: "There is no power or strength except in the Mighty and Exalted God."

Then Murjana, turning to Kawkab, said: "I shall give you an explanation for this. But by the name of Him who holds power on High, who executes His judgment on all people, if you make the least sound I shall, I swear, cleave you in two with this iron sword. Know this is no woman, but a man come to us from a distant land over hard and arduous paths, and none knows of him but I alone. I have granted him my protection, so that he is counted now among my dependents, and have given my solemn pledge to aid him as best I can in saving his wife and his child."

"My lady," Kawkab said then, "who, pray, is this man, and who is the wife you are striving with him to save?"

"His wife," said Murjana, "is our mistress Queen Munyat al-Nufus, daughter of King Qasim al-'Abous, who has long now drunk deep of anguish in this prison. As for him, he is called King Sayf Ben Dhi Yazan, the one of whom Queen Munyat al-Nufus told us, who has vanquished the mighty and valiant among men and jinn and made them bow down to him. His strength and prowess were clearly revealed to all the maidens when he struck the ball with the mallet; and we owe Queen Munyat al-Nufus too, my daughter, for past favors and kindness. It is no sin or shame that she journeyed from us to marry, according to the book and the law, and when she returned it was from a longing to see her people and her land once more, knowing nothing of the anguish and abasement that would befall her. By God, her sister's deeds toward her are the merest injustice and malice, as your own reason, Kawkab, will counsel you."

When Kawkab, the keeper of the prison, heard what the minister Murjana had to say, she turned to King Sayf Ben Dhi Yazan, saying: "What, King of all time, has brought you to this place?"

"I have come," he replied, "in search of my wife and son, to deliver them and restore them to my land, or else perish utterly for their sake. If I am to die in their stead, I shall rejoice at the outcome, embracing the decree of God, the Sovereign Lord. And if I am to deliver her, I shall have brought grief to the envious who oppose me."

"My lord," she said, "know that Queen Munyat al-Nufus was formerly matchless in loveliness and form. But now (I speak for your good, for my heart warms to you, and I shall aid you toward your goal) she has become lean of body, and her frame is grown spindly and weak; she has become like a corpse whose shroud has fallen into pieces over it, and her smell is like that of the rotting grave. I am now lovelier than she. If you wish to take me in her place, then here I stand before you, at your service, and I will go back with you to your country and be your companion there. As for Munyat al-Nufus, leave her to her suffering, so that this prison may be her grave, till her life ends at last and she returns to the Lord who made her."

"Kawkab," said King Sayf Ben Dhi Yazan, "my thoughts do not run on marriage or beauty, nor did I quit my land for the sake of any one of these maidens, nor indeed for her own sake. Rather I came to reproach her for her deed, in betraying me and deserting me and depriving me of my son; and when I have done that, I shall leave her there in her abode and return to the place I came from."

"King of all time," the wardress Kawkab said then, "I do not believe you would act in such a way. Queen Munyat al-Nufus has spoken to us of your gallantry and honor; and if you see her now, you will not leave her to suffer by the will of her sister, but rather deliver her through the sword, heaping vengeance on all who make themselves her enemies. When I hear you tell how you will reproach her, then go your way, as though you came only to gaze on the wretchedness of her plight, then that accords ill with what I have heard of you. But your wife is there before you, O King. Go in now, and see for yourself." And King Sayf Ben Dhi Yazan accordingly crossed the threshold of the prison.

Now as King Sayf was talking with the wardress Kawkab, the minister Murjana entered to find Queen Munyat al-Nufus prostrate on the ground, her son weeping by her side. That very day her sister Nour al-Houda had gone in to her and given her fifty lashes on the body, though she uttered not a moan from the pain of the blows. And now, when Murjana went in to her and asked after her condition, she replied: "Is there any need to ask, Murjana? I am as you see me. A while ago my sister entered and gave me fifty lashes, having no pity or mercy for me."

"My lady," replied Murjana, "you never knew rest in this land before your departure from us; always your spirit would rove. You could not, you would say, endure to remain in one spot, and you would set me to rule the kingdom in your stead, while you roamed hither and thither in your enchanted robe, till one day it was stolen and the attendants came without you; and when we sent them back with the feather robe they returned after some days, saying they had not found you. So I reported the matter to your father in the city of Marj al-'Aqiq, and he sent back word that your sister Nour al-Houda should sit in your place, then concerned himself no further with you. You came back of your own free will, though your father had been happy to see the back of you and was vexed to hear of your return."

Now what had happened was this. When King Sayf Ben Dhi Yazan had seized Munyat al-Nufus and the other maidens had returned to their city, Munyat al-Nufus had been queen of the city; and when her attendants returned to inform the minister Murjana that the queen had lingered in the Garden of Delights, Murjana had given them the second robe of feathers with instructions to hasten back to the queen and return with her. But when the attendants, returning to the garden and searching through the palace, still did not find her, the minister Murjana had no other course but to make her way to Munyat al-Nufus's chambers, night though it was, and go in to her sister Nour al-Houda. "Rise forthwith," she said, "and seat yourself in your sister's place while I assemble the dignitaries. If you do not do so, the kingdom will pass from your hands to others."

So Nour al-Houda rose, and Murjana summoned the elders of the land, who pledged allegiance to the new queen, while Murjana continued to serve as minister. Now there were in the city two old women who were sorceresses, one called Zaʿzouʿa and the other Sharahi bint al-Dawahi (meaning, Daughter of Disasters). And when Nour al-Houda had assumed the throne, sitting as queen over the city, she summoned Zaʿzouʿa and had her dwell there with her in the court, doing nothing except by her counsel.

Now King Qasim al-ʿAbous, as we said before, lived in the second city, along with sorcerers and magicians whose skills had been handed down from their fathers and forefathers. So it was that when Nour al-Houda assumed the throne of the City of Maidens, she said to the sorceress Zaʿzouʿa: "Go straightway to my father. Tell him my sister Munyat al-Nufus has left us and I reign in her stead."

"But how may I come to your father, O Queen," said Zaʿzouʿa, "when these are enchanted cities?"

"Sorceress," replied the Queen, "go to the river between the two cities, then cross and leave the letter on the other bank. One of the men will surely come to take it and bear it on to my father."

"I hear and obey," she said. Then, taking the letter, she set it down on the other side of the river, and there some men who were in the habit of walking out from the city picked it up and took it to King Qasim al-ʿAbous. When he saw it, he knew his daughter Munyat al-Nufus was lost, that one of the greatest of kings had come to love her and found a way to steal her enchanted robe of feathers, leaving her no means of return. At a loss what to do in the matter, he summoned the wizards and sorcerers, saying: "Read this letter, then learn for me in what corner of the world my daughter Munyat al-Nufus lies lost." With that they cast the sands and told him she had been seized by the Tubbaʿi king, who was sovereign ruler over cities and villages and regions, and that she would bear a king to succeed him who would found a city still greater than his father's. "Such is my desire," he said, and took not the smallest action in the matter thereafter, for this was a distant land and it was a hard and weary business to journey to such places.

When Queen Munyat al-Nufus returned, she went in to her sister and greeted her. And Nour al-Houda, seeing she had a small child with her, said: "Sister, a rampant male has entered you and you have given birth, which no virgin maiden should accept. But stay here with me still, till I have sent word to my father."

Being established now with the minister Murjana and her sister's former attendants, because she had ruled some while over them, she wrote to tell her father that her sister Munyat al-Nufus had returned with a boy child conceived by a man, with the intention of supplanting her; and if she succeeded in this, her son would perhaps grow to assume a mighty power. Thereupon her father sent back instructions to bind her in fetters of iron between four columns, with her son flung down by her side, and to go in each day to her sister and give her fifty lashes as punishment for treachery in that she had come with her son, the son of a king, to these lands.

Nour al-Houda rejoiced at this letter and, showing it to the city dignitaries, said: "Here is my father's command. His will is that I should seize my sister and rule as queen." And when they told her she should do as she deemed fit, she laid hold of her sister and set her in prison, wounding her in the head and giving her, that very day, fifty painful lashes. Munyat al-Nufus screamed out for help, but none was forthcoming, and she was left there in her prison, with her son by her side and this maiden Kawkab set as wardress over her.

So she remained all that day till evening, with her son now crying and now falling silent. But when the wardress Kawkab rose and lifted Prince Masr in her arms to gaze at him, she saw how he was white as fresh jasmine and how the mole on his cheek was like a disc of ambergris. Then God softened her heart toward him, and she went and unbound Munyat al-Nufus from the columns, saying: "Queen, return to this infant child. It may be that Almighty God will succor you for his sake." And when Munyat al-Nufus was unable to eat the food she brought her, she said: "Queen, if you do not eat, no milk will flow in your breasts." And so she induced her, through her kindness, to suckle the child.

When Munyat al-Nufus viewed herself and her child, bitter sorrow gripped her at the plight she had brought upon herself. "Kawkab," she said, "with my husband King Sayf I was the most honored of all women, and yet I tricked him to come to this land. And now the evil things decreed by the Lord of the Faithful have come to pass."

Then she slept till morning, when her sister came to give her fifty lashes as she had done the day before, and so things continued for many days and nights till, in due season, King Sayf stood at the prison gate and Murjana entered and talked with her. "Murjana," Munyat al-Nufus said then, "I it is who brought these deeds on myself, wronged though I have been." (Truly it is said: "Avoid inequity, that pathway to destruction leads, / the wheels of time revolve against the man of evil deeds.") "I am the one to blame," she said, "for I wronged my husband, taking his son from him; but my heart tells me, minister of all time, that my husband King Sayf Ben Dhi Yazan will not abandon me. He will never know rest till he comes in pursuit of me."

"The way is long, O Queen," said Murjana, "and you yourself came here on the wing. He has no magicians with power of spells and sorcery."

"That is not so," said Munyat al-Nufus, "for he has such as Barnoukh the magician, and the wizard Ikhmim, and the sorceress 'Aqila, each of them the equal of the people of our land. And as for his troops, and his standing, and the kings who acknowledge his sway, do not ask of them. Each of his commanders bears a sovereignty like that over the cities of my father and sister together, such is his might. And should he wish to come to this land, then he has a servant called 'Ayrud, son of the Red King, who serves him alone. If he rubs the tablet, the servant will come to him and fly off in any direction he is sent. And if it is his wish to journey himself to any place, this servant will bear him wherever he is minded to go. This giant makes a full year's journey in the space of an hour, and he has a sister among the jinn whose name is 'Aqisa, greater yet than 'Ayrud, who will venture into any place of danger for his sake and would lay down her very life for his. As for my lord King Sayf Ben Dhi Yazan himself, every shade of valor and bounty and gallantry is his."

"If King Sayf should come here striving to deliver you," said Murjana, "will you bear me with you to the seat of the kingdom and give me in marriage to one of the mighty champions?"

"By God, Murjana," Munyat al-Nufus said then, "indeed I will. And my wealth shall be yours, and I myself will supply your needs." With that she wept and, after invoking peace and prayer upon Taha the Messenger, recited the following lines:

> Life can bring a season of limpid happiness
> but if it lasts too long it can bring disaster.
> All wishes were fulfilled when I was with my beloved
> and the eyes of the watchers were closed in slumber.
> I was guarded by a bold lion, a king of kings,
> noble by his excellent and authentic lineage.
> His name was Sayf Ben Dhi Yazan, and his line
> has ruled Himyar since time immemorial.
> By stealth I recovered again my raiment of feathers
> and longing for them sought out my kinsfolk.
> I came to my place, but life dealt harshly with me
> because I betrayed my husband and neglected my duty.
> I fell into deep sorrow with no means of redress
> unless Sayf in his own person should seek me out.
> O Sayf, my lord, you gracious king of kings,
> master of all virtues and of courtesy,
> Do not blame me since, for what I have done,
> I have met with much grief and adversity.
> If you could see my grief and the strokes I receive
> and my humiliation, you'd witness a prodigy.
> And if you could see the downcast state of Masr, your son,
> imprisoned with his mother, weeping continually,
> With none whatever to have pity upon us,
> with no succor—and our minds distracted!
> Take pity upon us, come, let me see you
> before I encounter death and annihilation.
> If you should repine at coming because of distance,
> then let me beg your forbearance and pardon.
> Your virtue is forgiveness, to err is our nature,
> even strangers weep beholding our tears.
> Woe is me! My heart breaks parting from him,
> the more so if he's wrathful for what I've done.

As Queen Munyat al-Nufus uttered these lines, with the minister Murjana standing there before her, King Sayf stepped in through the door; and when he heard her verses, and saw the state into which she had fallen, her former loveliness and grace disfigured now by sickness and wasting, he grew beside himself with emotion, the tears flowing from his eyes. Then his Arab soul surged within him, and after invoking blessings upon the most beautiful, he recited the following lines:

> I've come to you, light of my eyes, have no more fear;
>   with much persistence I seek after you.
> I would forfeit my soul to save you from disaster,
>   indifferent to those who watch ready to blame.
> For every one of those who would injure you
>   I have prepared a sharp and cutting sword.
> With the edge of my sword I will and can guard you,
>   letting your enemies have their fill of its blade.
> So that you'll acknowledge as a doughty knight
>   who has seized by force of arms his heart's choice.
> Do not grieve, let the past go its way,
>   all this was written in the Book of Fate.
> Sorrow has now departed and happiness has returned
>   after a time of horror and disaster.
> Our enemies shall feel death at my hands;
>   some of them have fled like a flock of sand grouse.

When Queen Munyat al-Nufus heard him utter these words, joy suffused her heart; but making to rise, she faltered and sank back on account of her disease and utter weakness. "Queen Munyat al-Nufus," King Sayf said then, "what tempted you to this shameless deed, to take my child and scheme against me, obliging me to pursue you to this distant land over so many hard and arduous paths?" Then, drawing closer, he touched her, and she flung herself into his arms like a lioness, while he in turn clasped her to him; then they both fell into a faint, as though dead. When Murjana saw this, she sprinkled them with water, and they came to themselves, still locked together in their embrace.

"My lord," said Munyat al-Nufus, "do I truly see you there, living before me, or is this a dream? I adjure you, in the name of Islam, to tell me: are you truly King Sayf Ben Dhi Yazan? If you are indeed he, then do not leave me to return to the land of Yemen till you have placed me in my shroud. And if this be a dream, then I ask your forgiveness, and peace be upon you."

"Fear no injury, Munyat," said King Sayf Ben Dhi Yazan, "for here I forgive you all the things you have done, and let us have no blame or reproach more."

"My lord," she replied, "praise be to God, the Lord of Creation, that you view me here with your own eyes, captive as I am in the tyrant's prison. Strive to deliver me, King of kings and Crown of sultans."

"But for what cause," asked King Sayf, "were you cast in this prison by these cruel despots?"

"Now is not the time for words and questions," she said. "For your sake alone I was cast into prison. Seek now some way for us to escape this land."

"Here we are together, you and I," said King Sayf, "nor shall I again be parted from you, until you are set in your own palace in the midst of your slave maidens."

"And how shall I see that day, O King," she answered, "which is beyond even the world of dreams?"

Then King Sayf, taking out his goblet and covering it in the usual fashion, said: "I wish to have bread dipped in cow's ghee and bee's honey." And when he uncovered the goblet, lo, it was full of bread dipped in ghee and honey. Then he said to Murjana: "Minister, you and Kawkab and Munyat al-Nufus will eat with me."

"King of all time," said Murjana, "I see now Queen Munyat al-Nufus spoke truly of you. We shall now indeed eat with you and Queen Munyat al-Nufus, but tonight you and she will lodge in my house, for you alone in this land are dear to us now." So they ate together, then Murjana, removing them to her house which was near the prison, set food and drink before them there and honored them in the highest degree.

Now when a quarter of the night had passed, one of Queen Nour al-Houda's slave maidens came to the house of the minister Murjana, saying: "Minister of all time, the queen requires your attendance this very hour."

"I hear and obey," she said. Then, rising forthwith, she went to the Queen, who rose to greet her, saying: "Minister, know that in my sleep I saw fire raging in the city, and all the maidens within it crying out for help. Then a white bird descended and snatched me up in its claws, before flinging me down into the wilderness; and the instant I touched the ground, a beast snatched me and raced off with me, setting me down at length in my father's city. And I saw my sister Munyat al-Nufus riding on a grey horse, a sword glowing first in her left hand, then in her right, making sign to me and crying: 'Base, wanton woman!' I was minded to approach her, but a lion thrust itself at me, flinging me far back; and you, Murjana, were there beside my sister; and she was delivered from all injury and wretchedness, with a conquering lion at her back, thrusting all before it, beyond all our power to withstand. And what amazed me, minister, is that you should be there with my sister, abandoning me to my evil misfortune."

"Such a dream, O Queen," said Murjana, "can be interpreted only by one who is skilled in the secret sciences."

"You speak truly, minister," said the queen. "But be seated while I recover myself, for this dream has filled my heart with terror." Then, after a time, she said: "Summon the sorceress Za'zou'a forthwith."

When Za'zou'a had come and seated herself as instructed, the queen recounted once more the dream she had described to Murjana. "O Queen," said the sorceress, "I shall tell you the true meaning of this; but first I must cast the sands in your presence and show you what will be pleasing to your eyes." Then, when the queen had instructed her to proceed as she wished, she cast the sands and said: "I shall indeed speak, O Queen, but only when I have your pledge of safety." Again the Queen told her to proceed. Then she said: "Your sister Munyat al-Nufus has left her prison, released by the minister Murjana, who has taken her into her home; and the maiden Kawkab, the wardress charged with her guard, has accompanied them. With them is a man who is one of the great kings, a ruler of countries and realms, who, when he rides, rides with an army so mighty none can count or measure it; and this man is the husband of Queen Munyat al-Nufus and the father of her child. He has entered the city for her sake, and at his hands it is that the spells will be broken, and the men will mingle with the women, marrying and bearing children; and forthwith a mighty king and commander of troops will come to him, with a huge army in his train. Take care for yourself, O Queen, lest the enemy drive you down into your grave."

Then Nour al-Houda turned to Murjana, saying: "Do you hear what the sorceress relates?"

"These are mere words," replied Murjana, "that I neither heed nor set value on. I have taken a man into my house, she says, and delivered Munyat al-Nufus. How could a man enter our land when it is enchanted and has Watchers set to guard it? Had he attempted to enter, these would have given warning in the customary fashion."

With that the queen turned to the sorceress, saying: "The minister speaks truly."

"There is no truth in this argument, O Queen," said the sorceress. "I shall recount to you how the man entered this city." Then, having murmured spells over the sand, she said further: "Queen of all time, when the enemy first came to the land, he played with the ball and mallet alongside the comely maidens. Then he entered the city from the tower, and the minister it was who gave him entry."

At this Murjana fell into a fury, grasping the hilt of her sword. But Nour al-Houda said: "Sister, do not stir up an affray and kill this poor woman, for I do not believe her, nor do I accuse you of deceiving me." Then, turning to the sorceress, she said: "Rise and go your way, for I do not credit your account of events."

At this the sorceress rose, while Murjana remained with the queen, jesting with her till the gleaming morning broke. Then the queen said: "Remain today in the court so that I may sleep, for loss of sleep has left me anxious and perplexed."

"I hear and obey," said Murjana. Then she went into the court and seated herself there, while the queen went to her quarters under pretense of sleeping. But instead she disguised herself, and, going to the place where Munyat al-Nufus formerly was, and finding neither her nor Kawkab there, she went to knock at the door of Murjana's house; and when the slave maidens asked who was at the door, she said: "I am Zahra, slave maiden to my lady Munyat al-Nufus. I went to the prison and, not finding her there, enquired of the minister, who told me she was at her house, along with Kawkab and the noble husband of my lady Munyat al-Nufus."

"You speak truly, lady," the slave maidens replied. "But they are sleeping now. Where is our lady, the minister Murjana?"

"She is in the court," replied Queen Nour al-Houda. Then the queen returned herself to the court and, having seated herself there, gave command that Murjana be seized forthwith; and when the servants had seized her, she said in furious tones: "So, Murjana, you have hatched plots against us, taking the enemy into your house. I have been there, and learned of him."

"Is it for that, O Queen," said Murjana, "that you commanded me to be seized? Indeed there is no cause for secrecy here, for you have been to my house and learned of the enemy. Yet it is for love of you that I acted, not for love of your sister. He is her husband and she his wife, and he would have delivered her from you forthwith, striking off your heads with the sword. So it was that I was minded to trick him and bring him before you. But I see now you are a mad woman, and I shall not consider you wronged if you are slain or taken captive, for your enemy is the lord of the kings of all time and ruler over men and jinn."

"You will see now what I shall do," said Nour al-Houda. And with that she sent word to her father in the City of Men, informing him of all that had passed, then ordered the maidens to march on Murjana's house. Now King Sayf had risen in the middle of the morning; and he was gazing at Queen Munyat al-Nufus as she suckled her son, comforting her in her fretful impatience, when the maidens approached like swarming locusts. King Sayf laughed at the sight, saying: "How foolish your sister is, Munyat al-Nufus, that she thinks to fight against me using the maidens under her command. She will see now what I shall do." And with that he unsheathed his sword, shaking it till death crept along its exquisite blade, and cried out: "God is great!"

"O King," said Munyat al-Nufus, "do not go out to meet them. Or, if you go, do not stray far from the house, for the cunning of women will separate you and me, and you will cease to think of me, and so we may meet destruction at their hands."

"Have no fear," said King Sayf Ben Dhi Yazan, "for matters will not come to such a pass." And with that he fell upon the maidens with his sword, striking them with grievous blows and lunging with piercing thrusts, uttering cry upon cry against them till the immovable mountains shook. In the midst of the press he fought, slashing sides and breasts with his blade, protecting Munyat al-Nufus so that none could come to her. To and fro the enemy thronged, King Sayf sending heads spinning like balls and hands flying like the leaves of trees, while Queen Nour al-Houda charged forward, crying to her attendants: "This day is yours, for he is but one and you are armed in your thousands! Let your resolution remain firm and you cannot fail!"

With that the maidens hurled their lives into the fray, ready to endure all suffering. As for the queen, she summoned the sorceress Za'zou'a, saying: "Of you it is that I seek the capture of this man."

"I hear and obey," said the sorceress. Then, her hair hanging loose over her shoulders, she went to fetch a censer flaming with incense; and when she called out and the Watchers answered her, the lightning flashes and the rolls of thunder grew ever greater, and the city was convulsed from east to west, and all light was swallowed up in darkness. Then King Sayf found all his limbs grown limp, with no vigor remaining in them at all; and the maidens of the city surged forward, eager to seize King Sayf.

When Queen Munyat al-Nufus saw this and knew the fearful ordeal her husband faced, all because he had come to this land in pursuit of her, when she considered that his death would be on her account alone, she raised her eyes to the haven of prayer, which is the heaven above this earth, and, spreading out her palms to Him able to save her, cried out: "O God! O God! O God!" These words she uttered in submission and with an aching heart, her son raised up in her arms. Then, after invoking blessings and peace on Taha the Prophet, she recited the following lines:

> O that you should behold us and see our wretched state
>   and witness how we suffer horrors and change of fortune!
> O You the sole God, our Lord and Creator,
>   You who order the world and judge how it should go,
> O Lord! we are wretched and we have no succor,
>   our enemies are legion gathered around us.
> There's no one at all to have mercy upon us,
>   no one but You who can assuage our grief,
> ˙You who are unchallenged and without equal.
>   No one resembles You, no one can behold You,
> You, the Most Excellent to implore in disaster,
>   the alleviator of calamities when they come upon us.
> Show us the way, we are beset with hardships,
>   we have no strength, vision and hearing gone.
> I charge You by the grace of the holy Ka'ba
>   and the multitudes of pilgrims who circumambulate it,
> Send us a reprieve, O God, and grant us safety
>   from those evil beings who seek our blood.
> Frustrate their spite and on their own heads be it;
>   let them taste of misery and sorrow.
> I beg God's pardon for my ill word or deed,
>   for all sins I committed in act or thought.

Now as Queen Munyat al-Nufus uttered these words with her son raised up in her arms, the tears streaming down her cheeks and her eyes turned to the heavens for deliverance in her greatest need, and as she then gazed at her husband in his bitter anguish, it happened (and this is the strangest of all the things recounted in this book) that our venerable lord al-Khader Abu 'l-'Abbas had that very instant embarked on his wanderings. And since it was the will of the most Mighty and Glorious God that King Sayf's happiness should be fulfilled at his hands, he now cast his eyes to King Sayf and his plight and, gazing at what was written on the consecrated tablet, turned his steps, peace be upon him, toward the city of Dawariz, the seat of a ruler named Shah al-Zaman, who was the greatest king among the Persians.

"O Shah al-Zaman," he said, when he stood there before him, "repeat these words: 'There is no God but God, and Abraham is the Friend of God.' Then command all your ministers and men of state to say these words also, so that the Faith may be spread through your city."

Then God sent the light of guidance into his heart, and he became a Muslim in word and in heart; and all the dignitaries and ministers, and all those living with him there in the city heard him too, becoming believers in God. So it was that, in the space of an hour, the city was transformed utterly, as God guided his creatures to the true faith, away from the paths of infidelity and waywardness.

"Rise now," said the lord al-Khader Abu 'l-'Abbas, "and ride out with your troops; for you are called to fight in God's cause."

"I hear and obey," he said. And not staying to enquire where they were to go, he summoned his troops and commanded them to mount, then rode out at the head of them, saying: "Follow me, and let none look behind him."

After two hours had passed in this manner, they reached the City of Maidens, and he commanded his troops to enter it. Then the Watcher cried out: "People of the City of Maidens, sixty thousand knights are come to you from the city of Dawariz. They are from the ranks of the Faithful, and their king is King Shah al-Zaman. I shall be slain first, and the jinn shall find rest from all their weary labor."

No sooner had he uttered these words than the Teacher struck it, there on the turret of the wall, with the rod that was in his hand, so that it fell broken to the ground. Then the people of Islam entered the city, with the praise of Almighty God, the One and Immovable, ringing out; and God cast terror into the hearts of the maidens, causing them to flee through all the paths and byways, with tribulation pressing in from all sides.

When evening fell, King Shah al-Zaman met with King Sayf Ben Dhi Yazan at the forefront of the court and kissed his hands, saying: "Set me down, my lord, in the book of God's soldiers."

"And who, pray, are you?" he asked.

"My name, my lord," he replied, "is Shah al-Zaman, and I was given over to the worship of fire when your Teacher al-Khader came to me to instruct me in the faith of Islam and commanded me to ride out to this land, which I had never before entered." Then he heard a voice, which said: "O Shah al-Zaman, remain here in the service of the king of armies till all has been set in order in the city. Then you shall return to spend the night in your own city."

Meanwhile Munyat al-Nufus had delivered Murjana and taken her sister captive, setting her in chains. Then, seating herself alongside King Sayf on the throne, she said to Murjana: "Summon all the maidens here before me, saying I shall flay from head to foot any who delays till morning."

"I hear and obey," replied Murjana. Then, going out into the night with a group of her servants, she said: "People of the City of Maidens, it is I, the minister Murjana. I proclaim to you here that Queen Munyat al-Nufus has seized her sister and is restored to her rightful throne. If you will take wise counsel, present yourselves straightway before Queen Munyat al-Nufus; for any who delays will find only flaying awaits her. Come at once, all of you, and peace be upon you."

"I hear and obey," each of the maidens replied. Then they went all together to the court and placed themselves in the service of Queen Munyat al-Nufus. But when Murjana saw the sorceress Za'zou'a go up to beg favor along with the rest, she could not stay her hand, striking the sorceress full on the head with her sword and sending it cleaving down through her body.

Then King Shah al-Zaman approached King Sayf as he sat there on the throne alongside Queen Munyat al-Nufus, saying: "My lord, I ask, in the name of the religion of Islam, that should you ever turn your steps toward the kingdom of Dawariz, you will bestow on me the honor of serving you there. I cannot stay beyond this hour, for the Teacher has instructed me to depart. The journey to my country is a lengthy one indeed, and if the Teacher does not bear me there as he brought me, I shall not reach it in twenty years. I have, too, many troops with me."

"Remain here till morning," King Sayf said then, "so that you may take your share of booty."

"My lord," he replied, "keep the booty as my gift to you. For my part, I am content with Islam, which is my heart's desire."

While they were speaking thus, he heard the Teacher say: "Follow me, Shah al-Zaman." And with that he left the court by the way he had come.

"Follow me straightway," he said then to his troops. "Any who delays will not find the way again." With that the men mounted and followed him, and he returned to his land with all his soldiers. And when morning broke, he was once more on his throne by the blessing of al-Khader, peace be upon him, and we shall have more to say of him in the proper season.

As for Queen Munyat al-Nufus, she praised King Sayf Ben Dhi Yazan for pursuing her and striving to deliver her, without blame or reproach. "Tomorrow, my lord," she said, "I am minded to summon those who attended me and take the feather robes from them, and journey with them. The robe I had with me my sister seized when she imprisoned me."

"Munyat al-Nufus," King Sayf replied, "I have sworn a solemn oath not to quit this city till I have broken its spells and caused the maidens and the men to rejoin each with the other, and marry and bear children. Nor shall I ever break such an oath, though I were to remain here through all time."

"Such a thing is surely beyond you, O King," said the wardress Kawkab, "when others bolder and mightier have failed."

No sooner were the words out of her mouth than Munyat al-Nufus struck her such a buffet in the face as made her eyes start almost from her head. "She-dog," she cried, "what business have you to meddle in the presence of kings, you who are a beggar and the daughter of a beggar?" Then, turning to Murjana, she said: "Minister, can you not break the power of these Watchers over the city?"

"These Watchers, O Queen," she replied, "were, to my certain knowledge, established by the magicians at the command of your uncle 'Asim, when he asked your hand in marriage for his son and your father would not consent. The maidens, placed beneath a spell, all entered this city, while the men remained in the other, and from that day to this no woman has met with any man; and if, by God's decree, a woman went out alone from here and entered the stream, the men would pursue her and she would return only with her private parts wasted."

"I know indeed," said Munyat al-Nufus, "how these spells may be broken. Yet I fear the shrieking of the jinn."

"Tell me how it may be done," Said King Sayf, "and I will attend to the matter."

"Enter the place I came from with my sister," she said, "and raise the bed on which she sits. Beneath it is a tile of yellow marble different to those round about it; as you draw near it, O King, you will see on its edge a pointer of black lead. Rub this and the tile will rise, to reveal beneath, a floor with a stairway leading to it; then, if you descend this, you will find four tablets of lead in the four corners of the place that has a dome raised above, and in the center of the dome you will find a brass column, above which is a chair with a person of twisted form seated upon it. To his right you will find further persons and birds and certain other things, and high above his head a pair of scales. Look well then, O King. If the right arm of the scale is tipped down, then good fortune will be ours, but if it is the left that is tipped, then there is no remedy for us."

"And if the right arm is tipped down," said King Sayf, "what is then to be done?"

"In the front of the place," she said, "you will find a hammer and anvil of iron, inscribed with names and charms like clustering ants. Do not approach the hammer, but rather look to the wall, where you will find a brass bird; and if you rub this bird three times, then the hammer will descend tied to a chain. Unchain the hammer, then touch the anvil with it, but making no sound. When the two meet, the hammer will fly off and strike the person of twisted form between the eyes, so that he falls from the column; and after that the column will fall, and the trumpets of the other persons there will fall from their hands and the spirit will depart from them. With that the Watchers will perish, with no spirit remaining at all. Go then to the scales and break them, and all the spells too will be broken by the power of the Ancient and Everlasting One. Meanwhile I shall crucify my sister Nour al-Houda at the gates of the city, as an example to all."

"Let us go there before all else," said King Sayf. "And as for crucifying your sister, let it wait for another time." So he took her with him, and they took out the tile and, descending into the lower floor, went around all the various persons as Queen Munyat al-Nufus had indicated before; and when they had attained their goal, they returned to the palace.

The breaking of the spells brought abundant blessings in its wake, for the darkness was lifted from the eyes of the women; and as they grew aware of themselves, so the desire for union awoke in them and their blood stirred as nature spurred them on. Then, as the maidens were aroused and longing for the joys of love, Murjana said: "Summon the sorceress Za'zou'a." And when she had come, they said to her: "What is to be done concerning the longings of the women?"

"There is only one course, my lord," she replied, "and that is that the one who broke these spells should break those on the other city also, so that each man there may come and take one of these maidens."

"And what will break the spells over the men to this end?" asked King Sayf Ben Dhi Yazan.

"That, my lord," she said, "none knows but King Qasim al-'Abous, father to Queen Munyat al-Nufus. He can break them if such is his will."

"Our minister Murjana it is," said Munyat al-Nufus, "who shall take word of this to my father."

"I have no words, O Queen," said Murjana, "that I could use to sway him. The wiser course is to send your sister, Queen Nour al-Houda."

"By God, Murjana," said Munyat al-Nufus, "though my sister did me such wrong, and though I now have power over her, I cannot lightly permit harm to befall her. She remains my sister at last."

At that King Sayf Ben Dhi Yazan had Queen Nour al-Houda brought before him. "Know," he told her, "that I was resolved to strike your head from your body. But your sister would not permit your death, saying she could not endure any harm should come to you on account of her, even after all you have done against her; and I have summoned you accordingly to tell you of this. Are you now reconciled to your sister, as she to you, or do you still secretly contrive her downfall?"

"King of all time," she replied, "in the name of the One who formed the clotted blood, I hold my sister in no low esteem. Against my will it was that I beat her, and I would instruct the maiden Kawkab to be merciful and spare her pain. But for my father's tyranny over us, and the fear he struck in me, my hand would never have done her injury. Here I stand, King of all time, begging forgiveness and mercy at your hands. If my sister, in the goodness of her nature, recalls that I am her sister and forgives me for what I have done, then that will be a noble deed; and if she does not forgive, but is rather minded to slay me, then remember I did not slay her but beat her only. Let her accordingly beat me only, in the same measure that I beat her. But if she will requite my injuries with forgiveness, then I shall congratulate her this day on being rejoined with her husband."

"I have told you," said King Sayf Ben Dhi Yazan, "that your sister will permit no harm to befall you. Had she been so minded, she would have slain you the instant you fell into her hands."

At that Munyat al-Nufus rose and unchained her sister then, weeping, said: "By God, sister, I could see no harm befall you while I live." And at that Nour al-Houda stepped forward to be reconciled with her sister at the hands of King Sayf Ben Dhi Yazan.

"Nour al-Houda," he said then, "I seek your father, so that these spells may be broken at his hands."

"Know, King of all time," she replied, "that my father was vexed with my sister only when he learned she had betrayed you, coming here with your son. Should he know you have forgiven her, then he too will forgive."

"It is my will then," said King Sayf Ben Dhi Yazan, "that he should know of this."

"I must make my way to him through the air," said Nour al-Houda, "wearing my enchanted robe. For I cannot pass by the road on account of the Watchers."

"And where are the robes?" asked Munyat al-Nufus.

"They are in a box," said Nour al-Houda, "which is in my closet."

"Let neither wear them," King Sayf said then. "Neither you, Munyat al-Nufus, nor your sister."

"For what cause, King of all time?" she asked. "Have you not now forgiven me?"

"Indeed I have," he said, "but you are my wife, and I can no longer endure separation from you. As for your sister, I am minded to give her in marriage to one of the kings of the land, stronger than I myself in his religion and his faith; to a mighty king in truth."

"Do you speak perhaps of King Shah al-Zaman?" asked Munyat al-Nufus.

"Of him indeed," replied King Sayf. "I have said nothing to him on the matter, nor is there any covenant or promise between us. But he will not, I know, oppose my wishes in this; and if God's will be so, I shall give you in marriage to him on our return."

"King of all time," said Nour al-Houda then, "I have become of you and for you."

Now as they were conversing together, there was a tumult of drums and horns and men and horses, and lo, it was Munyat al-Nufus's father, King Qasim al-'Abous, come to meet with King Sayf. And when they had greeted one another, and each had learned who the other was, King Qasim said to King Sayf: "I learned this day that the enchantments over the city of maidens have been broken. It is my wish to do the same, and have things return to what they were before."

"Let it be so," said King Sayf. "And if it is the wish of any man to take one of the maidens in marriage, let him come and seek her at my hand."

"The first to seek marriage is I," King Qasim said then. "For I seek the hand of the minister Murjana."

The marriage was agreed accordingly, and each of the men in King Qasim's retinue acted in similar fashion, till all were married. Then the Watchers set around the city walls were removed, and the spells binding the city of men broken thereby, so that the men mixed with the women as in all other lands. And King Qasim al-'Abous rejoiced at the outcome, giving praise to Almighty God.

When all this was completed, King Sayf resolved to return to his own land, taking with him Munyat al-Nufus and his son Masr, who was now old enough to walk, and Nour al-Houda, who had been promised in marriage to King Shah al-Zaman. And so the four rode out on four splendid steeds, toward the place where King Sayf had parted from the giant.

Before they finally reached their goal, they passed through many trials and tribulations, and King Sayf fought many battles against sorcerers and infidels, joined by his son Dummar and his friends the sorceress 'Aqila, and the wizard Ikhmim al-Talib, and Barnoukh the magician, and Kings Abu Taj and Afrah and Shah al-Zaman, and the four commanders, Sa'doun al-Zinji and Sabik al-Thalath and Daminhour al-Wahsh and Maymoun al-Hajjam. And among the kings against whom King Sayf had to do battle before sitting on his throne in peace was the Emperor of China, Nahid's father al-Sammsaam, come to avenge his daughter's death. But they prevailed over all, and those who perished, perished, while others, al-Sammsaam among them, embraced Islam, turning to God in word and in heart. Then King Sayf ruled with justice over the lands, and before their appointed end came he and his sons had many more adventures, of which we shall speak in the proper season.

Glossary of Names and Places

NOTE: In the Glossary, "Sayf" refers to Sayf Ben Dhi Yazan, the hero of the tale, as opposed to the king of the Ethiopians, Sayf Ar'ad. In the early part of the tale the hero is known as "Wahsh al-Fala"

'Abd al-Khayr: servant of al-Jiza, ordered to kill Sayf. His own head is severed from his shoulders by a stratagem of al-Jiza's father, Ikhmim al-Talib (ch. 5)

'Abd Lahab (Servant of the Flame): an "outlandish man" who tries to trick Wahsh al-Fala into releasing a magic whip to him. Wahsh al-Fala tricks him instead and gains the whip (ch. 2)

'Abd Lahab (Servant of the Flame): son of the king of the magicians. He sends envoys to find Sayf and Barnoukh so as to avenge his dead father (ch. 10)

'Abīd al-Najm (Worshipper of the Star): sorcerer and king in the story related to Sayf by the jinn giant (ch. 13)

'Abd Nar: sorcerer who helps Saqardyoun prevent the "union of the two moles" (i.e., the marriage of Shama and Sayf) by creating the evil creature called the Snatcher (ch. 2)

'Abd Nar: subject of King 'Aboūd Khan who is ordered to kill Sayf. He is converted to Islam by a vision of al-Khader and becomes Sayf's ally (ch. 3)

'Abd al-Salam: pious shaykh dwelling in the land of the jinn. He helps 'Aqīsa find Sayf in order to deliver her from the Snatcher, then dies peacefully in the care of Sayf (ch. 3)

'Abd al-Samad (Servant of the Everlasting): formerly 'Abd Nar (Servant of the Fire). He embraces Islam and helps deliver Sayf from King 'Aboūd Khan (ch. 3)

'Aboūd Khan: son of Kalouth Khan, creator of the magic ring that slays the victim at which it is waved. He loses the ring to Sayf and is killed after his refusal to embrace Islam (ch. 3)

Abraham, Friend of God: taken as the first Muslim, forefather of all prophets in the Islamic tradition

Abu 'l-Nur al-Zaytouni: envoy of al-Khader who helps Sayf travel to the City of Maidens (ch. 13)

Abu Sinan: knight in the service of King Sayf Ar'ad; slain by Sa'doūn al-Zinji (ch. 10)

Abu Taj, King: saved from a fierce lion by Sayf. He then tries repeatedly to seduce Shama, but is foiled in his attempts and embraces Islam (ch. 8)

Aden: Yemeni province over which the Tūbba'ī kings rule

'Adnan: one of the two original Arab clans (the other being Qahtan). The Prophet Muhammad is from the clan of 'Adnan, from the tribe of Quraysh

Afrah, King: ruler of al-Dour. The infant Wahsh al-Fala is brought to his city from the wilderness, and Afrah rears him with his daughter Shama (ch. 2)

A'la Trous: wizard who created the treasure of Kush (ch. 13)

'Aqīla: sorcerer to King Qamroun, ruler of the city of Qaymar. She helps Sayf obtain the Book of the History of the Nile (ch. 3), and he later marries her daughter Tama

'Aqīsa: daughter of the White King and sister by suckling to Sayf. As one of the jinn she is empowered to help and protect Sayf, especially after he saves her from marriage to the Snatcher (ch. 3)

Asad al-Baīdaʾ: son of Shem

Asaf, son of Birkhiya: Sayf's ancestor through whom he acquires the sword of King Shem (ch. 5)

Ashkhas, King: king of the Valley of the Magicians. He frees his people from the destruction intended for them by Habis al-Wahshi (ch. 8)

'Atūmtūm Kharaq al-Shajjar: knight under King Afrah, given custody of Wahsh al-Fala. Trains him in the art of war but is awed by his prowess and banishes him to the wilderness (ch. 2)

'Ayrūd: servant of the tablet given to Sayf in King Shem's palace; son of the Red King of the jinn. He is under control of whoever possesses the tablet at a particular time

Bahr Qafqan al-Rif: Muslim minister of King Sayf Ar'ad. Informs King Dhi Yazan of Sayf Ar'ad's treachery in sending Qamariyya to poison him (ch. 1)

Ba'labek, King: a powerful king of whom King Dhi Yazan hears, pledging to defeat him. Dhi Yazan takes over his dominion (ch. 1)

Balqis, Queen of Sheba: queen of antiquity, noted for losing her throne by trickery

Banu Hashim: family of the Prophet Muhammad

Banu Himyar: Yemeni clan to which the Tūbbaʿī kings belong

Barnoukh: magician who rescues Sayf from the other magicians in the Valley of the Magicians (ch. 8) and subsequently becomes his ally

al-Batthaʾ (the Basin): expanse of water in which Sayf encounters a monstrous fish (ch. 9)

Bitter Mountain: home of the White King of the jinn

Book of the History of the Nile: book worshipped by King Qamroun of the city of Qaymar (ch. 3). Sayf is destined to take control of the book and so cause the Nile to flow through Egypt

City of Black Magic: original capital of the father of the ghouls (ch. 7)

City of Maidens: enchanted city ruled over first by Munyat al-Nufus, then by her sister Nour al-Houda. No men are allowed to enter it, and all of its maidens are trained as warriors (ch. 13)

City of Men: counterpart to the City of Maidens, ruled over by the father of Munyat al-Nufus (ch. 13)

City of Plato: home of magicians in the Valley of the Magicians (ch. 3)

Dahshana, Queen: wife of King Afrah

Daminhour al-Wahsh: knight in the service of King Sayf Arʿad, enlisted in the war against Sayf and his allies (ch. 10)

Dhi Yazan, King: father of Sayf. In the line of the Yemeni Tūbbaʿī kings

Diamond Isle: an enchanted island lying at the end of the world, home of Munyat al-Nufus and her father Qasim al-ʿAboūs

al-Dour: city of King Sayf Arʿad, ruler of Ethiopia

Dummar: son of Sayf and Shama

Estokan: ancient sorcerer whose power ʿAqīsa fears (ch. 10)

Ethiopia: land of King Sayf Arʿad

Forest of the Lions: home of Maymoun al-Hajjam, a warrior enlisted by King Sayf Arʿad in his struggles against Sayf (ch. 10)

Ghader (the Treacherous One): servant of al-Jiza and would-be assassin of Sayf. The attempt, ordered by al-Jiza, is foiled and he dies (ch. 5)

Ghaylouna: queen over the ghouls. Helps Sayf to escape from the Valley of the Ghouls, having destroyed the inhabitants. She then helps Sayf rescue Shama from the Valley of the Giants (ch. 7)

Habis al-Wahshi: king from the Valley of the Magicians who attempts to sacrifice the subjects of King Ashkhas after the latter has refused to give his daughter in marriage to his son. Ashkhas eventually defeats Habis al-Wahshi (ch. 8)

al-Hadid: city of King Afrah

Ham: son of Noah. His face is blackened by his father's curse, and consequently all his progeny are black. This is explained by Saqardyoun as the origin of black people (ch. 2). The descendants of Ham are to serve the white-skinned descendants of Shem

Hamra' al-Habash: city built by King Dhi Yazan in the Red Land (Ethiopia). Its presence angers Sayf Arʿad, king of Ethiopia, and incites him to attempt to destroy Dhi Yazan

Haris, King: ruler of Arwiqa, to whom the minister Kiwan turns for help in the story related to Sayf by the jinn giant (ch. 13)

al-Hatim: city of King Sayf Arʿad

Hidden One: magical guardian of the city of Qaymar, set to watch for the arrival of the man who will steal the Book of the History of the Nile (i.e., Sayf) (ch. 3)

Hijaz: central province of the Arabian Peninsula

Ikhmim al-Talib: pious wizard who leads Sayf to the sword of Shem (ch. 5)

Jann, people of the: the people under the rule of the White King who lives on the Bitter Mountain (ch. 3)

Jayhoun: one of the two rivers of God, running to the lands of the Turks and the Romans. These two rivers run overland. The two underground rivers are the Euphrates and the Nile

Jiyad: pious shaykh who tells Sayf of his true lineage and teaches him the ways of Islam (ch. 2) before dying in his care (ch. 3)

al-Jiza: daughter of Ikhmim al-Talib; destined to marry Sayf

Kafur, King: original ruler of Waq al-Waq (ch. 13)

Kalouth Khan: creator of the magic ring, which has the power to strike heads from bodies when waved at the victim. He passed it on to his son, 'Aboūd Khan, from whom Sayf takes it (ch. 3)

Karkar: land to which Ham flees after being exiled by his brother Shem. He settles there and marries a princess, giving birth to children who populate the area with black-skinned people

Kawkab: jailor of Munyat al-Nufus in the City of Maidens (ch. 13)

al-Khader: exalted teacher who persuades 'Abd Nar to convert in a vision and so saves Sayf from death (ch. 3). He later rescues Sayf again by leading King Shah al-Zaman to the City of Maidens (ch. 13)

al-Khayraqan: giant servant of the tablet given to Sayf by Abu 'l-Nur al-Zaytouni (ch. 13)

Kiwan: minister to the son of 'Abīd al-Najm in the story related to Sayf by the jinn giant (ch. 13)

Kush Ben Can'an: original owner of the treasure given to Sayf by Abu 'l-Nur al-Zaytouni (ch. 13)

al-Lat: one of the pre-Islamic goddesses of Arabia

Maymoun al-Hajjam: giant knight, marauder of caravans, in the service of King Sayf Ar'ad. Employed to defeat Sayf and his allies (ch. 10)

Mecca: birthplace of the Prophet Muhammad and home of the Ka'ba

Mount Abu Qubays: place of safekeeping of the Black Stone during the flood of Noah

Mountains of the Moon: home of the jinn

Muhammad: Prophet of Islam

Mulakim al-Rih (He Who Punches at the Wind): knight in the service of King Sayf Ar'ad (ch. 10)

Munatih al-Bighal (He Who Butts with Mules): King Sayf Ar'ad's envoy sent to ask King Afrah for his daughter Shama's hand in marriage. He is killed by Sayf's ally Sa'doūn al-Zinji (ch. 4)

Munyat al-Nufus: daughter of King Qasim al-'Aboūs. She is queen of the Garden of Delights (ch. 10), and also of the City of Maidens till replaced by her sister, Nour al-Houda (ch. 13). She becomes the favorite wife of Sayf

Murjana: minister of the queen of the City of Maidens, Nour al-Houda (ch. 13)

Nahid, Princess: daughter of the Emperor of China, kidnapped by the Snatcher, saved by Sayf and returned to China (ch. 3). Sayf subsequently marries her after curing her of blindness (ch. 9)

Noah: prophet of God and forefather of Sayf

Nour al-Houda: sister of Munyat al-Nufus; takes control of the City of Maidens after Munyat's marriage to Sayf (ch. 13)

Qamar: original home of Qamariyya, mother of Sayf

Qamariyya: concubine of Sayf Ar'ad sent to poison King Dhi Yazan. She gives birth to Sayf and makes repeated subsequent attempts on his life so as to try to keep his domains for herself

Qamar Shahiq: daughter of the king of Karkar; married Ham, son of Noah

Qasim al-'Abous: father of Munyat al-Nufus; ruler of the Diamond Isle (ch. 10)

Quraysh: the most important of Meccan tribes. The tribe of the Prophet Muhammad

Red Land: Ethiopia

Sabik al-Thalath: knight in the service of King Sayf Ar'ad, enlisted in the war against Sayf and his allies (ch. 10)

Sa'doun al-Zinji: warlord whose head King Afrah demands of Sayf as a bride price for his daughter Shama. Sa'doun and Sayf become allies instead and together defeat Sayf Ar'ad, King Afrah's overlord

Sanaa: province of Yemen

Saqardis: wizard in the service of King Sayf Ar'ad

Saqardyoun: wizard in the service of King Sayf Ar'ad

Saturn: planet worshipped by the Ethiopians and Sudanese

Sayf Ar'ad, King: ruler of Ethiopia, archenemy of Sayf

Sayf Ben Dhi Yazan: son of King Dhi Yazan and hero of the tale. The curse of Noah will come to pass at his hands

Sayhoun: one of the two rivers of God (the other being Jayhoun), running to the lands of the Turks and Romans

Shama: daughter of King Afrah, first wife of Sayf

Shahouta, Prince: son of 'Abid al-Najm, slain by Kiwan for seducing his daughter in the story related to Sayf by the jinn giant (ch. 13)

Sharahi bint al-Dawahi (Daughter of Disasters): sorceress of Nour al-Houda, queen of the City of Maidens (ch. 13)

Shem: older son of Noah, whose sword eventually passes to Sayf

The Snatcher: monster created by the sorcerer 'Abd Nar to take Shama from Sayf and so prevent the union of the two moles through their marriage. He is eventually destroyed by Sayf, using a magic whip

Solomon: son of David

Taha: another name for the Prophet Muhammad

Tahama: coastal plain of Yemen

Tama: daughter of the sorceress 'Aqila. She is eventually married to Sayf

al-Thurayya: castle of Sa'doun al-Zinji

al-'Uzza: one of the pre-Islamic goddesses of Arabia

Valley of the Ghouls: place to which the servant of the tablet, 'Ayrud, takes Sayf on the orders of Qamariyya

Valley of the Giants: place to which the servant of the tablet, 'Ayrud, takes Sayf's wife Shama on the orders of Qamariyya

Valley of the Magicians: place to which the servant of the tablet, 'Ayrud, takes Sayf on the orders of Qamariyya

Wahsh al-Fala: name given to Sayf as an infant after he has been found in the wilderness being suckled by a gazelle. The name means "Beast of the Wild"

Yemen: southern Arabian domain of the Tubba'i kings, of which Sayf is one

Zamzam: holy well outside Mecca

Za'zou'a: sorceress of Nour al-Houda, queen of the City of Maidens (ch. 13)

EPITHETS FOR GOD

All-Bountiful Sovereign
All-Conquering
All-Exalted
All-Forgiving
All-Generous
All-Glorious and Exalted
All-Great
All-Highest Sovereign
All-Kindly
All-Knowing Sovereign
All-Merciful
All-Powerful Sovereign
All-Vanquishing
All-Victorious
Almighty Sovereign

Beloved One
Benevolent One

Cleaver of Seed and Kernel
Compassionate One

Deliverer
Divine Sovereign

Eternal One
Everlasting Ruler of All

Guardian

Lord of Creation
Lord of Lords
Lord of the Earth

Mighty One
Most Blessed of Stays

Omnipotent One

Resourceful One

Sovereign Lord

Vindicator

Appendix

PAGE REFERENCES TO THE ARABIC TEXT

This appendix keys the chapters of *The Adventures of Sayf Ben Dhi Yazan: An Arab Folk Epic* to the following Arabic text: *Sirat Sayf ibn Dhi Yazan*, Parts 1–6 (Cairo: Bulak, AH 1294 [AD 1877]).

Contributors

JOHN HEATH-STUBBS, English poet, critic, and translator, took his first class degree in English from Queen's College, Oxford, in 1942 and lectured at the universities of Alexandria and Michigan, and at the colleges of St. Mark and St. John in London. He now lectures at the University of Oxford. Among his many writings is the long poem, *Artorius,* for which he won the Queen's Gold Medal for poetry in 1972. In 1978, he won the Oscar William-Jean Durwood Award. He has published a number of volumes of criticism, plays, and poetry—the latest of which is *Naming the Beasts* (1983). He has also translated from Italian *Selected Poems and Prose of Giacomo Leopardi* with Iris Origo, and with Peter Avery has translated *Hafiz of Shiraz* and *The Rubaiyat of Omar Khayyam* from Persian. In 1988 Carcanet published his *Collected Poems. Selected Poems* was published by Carcanet in 1990. His new volume, *The Literary Essays,* appeared in 1998, also with Carcanet.

LENA JAYYUSI was born in Amman, Jordan, to Palestinian parents, and educated in England, where she obtained an M.A. in economics and a Ph.D. in sociology from the University of Manchester, focusing on the pragmatics of language use. She later obtained an M.Sc. in film studies at Boston University. Currently, she is Director of Academic Programs at the Institute of Modern Media Studies at Al Quds University and Senior Research Fellow at Muwatin Palestinian Institute for the Study of Democracy. She was an Annenberg Scholar at the Annenberg School for Communication of the University of Pennsylvania, where she conducted research on the Palestinian Broadcasting Corporation; she has been awarded an SSRC Postdoctoral Research Fellowship to continue this research. Author of *Categorization and the Moral Order* (1984), Jayyusi is presently writing a book on issues of visuality. She is coediting (with T. Dunbar Moodie) *Enacting Democracy: Creating, Maintaining, and Transforming Public Spaces,* based on an Annenberg Scholars Program project on the theme of public space. As one of PROTA's readers and reviewers, Jayyusi has translated poetry and fiction for four anthologies of modern Arabic literature. Her PROTA translations include *Songs of Life* (with Naomi Shibab Nye, 1985), a collection of poems by Abu 'l-Qasim al-Shabbi and (with Sharif El-Musa) *On Entering the Sea: The Erotic and Other Poetry of Nizar Qabbani,* as well as selections of the poetry of Mahmoud Darwish.

SALMA KHADRA JAYYUSI taught at a number of Arab and American universities before founding the Project of Translation from Arabic (PROTA) in 1980 to disseminate Arabic literature and culture worldwide. She is noted for her poetry and critical writing. Her first collection of poems, *Return from the Dreamy Fountain*, appeared in 1960; her two-volume critical history, *Trends and Movements in Modern Arabic Poetry*, was published in 1977. As director of PROTA, Jayyusi has edited approximately thirty books, ranging from monographs to anthologies of modern Arabic literature, and including *Modern Arabic Poetry* (1987), *The Literature of Modern Arabia* (1988), *An Anthology of Modern Palestinian Literature* (1992), *Modern Arabic Fiction* (forthcoming), and *Modern Arabic Drama* (with Roger Allen, 1995). Since 1989, she has been working on a new anthology, *Poets of the End of the Century: New Voices in Arabic Poetry*, she is also preparing two collections of her critical work in Arabic and English.

HARRY NORRIS studied archaeology at Cambridge, and after serving in the Aden and Gibraltar governments, was appointed Lecturer at the School of Oriental and African Studies at London University with a specialization in Hassaniyya poetry. Later he became Professor of Arabic and Islamic Studies at the School and was appointed Dean of Undergraduate Studies. Now Emeritus, he devotes his time to research and translation. As an Arabic scholar, he attempted to discover new areas of study and to venture into regions unknown to other scholars. His research ranged from the study of the relations between Arabs and Berbers; to the history of South Arabia; to Moorish, Gibraltar, and Saharan studies; to the relations between the Arabs and medieval Europe. His many books are a testament to the originality of his life-long endeavors. In addition to many scholarly articles, which include several studies of the Sayf Ben Dhi Yazan folk romance, he has published *Shinqiti Folk Literature and Song*, *Saharan Myth and Saga*, *'Antar,' The Berbers in Arabic Literature*, *Sufi Mystics of the Niger Desert*, and *Islam in the Balkans* (forthcoming). At present, Norris is translating and annotating Abu Hamid al-Gharnati's travel book, *Tuhfat al-Albab*, which will be part of *The Medieval World through Muslim Eyes*, a new PROTA series.

CHRISTOPHER TINGLEY was born in Brighton, England, and received his education at the universities of London and Leeds. Following initial teaching experience in Germany and Britain, he lectured in the fields of English language and linguistics at the University of Constantine, Algeria, the University of Ghana, the National University of Rwanda, and the University of Ouagadougou, Burkina Faso. In the field of translation, he has collaborated with Salma Khadra Jayyusi on her work, *Trends and Movements in Modern Arabic Poetry*. For PROTA, he has translated, with Olive and Lorne Kenny, Yusuf al-Qa'id's novel, *War in the Land of Egypt* (1986); and he collaborated on a number of short stories in Salma Khadra Jayyusi's anthologies, *The Literature of Modern Arabia: An Anthology* (1977), and *Modern Arabic Fiction: An Anthology* (forthcoming). He has also provided comprehensive stylistic and scholarly editing for PROTA's volume of essays on Muslim Spain entitled, *The Legacy of Muslim Spain*, edited by Salma Khadra Jayyusi (1992).

Motif Index

NOTE: In the following index, "Sayf" refers to Sayf Ben Dhi Yazan, the hero of the tale, as opposed to the king of the Ethiopians, Sayf Ar'ad.

Bodily Marks:

Green mole on the cheek: Royal family sign found on both Sayf and his first wife, Shama, on their son Dummar, and on Masr, the son of Sayf and Munyat al-Nufus. The "union of the moles" through the marriage of Sayf and Shama unleashes the curse of Noah against the Ethiopians /15, 17–19, 23, 73–74, 129, 133, 143, 277

Burial:

Sayf buries the pious Shaykh 'Abd al-Salam with formal Muslim rites /68
Sayf buries the pious Shaykh Jiyad with formal Muslim rites /87–88
The jinn maiden 'Aqīsa gives burial to Ghaylouna, queen over the ghouls, after she dies protecting Sayf /146

Chivalry:

Knightly combat:
King Dhi Yazan against King Ba'labek /7
Sayf against his future wife Shama (disguised) /26–27
Sayf against his (future) ally Sa'doūn al-Zinji /28–30, 131
Sayf against his future wife Tama (disguised) /37–39
Sayf against King Sayf Ar'ad's knights /130, 205–210, 218
Sa'doūn al-Zinji against Sayf /28–30, 131
Sa'doūn al-Zinji against King Sayf Ar'ad's knights /131, 192–194, 197–198, 215–216

Knightly protocol:
Declaration of lineage before combat /56, 91, 202, 227
Formal invitation to combat /chapter 11 (passim)

Conversion to Islam:

By direct supernatural agency:
'Abd Nar, captain of King 'Aboūd Khan, is converted in a vision by the divine messenger al-Khader /76–77
The magician Barnoukh is converted in a vision by a divine messenger (unnamed) /152

By human agency, through formal reception into the faith:
King Dhi Yazan is received by his minister Yathrib /4
Sayf is received by Shaykh Jiyad /34
Princess Nahid and her companions are received by Sayf /64
King 'Aboūd Khan's counselors are received by Sayf /81
King Abu Taj is received by Queen Shama /155

Sabik al-Thalath is received by Sayf /212–214
Daminhour al-Wahsh is received by Sayf /212–214
Maymoun al-Hajjam is received by Sayf /219
King Shah al-Zaman is received by al-Khader /283–284

Disguise:

Man disguised as a woman:
Sayf disguises himself as a maiden (to enter the City of Maidens unobserved) /262–273

Woman disguised as man:
Shama, Sayf's future queen, disguises herself as a knight seeking combat (to make trial of Sayf's prowess) /26–27
Tama, Sayf's future queen, disguises herself as a knight seeking combat (as a means of identifying Sayf) /37–38
Queen Qamariyya disguises herself as a (male) messenger (as a means of coming to Sayf) /94
Al-Jiza, Sayf's future queen, disguises herself as a (male) military commander (in the course of capturing Sayf) /113–117

Other:
The magician Barnoukh disguises himself as the wizard Saqardis (in order to trick Queen Qamariyya) /158
Queen Nour al-Houda disguises herself as a slave girl (to ascertain the whereabouts of Sayf and his wife Munyat al-Nufus) /281
Sayf disguises himself as a slave boy (to escape recognition by the people of Qaymar) /52–53

Divination: *See* **Prophecy and Divination**

Divine Intervention *(see also* **Conversion to Islam***):*

Benefits bestowed:
The ring of King Qamroun is found inside a fish caught by Sayf and his ally 'Abd al-Samad /79
A wind is sent to shake a tree and send healing leaves to the wounded Sayf /102

Disease, disfigurement, etc.:
King Dhi Yazan is visited by disease when he attempts to dismantle the Holy House /3–4
Queen Qamariyya's arm is paralyzed when she attempts to murder the infant Sayf /16
King Abu Taj is disfigured when he attempts to ravish Queen Shama /154–155

Flying: *See* **Magical Travel**

Healing:

Sayf's wounds, received from Queen Qamariyya, are healed by applying the chewed leaves of a tree /102
Princess Nahid's blindness is cured by applying to the eyes a crayfish ground in rose water /160–161
Sayf's wounds, received in the City of Plato, are healed by ointments provided by the magician Barnoukh /165

Human and Non-Human, Blending of *(see also* **Monsters***)*:

Human and bird:
Shaykh 'Abd al-Salam and Shaykh Jiyad reappear as birds after death /101–102
Queen Munyat al-Nufus and her companions fly with feather robes and have some attributes of birds /170–171, 173, 177, 240–242

Human and fruit:
Fruit hanging from a tree in the form of maidens singing praises to God /248–249, 257–260
Fruit hanging from a tree in the form of men singing praises to God /248

Idolatry:

Creatures and objects:
Book of the Nile: Worshipped by Qamroun, king of Qaymar, and his people /31, 40–55, 84–86
Fire: Worshipped by Sayf's ally 'Abd al-Samad before his conversion, and by the magicians of the gully of fire /75–76, 78, 81, 151–153
Sheep: Worshipped by the giants in the Land of the Giants /134, 143–145

Pagan deities:
Al-Lat and al-'Uzza: Pre-Islamic deities worshipped by King Dhi Yazan (before his conversion) /2–3
Saturn: Worshipped by King Sayf Ar'ad of Ethiopia and his people /9–10, 17, 34, 213–214

Lineage:

Recitation of lineage:
Sayf recites his lineage before entering King Shem's palace /108

Magical Creatures:

Crayfish: Has the power to heal blindness if ground in rosewater and applied to the eyes /159–161
Rooster: Destroys the ghouls pursuing Sayf and Ghaylouna, queen over the ghouls, when its feathers are plucked and thrown at them. The last ghouls are destroyed by the throwing of the rooster's plucked body /139–143

Magical Objects:

Book of the Nile: Gives its rightful possessor (Sayf) power over the course of the Nile. When Sayf appears, the chest containing the book acknowledges him by spinning around three times then falling between his feet /31, 38, 40, 49–50, 53–55, 69–70, 84
Cap of Plato: Renders the wearer invisible. Sayf obtains it by trickery from the sons of the wizard Plato /72, 84–85, 226, 232–233
Deerskin girdle: Renders the wearer invulnerable in battle. Fashioned for Sayf by the sorceress 'Aqila /226, 231, 234
Emerald: Affords protection against extreme heat and cold and causes bedding to appear when moved to the right; given to Sayf by Shaykh Abu 'l-Nur al-Zaytouni before his journey to the City of Maidens /245–247, 262

Feather robe: Enables Queen Munyat al-Nufus and her companions to fly /170–171, 173, 176–177, 240–242

Goblet: Provides food and drink when covered with a napkin; given to Sayf by Shaykh Abu 'l-Nur al-Zaytouni before his journey to the City of Maidens /245–247, 249, 259, 262, 280

Ring of King 'Aboud Khan: Kills anyone at whom it is waved by striking his head from his shoulders. Sayf takes possession of it and turns it against its original owner /74–82, 84

Sword: Renders the possessor invulnerable in battle. Given to Sayf at the palace of King Shem /109, 110, 112, 147, 151

Tablet: Summons its jinn servant when rubbed. One is given to Sayf at the palace of King Shem (summoning the jinn servant 'Ayrūd), another by Shaykh Abu 'l-Nur al-Zaytouni before his journey to the City of Maidens (summoning the jinn giant) /108, 120–124, 161, 163, 231, 235, 236, 243, 246–247

Whip: Kills or lops off the limbs of those against whom it is cracked. Obtained by Sayf from an "outlandish man" and used by him first to maim then kill the evil creature called the Snatcher /22–23, 25, 65

Magical Travel:

Magical flight by wizards and sorceresses:
By the sorceress 'Aqīla /223, 225–226
By the magician Barnoukh /151–152, 155, 165–166, 236
By the wizard Ikhmim al-Talib /106–107, 110–111
By the magician sent to Sayf Ar'ad from the magicians of the gully of fire /188–189, 220

Humans borne by jinn:
'Aqīsa bears: Sayf /62, 67, 69, 70, 72, 82, 164, 244; Sayf and Queen Shama /145–146; Queen Shama and their son Dummar /145–147, 149; Sayf and the magician Barnoukh /154–155; Sayf and Queen Munyat al-Nufus /179, 181–182; Queen Qamariyya /236–237
'Ayrūd bears: Sayf /125, 127, 151, 157–158, 163–164, 244; Sayf and Queen Shama / 128, 133; Sayf and Queen Nahid /161
The giant bears Sayf to the City of Maidens /247–250, 257–262

Unspecified:
Al-Khader conveys King Shah al-Zaman and his troops to the City of Maidens to rescue Sayf and Queen Munyat al-Nufus, then returns them to their country /284–285

Magic Spells:

Spells leading to:
Creation of objects: The magician Barnoukh creates a sea around the city of Hamra' al-Yaman to block King Sayf Ar'ad's army /190–191
Darkness: The magician Barnoukh inscribes names and charms on a sheet of paper to bring darkness over Queen Qamariyya's palace /165–166, 187
Destruction: The sorceress 'Aqīla cuts eighty papers in human shape, then inscribes them in order to destroy the eighty evil wizards in King Sayf Ar'ad's army /225–226
Immobility and paralysis: The magician Barnoukh casts a spell of immobility on Sayf / 151–152; Barnoukh's inscription (see Darkness, above) prevents Queen Qamariyya

from moving her arm to rub the tablet of the jinn servant 'Ayrud /165–166, 187, 191; King Sayf Ar'ad's wizards cast a spell of immobility on Sayf and his followers /220–221, 225

Levitation: The magician Barnoukh murmurs a spell to effect magical ascent of the mountain of the gully of fire /151

Sickness: The magician Barnoukh brings sickness upon Queen Qamariyya by inscribing a sheet with a woman's picture and her name /157–158

Monsters:

Ghouls: Creatures formed by the combined action of a wolf's seed, smoke from a fire, and human seed in the body of a human woman. They inhabit the Valley of the Ghouls /135–143

Giants: Outsize humanlike creatures inhabiting the Valley of the Giants /133–134, 143–146

Water monsters: A sea beast, moving constantly from shore to shore, attempts to catch and devour the sun in its course /35–37, 86–87; a monstrous fish devours Sayf's boat and attempts to devour Sayf himself /159–160

Prophecy and Divination:

Prophetic foreknowledge (on the part of Muslim believers):
Shaykh Jiyad knows of Sayf's coming and destiny /33–34, 36
Shaykh 'Abd al-Salam knows of Sayf's coming and of his future destruction of the Snatcher /62
The wizard Ikhmim al-Talib knows of Sayf's coming and destiny /104–105

Divination through casting of the sands:
By Muslim believers: The minister Yathrib sees King Dhi Yazan is not the bearer of the curse of Noah /8
The sorceress 'Aqila foresees Sayf's marriage to her daughter Tama and learns of his release from the pit of King Qamroun /38–39, 40–41, 83
The wizard Ikhmim al-Talib foresees Sayf's marriage to his daughter al-Jiza, together with Sayf's future achievements /119, 123
The sorceress 'Aqila sees Sayf's plight in the battle against Sayf Ar'ad's army /224

By non-believers: The wizards Saqardyoun and Saqardis foresee the "union of the moles" through the marriage of Sayf and Shama, presaging the end of the power of Ethiopia / 17–19
King Qamroun's wizards perceive Sayf's presence in their city /43–49
King 'Aboud Khan's wizards foresee Sayf's arrival and his destruction of 'Aboud Khan /75
The father of Ghaylouna, queen over the ghouls, foresees the destruction of the ghouls /138
The sorceress Za'zou'a perceives Sayf's presence in the City of Maidens and his exploits there /280–281

Ritual Actions:

Sets of complex prescribed actions lead to the following:
Sayf obtains the tablet and sword of King Shem (*see also* **Magical Objects**) /107–109

Sayf releases the rooster whose magic properties will enable him to destroy the ghouls *(see also* **Magical Creatures***)* /138–140
Sayf breaks the spell ensuring the isolation of the City of Maidens /286

Spells: *See* **Magic Spells**

Suckling of Human by Non-Human:

The infant Sayf is suckled by a gazelle /16
The infant Sayf is suckled by the consort of the White King of the jinn. Her daughter 'Aqisa subsequently becomes Sayf's protecting "sister" /20, 60, 66

Trickery *(see also* **Disguise***):*

The sorceress 'Aqila tricks King Qamroun's wizards by creating grotesque situations, so causing their divination to appear absurd /42–49
Sayf tricks the sons of the wizard Plato into releasing their magic cap *(see also* **Magical Objects***)* by pretending to hold it as umpire while they contend for it /71–72
Sayf and his ally 'Abd al-Samad trick King al-'Aboud Khan into supposing Sayf dead, by exposing the limbs of a fair-skinned concubine 'Abd al-Samad has killed /78
Sayf attempts to trick al-Jiza with an elaborate account of himself as a shipwrecked mariner /116–117